TO THE FIRE OF
NORMANDY
— AND —
BEYOND

TO THE FIRE OF NORMANDY
—— AND ——
BEYOND

Behind Enemy Lines during World War II

Frank Kozol

Submitted for publication by Neil Kozol

This book is a work of non-fiction. Unless otherwise noted, the author
and the publisher make no explicit guarantees as to the accuracy of
the information contained in this book and in some cases, names of
people and places have been altered to protect their privacy.

Archway Publishing books may be ordered through booksellers or by contacting:

Archway Publishing
1663 Liberty Drive
Bloomington, IN 47403
www.archwaypublishing.com
1 (888) 242-5904

Because of the dynamic nature of the Internet, any web addresses or
links contained in this book may have changed since publication and
may no longer be valid. The views expressed in this work are solely those
of the author and do not necessarily reflect the views of the publisher,
and the publisher hereby disclaims any responsibility for them.

Scripture quotes marked (JPS Tanakh 1917) are taken from the Prayer
Book abridged for Jews in the Armed Forces of the United States.

ISBN: 978-1-4808-4302-8 (sc)
ISBN: 978-1-4808-4303-5 (hc)
ISBN: 978-1-4808-4304-2 (e)

Library of Congress Control Number: 2017938404

Printed in the United States of America.

Archway Publishing rev. date: 10/11/2017

In loving memory and respect to all of the men and women of the United States Armed Forces who have given their lives in defense of these blessed United States of America.

To the loved ones of these heroes who had to endure the pain and the heartache of their terrible loss.

To the veterans of our armed forces and their loved ones.

To the men and women who, at the time of this writing, serve with honor and distinction in the United States Armed Forces; local, federal, and state law enforcement officers; firefighters; rescue workers; clergy; and individuals who strive to help us in our everyday lives. God bless you all.

To our president, vice president, members of Congress, members of the Senate, and other local, state, and federal officials who serve our great country.

In loving memory and respect to the federal, state, and local law enforcement officers, firefighters, rescue workers, clergy, and individuals who gave their lives trying to save people at the time of the World Trade Center tragedy, as well as the Pentagon and airline tragedies, and to the surviving loved ones of these heroes, who try every day to cope with their terrible loss.

In loving and respectful memory of the innocent victims of these terrible tragedies and to the loved ones of these people, who are trying to cope with their heartbreak.

The reader might well ask, why are these groups included in a story about a war? This too was a war, albeit an undeclared sneak attack. It was a war just the same, hence this dedication.

May God bless our beloved United States of America.

In Adversity Lies Opportunity

Inspired by

With dedicated assistance from my favorite
proof-reader, my lovely wife, Ruth Kozol

My son Mark Stephen Kozol
In memoriam August 14, 1952 - October 15, 2014

My parents and my brother, Joseph Kozol, whose
support and photographs are very much appreciated
and his sons Jeffrey Kozol and Stephen Kozol

My son Neil David Kozol who edited and submitted
the manuscript to Archway Publishing.

My daughter-in-law, Neil's wife, Patti Kozol, who provided
hours of detailed editing, support and guidance on the book

My granddaughter Stephanie Lynn Kozol who
also spent many hours editing this book

My grandson Jonathan Carlin Kozol

My granddaughter Alison Marea Kozol

My grandson Adam Benjamin Kozol

My daughter-in-law, Joyce Kozol

And my second home, The New England
College of Optometry, Boston, Mass.

CONTENTS

PART I: The Boy Soldier 1

PART II: The Real Soldier 107

PART III: The Combat Soldier 211

PART IV: The Homecoming Veteran 493

INTRODUCTION

To my Grandchildren and all the Grandchildren of our Veterans

Once upon a time, there were people, most of whom we will read about, who were born and grew up in the twenties and thirties. As children, they experienced the terrifying time of the Depression. Many were out of work and had a lot of trouble finding ways to make ends meet, feed their families, and pay rent.

Daily newspapers cost two cents, and the Sunday edition went for five cents. Even that was too much money for many people who were poor. There was no Social Security, welfare, or Medicaid at that time. For those people who could afford it, a radio was the essential form of entertainment. Television did not exist at that time, and so families would cluster around the radio to listen to their favorite programs. For some fortunate families who could afford an automobile, transportation would be shared with many members of family and friends. The driver of a car would pull in to a gas station and have the attendant fill the tank with gasoline, check the tires, clean the windshield, and check the oil level. The driver would then pay a dollar and receive change as the attendant gave him or her a hearty "Thank you very much!"

Most people had an icebox to cool their food instead of a refrigerator. Periodically, a horse-drawn ice wagon would pull in to the neighborhood, and people would lean out the window and tell the ice man just how big a chunk of ice they needed. There were no supermarkets in those days. All essential food items, for the most part, were purchased at a corner grocery store. Milk wagons pulled by horses would also visit the neighborhood on a daily basis. A large candy bar such as a Milky Way, Baby Ruth, or Hershey bar cost five cents. There was no such thing as a computer, Palm Pilot, or calculator. These, along with television, were the subjects of speculative articles in various science and science fiction magazines. Rocket travel to the moon and planets was generally dismissed as fantasy.

If a person needed to have a printed report, it was necessary to use a manual typewriter. Electric typewriters would come along many years later. If several copies were needed, there would be the difficult task of inserting carbon sheets between the pages, in order to squeeze out as many copies as one could manage on their individual machine. Ballpoint pens and nylon stockings did not exist then, and contact lenses were hardly known to most of the population. And so, my children, in this once-upon-a-time story, this is how the people being written about lived.

To the Reader

When my wife and I first married, she asked me on several occasions why I did not write down my wartime experiences. I used the excuse that I was busy with my professional responsibilities as an Optometry professor which included writing, instruction and private practice and consequently could not find the time for a chore so potentially daunting. Furthermore, in those unenlightened times, all of my writing was done on a tiny Royal portable typewriter, which did not allow for typos. The entire text had to be made with several carbon copies, and an error of any kind had to be erased, painfully and tediously, one copy at a time. When my sons started to get older and became curious about their father, they asked the very same question.

Once, shortly after the end of World War II, an old army buddy and his family came to visit. As my good friend and I refreshed our memories, encouraged and helped on by generous quantities of scotch and bourbon, our reminiscences became even more colorful and embellished, thereby making the stories all the more fascinating to our children. At that time, I was totally involved with writing some technical articles that would later serve as the basis for an Optometric textbook. My excuses for not documenting these wartime experiences were reluctantly accepted by my wife and sons, and I was off the hook for the time being.

Happily, my sons got married, and ultimately, when my lovely grandchildren came along, once again an admonition came from my boys and wife: "Your grandchildren are going to want to know about your wartime experiences. Just wait and see!" The prediction was true, of course, and now I am asked on a fairly regular basis by my adorable grandchildren to relate these experiences. I have no alternative but to accede to their wishes. A word of caution, however; the passage of time has dimmed my memory somewhat, and so I am attempting to put down on paper what I can recall. Some of the experiences are mine, and some were experienced by others. They are all real and true.

There is a major advantage in being able to write this on a computer, what with spell check, cut and paste, and the other goodies with which computers come equipped.

Some other comments to the reader are necessary. I have changed some names here so as not to embarrass any individuals or make them feel uncomfortable. Historical figures, however, have been given the liberty of retaining their original names. Another important point is that I feel that since this is being addressed not only to my grandchildren but also to the multitude of other veterans' grandchildren, it is not necessary in the telling of this story to burden the dramatic content by adding profane, vile, or vulgar language. The story content will hold on its own merit.

Frank Kozol
Sharon, Massachusetts

NEIL KOZOL'S INTRODUCTION

Assuming my father's goal of publishing his work several years after his death in 2008, I fortunately found Archway Publishing. They were particularly patient with my lack of experience with the task at hand. I can not sufficiently thank them for their guidance and reassurance.

Not having had the privilege of serving in the military, I chose to neither add to nor remove anything from the story as presented by my father with the exceptions of the cover design, the epigraph at the front of the book, my introduction on on Page xvii, the oral history on Page 124 and the epilogue. I added to the photographs my father originally included with other photographs from my collection. The photograph at the top of Page 516 was provided by my uncle, Joseph Kozol, with his permission. Reviewing photographs of his war experiences, I found approximately two dozen people with whom he was associated. He made the decision of not using their real names and combining the protagonists into a smaller and more manageable set of participants. I tried not to use photographs of non-family characters to avoid concern regarding permission. It is evident in examining the photographs, that my father was attempting to reassure his family that he was safe while in the midst of war. In the story, the reader will see that the author reconciles the balancing act of describing his story without resorting to the grim realities of war nor devaluing the sacrifices made by our armed forces.

On October 14, 2000, during the occasion of his retirement party from The New England College of Optometry, my father received a very large framed commendation from the French Consulate thanking him for his service to the country of France during World War 2.

As my father repeatedly said, everything he wrote in the story is true.

Neil Kozol
Sharon, Mass.

Commendation from French Consulate Presented Oct 14, 2000

—Part I—

The Boy Soldier

—1—

On April 29, 1943, at seven thirty in the morning, Paul walked by the multitude of three-decker houses along Morton Street in Boston's suburb of Dorchester, heading toward the large thoroughfare Blue Hill Avenue. His mother, Becky, father, Charlie, and brother, Jerry walked alongside him. Becky's formal name was Rebecca, but many of the children in school had mocked her and called her Becky the Greenhorn (someone who just got off the boat from the Old Country), and so she had defensively decided to call herself Becky. His father had

Paul's parents

grown up in South Boston, and his biblical name, Shlamy, did not fit in with his friends, and so they decided to call him Charlie.

They all seemed solemn except for Paul. He was going to embark on a great adventure. Didn't they realize it? He was going to be fine. How could they be so upset when their son and brother was merely going off to war?

Earlier, on Middleton Street, they had passed the William Bradford Grammar School, where Paul had been a pupil. On the first day of school, he had reported dutifully with his new pencil box—and wearing a new pair of shoes and a new suit, if his parents could afford it. His mother had brought milk and cookies to the schoolyard for him during recess time, with a generous supply for all the kids he was friendly with. Many was the time he and his friends, after school, climbed over the locked fence to play stickball. They used the handle of a broom or mop as a bat, hitting a dimpled rubber ball that would travel far and wide.

There was a slight chill in the air, which was normal and expected for that time of year. As they approached Blue Hill Avenue, they could see a long column of streetcars, empty now, waiting for the soon-to-be members of the armed forces to board them. Paul paused to think about his good-byes to his loved ones. Especially dear and close to him were his maternal grandparents. He was a lucky boy to have enjoyed a particularly loving and close relationship with these beautiful people. The affectionate Yiddish terms for them were *Zadie* (grandpa) and *Bobie* (grandma).

Author's grandmother

Reminiscing, he could recall enduring the usual childhood diseases, and at times being confined to bed. Each and every time he was ill, his bobie would come to stay with him, not saying too much while she sat by him and knitted or crocheted. The very presence of this calm, strong woman gave him a lot of reassurance and actually made him feel better.

A few years earlier, Paul had broken his arm playing ice hockey. He did not dare tell his mother and father, who he feared would get very upset and severely chastise him. Rather, he went to his zadie, and without any fuss or bother, this kind and devoted old man calmly took him on the subway to seek proper medical care. Zadie braced Paul's arm with a Ping-Pong paddle to make him more comfortable and brought him to Boston's famed City Hospital.

The doctors had treated him without incident, and he came home with his broken arm wrapped in a cast, accompanied by his protective grandfather, who explained to Paul's parents that all was okay. Zadie sternly warned Mom and Dad not to scold Paul or carry on in any way.

Ruefully, Paul also remembered when he was about seven or eight years old and had in his possession at least a half a dozen cap pistols. He had just found another one—a particularly appealing cap gun—in a local variety store that he felt he just had to have. Mom and Dad firmly reminded him that he had more than enough and told him to forget about his yearning. When word about this got to his zadie, lo and behold, the new cap pistol mysteriously appeared one day on his bedside table. As soon as his parents saw the gun, they knew right away who the donor was, and Paul was chastised by his parents for being so selfish and inconsiderate. For the first time in his life, Paul became aware of the fact that his grandparents had only meager funds to live on.

Paul, his brother, and his parents finally arrived at the major intersection of Blue Hill Avenue and Morton Street. They joined a growing throng of young men, many of them accompanied mostly by parents and, in some instances, close friends. Paul did not want any of his friends to accompany him, feeling rightfully so that this moment should be shared exclusively with his parents and brother.

He had made his loving farewells to his grandparents the night before at their house and had enjoyed being visited there by most of his family of aunts, uncles, and cousins, as well as some close friends.

Time dragged on slowly, and finally the scheduled departure time of 8:30 a.m. arrived. All of the soon-to-be military people crowded around the trolley doors, and as Paul approached a streetcar, his mother asked plaintively, "Can't you wait a bit more?"

He replied, "Ma, it is time to go now."

Dad said tersely, "I'll pray for you every day," fighting back the tears welling up in his eyes.

His brother, Jerry, gripped him and said quietly, "Take good care of yourself."

He turned to his mother, all four feet eleven inches of her, and hugged her thin, bony frame tightly. She too fought a losing battle with her tears and kissed him on his forehead and the sides of his face. "Please, dear God," she invoked, "please bring him back to me."

Paul followed the line of young men boarding the trolley car and found himself a window seat so that he could wave to his little family. As soon as the car was filled with all of the seated passengers, it started to move slowly. This generated a lot of calls and shouts from the well-wishers seeing them off. The trolley moved slowly past the Morton movie theater on the left.

He recalled going to the movies once a week on "dish night." When leaving the theater, on presenting his ticket stub to an usher, he would receive a dish. These dishes were collected by his mother and put into a special set for "company only." Getting the dishes had been more enjoyable than watching the movies.

When he and his friends would each buy a ten-cent theater

ticket for upstairs, after the show started, they would wait for the usher's attention to be diverted. One at a time, they sneaked by him to a seat downstairs that cost fifteen cents. They tried to sit near one another so that they could congratulate one another on their skill and prowess at their accomplishment.

The presentations consisted of two feature-length films, the news, a serial, the coming attractions, several cartoons, and, most of the time, a Popular Science presentation. One of the films was the feature, while the second was of the B category and was likely to be a movie with the Marx brothers, Charlie Chan, Mr. Moto, Sherlock Holmes; or, if the boys were really lucky, a genuine action movie with Errol Flynn or John Wayne. These B

Paul in Seventh Grade
Age 12 during 1936

films were enjoyed by them most of the time even more than the feature film. If the feature was a tearjerker with stars like Sylvia Sidney, Bette Davis, or Joan Crawford, the boys were totally bored and usually went out to the lobby to check out the refreshment stand. The women and girls in the audience generally liked this sort of thing and spent most of the time happily snuffling into their handkerchiefs.

The trolley passed Brown's Jewelry Store on the right, where on occasion Paul would accompany his parents. He had been given his first watch by his parents, and he had selected it at this establishment. It seemed that the proprietor walked around with a magnifying loop permanently attached to his face.

The trolley car picked up a little speed and then passed the G&G Delicatessen on the right. After the movies, and on other occasions, Paul had gone there for a mouthwatering corned beef or rolled beef sandwich, which had always been heaped high with the delicatessen meat as well as a generous portion of half-sour pickles and tomatoes on the side. There was always a group of old-timers who also came down to see their friends. Some of them who did not have much money would order a glass of hot water and then produce a tea bag from out of their shirt or jacket pocket to flavor the brew.

The streetcar was now moving at a good pace and shortly went by Franklin Field on the right. There was a stone wall that ran the length of Franklin Field along Blue Hill Avenue. On the Jewish High Holy Days, following the service, or in some instances when occasional daring young men and women skipped the service, a throng congregated at the wall. The area was crowded with young people each eager to see and be seen. Some sat on the wall, and some congregated on the sidewalk in order to see old friends, meet new friends, and talk.

The trolley went by the Franklin Park Theater, which was across the street from the Franklin Park Zoo. Paul, along with his friends, had enjoyed many a day visiting the zoo, which held a variety of exotic wild animals.

In the warm weather, the many great bicycle paths were used by people of all ages so they could safely ride their bikes without worrying about pedestrians or automobiles. In the wintertime, a magnificent toboggan ice slide was set up where Paul and his friends enjoyed the delight of barreling down the steep hill of solid ice on their sleds and toboggans. A splendid golf course was in the park and was used by many people, young and old.

The trolley continued past Franklin Park and down a slight incline to turn sharply left at Seaver Street. The streetcar was moving faster, and the rest of the trip to South Station blurred into a series of waiting and then moving ahead until they arrived at the military registration area located at the rear of the teeming station. Various groups were then parceled off for their individually assigned units: army, navy, or marines. Paul's army section was brought inside of a separated walled-off section labeled with the notation "US Army Personnel." They were ordered to remove all of their clothing and were given a perfunctory physical examination. They joked among themselves that unless one was clinically dead, he was guaranteed to pass this exam. Once this was completed, they were made to walk through a battery of medical technicians who gave each of them a series of inoculations. The men were then ordered to dress and gather their belongings before being directed out to a train waiting on a track.

They boarded the train for their next destination, which they were told would be Fort Devens. This was a rather large military installation about fifty miles west of Boston. The cars were hot and dusty, and it was with some relief that they saw a corporal approaching carrying a large hamper full of what appeared to be sandwiches. "Got cheese, bologna, or turkey. What do you want?" He was followed by a private first class carrying a cooler full of milk cartons. Paul was in a dilemma. He had been brought up in a home that strictly observed the rules of *kashruth*, or only eating foods that were deemed to be kosher. Here he obviously had to make a choice that would avoid the meat sandwiches and let his hunger guide him toward an unappetizing-looking cheese sandwich on plain white bread. He noted that his fellow recruits eagerly grabbed for their particular choices of sandwich, and all of them wolfed the food down in short order.

When the train finally arrived at Fort Devens, Paul and his fellow passengers alighted. Milling around the train, they noticed a strong odor of burning coal that seemed to be coming from numerous stoves located in the many barracks buildings that surrounded the train site. It made sense, of course, with this being late April; as the afternoons wore on, a chill started to take place in the air.

The new soldiers were ordered to fall into line and marched to a nearby large wood-frame barracks building labeled "Reception Center." Here they were told that each of them would be issued army clothing and gear. Two sets of long tables were positioned on each side of the spacious room. They were heaped with piles of clothing and gear. There was one soldier—in some cases, two—positioned behind each cluster of items. The first soldier Paul came to in the line, a buck sergeant, identified by three stripes on the side of each sleeve, asked him for his name. The sergeant shuffled through a group of three-by-five file cards and handed him one with his name and a set of numbers on it. "This is your serial number," he cautioned. "You have got to remember this better than you know your own name. This is going to be the army's way of identifying you."

Partial copy of US Army Military Identification Card

As Paul and his group proceeded down the line, they were asked what their clothing size was as they drew trousers, shirts, shoes, etc., including various types of essential clothing and gear they would need until they reached their basic training station. There, they were informed, additional items would be supplied to them. Paul noted that by the time he had moved through both lines, he had accumulated the following: a mess kit; a canteen cup; a canteen; one set of toilet articles, including toothbrush, tube of toothpaste, hair brush and comb, razor, bar of soap, one large bath towel, and one face cloth; one large woolen overcoat; two neckties; one tan field jacket; one fatigue jacket; five sets of olive drab undershirts; five pairs of shorts; eight pairs of socks; two pairs of fatigue pants and shirts; fatigue cap; one wool knit cap; two khaki dress shirts; two pairs of dress khaki pants; one khaki dress blouse (army terminology for a jacket); one dress belt with brass buckle; one web field belt, one raincoat; one pair of dress shoes; one pair of field shoes; blanket; overseas hat; a garrison cap; and a duffel bag.

The supply sergeant, a heavy-framed ruddy-complexioned man, told the recruits to carry the bundle of their gear to a long row of benches lining the wall behind the tables. The sergeant ordered, "Try on these clothes and shoes and make sure they fit you right. You'd better understand that you are going to wear these things for the duration of the war. When you get to basic training, you will be issued the remainder of your gear."

My God, Paul wondered, *what else will the army issue me on top of all of this?* Frequently, at an earlier time, he had heard comedians on the radio joke about recruits getting fitted to the wrong size clothing. Abbot and Costello, two well-known movie comedians, had also based a lot of their humor around this. Paul was surprised to see that at least a half a dozen soldiers were going around the room to assist the new recruits in determining whether the clothing fitted correctly. The recruits then stashed all of their individual gear in their assigned duffel bags, filled out a tag with their name, rank, and serial number, and firmly attached the tag to their own duffel bag. They were then instructed to leave their duffel bags, which held their original civilian clothing, and were directed to proceed to an adjacent building. Once again, they filled out cards that were transcribed on to a machine producing dog tags. These were attached to a strong chain, and when they were issued them, they were told that these little slivers of metal were to be put around their neck and worn permanently until they were either discharged or died, whichever came first.

Once again they were formed into two lines, and they were brought next door to another building. Here a spacious room was set up with desks and chairs. At this point in time, they were given a battery of written tests, including what were apparently aptitude tests. After about two hours elapsed, a staff sergeant walked to the front of the room. His rank was obvious from the three stripes on each sleeve with a curved line at the bottom of the stripes. He said, "All right men. Turn your papers in to the people coming down your aisle to collect them. We are now leaving here and returning to the building housing your duffel bags. You will locate your own and meet in front of the building, where you will be assigned to a vehicle which will take you to your own barracks."

When they had picked up their gear, the staff sergeant called off a group of names and designated each man to a numbered truck that was parked outside. The men left the building at a reasonable pace and boarded their assigned trucks. These two-and-a-half-ton trucks held a surprising number of men as well as their individual duffel bags; they were packed nearly to the brim. Paul's truck, after a ride of about ten minutes, stopped in front of a two-story wood-frame barracks building. The same staff sergeant got out of the front of the truck and called off a group of names including

"Kramer, Paul." The sergeant then introduced himself. "My name is Sergeant Harold Williams, and I am in charge of this barracks building, number 3623. Follow me inside, and I will assign you to your bunks." He listed a group of names, once again including Paul's, indicating that this group was assigned to the first floor. A second group of names was called off and sent to the second floor.

As Paul entered the barracks room, he noted a group of neatly arranged bunks set on each side of the room. In front of every bunk was a footlocker. Atop of each bunk was a neatly arranged mattress cover, sheet, blanket, pillow, and pillowcase. Sergeant Williams assigned each man in Paul's group to a bunk and announced, "You are only going to be here for a short time. While you are here, empty the contents of your duffel bag into your footlocker and arrange the items neatly so that you can get at them easily. I will return in a while and assign you to your temporary duties that you will perform for as long as you are at this base."

Paul walked over to his assigned bunk and turned to the man next to him, who was already taking things out of his duffel and packing them into the footlocker. "Looks like we will be here for awhile," he said. "My name is Kramer."

The short, dark-complexioned man next to him held out his hand. "I'm Martino. I hear that we'll be out of here too soon to get comfortable."

Paul replied, "Maybe you are right."

As soon as he answered, he noticed that he was beginning to feel the pangs of hunger. He realized he hadn't eaten since the quick lunch he had had on the train.

As if reading his thoughts, Sergeant Williams returned and said "All right, men. This is it. We're going to form up in front of this barracks in ten minutes and then go to the mess hall."

Remarks of "It's about time," "I'm starving," and "Hope the

chow is decent," permeated the room. Ten minutes later, they formed loosely into two lines, the front line being the men on the first floor and the second line being the men on the second floor. On the company street, in front of their barracks, they were joined by two columns from the adjacent barracks. The four columns, in line, were marched down the company street by Sergeant Williams. He positioned himself at the head of the group and walked briskly, turning every now and then to make certain that the men were keeping up with him.

They arrived at the end of the street, where they came upon a large building marked appropriately, "Mess Hall." The cluster of four columns positioned itself behind several other columns of soldiers who had arrived earlier. The lines moved forward at a slow but regular pace and gradually came near the entrance. The four columns entered the spacious mess hall and then split into two groups as directed by a mess sergeant at the entrance. The two columns then went around each side of two long counters extending nearly the entire length of the room, set up in the center of the mess hall. On either side of these counters, positioned perpendicularly, were sets of long tables and benches, also extending the length of the mess hall. At the very beginning of the counters, massive stacks of metal trays were stacked up, and the GI's were told to take one as they moved along both sides of the counter. Several large signs were prominently displayed on the walls, reading, "Take all you want, but eat all you take."

Once again, Paul's dilemma came back to him. *What am I going to do now? The dishes are not separated for dairy and meat, according to the rules of kashruth. I can't eat any meat that's not considered kosher, so I'll eat as little as possible and get by on whatever candy bars I can scrounge.*

Paul followed the example of Martino, who was in front of him, and took a tray. As they moved down the line, they came to a set of dishes and coffee mugs that they placed on their trays. They then moved on to where a group of soldiers, dressed in white aprons to signify that they were mess personnel, stood over some steaming food containers. First there was meat loaf. Paul passed on that and went on to a heaping mound of mashed potatoes. *I guess I can't go wrong here*, he thought, and he took a sparing amount. Then there was a tray containing green beans, from which he also took a small helping. A large metal urn was filled with a heavy creamy liquid containing multiple chunks of something; it was being stirred around by one of the mess personnel with a giant wooden ladle. Paul noticed that as the soldier in front of him nodded for a helping of this, the liquid was poured over several pieces of toast on a metal plate and put on the soldier's tray.

"Is there any meat in that?" Paul asked.

"You bet," the mess soldier replied. "That's what the army calls SOS, or chipped beef on toast."

Paul shook his head. "I'll pass on that." he said.

"Too bad," he retorted. "That's good chow."

Following this, Paul selected a few slices of white bread along with several chunks of butter. Walking down the line, he came to a huge urn that apparently held coffee. As he poured a cup, Martino turned to him and commented, "Drink this coffee, and it'll put hair on your chest."

Paul followed Martino to a large mess table. As he sat down, Paul said, "I'm not going to go on calling you Martino. What's your first name?"

"Anthony is the name my mother uses to call me, but you can call me Tony," he replied.

"That's fine, Tony," Paul responded. "My name is Paul." They shook hands and then got down to the business of eating their food.

"What's the story, Paul? How come you didn't take any meat loaf or SOS? It tastes just fine," Tony remarked.

Paul replied, "I don't know if you are familiar with any Jewish people."

Sure," Tony replied. "We have plenty of them in our neighborhood in Jersey City."

"Well," Paul continued, "I was brought up in a very observant Jewish home that lived with strict dietary laws"

"I know about that," Tony said. "You guys call that kasher or kosher, right? But if you do that, aren't you supposed to wear that little beanie on your head? What do you call it?"

Paul replied, "The men in my family only wear a yarmulke— or, as you call it, a beanie—when we pray or go to religious services."

"So," Tony replied, "you just can't go through your time in the army eating a little bit of this and that. This may be a very long war."

Paul answered, "I've got some Hershey bars in my footlocker if I get hungry, and later on, when I can, I'll run down to the post exchange and load up on some more of them."

They completed their meal and proceeded to return the eating utensils and dishes to one clearly marked counter and the trays to another.

They followed the line of men out of the rear door of the mess hall and returned to their barracks. Sergeant Williams was waiting for them. He said, "All right, men. You've had a wild, crazy day and are going to hit the sack now. Tomorrow morning we'll get your rear end out of the sack real early, so snap it up! Lights out in fifteen minutes."

Paul and Tony busied themselves going through the various compartments of their respective footlockers. Both were looking for their toilet articles, including soap, toothbrush, and toothpaste, as well as a towel. This didn't take very long, and soon, at the end of their barracks room, they waited patiently in line in order to get at the row of sinks against the wall. As each group of men walked in, a corporal standing just inside the door announced, "There's paper towels on the shelf in front of the mirror. Clean up the mirror and sink after you use it. We don't want any slobs in this barracks."

Following their ablutions, Paul and Tony returned to their respective bunks and got busy making the beds. As soon as his head touched the pillow, Paul fell into a deep sleep.

It seemed that not more than five minutes had gone by when all of the lights of the barracks room came on and Sergeant Williams came storming down the space between the bunks. "All right, you guys, up and at 'em. Now! I said now!" he hollered.

Paul groggily rolled out of bed, grabbed his towel, soap, and toilet articles, and staggered toward the latrine. He found an open space on one of the benches, where he left his toilet articles, and then moved to a spot in the open shower area. The shower woke him up somewhat, and he became even more alert when he finished brushing his teeth. He noticed that many of the men were shaving. Paul had to shave only about two or three times a week at this stage, but he followed suit and went through the motions of shaving the very light beard growth he had accumulated in a few days.

Sergeant Williams poked his head inside the open doorway of the latrine. "All right, you guys. Uniform of the day is fatigues. I want you lined up in front of the barracks in five minutes!" Paul found that Tony was already ahead of him and partially dressed as he returned to his bunk.

They completed their dressing almost in silence, except for a few grunts and moans about how tough it was to lace up the field shoes. The men fell out in front of the barracks and formed up in the same rows in which they had been placed the previous evening. Sergeant Williams, now accompanied by several corporals, walked in front of the group and said, "Pay attention! Listen carefully. I am giving you your duty assignments for the next few days that you are here." He called off six names and said, "After chow, you men are going to report to the mess hall for kitchen police work. The mess people will give each of you a job to do. Uniform of the day is fatigues." He then called off the next six names, which included Kramer and Martino. "You men will report to the sergeant of arms for guard duty after you have finished chow. Dress uniform is the uniform for this duty, and you will report in front of your barracks for your schedule." The next group of men were assigned to "police-up" detail. Sergeant Williams said to them, "Your uniform of the day is fatigues. You are going to go out into the company street, right in front of all of the barracks. You will patrol the area in front of, alongside of, and behind each building. Pick up everything that doesn't grow. The army says that if you can't pick it up, then paint it. Everybody understand?" No one dared to answer. Williams then went on down the line until all in the barracks had been given an allotted job.

Paul looked over at Tony and asked, "How in God's name are we going to do guard duty? I have never held a weapon in my hand except for a cap pistol."

Tony grunted. "They'll think of something. They say the army always does."

The men marched off and reached the mess hall.

Once again, Paul agonized over what to do about the food. After he picked up his tray, he found several large platters filled with sliced white bread. *Can't go wrong here*, he thought, and he selected a few slices, along with a generous slab of butter. He then continued down the line to where he saw a mess sergeant stirring a giant urn containing what appeared to be the same concoction he had seen the previous evening.

"Is that SOS?" he asked.

"You bet," the sergeant replied. "Want some?"

"No thanks," Paul answered, and he moved on down the line.

Next Paul came to a large pan holding scrambled eggs. They looked underdone and watery, but he took a small ladleful. Following that, there was a large pan holding strips of bacon, which he skipped, going on to another large pan, which held something that looked like fine, white cooked cereal.

"That's hominy grits," commented one GI as he moved along next to Paul.

Most of the men in Paul's group, being from New England, skipped the grits, with which they were unfamiliar. Moving on down the chow line, Paul came to a large platter of home fries, of which he accepted a ladleful. This seemed to be a popular item, he noticed. There were a number of other foods set out in large pans, none of which appealed to Paul, considering his concern about his dietary restrictions. The other men alongside him took these choices with some enthusiasm, he noted.

Following their meal, the group assigned to kitchen police duty walked over to the mess sergeant to report. Kramer, Martino, and the others assigned to guard duty adjourned back to the barracks. They hurriedly changed into their dress uniforms and lined up in the street in front of their barracks. Sergeant Williams was there to send the individual groups off to their appointed duties.

A three-stripe sergeant standing alongside Williams stepped forward. Somebody muttered "buck sergeant." The sergeant called out, "All of those men assigned to guard duty, front and center." Kramer, Martino, and the other men designated for guard duty stepped forward. "My name is Dever," he announced, "Sergeant Dever. Follow me over to that truck." He gestured toward a three-quarter-ton truck that was parked alongside the barracks. Dever pointed to the driver of the truck, who was also a three-striper. This is Sergeant Andersen. He and I are sergeants of the guard." Sergeant Dever directed the men to climb onto the back of the truck, which had some hard wooden benches along each side. Both Andersen and Dever were wearing MP brassards. When the truck was loaded, Sergeant Dever pulled up the loading gate at the back of the truck, fastened it in place, and got into the cab of the truck alongside Andersen. Dever was a tall, thin person with pale features. Andersen was his exact opposite—short and stocky, with a ruddy complexion.

The vehicle started off slowly at first, and then, with a whining of the gears, it picked up some acceleration and headed down the long company street. The truck went by a building that did not look like a barracks. It was substantially larger than the usual barracks structure, and a large sign in front proclaimed that this was the "Post Exchange." Under this sign was a smaller one with the word "Canteen" on it. *Got to stock up on some more Hershey bars sometime soon*, Paul mused to himself. The truck continued along this street, which seemed to be a main thoroughfare, and arrived at what appeared to be the perimeter of the camp. It was delineated by a ten-foot chain-link fence attached to thick metal fence posts at about twenty-foot intervals extending in both directions as far as one could see.

The truck stopped, and Sergeant Dever ordered everyone out. He formed them up into a single line and then stated, "You are going to be issued a shotgun and patrol this area of the perimeter. The boundaries of your patrol are designated by yellow flags attached to the fence post. You will walk from here to the yellow flag, turn around, and come back to this spot. Then you'll turn around and do it again, until you are relieved. You are going to be two hours on and four hours off. When your relief gets here, the truck will take you back to your barracks. You can stay there as long as you want or walk down to the PX. It's only a little less than a mile from here. But remember: I want you out in front of your barracks fifteen minutes before your time is up. I don't want to run around looking for you. Be there! If you are worried about carrying around a weapon you're not familiar with, forget it. There's no ammunition in these guns anyway." He smiled. "If someone comes along, you holler out 'Halt! Who goes there?' If they don't answer or keep walking, you yell out, 'Sergeant of the Guard!'" Dever had in his hand a number of whistles attached to thick black cords, and he passed one out to each man. "When you yell for the sergeant of the guard, you will follow it up by blowing on this whistle. It'll bring me faster. I've got a real gun here that shoots," he said as he patted a Colt .45 in a holster attached to his belt. Dever selected two men to begin the assignment and handed each of them a shotgun.

"Remember," he told the men, "it is now 0800 army time, which is 8:00 a.m. civvy time. You will be relieved at ten hundred hours. Let the gun rest in the hollow of your shoulder, and don't press down on it, so it'll be less of a problem carrying it around for two straight hours." Sergeant Andersen left the truck, walked over to the two men, and repeated the instructions they had just been given by Sergeant Dever. The other remaining GIs, including Kramer, were then directed by Dever and Andersen to get back onto the truck. Sergeant Andersen remained with the two men assigned to guard duty.

Sergeant Dever supervised the loading of the truck and then got into the front seat and drove off to return to the barracks. It seemed to those riding in the truck that the distance back was considerably shorter. And as soon as they arrived and disembarked, Kramer and Martino were told by Dever that they would take the next shift. This tour would be from ten hundred hours to twelve hundred hours. They were instructed to be out in front of the barracks by zero nine thirty, ready to be picked up. They were reminded that after they completed their two-hour shift, they would have the next four hours off. The remainder of the group was paired off and given their individual assignments. "One more thing," Dever said. "Latrine rumors have it that you are all going to be shipped out for basic soon. This can happen at any time during the next few days. When you hear 'This is it!' be ready to go."

With that, the men trooped into the barracks, with some sitting on the edges of their bunks and others stretched out full length, trying to doze for the time they had until they had to go on duty. A few men got out a deck of cards and set up a five-card stud poker game. Paul watched with interest but did not feel he knew enough about the game to risk the paltry few dollars he had. Tony echoed his sentiments with the comment "These guys look too sharp for me."

Paul glanced over at Tony, who was already stretched out on his bunk, apparently napping. He followed Tony's example and lay down on his bunk with his arms folded behind his head.

Paul started to doze off, and a short time later, he glanced up at his watch on his wrist to make sure he was not going to be late. He dozed in fits and starts, waking periodically to check on the time. It seemed that before he knew it, it was time for them to move out in front of the barracks. He leaned over and nudged Martino. "Okay, buddy. Up and at 'em!"

Tony stretched his arms out and yawned. "What's going on? I just fell asleep two minutes ago."

Paul replied, "It's nine thirty now, and Dever wants us in front of the barracks, waiting for him."

They both swung their feet out from their respective bunks, got up, and walked toward the front door of the barracks. Sergeant

Dever was impatiently looking out of the cab of the truck, which was already parked in front of their building "All right! Move it!" he hollered.

Martino and Kramer bolted down the stairs and hopped onto the back of the truck, which started moving precisely at the time their feet touched the floorboard. When they arrived at the guard post, Andersen was there, looking at his watch, and he greeted them with a perfunctory nod. It took several minutes for the men on guard duty to return from their rounds. It took less time for them to turn their weapons over to Kramer and Martino. They also handed over the whistles, which Paul and Tony promptly hung around their necks. Sergeant Dever then turned to Sergeant Andersen and formally announced, "You are now relieved." Andersen signaled the relieved GIs to get into the back of the truck, and then they drove off.

Dever said, "Follow me," and walked to the center point of the guard post. He instructed Paul and Tony to turn so that they were back to back and then told them, "Walk until you reach the fence post with the signal flag on it. Stop, and then turn around and return here. You will do this until I come and get you. Any questions?" Neither Tony nor Paul ventured any comment. The sergeant then repeated his earlier instructions by saying, "If anyone shows up except me, you will call out, 'Halt. Who goes there?' If the person does not comply with your command, blow on the whistle and yell out, 'Sergeant of the Guard.' I will be near this post at all times."

Paul started out in his direction while Tony walked in the opposite direction. It seemed to be an endless, boring job. Paul mused, *Who is going to try to get onto a secure military post? But these guys must know what they're doing.* After about the tenth rotation, he heard Tony shout out, "Halt, who goes there?" He turned to see a GI who had wandered onto Tony's route. Paul followed Tony's example by leveling his weapon at the man. The soldier called out, "I know those guns are not loaded, so buzz off. I'm going over the hill!" With that, he bolted toward the fence. Both Tony and Paul simultaneously blew on their whistles, and Sergeant Dever came running up. He had already pulled out his .45 and pointed it at the soldier. "You'd better stop, soldier, or I'll blow your head off!" he shouted. Dever then turned to Tony and Paul. "Good job, men! I'll get this character off to the guardhouse and be right back." He produced a pair of handcuffs, holstered his pistol, and handcuffed the would-be AWOL soldier. Dever nudged him over to the passenger side of the truck. Tony and Paul resumed their duties as the truck drove off. A short time later, it returned, and Dever walked over to them. "I never thought we would have a guy trying to get out of here. Always thought someone would be trying to get onto our base. Go figure."

The guard duty seemed to be without end until finally Dever walked over to them and announced that he was going back to get their relief. A short time later, the truck returned, this time with Sergeant Andersen driving and the two relief guards in the back. The new guards hopped out of the truck, and Andersen called Paul and Tony together. "You are now relieved," he said. "Be just a minute for me to get these men going, and I'll take you back to your barracks." After giving the new guards their instructions and setting them off on their tour, he returned to Tony and Paul. "Okay, jump in the truck and I'll get you back in no time."

"Sergeant," Paul said, "is there any chance you could drop us off at the PX and let us return to our barracks on our own?"

"What's up?" Andersen asked. "You guys looking for the dance? It's not until the weekend."

"I just want to buy some candy bars, Sergeant," Paul said.

Tony added, "I'd like to go along as his bodyguard, if that's okay with you."

"All right, I'll drop you off at the PX, but I want to warn you that I heard that most of your barracks is going to be put on alert in the next few hours. Get back as soon as you can."

The stop at the post exchange did not take long. Paul approached a glass counter under which there was a fairly large assortment of candy bars, chewing gum, and cigarettes. Paul pointed to a carton of Hershey bars. How many can I buy, sir?" he asked a kindly looking middle-aged gentleman in civilian clothing behind the counter.

"Sonny," the man replied, "I've got twenty cartons in the back. You can buy as many as you want for a nickel apiece."

Paul fished in his pockets. He had a total of twenty dollars and change. "Can I buy a dollar's worth, please?" he asked. The man counted out the candy bars and then turned to Tony, who wanted to purchase some chewing gum.

Their purchases completed, both of them spun around and headed back to the barracks. They were met on the front steps by Sergeant Andersen. "About one hour from now, the official word will be coming through, putting you guys on alert. As of now you are confined to the barracks. Better get ready and start emptying out your footlockers into your barracks bags. Whatever doesn't fit gets dumped." He then added, "Take off the sheet and fold it up. Do the same with the blanket and pillowcase, and leave them in a decent pile at the head of the bed." Tony and Paul went into the barracks and busied themselves packing their duffel bags. It did not take long, and shortly thereafter, with their tasks completed, each of them stretched out on his respective bunk, awaiting the next line of events. It did not take long.

Perhaps twenty minutes had gone by when Andersen returned. "All right, men. This is it!" he called out. "This outfit is now on alert, so get yourselves ready. You will be directed where you are going when I return." He came back about twenty minutes later and hustled the men out into the street.

Sergeants Andersen and Dever, respectively, called out various groups of names from several rosters each of them held and had the clusters of men they called out line up in separate formations. Paul was pleased to find that he and Tony were in the same group. Andersen walked over in front of their group and called out, "You men are assigned to group A. The convoy of trucks will come by soon, and they will have signs on the passenger window. Get into any truck that is marked *A*. Make sure you get into the right truck, because they are not all going to the same place. Don't forget your truck letter." He then headed to another group to give them their instructions.

Sergeant Dever was on the opposite side of the street, giving orders to other groups.

"All right already. Where are the blasted trucks?" someone in Paul and Tony's group griped.

"Sure," someone else joined in, "it's hurry up and wait, just like it always is in the army."

After what seemed to be an interminable amount of time, a long column of two-and-a-half-ton trucks turned onto their street and moved all the way to the end before they came to a halt. Large-lettered placards were in the front of each window. Tony and Paul simultaneously spotted the trucks marked *A*. "Here we go." Paul called out jubilantly.

They shouldered their heavy duffel bags and followed the men in front of them, heading for the appropriate trucks. As they approached the rear of the truck, each man swung his own duffel bag off his shoulder and onto the tail end of the truck. He then followed the bag by climbing onto the open tail gate—which was no easy task, considering its height. Tony and Paul found an empty spot on the bench on one side of the truck and sat down next to one another. More men crowded in until the truck was full. With the men and their duffel bags squeezed into the back, there was very little room to move.

Sergeant Andersen came by once again. "When we get down to the train station, wait until I give you the order to jump off. Then you'll wait again until we tell you what car to get on," he said.

"Where're we heading, Sarge?" someone asked.

"Never mind," was his rejoinder. "You'll find out soon enough."

The vehicle started moving, followed by an entire column of trucks marked *A*.

They drove to the road skirting the perimeter of the camp and then out the main gate and onto a bumpy road that seemed to be filled with giant potholes. The ride seemed as if it would never end until finally they pulled in to a train station. Judging from the diminutive size of the station, Paul assumed it must be for one of the small towns near the camp. A very long group of railroad coaches was at the station platform, and as the men disembarked from the trucks, group by group, they were directed to various cars.

As soon as a group of men were seated, some of them started to chant, "Where's the chow?"

Others yelled, "I'm starving. Got to have something to eat!"

This went on for a while, and shortly thereafter, a corporal came through the car. "Knock it off, you guys!" he hollered. "Once we get moving, you'll get fed."

Someone else shouted after him, "Where're we going, buddy?"

The corporal did not answer. In fact, he did not even turn his head while moving on to the next car.

One of the seated GIs yelled after him, "I'll have my steak medium rare." The train did not move for a long time. Some of the men produced decks of cards. Others tried to nap, which was difficult to do with four men seated two on each bench, facing each other. There was no place to put their legs, what with the space-grabbing problems of the bulky barracks bags. Paul and Tony followed the example of other GIs by placing their barracks bags on the floor between the two seats. In this way, they could carefully stretch out their legs without disturbing the soldiers sitting opposite them.

With an almost imperceptible bump, the cars slowly began to roll ahead. Almost no one noticed it at first, but after a while, the train picked up momentum. The scenery outside the windows changed to that of typical countryside with some scattered farmlands. Paul gazed out of the window and wondered aloud, "Where do you think we're heading?"

Tony answered, "Only God and our officers know that. Just relax and enjoy the ride."

—2—

The train door slid open with a resounding bang, and a metal cart holding a giant urn rolled into the car, propelled by a portly gray-haired gentleman. The man was wearing a Salvation Army uniform, and he stopped the cart at the first row of seats. "Would you like some coffee, gentlemen?" he asked cheerfully.

"You bet your life." was the willing reply

"We've got smokes for those who want them, and the donuts are coming up right behind me." the older man offered. He started pouring the coffee into the cups and handed them out quickly to the eager outstretched hands of the waiting GIs. Squeezed in next to the coffee urn were several cartons of cigarettes, a few clinking glass bottles of milk, and a box of granulated sugar cubes. He moved forward, and when he was about halfway down the car, the door slid open, again with a resounding clang, and another metal tray was pushed into the car by an attractive young woman, also attired in a Salvation Army uniform. She was short and thin, without a touch of makeup, and although her hair was primly pulled back in a bun, she was very pretty. She was in no way intimidated by the appreciative whistles and stares that came her way, and she busied herself passing out donuts and napkins to the grateful soldiers who were now taking serious notice of their benefactors.

The older gentleman turned around and called out, "This will be followed up with sandwiches, coffee, and cold drinks in a little while." A number of the soldiers voiced their thanks for the bountiful refreshments. Some just tried to get the girl's attention. The sight of this very attractive young woman serving them some greatly appreciated refreshments cheered them all. The train rolled on interminably, and after a while, the sun started to set and the lights in their car came on. Just about at that time, another Salvation Army person, a young man, wheeled a large metal cart containing sandwiches into their car.

"Okay, guys, what's your pleasure? We've got ham and cheese; turkey; lettuce, tomato and cheese; or bologna. And to save your having a headache on choosing, they're all on white. Soda is coming up." Paul took the lettuce, tomato, and cheese sandwich. Tony opted for the ham and cheese. They had both started munching on their food when the car door slid open again and a cart holding a variety of soft drinks was wheeled in.

"All right. What do you want?" he asked. We've got hot coffee, Coca-Cola, orangeade, Moxie, or root beer." Paul and Tony both selected a root beer, and they settled down to enjoy their dinner.

By this time, the sun had completely set, and the train sped on into the dark of night. The men all dozed fitfully, awakening at different intervals, rolling over in their individual cramped spaces and napping again. Paul awoke with a start. The train had stopped, and he looked out of the window anxiously. They seemed to be in some sort of a railroad yard with long columns of freight trains on adjacent tracks. Through the gloom of the darkness, faintly illuminated by some weak streetlights, he could make out the outline of some soldiers who were patrolling on either side of the train. Tony stirred for a moment and then awakened also.

"What's up?" he asked drowsily.

"I don't know," Paul replied. "Maybe they're taking on some

coal or something." Both men glanced at what little could be seen through the windows, and then the train started moving again. Feeling somewhat reassured, they both fell asleep again almost simultaneously. What seemed to be many hours later, the train stopped again as the sun just started to peek over the horizon. The jolt of the stopping train awoke many of the soldiers.

"Where are we?" asked one.

Someone else commented, "I see a small sign beside the station that says 'Blackstone, VA.' Where in God's name could that be?" The train door slid open, and a sergeant stepped in.

"All right. Everybody out. Now! Form up in a single-line column in front of this car." he ordered. The men complied with his command, gathered up their duffel bags, and slowly started to shuffle out of the car and onto the station platform.

July 1943. Basic training at Camp Pickett, Virginia. Note the helmet liner and necktie in the background that were removed because of the sweltering heat.

There was a long column of buses, painted in the usual army olive drab color. As the men exited the train, noncoms holding rosters called out names and formed the men up into double lines that were then led by another noncommissioned officer directly to their designated bus. Tony and Paul were some of the first to board their bus, and they grabbed a seat up front. Tony nudged Paul. "Will you take a look at that?" he asked, pointing to a large sign in the front of the bus, just above the windshield. Paul looked at it in amazement. The sign read, "Whites in front, Blacks in the rear."

One of the GIs joked, "What place is this? Are we still in the

US of A?" Tony and Paul, along with the other recruits, were stunned. They were all from New England and had never in their wildest imagination dreamed that anything like this could exist, especially in this modern enlightened year of 1943. It was true, of course, that in Nazi Germany racist concepts prevailed; but in this country, how could anything like this happen? The bus driver paid little attention to the comments, apparently having heard this many times before.

When the bus was filled, a staff sergeant jumped into the front of the bus and positioned himself alongside the driver, which apparently was a signal for the bus driver to close the front doors and drive off. As soon as the vehicle started to move, the sergeant called out, "Knock it off, you guys! Pay attention! The place we are heading for is called Camp Pickett, and if you haven't figured it out yet, you are in the great state of Virginia. You have to be wiped out from your long, dragged-out train ride, and most likely hungry. So we're going to take first things first. We are going to a mess hall now, where you will all be fed. Leave your barracks bag on your seat. As you leave this vehicle, check the number on the front of the bus. After chow, you will return to this same bus. This vehicle will take you to your barracks, where you will be assigned a bunk, unpack your duffel bag, and be given a few hours to relax or sack out." A very short time later, the convoy of buses stopped by a large building to which was attached a huge sign that read "Mess Hall." The men piled out of the bus and were lined up by a sergeant.

The entire column of buses had come to a halt by now, and each group was being efficiently lined up by the noncom in charge of their individual vehicle. The lines of men were marched informally to fall in behind other columns of men in front of them. Slowly, and gradually, the men moved into the spacious mess hall and walked along double-sided mess tables staffed by numerous mess personnel. The mess people at the heads of the food tables handed out eating implements, while others farther down the line dispensed heaping portions of food. In spite of his hunger, Paul accepted only a small quantity of home fries and an equally small portion of scrambled eggs. He skipped the platters of bacon, ham, and sausages and stopped at a huge coffee urn to fill his mug with steaming brew. Tony, alongside him, was helping himself to generous portions of all of the food and glanced over at the sparse amount of food on Paul's tray

He exclaimed, "For crying out loud! Are you crazy? You'd better eat something or you'll end up getting sick!" Paul did not answer, and in silence they headed for an empty table. They were followed by a mess sergeant who sat down beside Paul and asked, "What's the matter, soldier? Something wrong with our food?"

Tony interjected, "There's nothing wrong with this chow. It's great! He has a problem with his religious laws that won't let him eat most of the food you've got here."

"I understand," answered the sergeant. Are you Muslim, Jewish, Hindu, or something else? They all have religious laws about food, I believe."

Paul answered, "Thank you for asking, Sergeant. There is absolutely nothing wrong with this great food. According to my beliefs as a Jew, I need to eat kosher food on kosher dishes, if you understand what I am saying."

"I know what you're saying, soldier, and you are not the first GI who has come here with this problem. Let me see what I can do. Give me your name and bus number." Paul gave him the information he asked for, and the sergeant walked over to several of the noncoms holding rosters. He went from one to another until he finally found one who had Paul's name.

The sergeant returned with a satisfied grin on his face. He said, "We'll have this settled in no time. Don't worry about it."

Paul said apologetically, "I don't expect the army to cater to me; I'll just have to deal with it."

The sergeant said, "No sweat, soldier, but if you are having a problem with our food, it becomes our problem too. We'll fix it someway." He then walked back to the food tables. While the men ate, the soldiers holding the rosters walked to the front of the room.

One of them called out, "Knock it off, you guys! Pay attention here. When you finish chowing down, stack your trays on the pile of other trays at the end of this table. Put your silverware in the designated bin and your dishes in the bin with the other dishes. Then return to the bus that brought you here. If you forget your bus number, one of us can help you."

When Tony and Paul left the mess hall, they found their bus was parked third from the front of a huge line of waiting conveyances. They boarded it and returned to their original seats, moving the heavy barracks bags out of the way so they could sit down. After about fifteen minutes, the bus was filled, and a tall, thin, bony corporal got on board.

"Men," he announced, "my name is Corporal Sanders, and I am your barracks leader. Everyone on this bus is going to barracks number 3521."

Sanders instructed the bus driver to proceed, and the bus started with a slight lurch and then traveled slowly down the street to an intersection. They drove for about five minutes to another company street and stopped in front of a characteristic two-story barracks building with a sign indicating that this was, indeed, Barracks 3521. Corporal Sanders assigned the men to either the first or second floor, telling them to take the first empty bunk that they found available. Paul noted, with relief, that he and Tony were on the first floor. Actually there would be no problem with climbing the stairs to the second floor, but he just felt it probably would be a nuisance to be continually climbing up and down the stairs.

As soon as they entered the building, they were somewhat startled to see a captain standing by the first bunk. His connected silver bars were bright and shiny, indicating either that he had not had them for very long or had been busy polishing them. He was about five feet eleven inches—approximately the same height as Paul. The man was somewhat on the stocky side with a moderately fair complexion, and he had a neatly trimmed mustache adorning his upper lip.

Corporal Sanders, who entered the room, upon seeing the officer called out "Attention!"

The captain smiled, "At ease, men," he said. "I am Chaplain Rose—Herbert Rose, that is—and I just thought I would drop in for an informal visit. I am the Jewish chaplain for this outfit, and I have been told that there are several of my coreligionists here. I, however, will be happy to talk to anyone who has a problem or something on his mind." He opened a briefcase he was holding and took out a sheet of paper with several names on it. "Is there a Paul Kramer here?" he asked. Paul stepped forward. Chaplain Rose held out his hand, and Paul took the proffered hand in his. "Nice to meet you, Chaplain," said Paul. Captain Rose suggested, "Why don't you get on with unpacking your gear and stowing it in your footlocker. We can chat while you are doing this."

Tony walked over to them. "I don't want to interrupt this conversation, but I've located two free bunks near the back. Why don't we grab them?"

Wordlessly, the three of them walked over to the bunks Tony indicated, and both Tony and Paul got busy unpacking their duffel bags and packing everything they had into their respective footlockers.

Captain Rose opened his briefcase once again. "I have two army prayer books for you, Private Kramer." He held out two small brown books to Paul. One of them had the printed notation on the cover, "Prayer Book abridged for Jews in the Armed Forces of the United States." Paul paged through it briefly and noted that it included prayers for Sabbath services, daily services, High Holy Day services, festival services, and special occasions, as well as some patriotic hymns. The second book had a printed and signed inscription from President Franklin Delano Roosevelt on the inside cover page and contained readings from the Jewish holy scriptures.

The chaplain joked, "If you keep one of these in each of your breast pockets, you will double your chances of getting through combat." Paul took them, mumbled his thanks, put them into one of the top compartments of the footlocker, and continued on with his work.

Captain Rose said, "There is one more thing I would like to talk to you about that is somewhat personal. Perhaps you would like to go outside and talk it over with me privately." Paul left his chores and turned to the chaplain. "After you, sir," he said anxiously, wondering what personal problem this man had to discuss with him.

As they stepped out on to the company street, Captain Rose turned to him. "May I call you Paul?" he asked. "Certainly," Paul replied. "As a matter of fact, I would appreciate it, sir." "I understand you are having serious problems about a major conflict between your religious convictions and the army food that is available. Is that right?" "Yes, sir," Paul replied. "I was brought up in a kind of Orthodox tradition, where we not only ate food that was strictly kosher but also used separate dishes for meat and for dairy. We even changed our dishes during the Passover holiday. We didn't eat any shellfish, pork, ham, or bacon. Now, most of the food that the army serves includes these foods. I've been figuring that I can get by eating a little bit of dairy in the mess hall and filling myself up with candy bars. I don't feel that the army should worry itself over the problems of a lowly private."

"You are wrong, son," the captain replied. "The army is very much concerned with this type of problem. Most of the major religions of this world, including Christianity, Islam, Judaism, and others, teach that God created man, as well as all of the creatures of this earth. These religions are closely intertwined, and their basic tenets are very similar. They all teach that it is a cardinal sin to harm a human being or harm yourself, since God created you. If there is no alternative but to defend yourself, as we are now doing, we must fight these evildoers to the bitter end. In this terrible conflict, we are trying to survive and preserve our precious democratic way of life. We in the United States find ourselves up against a powerful and determined enemy who wants to destroy us and our American way of life. They also want to destroy freedom-loving people all over this planet. Each and every one of us must pull together in this terrible war, and God willing, our democratic way of life will prevail.

"Getting back to you personally, if you go on depriving yourself of food and nourishment, you may be inflicting serious injury to your body and will in effect be committing a major sin in the eyes of God. And so, for the duration of this war, you will eat whatever food the army gives you. After the war is over, Please God, and you become a civilian again, go back to whatever religious convictions your conscience leads you to. Remember that, for now, you are not violating any of your religious beliefs or obligations by giving your body proper nourishment. Do you understand that?"

"Yes, sir," Paul replied, laughing. "I guess I can ease back on buying more candy bars."

"Another thing," the Chaplain added. "We have Friday night Sabbath services in the post exchange at 7:00 p.m., followed by Saturday morning services at 9:00 a.m., also in the post exchange. I would appreciate it if you would join us."

"Sure thing, Chaplain," Paul responded, and they both returned to the barracks. Chaplain Rose then went upstairs to look for another coreligionist.

As soon as he entered the large room, Paul saw Tony, sit up from lounging on his bunk. "So what's the story? What was that all about?" Tony asked. "Aw, he told me that I was dead wrong about not eating the food in the mess hall. Something about it being a sin to starve myself." Tony rejoined, "We have the same belief in the Catholic faith. We believe that it is a mortal sin to commit murder or suicide or to cause any harm to your own body." Paul laughed. "I was born in the Saint Elizabeth Hospital in Brighton, Massachusetts, and so that makes me part Catholic anyway." Tony replied "I could have saved you the trouble of talking to the Chaplain and told you the same thing. Forget this baloney about living on candy bars. The chow is good, and you'd better make up your mind to start enjoying it!"

Paul said, "The Chaplain also gave me two religious books; one is for daily prayers, and the other is the Bible." Tony held out his hand and said, "Let me see them." As he paged through them, he exclaimed, "We have a lot of the same passages in our New Testament," and he turned them back to Paul, who stretched out on his bunk and clasped his hands behind his head.

He had just started to doze off when he was startled by a shout from Corporal Sanders. "All right men! Listen here. This is the first day of your medic basic training. We are going to give you until noon to put your gear in order and relax. After that I will march you to the mess hall, where we will eat and then return for our afternoon assignment." With that he spun around and headed for the stairs, presumably to give the same message to the men on the second floor.

Paul turned to Tony. "How about a Hershey bar?" he jokingly asked. Tony laughed and went back to lounging on his bunk. Both of them had long since carefully stowed away their clothing and equipment. Some of the men dozed off, and others just sat on their bunks or lay down looking up at the ceiling. Paul wondered if their thoughts were the same as his; he was thinking of home and family and friends.

Several hours later, Corporal Sanders walked into the barracks room. "Okay, men. Up and at 'em! Let's go, and let's go now!" he shouted. The men piled out onto the company street and lined up according to Sanders's instructions. As soon as they were formed up, he proceeded to march them toward the mess hall.

Tony looked over at Paul. "Okay, big boy. I'm going to have my eye on you. No more baloney about passing up the chow or I'll get all the chaplains after you." As they entered the mess hall once again, the appetizing aroma of the cooking food got to Paul, and he started to salivate.

"Here I go, buddy," he uttered, and he approached the food table in a determined manner. A short time later, as they returned with full stomachs to the barracks, he uttered a sigh of contentment. "That chaplain knew what he was talking about," he said to Tony, who just grunted in the affirmative. As they approached the barracks, they found Corporal Sanders waiting for them on the front steps.

"Go to your footlocker, and take your barracks bag with you. Meet me out front immediately, if not sooner," he ordered.

As each GI returned, he, in turn, sent them on the same errand. When they reported outside, he formed them into a column of two's and then told them to stand at ease. When the final group of stragglers got back, retrieved their duffel bags, and fell in line outside, Sanders called them all to attention.

"We are going to have some more testing and classification evaluations in the classroom building for the next several hours. After that, we are going to draw some more gear and equipment. Okay, men. Forward march."

He led them down the company street and on to the main camp road. They turned off after they had passed several streets until they came to a two-story barracks building marked "Classrooms." The men were directed to an auditorium in which each seat had a folding desk. Several other noncoms were waiting for them, passing out testing booklets and pencils. The men were given a battery of tests, and as soon as one was completed, they were handed another.

When the tests were finished, they left the building and were directed to an adjacent one that was marked "Quartermaster." Here they were issued a helmet, helmet liner, pair of leggings, gas mask, mess kit, eating utensils, canteen cup, backpack, entrenching tool, shelter half, and first aid kit. These items were stuffed into their barracks bags, and every man shouldered this new gear and once again formed up into a column of two's that was directed back to their barracks by Corporal Sanders.

While they were unloading the contents of their barracks bags into whatever space they had left in their footlockers, Corporal Sanders announced, "Tomorrow is the first day of your medic basic training activities. You will haul out of the sack at 0430 hours and be cleaned up, dressed, and standing in formation for reveille at 0500 hours. Uniform of the day until further notice will be fatigues. We will stand formation in front of this barracks for roll call and inspection. Salute the flag as it is raised. You will then be marched to the mess hall for chow and return to the barracks no later than 0630 hours. We will then learn close-order drill."

The rest of the day was spent putting clothing and gear away. Some long pegs hung beside each bunk were used to hang certain items of clothing, while other items were folded neatly and put into the footlockers.

After chow, the men fell into their bunks, exhausted by their activities during the day. A neighbor of Tony and Paul turned to them and remarked, "If you think this day was rough, wait till tomorrow. I hear that basic can run you into the ground." Tony smiled noncommittally and said, "We'll see."

It seemed that no sooner than he fell asleep, Paul woke up with a start. It was still dark outside, but he heard a lot of activity outside of the building. The lights came on suddenly, and Corporal Sanders was hollering.

"All right, you guys! Up and at 'em! Get out of that sack, now!"

Getting dressed, marching to the mess hall, and returning was all part of a sleepy blur. Before he knew it, he was standing in formation in front of the barracks. The men were lined up in a column of three's, and Corporal Sanders marched to the front of the column, facing the middle of the street. Acrid fumes of smoke from each barracks stove and chimney pervaded the company street. Sanders was holding a clipboard, and from this he read the names of the men on his roster. They had been instructed to answer loud and clear when their name was called. They were supposed to call out "here," but most of them yelled "yo." Following the roll call, he spun around neatly and saluted an officer wearing a single silver bar.

"All present and accounted for, sir," the corporal reported. This man, as the men had been told earlier, was the company commander, Lieutenant Beauregard Danville. Lieutenant Danville was short, about five feet four inches, and had sandy-colored hair and a fair complexion and slim build. He spoke softly, with barely a trace of his native Alabama accent, and was obviously well liked and highly respected by his men. As soon as he took the salute and report from Corporal Sanders, he turned sharply and moved down the street to another squad. When roll call for the entire company was completed, the men were introduced to a very stirring and beautiful ceremony—that of reveille. As the bugler blew the notes of reveille, the men stood at attention and saluted while a huge flag was raised on a pole at the end of the company street. The men all enjoyed participating in this observance, and at the completion of the bugler's sounds, the men were ordered to "recover" from the salute and ordered to stand at parade rest. This involved folding their hands behind their backs and moving their feet slightly apart.

Lieutenant Danville moved to the center of the street and said, "Welcome to Camp Pickett and the beginning of your medical basic training. If you encounter any problems, bring them up with the noncom in charge of your barracks. If you are still not satisfied, come on down to my office. Tell the company clerk what your situation is, and if he feels that it is warranted, he will bring you in to see me. On behalf of all of your training officers and noncoms, we wish you every success. Get used to the fact that every day, all day, you are going to work hard. What you learn here will go a long way toward saving your life and saving the lives of the wounded GIs you will care for when you get into combat." He then called out to the noncoms, "You may dismiss your men."

Corporal Sanders turned to his squad and called out, "You can fall out for a ten-minute break. Smoke if you've got them. Then we will re-form back here."

A short time later, when the squad had re-formed, Corporal Sanders called out, "Pay attention, men. We are going to learn the basics of close-order drill." He then taught them how to respond to the orders of "forward march," "halt," "about face," "by the right flank march," "by the left flank march," "to the rear march," "column right march," "column left march," and a number of other commands. The men followed these directives until, after a reasonably short time, they were marching and responding to their orders in a satisfyingly cohesive manner.

Sanders halted the group and then called out, "I now want someone to volunteer to put this squad through the paces. The men had learned at an early stage of their army career not to volunteer for anything. He looked directly at Paul. "Hershey bar," he called out. "You look like a good prospect. Front and center!" Paul's reputation about his chocaholic addiction was becoming well known in the barracks. Paul shrugged and marched to the front of the column, turned to the front, and saluted Sanders.

Corporal Sanders loudly corrected him.

"You never salute a noncommissioned officer, soldier; get that?"

"Yes, sir," Paul mumbled.

"And another thing, you never call one 'sir!'" Sanders commanded.

"Yes, Corporal," Paul answered.

"That's better," Sanders replied. "Now put this squad of men through their paces. Go through every command I have taught you, and yell out your orders in a loud and clear voice so they can hear you. Got that, soldier?"

"Yes, Corporal," Paul answered, smiling. He was inwardly amused by the fact that at Boston's Dorchester High School for Boys, he had been a student cadet, and like so many others, he had been meticulously taught close-order drill by Major Willy Moulton. Major Moulton was a tall, stately individual who always walked as if he were on a parade ground. Rumor had it that Major Moulton was a graduate of West Point, but the boys were never able to confirm this.

In a loud and clear voice, Paul called out the commands and put the squad through the entire drill repertoire they had just been practicing. As he did this, Paul reminisced about his proclivity for this and how, as a result, he had been promoted to cadet captain of a company. Later, after Dorchester High School had won the first prize award for being the best marching unit in Boston's street parade, he was promoted to major of his own battalion.

One time, as captain, he had been drilling his company out in the school yard when a sudden thought occurred to him. A cute girl he wanted to impress attended Dorchester High School for Girls, just a few short blocks away. What better way to impress her than to march his company around her school? He impulsively marched the company out of the schoolyard, down Peacevale Road, onto the main thoroughfare, Norfolk Street. This caused a good bit of commotion, with cars having to slow down and drivers leaning out of their windows, some yelling shouts of approval and others cursing the boys out for the delay. Paul marched the company through the busy intersection of Codman Square and into the schoolyard of the girl's school. He marched the company around the school building with some interested girls looking out of the windows, waving, or calling out to a special boy they knew. Paul tried to keep his eye on his company but kept stealing glances at the open windows, looking for his young lady. It wasn't too long after this that some of the teachers noticed the commotion and shooed the girls away from the windows. They then called out to the boys to get out of the schoolyard. Without skipping a beat, Paul calmly marched his company back through Codman Square, down Norfolk Street to Peacevale Road, and back into the schoolyard. Some of the boys who attended Dorchester High School, wanting to impress a new friend, would claim that they attended "Peacevale Prep."

As they entered the schoolyard, Major Moulton was waiting for them, his arms folded akimbo and a disapproving look on his face. "What's the meaning of this, marching your company out of the schoolyard?" he sternly asked. Paul replied that he didn't see any harm in continuing the close-order drill out of the school grounds and showing off his great company to one and all. A hint of a smile appeared on Major Moulton's face, who tried unsuccessfully to frown at the same time. He countered with, "You were trying to show off your great outfit to the girls—or was it a special girl? Whatever it was, don't ever do that again, Captain, or I'll bust you down to a private." Paul saluted him and returned to his duties.

Suddenly, now, he was brought back to reality when he realized he had his squad marching directly toward a barracks, and their collision seemed to be imminent. He snapped out of his daydream and shouted out, "To the rear march!"

Another wild thought occurred to him. As a student cadet, he had been taught the intricacies of marine close-order drill. This was a step up from the ordinary maneuvers, but with a squad such as his, which was showing good coordination and an ability to follow commands correctly, he impulsively gave the commands to put them through the sophisticated paces of close-order marine drill. As the squad marched in a very snappy way to their new set of commands, efficiently and with flair, Captain Danville walked over to observe what was going on. He turned to Corporal Sanders, standing slightly behind him, and in a soft drawl said, "Tell that soldier enough of this fancy-pants drill!"

Sanders strode over to Paul. "Halt the squad now, soldier, and return to your place!" he commanded. Paul shouted out, "Squad halt!" Then, flustered and embarrassed with his orders, he made his way back into the formation, to the accompaniment of laughter and good-natured kidding from some of the men in the ranks. Sanders looked at the men angrily, especially focusing on Paul.

"At ease there," he bellowed. "There'll be no more of this kind of shenanigans." Then he selected another soldier from the squad to put them through the drill procedures they had been practicing.

Later, when they returned to the barracks to wash up for lunch, Tony turned to him. "Where did you learn those fancy drill moves?" "It's a long story," Paul laughed. "To make a long story short, I learned this in high school."

Again Paul thought back to what seemed to be the distant past, when he was a senior at Dorchester High. The school cadets had won first prize in the annual drill parade, which had been held in a soaking rainstorm. All of Boston's high schools participated in this event. The cadets had all marched in perfect formation, in spite of the weather, and won high accolades from the judges, who sat in a sheltered booth, watching the performance. Dunbar Academy, a name jokingly given by many of Dorchester High School's students, won singular honors that memorable day. Dunbar Avenue was a street that adjoined the school.

When the squad returned from lunch, they found Corporal Sanders waiting for them in front of the barracks.

"Get into your footlockers and pull out your gas mask and case, and fall in front of this barracks immediately, if not sooner! Hurry up! Get with it!" The men rushed into the barracks and started scrambling around in their respective footlockers for the gas mask cases and gas masks. As soon as each soldier located what he was looking for, he rushed out into the company street and got into the usual formation. Corporal Sanders first noted that all were present before he addressed the group. He held up a gas mask and said, "Men, this is an M1A1 GI gas mask." He then went through, in meticulously slow detail, the mechanism of removing the mask from its case, positioning it on the face properly, tightening the adjustment straps, and removing it. He repeated the procedure several times. When he felt that they all understood the step-by-step procedures, he had the men follow him, by the numbers, in a precise review of the procedure of donning and removing the gas mask.

The procedure was repeated again and again until the men felt that they could do this blindfolded. When the corporal was satisfied that all of the men demonstrated ability and competence in this exercise, he ordered the group to attention and directed them to the end of the company street. Marching onto the main street, he ordered the men to "double time" (quick march), and they continued this until they arrived at a large single-frame building where he ordered the squad to halt.

"All right men," he called out, "this building houses the gas room. Pay careful attention here! At my command, you are going to enter the room, which is the only room and is marked by a large sign reading, "Gas Room." Your gas mask will still be in your case. Once you are all in place, someone is going to set off a tear gas canister. At that point, I will yell out 'Gas! Gas!' When you hear this, and only when you hear this, you will hold your breath. Shut your eyes tightly, locate the mask in its case, and put it on as fast as you can, just as we have practiced. Make certain that the straps are adjusted properly so that it fits tightly and smoothly on your face. If someone in your vicinity seems to be having trouble, be sure that your mask is on right before you try to help him. Got it?"

Some of the men grunted affirmatively, while others did not even bother to reply. Several other noncoms appeared and helped Sanders to direct the men into the room. They were formed in a single line around the perimeter of the room and waited apprehensively. When all had entered, the door swung shut ominously. A large bang went off as a gas canister exploded in the middle of the room. Simultaneously, someone shouted "Gas! Gas!"

Paul shut his eyes tightly, held his breath as he reached into the gas case, pulled out the mask, and put it on easily, just as he had been taught earlier. After his mask was on, he noted that Tony, standing beside him, had had no difficulty with the procedure either. A GI not far from them was obviously panicking because he was having difficulty putting his mask on. Both Tony and Paul moved to either side of him and helped him position the mask properly on his face. Simultaneously, two noncoms moved to assist and moved the man to the door, since he seemed to have ingested enough of the tear gas to give him continued difficulty.

After they saw him out the door and called several other noncoms over to assist the man, they returned inside the room. They checked each soldier to make sure that he was all right. After the last man had been observed, they moved the men outside, where they were permitted to remove their masks. They all waited while the man who had had difficulty earlier was given a review of the procedures. They then marched him back into the gas room to ensure that he could perform the task at hand competently. A few minutes later, he emerged smiling, indicating that he had successfully completed the exercise.

The men were then marched back to their barracks and given a fifteen-minute break.

Fifteen minutes to the second later, Corporal Sanders walked in and ordered, "All right, men! Make sure that your gas mask and case are stored away. Find your entrenching tool and line up out front." The entrenching tool was a hinged shovel that folded up and was easily attached to a backpack.

After the men lined up in their usual formation outside of the barracks, Corporal Sanders held up an entrenching tool. "You see this here piece of equipment?" he said. "This can save your life if you use it right. When you are in combat, pieces of shrapnel can take your head off or cut you in half. That is besides the bullets that the Jerries will throw at you—and take my word; they have very good aim and very good equipment. Their machine gun, the Schmeisser, is better than anything we or our allies have. You have got to learn to dig a foxhole fast and deep enough so you can get your head and your butt down under cover."

He then marched the squad to a large open field and called out, "You are going to become real good friends with your shovel and learn how tough the red clay of Virginia really is. Space yourself well apart from the guys on either side of you. Then dig yourself a foxhole that is at least six feet deep and six feet wide so you have enough room to jump down into it. All right, men! Get to work!"

They all started with a vengeance, but the very hard soil and the sun bearing down on them made the work extremely difficult. The men persisted, however, and after a reasonable amount of time, their work began to show results. Paul found that he was working up a sweat and paused occasionally so that he could take a sip of water from his canteen and catch his breath.

He noted with satisfaction that the other men were also taking breaks either for a sip of water or to just rest. Corporal Sanders noticed this too and at first did not comment. After a while, however, he called out "No goofing off, men. Try to imagine that you are in combat and your life depends on how fast you can get down into that hole." When Paul finished his task, he tested his work by sliding down into the hole. He happily observed that he could crouch down so that the top of his head was well below the rim of the hole. He paused for a few moments to savor the satisfaction of his achievement.

No sooner did he happily relax than the voice of Corporal Sanders reached his ears. "All right, men. You all did an okay job. Now get to work and fill it back up to the top and then smooth over the earth so no one will kill themselves walking over it." The men all wearily picked up their shovels and proceeded to fill in their foxholes. Some were griping and moaning, while others went about the tiresome job silently. By the time he was finished, Paul realized that he was exhausted and did not look forward to the march back to the barracks.

It has to be close to chow time, he thought to himself. It was either that or he had worked himself up a gigantic appetite. When the group had all completed their arduous task, they were formed back into a column of two's and marched back to their barracks. Tony turned to him and murmured, "My aching back. What else do they have in store for us?"

A few of the other men were talking back and forth when Sanders called out, "Knock it off, you men. Keep moving!" Finally, when they arrived at their destination, much to their relief, the men were told that they could take a half hour break to shower and change. Their soiled clothing was thrown into their individual laundry bags to be brought down to the laundry room at a later convenient time.

By now it was late in the afternoon, and the men were lined up in formation outside of the barracks. A bugler at the far end of the street sounded the notes of Retreat; the men stood at attention and saluted as the company flag was lowered. Paul was very touched and stirred by the beauty and significance of this simple ceremony—so much so that the hackles on the back of his neck stood up. When the bugler finished and the lowered flag had been properly folded and stored away, the men were marched to the mess hall.

While they were eating, Tony, seated next to Paul, asked, "Would you like to go down to the recreation hall after chow?" There was no alternative but to sit on one's bunk, write letters, or just relax. Paul replied, "Good idea."

Rather than walk close to a mile to the rec hall, they opted to board the bus that stopped near their barracks at frequent intervals. They found a pair of empty seats close to the front. They jokingly noted that since all of the barracks were identical, if one was returning in a sleepy or drunk condition, one could spend an eternity trying to find the way home. At the very next stop, a middle-aged black woman, carrying a large and seemingly heavy shopping bag in each hand, got on. The driver did not wait for her to sit down but, as soon as she boarded, lurched the bus ahead. She started to fall, and Paul leaped out of his seat and wrapped his arms around her, easing her into his seat.

"No, you mustn't!" she exclaimed.

"Why?" Paul asked. "Can't I give you my seat if I want to?" Wordlessly, she pointed to the sign above the driver, which read, "Blacks to the rear; Whites in the front."

Simultaneously, a soldier sitting several rows behind them started to mouth some obscenities. Another yelled out, "What's that black —[expletive deleted]—— doing sitting in front?"

"Watch your mouths, you guys!" Paul called out. Tony enthusiastically joined Paul in objecting to the vulgar language.

The poor lady was very distressed and said desperately, "Young man, you'd better let me get out of this seat."

"You can if you want, lady," Paul replied, "but we are not going to put up with that kind of garbage talk."

Tony and Paul then walked down the aisle to one of the soldiers who had been mouthing epithets.

"Watch your mouth, soldier!" Tony said menacingly. The man responded by pushing Tony back and then taking a swing at him.

"Dear Lord," the lady exclaimed. "Please make them stop." Tony, who did not shy away from a fight, responded by clipping the man on the chin with an uppercut.

The other soldier went after Paul, who hit him with a hard right jab on the chin. The bus driver, who saw what was going on, stopped the bus and ordered everybody off. The surge of the soldiers pushing and shoving so that they could rapidly exit caught both Tony and Paul up in it, and before they knew it, they were out on the street, surrounded by cursing GIs, each of whom was trying to punch them. Some of Tony and Paul's barrack mates ran back to the barracks to bring help. Some other barracks emptied out to join the fray. Some joined sides with Tony and Paul, and others aligned with the group trying to hit them. Shrill whistles then sounded as several squads of tough-looking military police moved in to break up the fray. Both Tony and Paul were by this time on the bottom of a pile of battling GIs.

One of the MPs grabbed Paul by the nape of his neck. "Did you start this fight, soldier?" he asked.

Paul replied, "I guess I did."

Tony joined in. "I started it too," he proclaimed.

"Okay," the MP answered. "Both of you come with me." He pushed them into the back of a jeep that was marked "Military Police." "What's your barracks number, soldiers?" the MP asked. They responded and were swiftly driven to the office of their company commander, Lieutenant Danville. They were ushered into his office and told to sit down in the chairs that were offered them. The lieutenant walked to his chair, sat down, and silently stared at them for a few minutes, apparently pondering the problem at hand.

"Did you two start this fight?" he asked in his gentle Alabama drawl.

Tony and Paul both answered in unison, "We did, sir." They had a lot of respect for this recent West Point graduate, who had a reputation of being a good leader as well as a fine soldier. "Can you explain the reason for this?" Lieutenant Danville asked.

Paul replied, "Some men, sir, were using language that is unacceptable in front of a lady." Tony added, "We could not sit by and let something like that go on, sir."

Beauregard Danville sighed. "Tell me that you won't ever do this again, and we will forget about it." Tony and Paul both respectfully objected.

"We can't do that, sir," Paul said softly. Tony added his objection respectfully.

The lieutenant paused for a moment and then said, "Soldiers, get out of here."

Three weeks later, by coincidence or otherwise, the hateful signs were removed from the buses. The very next day, Sunday, the troops were on their own. Tony went to Mass, and Paul wrote several letters to his parents, to his brother, and to his grandparents. When Tony returned, they both decided to take the bus into town in order to get a different perspective. After all, during the previous week they had spent arduous hours doing calisthenics, including lots of push-ups, digging foxholes and slit trenches, and forced marches. The trip took about a half hour, after which they were deposited into the tiny little town of Blackstone. The very first thing that they noticed was a water bubbler on the sidewalk near the bus stop. Attached to the base was a large sign that read "Whites only." They proceeded down the sidewalk and came to a ramshackle-looking restaurant that had a large sign in the window reading, "Whites only." Tony asked, "You seen enough, buddy?" "Let's get out of here," Paul replied angrily. They had to wait another half an hour at the bus stop before their conveyance arrived. It was with a tremendous amount of relief that they boarded the bus to take them back to the camp, and it seemed another eternity before they arrived back at the site of their barracks.

The previous day, Saturday, Paul had attended the Saturday morning Sabbath service, and to his satisfaction, he had been called up to read from the sacred scrolls, the Torah. The chaplain had been delighted to see him and greeted him enthusiastically. Paul made a mental note to let his parents know that he had been given an "Aliyah" (it is an honor to be called up to the front of the religious service). This would please them a great deal. They would also be happy to learn that he had also attended the Friday-night Sabbath service as well.

They decided to go to the recreation hall, which also housed the post exchange, and by mutual consent took the fairly long walk to their destination.

The very next morning, as usual, the lights came on at the ungodly hour of 4:30 a.m. Corporal Sanders walked down the open space between the bunks on either side of the room. "All right, men! Up and at 'em!" he called out. "This is it! Uniform of the day is fatigues, helmet liner, and helmet. Snap to and get going!" One of the men muttered, "Latrine rumor is that today we go to the obstacle course!"

Sure enough, after reveille and chow, the men were lined up in formation, and Lieutenant Danville paused briefly in front of each squad to consult with the squad leaders. They in turn announced that they, in fact, would be going to the obstacle course. They were ordered to "right face" and then, in their usual column of two's, they double-timed down the company streets to their destination some two miles away, near the perimeter of the camp. Finally they came to a large open field that had a series of large posts about two to three feet high driven into the ground. A series of barbed wire clusters were attached to the posts so that they roughly formed an open roof over the ground. Several GI's were grouped around a .50-caliber machine gun positioned at one end of the field.

Sanders called out, "Listen here, men. This is the starting point, where the machine gun is. When I say go, we will send you out in groups of two to crawl down to the end of the barbed wire enclosure, and then you will turn around and crawl back. When you crawl, remember that this here machine gun is shooting live ammunition over your head, so keep your head down and your butt down. Crawl as close to the ground as you can get! Do not try to raise your head, or it will get shot off!"

The machine gun started to fire, and the horrendous noise was deafening. Standing next to one another, Tony and Paul were paired off, and in no time, it was their turn to start. They both got down on the ground as flat and as low as they could and started to crawl forward with their arms and legs spread out to propel them. As they moved along, they came across a GI in front of them who seemed to be frozen in fear and starting to panic. This was the same soldier who had been in dire straits in the gas room. As if by mutual consent, with no word passing between them, Tony and Paul moved to either side of him. They convinced him to crawl with them, giving him words of encouragement. For a few moments, it worked; and then suddenly, he started to try to get up! They both exerted all the energy they had to keep him down and get him to move forward once again. At long last, they reached the end of their prescribed route.

Corporal Sanders anxiously directed two GIs to help the trembling man up. The poor man was shaking and just beginning to realize the impact of what could have happened if he had followed his impulse to stand. Any one of the .50-caliber bullets could have literally torn him in half.

"You'll be all right now, soldier," Sanders said encouragingly.

The man turned to Tony and Paul. "Thank you for saving my life." he murmured.

Sanders directed his attention to Tony and Paul. "You most likely saved this man's life. Great job!" he said sincerely, adding, "For that, you two can have the rest of the day off."

Without a further word, the two of them ran back to the barracks, showered and changed, and then headed out for the recreation hall. Tony headed for a billiards table, while Paul spotted an upright piano in a corner of the large hall. Since there was no one playing the piano, Paul sat down, ran his fingers over some of the keys, and started to play some of his favorite songs. He varied his selections from classical music to jazz and reminisced about how, at the age of seven, after an unsuccessful attempt to learn how to play the violin, his parents had purchased a baby grand piano. They hoped he would show some affinity for music and enrolled him in music lessons. Paul had seemed to have a natural talent for music, and especially the piano.

Paul's father was a great tenor who at a young age sung in

a choir and later joined a Yiddish theater group with which he performed in many cities in the Northeast.

Paul's elementary lessons segued into classical music, and he developed a deep and abiding love for many varieties of this type of music. By the time he reached the age of fourteen, he discovered that just about all of the cute and attractive girls of his age simply liked jazz and boogie-woogie, and had little use for longhair music. Even though he was scheduled to give concerts by his teacher, he had made the momentous decision to discontinue his classical music studies and instead study jazz. His parents were both deeply disappointed but respected his wishes and made arrangements for him to study with an instructor who had himself been a protégé of Art Tatum. Within a year, Paul was playing great jazz music and was especially appreciative of the fact that his teacher had included transposing and arranging with the lessons as well.

One sunny spring afternoon, as he was practicing some of his jazz repertoire, his mother entered the room and opened several of the windows in the parlor where he was playing. A short time later, the doorbell rang and a young man explained to Paul's mother, when she opened the door, that he appreciated the great musical sounds emanating from the Kramer apartment. Paul's mother invited him in, and he introduced himself as Harry Roberts. He explained to Paul and his mother that he wanted to talk about the possibility of Paul joining his jazz band. Harry already had a drummer and a saxophone player, while he himself played the trumpet. Harry, himself about sixteen years old, explained that he had several prospects for jobs, and getting a good piano player was number one in his priorities.

Harry wrangled permission from Mrs. Kramer for the band to practice in the Kramer parlor, since it was so spacious. In a few days, after school, the band assembled in the Kramer home, set up their instruments, and started to practice. It seemed that because the boys had no money, they could not afford to buy arrangements. It was decided that they would purchase a single sheet of each song, and then, because of Paul's knowledge, he would transpose the music for each instrument and then arrange it as well. They had played only a few selections when the doorbell rang.

"Oh my goodness," Mrs. Kramer exclaimed, "the neighbors must be upset about the racket going on!" Instead it was a group of teenagers who asked if they could come in and listen to the performance. Mrs. Kramer scrambled to bring in kitchen chairs, bedroom chairs, and stools—practically anything that would accommodate the boys and girls who tried to crowd into the parlor. The other kids out in the hall asked that the windows be opened so that they could listen to the "jivey" music out on the street.

One afternoon, Harry entered the apartment all excited. "I have great news!" he proclaimed. "We have just been offered a job for the summer at a resort in Millis."

"We are just going to play in the band all summer?" Paul asked. "Well, not exactly," Harry sheepishly replied. "We also have to do some other chores to earn our salary and pay for our keep." "Just what does that involve?" Paul's mother asked. "Well," he answered, "we have to work as busboys and waiters too, but we'll play in the band six nights a week." Sensing some disappointment, he added, "We'll be getting tips besides a salary." Paul asked, "How much of a salary do we get?" "The pay is eleven dollars a week, plus the tips we get waiting on tables and playing in the band." he answered.

Lengthy discussions followed with all of the boys' parents, some of whom were reluctant to approve. Finally the boys' wishes prevailed, and a few weeks later, a small convoy of automobiles headed for the tiny suburb of Millis, some thirty miles west of Boston. This was a small farm community that boasted one gasoline station, a small variety store, and a few resort hotels.

The cars all stopped at the main building, where the boys checked in to see where they would stay. Some of the parents thought they would be staying in the main building, but their ideas were shattered when the boys were escorted onto a narrow path behind the building into a cluster of trees. A little farther into the woods was a ramshackle cabin in a clearing.

The young woman who guided them to this spot announced, "This is your living quarters." Some of the parents who accompanied the group started to object, but the boys silenced them with icy stares. As they entered, a few field mice clattered along one of the roof beams. The boys got busy unpacking their things while the parents bade them a fond and sad farewell.

Later the boys were told about their schedule. They were to arise at 4:30 a.m., dress quickly, and report to the kitchen by 5:00 a.m. They were to set up the tables for breakfast, serve breakfast from 8:00 a.m. to 10:00 a.m., clear the breakfast dishes, set up for the midmorning snack from 10:30 a.m. to 11:00 a.m., set up the tables for lunch, serve lunch at 12:30 p.m., clear the tables, serve mid-afternoon snacks from 3:30 p.m. to 4:30 p.m., set the tables for dinner, serve dinner from 6:00 p.m. to 7:30 p.m., clear the tables, be showered and changed by 8:30 p.m., and report to the bandstand at 9:00 p.m. to play until midnight, six nights a week. Friday night being the Sabbath eve, there would be no dancing, but informal card games would be held in the dance hall area.

One of the boys cracked, "What do we do in our spare time?"

The dining room tips ranged from poor to generous. In the dance hall, the boys at an early stage found that the maître d' would cue them in on whose birthday or anniversary it was. They would single out the lucky person or persons and play an appropriate tune. When they did this, the tips were more substantial than usual. Still another source of tips was from grateful parents who had a teenage daughter standing sadly on the sidelines, watching the dancers. The boys would take turns dancing with these damsels, which always evoked a grateful response from one or both parents.

"Hey soldier!" A loud voice interrupted Paul's reverie. A GI standing alongside the piano was trying to get Paul's attention. "Can you play 'Stardust'?" he asked. Another called out, "How about 'Elmer's Tune'?" More voices were clamoring for "Chattanooga Choo Choo," "Tangerine," "One O'clock Jump," "Boogie Woogie Bugle Boy," and more. He could play most of the songs. Time passed quickly, and after a while, he noted that it was getting late. Time for Chow.

He got up amid a chorus of complaints like "Don't go yet, buddy" and "How about just one more?"

"Sorry, guys, almost time to feed my face." He grinned as he got up and headed for the door.

The days passed quickly, including many twenty-five-mile forced marches in the hot Virginia sun undertaken while carrying a kitchen-sink pack. This included almost everything in their footlockers as well as the shelter half that they had been recently issued. The men had been limited to one sip from their canteen during the brief breaks they took. The water, which had been treated with some foul-smelling medications, was not very appealing even when they were thirsty.

Corporal Sanders reminded them that they were limited to one sip from their canteen each time they took a break. He issued each man some salt tablets and had them take one before they started, and they were to take another every two hours. One man, Private Long, grumbled that the salt tablets made him sick to the stomach and refused to take them. About two hours into the march, with everyone perspiring heavily, Long started to stagger and stumble, and finally he collapsed. Paul and Tony dragged him under the shade of a tree and removed his shoes, socks, and backpack. Tony pulled out a clean handkerchief and soaked it with his open canteen. They sponged his face, neck, feet, and ankles. Paul held his open canteen to Long's lips, pouring some water into his mouth. After a few seconds, he revived and tried to get up. Paul and Tony held him down until they were certain he was fully conscious. They then replaced his shoes and socks and got him to his feet, and each took turns carrying Long's backpack as well as his own. While taking turns holding on to Private Long and keeping him steady on his feet, they were able to join the rest of their group. Corporal Sanders came over, noted that everything was under control, and proceeded to direct them all back to camp.

Author at one of the camps where he received training

One morning, following retreat, Corporal Sanders ordered Paul and Tony to report to the company commander's office. "What did we do wrong this time?" Tony asked. Paul replied anxiously, "We'll find out soon enough," as they raced to their destination.

They reported to the sergeant of the day, who bade them to sit down in the outer office. After what seemed like an eternity, the sergeant called to them and bade them to enter the inner door to the commander's office. As they entered, Lieutenant Beauregard Danville arose from his seat, smiling, and beckoned them to two chairs in front of his desk. Paul and Tony were immediately put at ease by the smiling person who faced them. "I want to say that from the outset, the two of you have demonstrated admirable leadership qualities, as well as a high level of self-discipline. This includes your recent actions in the bus incident. Although I cannot condone your getting into a brawl, your efforts to defend that woman were commendable. In addition to that, your initiative in helping that soldier during the gas mask drill and later helping this same man on the obstacle course without regard for your own personal safety singles you both out as individuals with good potential leadership qualities. Your handling the situation of the soldier who suffered from heat prostration was highly commendable. You have both demonstrated integrity, competence, ability, and responsibility under pressure. For all of these reasons, I am contemplating recommending you both for officer candidate preparatory school, and following that, officer candidate school—that is, unless either or both of you have any objections."

Tony was the first to comment, "With all due respect, sir, I simply cannot see myself as an eighteen-year-old ordering around a bunch of men, most of whom are older than me." Paul joined in, saying, "With your permission, sir, I very strongly agree with my friend Martino."

The lieutenant looked at them carefully. "I respect your feelings, men, and in this case, I am going to recommend that you both be sent to the medical and surgical technicians school at Fort Benjamin Harrison in Indianapolis, Indiana. This will be a continuation of the medic basic program you have just about completed. And I am sure that you both will be of greater value to the army with this education." He stood up and held his hand out to Tony and Paul. They eagerly took turns shaking hands with him.

He handed them a sheaf of papers. "Sign the top form and hand them back to me. This indicates that I have explained all of your options and you have opted to take the training program at

Fort Ben. At the conclusion of your basic training here, you will be given a thirty-day furlough, with travel vouchers and orders that will get you to your home and from there to Indiana. Good luck, men."

Tony and Paul stood at attention, saluted him, smartly about-faced, and jubilantly walked out of the office.

— 3 —

After a trip of seventeen hours from Richmond, Virginia, the train pulled into Boston's South Station. Paul hoisted his jam-packed duffel bag onto his shoulder and made his way into the teeming station.

A white-haired older gentleman wearing a Salvation Army uniform approached him. "Can I help you, soldier? Do you need directions, or could you just use a cup of coffee and a donut?"

"Thank you, sir," Paul replied. "The coffee and donut would go great just now, sir. I am from around here, so I am all set as far as directions go. I thank you for your hospitality as well as your helpful offer."

He took the proffered coffee and donut gratefully and thanked the man again while practically inhaling the fresh, tasty donut and wolfing down the steaming coffee. The food on the train had been stale and sparse. Paul found a pay phone, deposited his nickel, and called his mother.

"Ma, I am at South Station and going to take the subway home. No, Ma, please do not come and get me; I'll be fine, and I'll be home soon. First, I am going to stop off at Bobie and Zadie's before I get home. Okay, Ma. My nickel is up. Love you. See you soon."

He hung up the phone and walked rapidly to the subway

station. The subway train took him to the Washington Street station. There he departed the train and connected with a different subway line, where he boarded an Ashmont Station–bound train. As the train pulled out of the tunnel, he glanced out of the windows across Dorchester Bay, reminiscing about the many frequent trips he had taken on this subway line with his mother or his mother's sister, Aunt Estie. She had been like a second mother to him and, on many occasions, had taken him into town for a treat in order to go shopping, sometimes watch a movie, and eat lunch. She had always purchased him a souvenir of the trip, such as a new toy, shirt, or whatever.

Estie's husband, Ted, was also a loving uncle who was generous with all of his nieces and nephews, and he had bought Paul his first pair of long pants. In the summertime, at Nantasket Beach, Uncle Ted would fill the back of his truck with neighborhood kids, take them down to the famed Paragon Park, and buy strips of tickets for all of the children, who enjoyed the many and varied rides and amusements in this great amusement park.

It seemed to be an incredibly short time for the train to arrive at Ashmont station, where he debarked and took the Norfolk street bus. Another short distance was covered before the bus let him off at the corner of Morton and Norfolk streets in front of a popular drug store on the corner. The soda fountain there had boasted of providing the best frappés and hot fudge sundaes in the neighborhood. He crossed Norfolk Street and in no time made it to the corner of Middleton Street. On one corner was the familiar family-run grocery store, and on the opposite corner was a small Jewish temple called Congregation Beth Jacob. Many years before, his beloved grandfather, Zadie, had scraped together whatever monies he could and made a donation that would allow this modest little building to open.

The grocers, Irving and Shirley Cohen, spotted him from their large front window. They excused themselves from their customers and came out to greet him. Shirley gave him a resounding kiss on the side of his face, and Irving grabbed him in a giant bear hug. They reluctantly released him, telling him, "Go to your loved ones." As Paul walked down the gentle hill of Middleton street, he remembered the great times he and his friends had experienced in the wintertime on their sleds, coasting down this same slope. He stopped at the house numbered 16, the home of his grandparents. This edifice housed not only his Bobie and Zadie, but also Aunt Sarah; Uncle Israel; their daughter, his cousin Shainaie; Aunt Estie; Uncle Shlamy; and their children, Charnette and Yosel. It was a rambling two-story home with a curving banister and stairs that connected the two floors. The kids all had a grand time sliding down the banister when their parents were conveniently on the other side of the house. The delicious aroma of food greeted him, even as he bounded up the front steps. His darling grandmother, Bobie, her eyes filled with tears of happiness, met him on the front porch. His grandfather, Zadie, was close behind her, and the three of them just hugged each other without saying a word.

Zadie murmured, "Welcome home, my beautiful *Aynekel* [grandchild]."

They ushered him into the parlor, which also served as a dining room. A huge platter of steaming potato latkes sat next to an equally large tureen of matzo ball soup. Another large platter held meat and potato knishes.

"Ess mine tiere kind [Eat, my precious child]," Bobie urged. As soon as he finished the soup, Bobie brought in a large platter heaped with stuffed brisket. This was followed by Zadie bringing in a huge dish of *Tsimmes* (carrot, meat, and potato casserole), followed by many more mouthwatering side dishes. They gazed contentedly at him as he wolfed down the food. His basic training had done a lot to increase his appetite for food.

This reminded him of Tony telling him about visits to his own grandmother's home, where she too would press food on him, telling him to *Mangia* (eat) while enthusiastically plying him with all sorts of delicious Italian home-cooked delicacies.

As Paul ate, some of his relatives crowded into the room to greet him, interrupting his feast with lots of hugs and kisses.

In the middle of this clamor, somebody called out, "Give the kid a break! How about letting him go on down to his mom and dad. Give them a break. And how about his brother?"

Paul had barely finished wolfing down his food when his bobie and zadie urged him to get up. "Gai mine kinde [Go, my child]," Bobie whispered, hugging him and kissing him. Zadie murmured a prayer of thanks, gave him a fierce hug, and kissed him as well.

Paul reluctantly moved to the door, amid lots of loving clamor, and headed back out onto the street.

He turned to them all and promised, "I'll be back real soon," as he headed back down Middleton street. As he moved along, he was greeted by neighbors and friends along both sides of the street.

His mother, father, and brother, as well as some friends and neighbors, were waiting for him in front of the stoop of their first-floor apartment. His mother rushed to him, clasped her arms around his neck, and murmured, "Dear God, thank you for bringing him home safely."

His father and brother also hugged him while the group gathering around them took turns welcoming him home and ushered him into their spacious apartment. The delicious aroma of cooking food and freshly baked pastry struck him in the hallway before he even entered their home. His mother had prepared just about everything his grandparents had served him, with a few more refinements, such as a huge platter of gefilte fish, kasha and *Varnishkes* (bowties), potato kugel, *Gribbenes* (rendered chicken fat), more tszimmes, and an impressive variety of cakes and cookies that included *Tayglach* (delicious pastries covered with honey). Paul realized he had thought about this moment often during his basic training. Now, with of a full thirty days of leave coming to him, he basked in the luxury of the prospect of sleeping late, getting all of his favorite foods, and seeing all of his family and friends.

The late August days were hot and muggy, and so even with gasoline rationing in effect, his father had scrimped and saved his gasoline ration coupons so that they could manage a trip out to Paul's favorite summer spot, Nantasket Beach. Nantasket is a small peninsula located about halfway between Boston and Cape Cod, and for many years it was a popular summer attraction for many New England residents. The beach itself consisted of miles of mostly smooth white sand, and at low tide, the firmly packed sand became a great place for marking out a baseball type of diamond and playing ball. The kids, boys and girls, used a soft rubber ball with bumps on it, and it was called a pimple ball. No bat was used, but the batter simply held the ball in one hand and hit it with the fist of the other hand.

As they approached the long curving road leading into Nantasket proper, the huge roller coaster of the famed Paragon Park, a very popular amusement center, came into view. With wartime gasoline rationing, the usual heavy crowd had noticeably diminished. The trusty 1941 Plymouth made its way down the main thoroughfare to Nantasket Avenue and over to Revere Street, turned left, and drove all the way down to the bay, where Mom and Dad had rented a cottage for a few days. They could not stay longer, since Dad had to get back to work at Roger's Furriers in Boston. They did not have enough gasoline stamps to permit him to commute back and forth.

As soon as they unpacked, Paul hastily donned a bathing suit, grabbed a beach blanket and the family's prized portable radio, and headed up Revere Street toward the beach. This was just one block from Kenberma street, where both areas on the beach were very popular locations for the teenage crowd. In no time, Paul approached some high sand dunes topped by sparse long grass, which fronted the ocean.

He could hear the pounding of the surf even before he saw the dark blue ocean. He walked through an opening between the dunes and saw spread out before him the unblemished soft white sand and sparkling dark blue waters of the Atlantic Ocean. Disappointingly, but understandably, because of this terrible war, very few of his old friends were there. Paul greeted the few who were there and spread out his blanket near them, taking care to position the precious portable radio on the blanket. Tuning the radio to a popular radio station setting that delivered all of the popular music of the forties, he lay down to enjoy the hot sun and the aroma of the salt air. The marvelous sounds of the orchestras of Louis Armstrong, Harry James, Benny Goodman, Count Basie, Tommy Dorsey, Jimmy Dorsey, Artie Shaw, and Duke Ellington permeated the air. Great singers like Frank Sinatra, Roy Eberle, Billie Holiday, Billy Eckstein, Louis Prima, Sarah Vaughn, and a host of others made him happily forget the war for a few precious moments. The pounding of the waves almost instantly had him drowsing off.

In just a few minutes, perspiring heavily, he jumped up and ran down the smooth, wet sand to the water's edge. The ocean was characteristically frigid—so cold, in fact, that when he walked in up to his knees, they became numb with the cold. He persisted nevertheless until he was waist deep; and then, after taking a deep breath, he plunged into the water. The intense cold was shocking but very refreshing, and he swam a number of strokes parallel to the shoreline. There was a hint of the usual undertow, and he did not want to take any chances of fighting this powerful force. After a short time, he stood up and walked toward the shore.

Most of his old friends were gone, many of them having joined the armed services. Some of the young women he knew had enlisted in the Women's Army Corps (WAC), or the women's branch of the US Naval Reserve (WAVES). Practically all of the young men he knew were in the armed forces. The carefree, happy world as he knew it before the war would never be the same.

The days at home flew by, and before he knew it, time was at hand to return to his army duties. His mother insisted on packing all of his things, folding carefully everything that she had previously washed and ironed, including his handkerchiefs. She even insisted on ironing his shorts and T-shirts—something that would amuse his buddies when he told them later on.

She fretted about Paul not taking one of the many suitcases she offered him, but she submitted to his insistence that everything be packed into his barracks bag. The small amount of gasoline available had been used up in the trip to Nantasket and other small essential trips, and so his parents and brother Jerry once more walked with him down to the trolley on Blue Hill Avenue. As they proceeded, Paul's father confided to him that he had tried to enlist but the recruiting noncom had sympathetically explained that he was needed more on the home front to take care of his little family.

Just as they spotted the next trolley coming over the hill of Blue Hill Avenue, his mom, dad, and brother all took turns hugging him and wishing him well. He jumped onto the platform of the streetcar and put his hand out to drop the necessary coins into the receptacle. The conductor put his hand over it and said, "Not for you, son. We don't take money from people who are serving our country." Paul thought for a minute. He took his uniform for granted most of the time, but it dawned on him that there was a tremendous amount of respect and esteem that the public held for members of the armed forces.

The ride was uneventful, and in no time he found himself once again at Boston's South Station. The place was jam-packed with throngs of people—mostly servicemen and servicewomen, along with a few scattered civilians. Paul spotted the Salvation Army booth along with the cheerful middle-aged gentleman in it who welcomed him with a proffered cup of steaming coffee.

"You, heading back to camp, young man?"

"Yes, sir. I have travel orders and vouchers to go out to Fort Benjamin Harrison in Indiana."

"Why don't you get out your travel vouchers, and we will go over to the ticket office and get you on your way. I believe they will route you through New York City."

They waited patiently in a long line of people, and Paul anxiously asked, "Aren't you worried about attending to your booth?"

"If I spot any service people who look like they need help, I will scoot over. In the meantime, we will get you on your way."

Finally they made it to the ticket window, and in no time the travel vouchers were converted to tickets and schedules that would take him to New York City and then transfer him to another train. The final destination would be Indianapolis, Indiana. The Salvation Army man turned to him, shook his hand, and said, "May God bless you. Have a safe and pleasant trip, and may the Lord keep you safe in this conflict."

Paul thanked him, hoisted his barracks bag onto his shoulder, and headed for the track he had been directed to. There might be a little wait, but he didn't mind. Almost at that instant, the loudspeaker blared out with the announcement of his train and its number, as well as the track it was leaving from. As he walked down the track, a conductor greeted him, asked to see his ticket, and directed him to one of the cars.

"This train is going to take you all the way, soldier. When you get to New York, just stay aboard. People will unhook some cars and add on others. This car you are going to board, no matter how many stops, will finally get you to Indianapolis. Good luck."

"Thank you, sir," Paul replied, and he made his way onto the railroad coach. There seemed to be a substantial number of empty seats, but it was early, and he knew that long before the train pulled out, most of them would be filled. He selected one in about the middle of the car, swung his duffel bag up to the luggage rack, and seated himself next to the window. Sure enough, in a short time, the train started to fill. He heard the conductor shout "All aboard," and in a fairly short time, the train started to move out of the station. Paul looked out of the window, taking in the downtown Boston skyline, the theater district, and, closer by, the immediate area of Chinatown. Further back, the taller buildings of Boston's financial area loomed. The train made its way slowly, with ever-increasing speed through the South Station railroad yards, past some of the backwaters surrounding the tracks, and on to Back Bay Station. Here there was a brief stop while another crowd of people came aboard, and then the train was off and quickly coming up to speed. At the Route 128 station, still another crowd of people surged aboard.

The train sped on and stopped again in Providence, Rhode Island. Now the seats had all long been filled, and there were some people standing in the aisles. Paul chuckled at the fact that the train had been advertised as "nonstop."

Paul had started to doze off, but he opened one eye when the train lurched slightly. He saw an elderly lady trying to lean on the seat for support. He immediately got up and offered her his seat. "No, no, no," she insisted, "I want you to stay put." "Please, ma'am," Paul replied, "I insist."

She reluctantly took the empty seat, but not before some younger man started to go for it as well. A stern look from Paul was all it took to get him to back off and let the woman sit down. The woman and a civilian next to her struck up a conversation with Paul. Time seemed to pass very quickly, and it seemed that in no time the train arrived at Grand Central Station in New York City. Most of the passengers disembarked, and an equal number then boarded, filling up the cars once again. The train got under way once again, preceded by a series of jolts, jerky starts, and sudden stops. Once out in the railroad yards, it stopped. There, one engine was shunted off, and another joined the front of the train. Paul dozed fitfully and kept wakening, worried that he would sleep through his scheduled stop in Indianapolis. A conductor, sensing his concern, walked over to reassure Paul that he would let him know when they arrived. He then slept more peacefully for several hours. There was a tiny washroom, where he was able to wash his face and brush his teeth. He knew that he could go for several days without shaving since he had such a light beard. The passengers were notified that there was a dining car on the train, but he learned from some of the more experienced travelers that this was pricey, and so he contented himself with the sandwiches and drinks that were frequently supplied by Salvation Army people.

At long last, at about six o'clock in the morning, the train arrived at the main terminal of Indianapolis. Paul, with a tremendous feeling of relief and appreciation for the fact that he had finally arrived, grabbed his duffel bag off the rack, where it had waited for such a long time.

He headed for the large information booth in the center of the station, but before he even had a chance to speak, a young woman behind the counter said, "Soldier, the bus for Fort Benjamin

Harrison is just outside. There is a sign in the front of the bus marked "Fort Ben."'"

"Thank you, ma'am," Paul replied, and he headed out of the door to find the waiting bus, which was already being boarded by some GIs. Most of the men appeared to be exhausted, like Paul, and so there was little conversation as the bus filled and then departed. In a very short time, the bus arrived at the outside gate of the camp. Two MPs were at the open gate, carefully checking the papers of all of the soldiers who wanted to enter, and directing them to the appropriate bus waiting just inside the gates. Paul was directed to Bus 4, which would take him to the Fifth Battalion, Company A Orderly Room.

He swung onto a seat near the front and heard a familiar voice say "Hey, buddy, what are you, stuck up or something? Aren't you even going to say hi?" Paul swung around, and in the very seat behind him was Tony, as jovial as ever. They shook hands vigorously and then simultaneously moved out into the aisle until they agreed on an empty double seat, and slid in side by side. They eagerly started to relate the great times each one had had with his family. Before they had a chance to complete their stories, the bus stopped at a building that looked like a huge barrel that had been cut in half, with the widest part of the barrel on the ground. One of the men commented that this was called a Nissen hut. In front of the Nissen hut was a large white sign that read "Company A, Fifth Battalion, Orderly Room." All of the soldiers got off and informally lined up at the front door. Tony and Paul, being in no hurry, got in line toward the back and continued to talk about their furlough experiences. Little by little, as one man came out, the next one moved in. Finally it was Paul's turn.

"Private Paul Kramer, reporting as ordered," he said as he handed his travel orders to the three-stripe sergeant sitting behind the desk in front of him.

The sergeant took his papers, scanned them, and then said, "Welcome to Fort Benjamin Harrison and the start of your medical and surgical technician training program. You are assigned to Barracks 4190, which is the third building down on the left from here. First you will go down the corridor behind me to a large room. Take a seat there, and you will be given an orientation presentation very shortly.

Paul headed down the corridor and entered a large room that held desks and chairs, along with a large blackboard on the front wall. He took a seat near the front and saved one for Tony, who joined him just a few moments later.

After a few minutes had passed, the sergeant entered the room and took a position in front of the blackboard.

"My name is Sergeant Wilinsky, and once again I want to welcome you to this program. It will be very intense and require a lot of hard work on your part, because you are being trained to save lives. You will be given the best tools, materials, and equipment that we can come up with. You have already completed your medic basic and had to cope with not being trained in the use of weapons." A few of the men laughed. He continued. "Your

October 1943. Fort Benjamin Harrison, Indiana at the Medical and Surgical Technicians School.

weapons will be medications and instruments that will be critical for the survival of our wounded personnel. Starting tomorrow, you will attend classes in this room from 0800 to 1200, break for chow, and continue with classes from 1300 to 1600. You will then be given close-order drill until 1700, at which time you will stand retreat and then go for chow. When you are dismissed, you will bring your gear to your barracks—as I told you, Barracks 4190. Get yourself a bunk, stow your equipment and gear, and then report back here to draw your school supplies. Any questions?"

No one said anything, and so the men were dismissed. Paul and Tony headed out the door and moved quickly toward their assigned building. Some of the men lagged behind, but Tony and Paul were eager to grab a bunk on the first floor. The barracks buildings they saw were typical two-story buildings similar to the ones they had seen at Camp Pickett. As they entered the first floor, fortunately, they found a couple of unoccupied bunks near the front. Their availability was characterized by the mattresses being folded up over a pillow at the head of the bunk. The mattress cover and pillowcase were at the foot of the bed. They both got busy unpacking their duffel bags, and each took care to store his clothing and gear neatly. Then came the task of pulling the mattress cover over the mattress and then slipping the pillow into its case. With that done, they headed back to the orderly room.

They were directed to the rear of the building that served as a supply room. Here there were stacks of textbooks, notebooks, pens, pencils, and scratch pads. There was also a pile of mimeographed papers stapled together listing the academic schedule and various courses they would be taking, along with course descriptions. The men were handed an item from each pile while a noncom checked off their names.

Another noncom had them sign for the materials they had received. They were then instructed to return to their barracks and lay out the materials they had received on the set of shelves behind each cot. A tec 5 (a corporal with a *T* under his stripes) entered the room.

"All right men. Pay attention here! My name is Corporal Rutkowski, and I am your barracks chief. I have the first bunk on the first floor here. If you have any questions or problems, come and see me. If I am not in the barracks, I will be up at the Orderly Room. We are going to form outside of this building in fifteen minutes. Uniform of the day is fatigues."

The men all returned to their tasks, and those who were in a class A uniform changed to fatigues, including the floppy-brimmed fatigue hat.

Corporal Rutkowski formed the men up in front of the barracks in a column of three's. He then marched them down to another Nissen hut that was marked "Quartermaster Supply Room." Two clerks were behind a long counter; one was a three-stripe sergeant, and the other a private first class (PFC). Here each man was supplied with towels, soap, and still more underwear and socks. They then carried this back to their own barracks and got busy putting away these items.

Paul and Tony finished their tasks rather quickly and started to peruse the titles of their textbooks. Some of their titles were *Materia Medica, Basic Pharmacology, Mathematics including Basic Algebra, Human Anatomy and Physiology, Treatment of Wounds, General Pathology,* and *Army Training Manual for Medical and Surgical Technicians.*

Tony commented, "My God, I didn't think we were going to medical school."

Paul nodded in agreement, and they both came to the conclusion that they were pleased with the intense level of instruction that was apparently planned for them. Some of the men headed for the showers and latrines that were located in the front of the room. Others busied themselves packing away their things or writing letters. Tony and Paul, having finished with their chores, went outside to look over their company street.

There were several more Nissen huts, with signs in front of

them designating them as classrooms. Each classroom seemed to hold about fifty chairs and small desks.

They returned to the barracks to find the new men settling into their bunks and putting away their gear. They were then marched down to the supply room for their academic materials and returned shortly thereafter.

When they entered the barracks, corporal Rutkowski announced, "We have a little more time to get oriented, and then we are going to line up outside for retreat. At 1700 we will march out for chow. After that, you are on your own until lights out at 2000. At that time, you will be in your bunk. Reveille tomorrow morning is at 0500, followed by chow at 0530. Uniform of the day, unless otherwise ordered, will be fatigues. You will line up in front of this barracks at 0715 to be marched to your classroom. There is no excuse for being late for class, nor is there any for missing a class. All courses will be graded by written and oral examinations. If a soldier fails a single course, he will be shipped out of here immediately, if not sooner." He looked around the room. "Any questions?" he asked.

When no reply was forthcoming, he did a smart about-face and strode out of the room, apparently to go upstairs to deliver the same message to the soldiers ensconced there.

After the bugler awakened everybody early the next morning, the men piled out of their cots and made themselves ready for this first day of intensive class work. Tony and Paul were both eager to get started, and as soon as they returned from chow, they put together whatever texts were indicated from the class schedule, as well as their necessary notebooks and writing implements. A short time later, they were marched down the Company street to the first Nissen hut housing the classrooms. Tony and Paul selected a seat in the front row so that they could hear everything and have a better view of the blackboard. They all waited patiently, having some hushed conversations among themselves, which came to a halt when the door opened and a short, stocky, older-looking staff sergeant entered.

The staff sergeant deposited his books on the desk at the front of the room and said in a crisp, clear voice, "Good morning, men. I am Sergeant Oliver Jones, and I will be teaching your first course this morning, which happens to be Anatomy and Physiology. I want you to take good notes and make clear illustrations, which will all be reviewed by me at the end of the term as part of your grade. I will be teaching several other courses as well. The lectures will be fifty minutes in duration, at the end of which time you may leave the building to have a break and smoke if you've got them. The latrines are in the back of this building. My attitude is that you are here to learn and I am here to teach you, so let's get on with it. Remember that there is no such thing as a dumb or stupid question. What you are going to learn here will determine whether or not you can save some soldier's life in combat. Pay careful attention, and if you don't understand something, or you need me to repeat whatever was said, speak up. Your questions will also benefit everyone in this room, so remember that too."

As they arrived at the time for a break, it was noted that one of the men in the back row was sound asleep. Sergeant Jones said softly, "I don't expect he is going to be with us for long." Sure enough, the very next day, the man was gone. Rumors had it that he was transferred out to a repple depple (replacement depot)

The lectures were intense, interesting, and well presented. Sergeant Jones and the other teachers might well have been experienced professors on the faculty of a top-rate university, with the well-organized, detailed, and thorough presentations that were made.

Tony and Paul took to their studies with ease, and in a short time, various classmates were asking them for tutorial help with several of the courses. Tests, quizzes, and exams were given frequently. Thus the men had to be well up-to-date with their studies. Much knowledge and many practical, useful, and helpful skills were imparted to them during training sessions.

In the case of a twisted ankle, which was expected to be a common problem with infantrymen, the key ingredient to helping to reduce the painful swelling would be ice. But there was no way that ice could be supplied at the front lines, and so other emergency procedures would have to be used in order to make the soldier mobile. The patient's foot would be elevated and fully extended, after removing the boot and the sock. A liberal amount of tincture of benzoin was applied to all of the foot and ankle. Then strips of adhesive tape would be put on the ankle, starting at the very base of the ankle, one going horizontal and one vertical, forming what was called a basket weave.

Tourniquets, as a means of combating bleeding, were explained in detail. This would be a prime emergency measure designed to save a soldier's life.

They were taught how to clean a wound with hydrogen peroxide and then to swab the sides of it liberally with tincture of Merthiolate. In dealing with open or gaping wounds, their instructor told them to sprinkle liberal amounts of sulfanilamide powder into the wound, while two tablets of sulfathiozole would be administered orally every four hours. Then a sterile four- or six-inch gauze pad would be fastened into place with adhesive tape. The edges of smaller wounds could be brought together with a butterfly bandage. This was performed by taking a wide strip of adhesive tape and cutting the middle section of the strip and folding it over to narrow it, and then placing one end on one side of the wound, pulling the wound closed, and attaching the other end of the strip to the opposite end of the wound.

For burns, they were equipped with butesin picrate ointment.

A major lifesaving procedure was mixing plasma powder into sterile water and then injecting this into a vein. Later on in combat, this in itself would save many lives. Care and treatment of foot ailments were presented in detail, especially trench foot and athlete's foot. The use of morphine syrettes for controlling pain, all of the particulars for making splints for limb fractures, and the filling out of the emergency medical tag (EMT) for wounded GIs were also taught.

The days flew by, and then the weeks also. Before they knew it, the training program was drawing to a close.

One early evening after retreat and chow, Paul decided to walk to the recreation hall. After he had taken but a few steps, an olive drab camp bus stopped near him to pick up passengers, and so he took this opportunity to climb aboard. As he took a seat, he involuntarily looked toward the front of the bus, and he noted with relief and gratitude that there were no hateful signs proclaiming that whites were to be seated in the front and blacks in the rear.

Paul thought back to a time eleven years prior, when he was celebrating his seventh birthday. At that time, because of the terrible fear of the dreaded disease poliomyelitis, most of the children were adorned with a piece of camphor attached to a string or cord around their necks. Families hoped that this would ward off the terrible sickness. Paul's mother made arrangements for a party and invited a group of his classmates he was friendly with. Mom prepared some dishes of ice cream along with an assortment of delicious home-baked cookies.

After he had blown out the candles, the boys settled down on the living room floor to play with an Erector set that had been passed down by an older cousin, Jerry. For a time they got along well, until one of the boys wanted a part that another one held in his hand and stubbornly resisted surrendering it.

"Hand that over, you stupid n———!" the boy shouted.

The victim of this tirade was Emanuel Puryear, who happened to be black.

Paul's mother, who heard the argument, rushed into the living room.

"What you said to Emanuel is a terrible hateful, and hurtful thing! Now you apologize this instant!" she exclaimed.

The bully—in this case a stocky boy named Franklin Hackins, who was larger than his years would warrant—looked sullenly at her.

"I'm not going to apologize for something I'm thinking," he snarled.

"Very well then," Paul's mother replied. "I want you to leave this house and remind you that you will never be welcome here! As a matter of fact, I have a good mind to have a talk with your mother about this."

Franklin looked at her with tears in his eyes. "I'm sorry I upset you," he muttered.

"You tell Emanuel you are sorry and shake his hand," she scolded.

Franklin held his hand out limply to Emanuel, who took it briefly, and the handshake was completed.

"Now let's all go into the kitchen and have some fresh-baked chocolate chip cookies and some ice cream," she said with relief.

The bus came to a lurching halt in front of the recreation hall and broke off Paul's daydreaming, bringing him up to the present with a start. The building housing the recreation hall also had a post exchange, where soldiers could buy various and sundry items like toilet articles, cigarettes, candy bars, and soft drinks. The large main hall was used as a dance floor, or just a place where the men could hang out. Several pool tables and Ping-Pong tables were on the side of the room, as well as an upright piano. A juke box would play all of the tunes of the popular orchestras and singers of the day.

When the juke box was not playing, Paul busied himself playing the piano, and invariably a group of young men and women would join around the piano with requests for special songs or just enjoy the pleasure of listening.

One room off the main hall served as an interfaith chapel. On one of the occasions when Paul was playing the piano, he was approached by the Catholic chaplain.

"I am Father Murray, and I enjoy your piano playing. Would you help me by playing for our Catholic Sunday service? We have a small field organ in the chapel that is used for all three faiths: the Protestant, Jewish, and Catholic services."

Paul replied, "Father, I will be happy to oblige, but I want you to understand that I am not Catholic."

The chaplain smiled and said, "Son, you will be very much appreciated. Each of us prays to God in his way, and you will be a great help in our prayer service. Paul explained to him that he was very much at home participating in a Catholic service, since his Father had grown up in Boston's suburb of South Boston. Many of his father's friends were Catholic, and his father attended services with them on many occasions. After Paul was born, his father brought him along with him.

Shortly afterward, the Protestant chaplain, Reverend Thompson, sought Paul out in his barracks.

"Father Murray has told me about your musical talent. I know that you would give us a great hand with our congregational Sabbath observance." Since the times of the services did not conflict, Paul happily agreed, and the following weekend he was playing for both the Protestant and Catholic services.

It was no surprise when the Jewish chaplain, Rabbi Rose, sought him out and told him how happy he was to see him once again.

He said, "My friends the Catholic and Protestant chaplains

tell me that you are playing for their services. How would you like to play for the Jewish Sabbath services on Friday night and Saturday morning?"

"I would be happy to oblige, chaplain," Paul replied. "There is one favor I would like to ask. The next time the three of you are together, would you all say a special prayer for me? I think that, coming from the three of you, the prayer will have a lot more clout."

"Consider it done," the chaplain replied, grinning.

"Remember, Rabbi, if I don't get to heaven, I will be coming back to the three of you with lots of gripes."

The weekends were subsequently filled with Paul's volunteer duties. His time during the week was taken up with going to class, taking voluminous notes, studying, and preparing for the following lectures and labs.

One Sunday afternoon, Tony and Paul decided to take a walk into Indianapolis. There was a bus leaving from camp, but it was only about two miles to town, and so they decided to walk. They had not gone five steps when a car stopped beside them. A middle-aged couple looked out of the window and said, "Going into town ?"

"Thank you, sir" Tony replied. "We thought it would be a good idea to take a walk. We appreciate the offer just the same."

The lady said, "Come on, boys, and get in the car. Save your energy for some other time."

The boys looked at each other, shrugged and did and as they were told. When they were seated and the doors were closed, the car started up slowly, and the woman turned around from the front seat to face them.

"Our son is in the service. He is somewhere in the South Pacific right now. It makes us feel good to do something for the servicemen and servicewomen, and besides, it's the least we can do for you. We travel up and down the road to and from town, giving soldiers lifts, until we use up our gas rations"

The man spoke over his shoulder. "Whereabouts do you boys want to get dropped off? If you are not familiar with the place, we suggest the center of town. There is a big fountain there, and most of the GIs like to congregate around there."

"Sounds good to me," Tony replied.

In just a few minutes, they were dropped off at their destination, and the couple drove off to give other soldiers lifts. Right across the street from the huge fountain that adorned the center of the square was a movie theatre. On the marquee was advertised a Bette Davis movie, but what caught their attention was the listing of the second feature, which was a Charlie Chan movie. They crossed the street to the box office and inquired when the Charlie Chan movie would be playing.

The movie would cost them twenty-five cents each, which was a bit more than both of them were used to paying. However, seeing Warner Oland solving another crime would be worth it. They were informed that this would not go on for another hour, and so they settled for an ice cream parlor next door to the movie. Paul ordered a giant hot fudge sundae drowned in hot fudge with extra nuts and lots of whipped cream. Tony settled for what was called a Banana Boat Supreme, which was sinfully laden with all sorts of ice cream, whipped cream, and other goodies. They dawdled over the ice creams, killing time until they had about fifteen minutes to the start of the movie. Then they reluctantly got up and headed out to the theatre, enjoyed the movie, and started back for camp.

Another car stopped beside them, this time driven by a teenage boy.

"You soldiers want a lift back to camp?" he asked.

Paul answered, "Thanks just the same. We're going to walk it."

"Okay," the young man replied, and he drove off in search of other soldiers needing rides back to camp.

"These people are the greatest," Tony observed.

"You got that right, buddy," Paul responded.

When they returned to the barracks, there was a large notice posted on the front door: "Attention all men of Company A, Fifth Battalion. You are hereby placed on alert. All day passes, weekend passes, and other leaves are cancelled. You will be shipping out in a few days at the close of your classes. Start packing all of your gear into your barracks bag. Books and school equipment will be returned to the quartermaster on

November 1943. Having successfully completed the ten week course at the Medical and Surgical Technician's School at Fort Benjamin Harrison, Indiana, I proudly wore my Cadeuceus badge as a full fledged Medic.

the last day of class. Per order of the Commanding Office."

Sure enough, the very same announcement was made in class, but they were given permission to keep their notebooks. The instructors all made brief encouraging speeches. The final days passed even more quickly, and suddenly it was time to ship out. No one could tell them what their new destination would be, but latrine rumors had it that they would be moving to a staging area or a port of embarkation (POE).

— 4 —

Camp Shenango in Western Pennsylvania was a characteristic US Army installation. The late fall brought in some cold winds that promised a wintery environment in the very near future. Most of the barracks stoves were kept burning, with the result of a heavily pervading odor of coal smoke throughout the facility.

The men had been brought into a large auditorium, causing many to speculate on which army training film would be shown to them next.

Tony, sitting beside Paul, commented, "I think we are going to get the straight poop here."

Paul grunted in reply, not knowing for sure what was to transpire.

A top sergeant came out onto the open stage with a floor microphone in his hand. "All right you guys," he shouted. "Knock it off! Quiet down!"

As soon as the crowd settled down, a major joined the sergeant on the stage, took the proffered microphone, and said, "Men, you all want to know what is going on. This camp is a staging area. You are all going to be here for a few weeks until the unit comes up to strength. Soldiers will be shipping in here from camps all over the USA. When we have reached our quota of men, we will be shipping out, most likely to some POE. In the next few days, you will be turning in your light summer uniforms and be drawing heavy-duty khaki shirts and pants. You will also turn in your gas mask for a newly issued one. You will be given some field rations to take with you for your trip to your next destination, wherever that will be."

Some of the men groaned. The field rations were not the greatest in the world. One had a small container of processed cheese and bacon, along with some biscuits, and another contained a large, hard piece of concentrated chocolate.

"Your time will be taken up in short-order drills, forced marches, and orientation lectures on living in the field," the major commented. Some of our drill noncoms particularly like to work out with lots of push-ups. So I can promise you, you will get lots of exercise to keep you in shape. Keep your nose clean, follow orders, and you'll get along fine here."

With that, he did a smart about-face and strode off the stage. The men were brought to attention and then dismissed.

As Paul and Tony left the auditorium and proceeded back toward their barracks, two familiar-looking officers approached them. Tony and Paul saluted them, and one of them commented, "Don't you remember us?"

It was Father Murray and Rabbi Rose. The four of them enthusiastically shook hands.

Tony queried, "What are you fine chaplains doing in a place like this?"

"We heard from the grapevine," Father Murray said, "that this outfit is going to be sent to a POE, and we want to go along for the ride."

"We can't let you great soldiers go overseas without us," Rabbi Rose observed.

"So where is the third musketeer?" Paul asked.

"The Reverend Thompson is shipping out from Fort Ben in a few days and will be joining us," Chaplain Murray explained.

Just three days later, when walking down to the recreation hall, Paul and Tony spotted Chaplain Thompson leaving the officers' club.

"Welcome to Shenango, Chaplain," Paul said.

"Any news on where we are heading from here?" Tony asked.

"Since we are near the East Coast, we probably will ship out to Iceland, England, or Africa, but, you never know. We could be sent out to the West Coast and from there out to the South Pacific or Alaska. It's better to flip a coin to decide where we'll go and when we'll go."

Tony replied, "We happen to be turning in our lightweight summer uniforms and drawing heavyweight clothing. That could mean Alaska or England."

Paul commented, "We sure won't have long to find out, most likely."

Sure enough, just two days later, with several hours' notice, they packed their gear and were loaded on to two-and-one-half-ton trucks. The heavy canvas flap in the back of their truck was pulled down so that no one could look out of the rear of the vehicle. As they approached the highway, through an opening in the flap, they could see that the convoy of trucks extended for several miles.

Some of the men got busy opening up their rations. Others gazed straight ahead, while some closed their eyes and tried to sleep in spite of the bumpy ride.

It seemed to take forever for them to arrive at a military facility. Some of the men peeking through the canvas flap in the back of the truck saw a large sign posted on the front gate that read "Camp Shanks, Orangeburg, New York." Then came the expected comments: "This is it! This is a POE, and we are going overseas, like now! Get out your water wings, buddies; we're going sailing."

The convoy entered the camp and drove several miles to an area of barracks that apparently was not inhabited by any soldiers. The trucks stopped in the middle of each barracks street, and the process of emptying their cargo of soldiers and barracks bags began. Tony and Paul were directed to a barracks by a noncom holding a roster attached to a clipboard in his hands. As if out of habit, the two of them found a pair of unoccupied bunks on the first floor and started to unload their gear and pack this into the familiar footlocker at the foot of the bed.

A tec 5 corporal walked into the barracks and called out "Kramer, Paul! Is there a Paul Kramer here"?

Paul stood up and answered, "Here, Corporal."

"You are a tough person to get a hold of. This here telegram just missed you at Camp Shenango. It did some fancy tracking to locate you here."

"Did you say I have a telegram?" Paul asked apprehensively.

"Right here, soldier." The corporal held it out to Paul, who grabbed it fearfully and ripped it open with Tony peering over his shoulder.

The telegram read, "Dear son, I don't want to frighten you, but your grandfather has been seriously ill and has taken a turn for the worse. As a matter of fact, he is not expected to live and is asking for you. Is there any chance that you could get some emergency time off so that you could come up here and see him, even if it is just for a little while? Please get back to me as soon as you can. Love, Mom."

Tony spoke first. "Corporal, where is the company commander's office?"

The corporal replied, "Follow me."

Tony and Paul completely forgot about their gear, some of

which was lying on the floor, and rushed out of the door after the corporal. They proceeded at a run, and it didn't take long for them to arrive at a building marked "Orderly Room."

A three-stripe sergeant greeted them at the front desk and inquired, "What is your problem, soldiers?"

The tec 5 said that they had some kind of emergency problem that they needed to talk to the captain about.

Paul held out the telegram to the sergeant, who took it, read it, and then knocked on a door marked "Captain Evan D. Wright, Company Commander."

"Come in," a booming voice said from the other side of the door.

The three of them entered, and as they approached the captain's desk, they came to attention and saluted.

Captain Wright returned the salute briskly. He seemed to Paul and Tony to be a middle-aged man, somewhere between thirty and thirty-five years old. He was husky but did not seem to have any extra fat on him, and he had a light complexion and sandy-colored hair.

The sergeant held the telegram out for Captain Wright, who took it and studied it intensely.

"Which one of you is the soldier in question here?" Captain Wright asked.

Paul held his hand up.

"Looks like you have some serious problem back home, soldier," Captain Wright commented.

Paul said, "Sir, I am not trying to get out of any army duties, but my grandfather means a lot to me, and I am anxious to see him before he passes away."

"I understand, son, but we here at this port of embarkation have to look at this realistically. At any minute, your unit can be placed on alert to be moved to the nearest port of embarkation.

Under these circumstances, I cannot justify issuing a weekend pass or even an overnight pass. What we do have in place is a protocol to have a representative of the Red Cross rule on the justification to allow you time off to get back home."

"I will call him and get him over as soon as possible so that he can be made aware of the situation and make a decision. Why don't you soldiers have a seat out in the front room, and I will try to get him here as soon as possible."

Paul and Tony came to attention again, did an about-face, and stepped into the front office. They sat down on two of the available chairs, and it seemed that they waited there for a very long time. Paul was tormented by the fact that he had not yet been able to get in touch with his family and was sure that they were anxiously waiting to hear from him.

Finally the door flew open, and a civilian, stocky and bald, and carrying a tattered briefcase, hurried into the room and identified himself as Charles Roberts with the Red Cross. The sergeant knocked on the captain's door and ascertained it was all right to bring Mr. Roberts into his office. Before entering, he spun around toward Tony and Paul.

"Is one of these people the person in question?"

The sergeant answered in the affirmative.

"You two stay put until I instruct you to come in," Mr. Roberts said in a fairly hostile manner.

Tony muttered, "I don't like this guy or his attitude."

"Maybe he is upset with something else, or maybe he is ticked off at being routed out of whatever he was doing and brought down here," Paul answered.

A few minutes later, the sergeant was asked to bring Paul and Tony into the captain's office.

Captain Wright said to Paul, "I am sorry, soldier. This man refuses to recommend that you be granted an emergency leave."

Paul was stunned, "How can that be, sir?" he asked. "This is a real emergency in black and white."

Mr. Roberts said curtly, "The telegram does not say that your grandfather is dying. It simply says that he is not expected to live. I have no alternative but to recommend against your request."

Paul's eyes brimmed up with tears of frustration, anger, and grief. "How can you do this?" he blurted out. "I'll never forget you or what the Red Cross is doing to me."

Tony blurted out, "What's the matter with you? Are you blind? Can't you understand what this telegram says?"

"I have made my decision and will not discuss this any further," Mr. Roberts said brusquely. He then turned and walked out of the door.

Captain Wright put his hand on Paul's shoulder. "I am deeply sorry, soldier, but I have no alternative but to follow through with established protocol. I will, if you will let me know your religious faith, contact a chaplain to give you some counseling, and I will permit you to use this office phone to call your family."

Tony said, "He is Jewish, Captain, and if it is all the same to you, I would appreciate your bringing the Catholic chaplain too. I am so teed off I need some counseling too—and a lot more than that. This whole thing stinks, if you'll pardon my expression, Captain."

Paul replied over his shoulder as he left the office, "I'm just going to go over the hill, then."

Captain Wright rushed after him and caught him by his arm. "Kramer, you cannot go absent without leave now. You would be arrested and put behind bars. You would be court-martialed, and think of the added grief that this would cause your loved ones."

Paul replied, "Thank you for your concern, sir, but I have to do what I have to do."

With that he rushed out of the door, his eyes so filled with tears that he missed the front step and nearly fell down. Tony grabbed him to steady him, and the two of them hurried back to their barracks. Deep in the bottom of his barracks bag, Paul found a small leather bag with two handles and started to throw some odds and ends into it, including his toothbrush, toothpaste, shaving gear, and several changes of underwear. He had no sooner completed this task than someone in the barracks shouted out, "Attention!"

Everyone came to attention as Chaplains Rose and Murray anxiously approached Paul.

"What's this, Private Kramer?" Chaplain Rose asked anxiously. "We no sooner join up with you again than we find you about to get into some real serious trouble."

"Captain Wright explained the problem to us briefly when he contacted us, so why don't we go back to his office and try to settle this situation the best way we can," Chaplain Murray suggested. "It's good to see the both of you again, even though it is under these very trying circumstances." He turned to Tony. "You backing up your friend?"

"You bet, sir," replied a clearly concerned Tony.

The four of them left the barracks and headed for the company orderly room.

The sergeant ushered them into Captain Wright's office.

"Chaplains, thank you for coming here," Captain Wright said, proffering his hand to Father Murray and Rabbi Rose. "We are locked into a protocol that was decided upon long before I got here, and so my hands are tied," Captain Wright commented.

"Maybe we can arrange for Private Kramer to meet his parents someplace not far from camp." Chaplain Rose suggested.

"We are fairly close to New York City," Chaplain Murray said. "How about having Kramer's folks meet him at, say, Grand Central Station?"

"Begging your pardon, sirs, but I want to get home and see my grandfather," Paul said vehemently.

"That's not going to happen, soldier," Captain Wright said. "We may be placed on alert at any time. The only reasonable thing we can do is go along with the suggestion made by these gentlemen. In that case, you could at least see your folks for a little while anyway. It will probably be a long time before you see them again. Even then, I will be sticking my neck out giving you a pass off the base for a little while."

"How am I going to get in touch with them?" Paul asked.

"You can use my phone to call home, but make it short. You have a trip of about forty-five minutes to the city and forty-five minutes back, and I can squeak out two hours for you to meet your family in the city," Captain Wright said.

Tony spoke up. "That sounds like the best deal you can ask for, buddy."

"There is a bus that leaves for the city every hour on the hour at the front gate," Captain Wright said.

"We—that is, Chaplain Murray and myself—have made the acquaintance of a Salvation Army major," Chaplain Rose said. "I believe that he has some form of transportation available. Maybe we could prevail on him to give Kramer a lift into town and bring him back."

Captain Wright held out the telephone on his desk to Paul. "Call up home and see if your parents can arrange to come down to Grand Central Station and get a ballpark idea on how long it will take them to get here. Then we will work around that time frame."

Paul picked up the phone and, feeling somewhat uncomfortable, dialed for the operator to route him through long distance to dial up his home telephone.

"Hello, Ma, is that you?" he asked.

"Paul, how are you, darling? Are you all right?"

"Yes, Ma, but I can't get up to see Zadie. How is he doing now?"

His mother's hesitation was very brief, but as soon as she replied, he knew instinctively that she understood what situation he was in and was trying to allay his fears "Your Zadie is doing better, Paul, and I am sure he will understand if you cannot get up here."

"Ma, is there any chance that you, Dad, and Jerry could get over to South Station and take a train to Grand Central Station? I have permission to leave camp for a few hours and can meet you there."

"Paul, wait just a minute. I have a train schedule here in my kitchen. Let me take a look. Here it is. There is a train leaving here in about two hours. That gives me time to take Jerry out of school and meet Dad in town and be at South Station in time for that train. The normal traveling

Paul's family at home while he was away during WW2

time is five hours, give or take. We're on our way, darling. We will see you at Grand Central Station, where, God willing, we will have no real delays and be able to see you, if only for a little while."

Paul hung up the phone and explained what his mother had just told him. Chaplains Murray and Rose had already left the building, but they returned a short time later with a Salvation Army major with them. He introduced himself to all present in the room.

"My name is Major Underwood, and I have already been briefed on the situation. I will be more than happy to take Private

Kramer into the city, wait for him, and bring him back here safe and sound—that is, if it is all right with you, young man."

Paul blurted out his thanks and shook the man's hand in gratitude.

Major Underwood drove Paul into New York City and, fortunately, found a convenient parking spot close to the station. He accompanied Paul to one of the many doorways to the station and said, "I'll wait right here for you, son. You take as much time as you want with your family. I will square it with the captain."

Grand Central Station appeared to Paul as a monstrously huge building with its cavernous inside filled with benches, ticket offices, and shops. He found out from the people at the information counter which track the expected train from Boston was due to arrive on. It was supposed to be fifteen minutes behind schedule, which, considering the record of on-time trains, made it a highly unlikely pleasant surprise. Amazingly the train arrived exactly at the time the information person had predicted. Paul waited anxiously just inside the door to the track and scanned the railroad cars as far as he could see, looking for his family. He spotted his mother carrying some bundles, supported by his father and brother. Paul ran down the track and grabbed them all up in a huge hug. With people pushing and shoving by him, some snarling at them and blocking the way, they all decided it was better for everybody for them to move into the station.

Mom spoke up first. "How are you, my son? Are you still eating well?"

Paul assured her that his appetite was as hearty as ever, and in answer to his father's question as to how he felt, he said, "I've never felt better in all my life." He added anxiously, "So how is Zadie?"

Mom looked him straight in the eye and said, "He is feeling better, and Bobie and Zadie send their love along with everybody in the family." She turned to her bundles and brought out a bottle of milk and some Shirley Temple glasses. She confessed, "I was so flustered when I left the house that I opened the icebox and turned to the first thing I could find, which was a bottle of milk. Here, you and Jerry drink the milk." She handed Paul and Jerry each a glass, just as she had done for every day of his life, urging her children to take something nourishing. She added, "It just so happens that when you called, I was making up a fresh batch of chocolate chip cookies and brownies, so take these and make all gone." She held out two huge bags of cookies and brownies. "And I also brought a batch of Aunt Estie's fudge—your favorite, Paul, and yours, Jerry."

Jerry commented, "If Ma could have, she would have baked enough cookies to feed the whole army."

"I really would, you know," Mom laughed. "Paul, darling, take these back to camp with you. There may be a few more soldiers who would like a little snack from home."

Dad spoke up. "I know I told you before, but I tried to enlist. I went down to the army recruiting office. They were very nice to me and told me that my job was to stay on the home front and take care of my family. So I signed up with the civil defense outfit, and now I am a full-fledged air raid warden."

Mom added, "You should see how much fun he has going around the neighborhood, yelling for people to put down their shades and shut off their outside lights. He has a great time. And by the way, I am doing my bit for the war effort too. You'll be happy to know I joined the Red Cross as a volunteer and am doing whatever I can to help out."

Paul did not have the heart to tell her about his recent experience with the Red Cross representative. *Of course*, he mused to himself, *this man does not represent the entire organization.*

Jerry chimed in. "I'm doing my bit for the war effort too. I go around the neighborhood and pick up newspapers and tin cans. I bundle up the newspapers and clean up the tin cans, and I bring them to a collection point where a truck picks them up once a week."

Dad asked, "What is your situation ... or can't you tell us?"

"I'm not sure, but we expect to go on alert in maybe the next few hours," Paul replied.

Jerry asked, "Do you think you will go to the European theater or the South Pacific?"

"My guess is that, being on the East Coast, we will more than likely go to the European theater—that is, either Africa or England, most likely," Paul responded.

Mom cautioned, "Maybe with all these people around we'd better not talk about this. Who knows who is listening?"

Jerry interjected, "Do you know that Frank Sinatra is making a new album? I'll be down at the record store waiting at the door before they open so I can get it. Do you have a record player where you are, Paul?"

Paul laughed. "Yes, but it won't fit into my barracks bag."

They all nervously laughed at that.

Mom asked anxiously, "How much time do we have with you?"

Paul reluctantly looked up at the big clock on the balcony of the station. We have about another half hour. What time does your next train go back to Boston?"

"In about one hour, from track eleven. They will be boarding just about the time you have to leave," Mom replied. "There is no problem with our taking the next train. We can stay as long as you like."

"I think it would be better for you to take this train so you won't have the hassle of hanging around here another couple of hours for the next one," Paul suggested.

"Wouldn't it be wonderful to pull you on to the Boston train and take you home with us?" Dad said. "But that's a pipe dream, son. You have to go off to war, and we are going to be busy praying for you every day."

Mom clutched Paul's hands. "I will pray to God for you every waking minute I have. May you be well and safe and free from harm. I feel as if I have to take a deep breath and will not really be able to take another breath until I see you again."

Paul hugged her and kissed her on her forehead.

"Ma, I'll be fine. Don't you worry."

His father grabbed him in a fierce hug and assured him, "I'm going to make special prayers for your being well and coming out of this terrible war in one piece."

Jerry grabbed his arm. "Paul, you take care of yourself. And guess what? I'll be joining the line of people praying for you."

As if on signal, the four of them got up and started to move toward track eleven. With Mom and Dad on each side of Paul, holding him tightly as if they could not let him go, Jerry followed closely behind.

Mom turned to Paul. "I am sure it was not easy for you to be able to get away, judging from what I feel in these circumstances. Please tell those people who made it possible for you to come and see us that I send my deepest gratitude."

Dad chimed in. "Me too."

Jerry chorused the sentiment.

They reached what apparently was the car they were supposed to board, and it was already beginning to fill up with passengers.

Once more they kissed and hugged while Paul grasped the large bags of cookies, brownies and fudge. He forcefully pulled himself away and started back down the track toward the station. He stopped once and turned around, and there were the three of them, peering out of the doorway and waving amid the jostling and complaints of those trying to board. He steeled himself with as much willpower as he could muster up to turn around once more and head back to the station as fast as he could move. Major Underwood, waiting patiently by the door, greeted him as he hurried toward his car. He asked him how everything had gone. Paul extended his gratitude and that of his family for his kindness.

The major replied, "Bless you, my son. That's what we were put on this earth for—that is, to serve and help mankind."

Paul offered him some cookies, brownies and fudge. The major gingerly lifted a piece of fudge out of the bag and said, "I'll try the brownies when we return to camp."

The ride back did not seem to take as long as the trip into the city. The major soon deposited Paul at the orderly room, and they both entered to find Captain Wright and the Sergeant having a spirited conversation in the front room.

"Ah, you're back, Kramer. Good. Thank you, Major Underwood."

The major smiled and stepped aside for Paul.

"My family asked me to extend their heartfelt thanks for your having made this all possible. My mother sent you folks a little treat." He held out the open bags.

They took one look at the open bags and each grabbed a brownie and a piece of fudge.

Captain Wright turned to Paul. "We have just been placed on alert. I was discussing getting out the word to all companies in this regiment with our sergeant as you walked in the door. Bring those delicious refreshments back to your barracks and enjoy them while you start packing, pronto."

As Paul walked into the doorway of his barracks, a tec 5 followed him and shouted out, "This is it, men. We are on alert. Uniform of the day is fatigues. Pack your gear into your barracks bag immediately, if not sooner, and form up in front of this building thirty minutes from now!"

Paul handed the bags of goodies first to Tony, who then took charge of distributing them throughout the building. Paul was so excited he momentarily forgot about the brownies and fudge Then, realizing he had not taken any for himself, he scrambled into the crowd that was grabbing them from Tony. Luckily he managed to get what he wanted, and he then moved back to start packing. Tony complained, "Those chowhounds made short work of what we had, but I think everyone here got fed." He then got back to his bunk and briskly starting putting his clothing and equipment into his own barracks bag.

In less than a half hour, all of the barracks personnel were standing in smart formation, waiting for further orders. An hour from then they were still standing but were not so well organized. Some had squatted down on their haunches and lit up cigarettes. Others had clustered off to the side to determine which latrine rumor was most likely.

One of the men commented, "Just like the army. Hurry up and wait. That should be our motto."

A short time later, in a familiar pattern, a convoy of two-and-one-half-ton trucks drove down the company street and the men, barracks by barracks, were loaded into the backs.

Once again, a canvas was dropped over the back of the truck, making it almost impossible to see out. Occasionally one of the men near the back peered out of the narrow opening between the canvas and the truck frame to comment on where they appeared to be. Eventually someone shouted out, "Hey, we're in the city!"

"What city?" said someone sitting near the cab of the truck.

"New York, you jerk! What other city is there?"

"We're heading down toward the docks!" was another comment.

One enterprising GI rolled up the canvas so that most of the men in the truck could see where they were and where they were going.

Finally the convoy pulled up and stopped alongside a dock

that seemed to stretch farther than they could see out into the water. Alongside the dock was a giant roof set on steel beams that seemed to cover the entire length of the dock. There were no walls to this structure. Large speakers were attached to the tops of alternate beams, and emanating from these was some wonderful music. First they all heard, loud and clear, the great Andrews sisters singing "Boogie Woogie Bugle Boy." This was followed up by Dinah Shore singing "Night and Day." Glenn Miller's "Moonlight Serenade" was next, and one fantastic hit followed another. Not far from where their truck had stopped, Paul and Tony could see a fairly small building inside the cover of the roof with a neat sign posted in front that read "post exchange."

"This is it," one of the men said.

"I guess we're going sailing," somebody else suggested.

Slightly to the side of the PX was a small shack with an open counter that had coffee pots arranged in a neat column and stacks of donuts. This too had a sign that simply read, "Red Cross."

The soldiers were ordered to leave the trucks and form up alongside them. Each helped the others dragging their heavily loaded barracks bags down with them.

Tony said, "Hold on to my bag, and I'll get us some coffee and donuts."

Paul grunted, "Sure."

A three-stripe sergeant walked over to where Paul's platoon was waiting.

"You're going to be here a while, so relax and take a break. Smoke if you've got 'em." With that he moved off to deliver his message to the next group.

Just about that time, Tony returned with two cups of steaming coffee and a couple of donuts.

"See, Paul? The Red Cross isn't all bad," he commented.

"Yeah, yeah, yeah," Paul reluctantly agreed.

Someone in Paul's platoon called out, "Guys, there's a poker game going on. Who feels lucky?"

Not far from where they stood, Tony and Paul could see a small group forming into a circle.

Tony said, "Not me. I've got a few bucks that I'll save until we get paid again."

Paul laughed. "I've got five bucks in my pocket that is burning a hole there. Let's see what I can do."

He joined the circle and laid out his five one-dollar bills in front of him.

The game was seven-card stud, with aces, deuces, and jacks wild. Paul had played seven-card stud poker before, but never with any wild cards. That seemed to make the game more interesting. The cards just seemed to fall his way, and before he knew it, he had accumulated twenty-five dollars.

"This is it," he called out as he scooped up the money. He brought it over to Tony and asked if he needed some.

Tony said, "I'm all set, buddy. Thanks just the same. But while you've got the bucks, why not head over to the PX and stock up on your candy bars?"

Paul hadn't thought about it but realized that it was a great idea. "Do you want something?"

"Yes, how about a half dozen Baby Ruths?" Tony replied.

Paul bought a dozen Baby Ruth candy bars for Tony and spent the rest of his money on Hershey bars for himself.

The clerk accommodatingly put all of the candy into a small cardboard carton, and Paul hurried back to Tony with his treasure. They got to work opening their respective barracks bags and stuffing the candy down into the little remaining space that was left.

The sergeant returned a short time later. Almost coincidental with his arrival, the speakers clicked off.

"All right, men, hoist your bag on your shoulders, get back into line, and on my command start marching down toward the end of the dock. We will join up with another line there and proceed to amidships, where you will be checked off on a roster and board the ship."

Someone called out, "What ship?"

He laughed and pointed to what had seemed to be an enormous gray wall alongside the dock. "That's your ship, men." He laughed again.

Some of the men moved out from under the roof of the open building, and sure enough, they saw towering above them the sides of a tremendously large ship. All of the portholes had been painted over in the same gray color as the rest of the ship.

"I never saw anything afloat that is as big as this," Tony commented.

Paul and a few others agreed while looking in awe at the gigantic vessel.

They were ordered to start marching down toward the end of the dock, where they followed into a line already started. One of the men said, "I was just talking to an English sailor. That is the RMS *Queen Elizabeth*. The name was painted out for security reasons."

A GI standing next to Paul called out, "Hitler has offered a million reichsmarks, or the equivalent of two hundred fifty thousand dollars, to any Nazi sub commander who sinks this boat."

Someone else yelled out, "You'd better make sure your GI insurance is paid up!"

No one laughed.

Several English sailors positioned themselves alongside the lines of soldiers. One of them said, "Yanks, the German Luftwaffe is going for a welcoming that we won't like. They are patrolling the waters around the harbors in Europe, and for some distance out into the Atlantic. They especially like to hit the home ports of our *Queens*—the *Mary* as well as the *Elizabeth*—wherever they go, be it England or the Mediterranean or North Africa. Their Stuka dive-bombers are a nasty lot, but they are so slow that our RAF chaps have been giving them a real drumming. So you blokes hang in there."

"Yeah," the other one said, grinning, "but it's the bloody Nazi sub wolf packs that we have to watch out for. But don't worry mates, we'll get you there safely."

The column of men approached amidships, where two large gangways were set up from the dock into the innards of the ship. Tony and Paul were in one column and gave their names to a master sergeant with a roster on a clipboard.

He grunted in approval as he found their names, checked them off, and signaled them to board the ship.

With a bit of a sigh, Paul adjusted the position of his barracks bag straps more firmly on his shoulder and started to trek up the gangplank.

—PART II—

The Real Soldier

— 5 —

As Paul made his way up the gangplank carrying the heavy barracks bag over his shoulder, he paused briefly, looking toward the stern of the vessel. He saw that two more gangplanks had been set up halfway between him and the stern, while two more were positioned about halfway from his position to the bow. All three of the gangplanks seemed to come onto the ship about one deck above the waterline. They were all filled with a mass of GIs struggling to get up the fairly steep passageway and onto the ship. As he arrived at the top of the gangplank, Paul saw still more being installed at the bow and stern of the ship at a level several decks higher up. As Paul stepped aboard, he found the deck to be well below the level of the gangway. He swung his barracks bag down first, as he had seen the man in front of him do, and then jumped lightly onto the deck. A British naval noncom alongside a three-stripe US Army sergeant directed Paul and the column he was in, including Tony, to the entrance of the passageway. Heavy blackout curtains hung on either side of the doorway, and the column of men moved to a large, wide staircase. Some beautifully etched glass panels lined the entire wall of the staircase—a reminder of how luxurious this great ship had been in its peacetime days.

Another pair of servicemen, one American and the other

British, told them to go down two decks to D deck. One of the men objected.

"Hey, one deck below us is the waterline. You're sending us below the waterline. And you're sending us to the deck below that!"

The American sailor simply ordered, "Keep moving! Keep going!"

The English sailor standing alongside the first one spoke up: "It's not so bad, mate. If a torpedo hits us, you'll be the first to know." He chuckled.

One of the men in line said, "Why don't you limeys learn how to speak English?"

The sailor did not respond this time but simply assisted in waving the men to their destination.

When the line of men reached D deck, they were directed down a companionway that was well lighted. Standing in the doorway of a room was yet another pair of military personnel: one an American second lieutenant, and the other an English sublieutenant. Roughly they were about equal in rank.

They counted off twelve GIs and ordered them into the room.

The lieutenant spoke out, "My name is Lieutenant Thomas. This English gentleman is Sublieutenant Brooks. We are in charge of the group of cabins in this section of the ship. Grab a bunk, and use your barracks bag as a pillow. You won't need blankets down here. We will be back to orient you. The latrine is a few doorways down this corridor. Stay put until we come back to give you more complete information. The only reason for you to leave this cabin, for the time being, is to use the latrine. Then get back as fast as you can. Don't unpack any more than you have to. Locate your mess gear and keep that on the top of your bag, along with your toilet articles. If you need a drink of water, bring your canteen and canteen cup with you when you go for chow. They have a Lyster bag there so that you can fill your canteen up. Do not drink the water from the taps in the latrine. It is good enough to brush your teeth, but don't swallow it. If you need to get a drink sooner, let me know now. You are going to live out of your barracks bag for the time it takes us to get across this ocean."

No one apparently needed to get a drink, and so without any further delay, the two officers left to supervise the next group of GIs, who were following.

All four walls of the cabin were lined with bunks from ceiling to floor. Tubular steel frames supported sheets of canvas that had been attached by ropes laced through grommets running the length and breadth of the canvas. The bunk did not look overly comfortable, and it later proved to live up to its expectations. But then again, this was not designed to be a luxury cruise. At the foot of each bunk was a life jacket. The men noted that none of the cabins had doors on them. They assumed this was for fast and easy entry and egress. They all settled down on the bunks. Paul's was a bottom bed, and he noted that his face was only inches from the canvas above him. Tony was across the room from him, also on a bottom bunk.

Tony commented, "I hope that the guy above me is not big and fat and brings his bunk down onto my kisser."

Paul readily agreed.

In a moment, their wishes were answered. The beds above each of them came to be occupied by some thin guys, just like themselves.

In order to get at the contents of his barracks bag, Paul had to pull it out onto the floor beside him and then open it.

He fished through some of his things, remembering that the precious candy was near the top. He pulled out a Hershey bar for himself and stepped across the room to hand Tony a Baby Ruth.

Happily for Paul and his wish to hoard his precious cargo, only one of the other men asked for a Hershey bar.

Brooks and Thomas returned a short time later. Lieutenant Brooks called out, "Listen here, you chaps. You are on D deck. We have two more decks below us. Below that is the engine room; that is off limits to you Yanks. We are in what you call the front part of the ship. That is forward, on the port side, which is the right side. The decks go all the way up to A deck and then they go on up from there with AA, BB, and so on above that deck. The top two decks are off limits to you also. That is reserved for strictly officers and nurses."

He then turned to Lieutenant Thomas, who said, "We are going to have a chow line from ten to twelve in the morning and four to six in the afternoon. Don't ask me what the menu is, because I don't want to know myself. After the ship leaves the dock, you are required to wear your life jacket whenever you go out of this cabin. I want you to start putting it on now whenever you leave here. As of this time, you can go up to A deck, which goes all around the ship. There is absolutely no smoking on deck from one half hour before sunset to one half hour after sunrise. A lighted match can be seen for many miles out there, as can a lit cigarette. We don't want to attract any unwanted attention."

"Make certain that the blackout curtains are kept properly closed so that there is no chance any light will come out of the doorway. Even a tiny sliver of light could end up as a strong signal to anyone out there, saying, "Hey, you guys, here we are." It could end up getting us all killed. We don't know the exact time we are leaving, but we expect to cast off in a little while. Important announcements will be made from time to time on the speakers on the wall of the companionways and in the cabins."

"For something more urgent, Lieutenant Brooks and I are available at the end of this companionway, as we call it. For the time being, you're on your own. Keep your nose clean, and enjoy the ride."

He then left the cabin with Brooks in tow and went on to the next occupancy to deliver the same message.

Paul and Tony mutually decided to go up on deck. Some of the men simply laid down on their bunks and began to doze off. Paul and Tony donned their life jackets as previously ordered, even though the ship had not started to move yet, and walked toward the staircase. For the two of them, climbing the two flights of stairs was a breeze, and by mutual consent they took the steps two at a time. After reaching level A, they carefully closed the blackout curtains behind them as they came out on deck. Paul and Tony made their way to the railing and noted that the lines were still attached from the ship to the dock but most of the gangways had been removed. Looking forward toward what appeared to be the bridge deck and then back toward the stern, they observed a number of twenty-millimeter anti-aircraft guns, as well as forty-millimeter guns in twin mounts at various intervals on the deck. They assumed an equal number were on the opposite deck as well. There were more guns mounted in front of the bridge, and still more were mounted on the afterdecks. This should give them a fighting chance against surface raiders, submarines, or aircraft.

"I guess we are going to leave soon," Paul commented.

Tony turned around and raised his head to breathe in the pungent salt air of the harbor. He closed his eyes and said, "If I imagine it, I can believe that we are at Coney Island or Rockaway Beach."

Paul rejoined, "The sea air smells just like Nantasket Beach to me."

Tony pointed over the side.

"Look; they're taking in the gangplanks."

Paul looked, and sure enough, the gangplanks were being removed, cutting off their last connection to the shore. Almost as soon as the last gangplank was removed, the ship slowly, nearly imperceptibly, started to glide away from the dock. Disappointingly, there was no fanfare as they left.

There were no bells, no whistles, and no throwing of confetti. Without ceremony, two large tugs attached to the forward section, and two equally large tugs attached to the stern, slowly moved the massive ship out away from the dock and into the harbor.

As they reached mid-harbor, one of the tugs at the front and one at the rear detached and moved to the midship area of the boat. They positioned themselves so that one was on the port side and one was on the starboard side. A sailor at each of these stations on the *Queen Elizabeth* threw out a line that was expertly caught by one of the tugboat crew who looped the heavy rope around bulky posts on the respective tugs. Now attached to the huge vessel was a tug at the prow, one on either side, and one at the stern.

As they moved down the harbor toward the open ocean, a subdued but nevertheless noticeable throbbing started up, indicating that the engines were now starting to take over. A huge navy blimp first soared over the ship and then took up station just a little bit behind the stern of the vessel. A Coast Guard seaplane with floats attached to the wings flew over and around them. Almost at the same time, four US Navy destroyers moved into positions around the ship but at a respectable distance. They sped back and forth around the sides, prow, and stern of the great ship. At first there was no apparent motion as the giant *Queen Elizabeth* seemed to glide on a sea of glass.

Paul and Tony spotted Lieutenant Brooks standing nearby. Among his many duties, he apparently was supervising some naval enlisted personnel in hooking up with the tugboats.

"Hello there, Lieutenant," Tony called out, saluting him.

"We don't need any of that on board, Yank," Brooks said, returning the salute.

"Got a question," Tony said. "Isn't there a sister ship to this called the *Queen Mary*?"

"That's right, mate," Brooks answered. "They were both built with the same specifications, with the one major difference being that this has two smokestacks and the *Queen Mary* has three. The two ships have been converted to troop transports. What would normally be a full complement of approximately thirty-five hundred people, passengers, and crew has now become close to what I hear is sixteen to seventeen thousand."

Paul asked, "Where is the rest of the convoy?"

Brooks laughed. "This is it, soldier. What you see is what you have got." He pointed to the plane and the blimp. "A half a day out and we lose the plane; and two days out, the blimp leaves us. A bit after that, the destroyers head back, and from then on, the only company we may get is Jerry subs. When we are about a day's journey from wherever we are heading for, we will pick up Spitfires flying escort for us, and shortly thereafter we will have a ring of destroyers and other ships scurrying around us, providing good anti-aircraft and submarine cover. Commodore Farnum, the captain of this ship, is probably opening his sealed orders around this time. That means that even he doesn't know where we are going yet."

"So where do you think we are going?" Tony queried.

"S' God's truth, I really don't know. But you will land somewheres in Jolly Old. You can bet on that unless the powers that be decide to bring us up to Iceland and on down east to North Africa, or around South Africa to the CBI [the China, Burma, India theatre of war], or down the East Coast of the USA, to the Panama Canal, and over to the Pacific. Take your choice. We have brought troops to all of those places, y'know."

The late-afternoon mid-December ocean breeze promised there would be high waves waiting for them beyond the shelter of the harbor.

"What about Chow?" Paul asked.

"Since we embarked kind of late, in a short time, the loudspeakers will announce that everyone on each deck should start to queue up for mess. A galley—or mess hall, as you call it—has been set up on every other deck. Don't forget to bring your mess gear."

They noticed that the tugboats had detached themselves and that they were now moving at a more rapid pace. As they headed out of the harbor, an ocean swell seemed to lift up the prow of the ship and then gently let it down again. Large white-capped waves were all around them.

"Thanks for the info, sir," Paul said.

They mutually agreed to return to their quarters and wait for the chow signal. The effect of the candy bars had worn off, and the both of them were now getting hungry again.

They had returned to their cabin only for a short time when the speakers sounded. "Attention! Attention! Mess call! You will leave your cabin with your mess gear in hand. Don't forget to put on your life jacket every time you leave your quarters. Those on the portside of decks D and C will eat in the portside midships galley on deck D. Those on the starboard side will be fed at the starboard-side midships galley on deck B. Decks B and A will be fed at the midships galleys on deck A. Decks AA and BB will mess at the midships galleys on deck BB, and so on. Remember to bring your mess gear with you, including canteen cup and eating utensils. Alongside each galley is a quartermaster that will issue, on request, K rations and D rations. Carry on." The speaker clicked off.

As they headed away from the coast and toward the Atlantic ocean, the ship started to rock in a predictable rhythm. First the bow went up and then down, followed by the port side turning downward and then back up again. That was followed by the starboard side doing the same thing. This became more pronounced the farther they got out into the North Atlantic. The motion became even more intense when the ship started to zigzag.

Paul and Tony located their canteens, canteen cups, and eating utensils, as well as their mess kits, and joined the already formed line out in the corridor. The line moved slowly back toward the staircase and then up the stairs to deck C. They made their way into a cafeteria-style mess hall that seemed to be a modified dining room. On entering the large room, which held about twenty-five hundred men at one sitting, each man was handed two lengths of wire and instructed to loop one through the handles of his knife, fork, and spoon and the other through the D rings of his mess kit. They also balanced the canteen cup with whatever grip they could utilize. The line of men split into two groups, each going to either side of two long tables set up in the middle of the room.

Each table had several huge, steaming vats on it, with an English sailor stationed behind them. He ladled the contents into the mess kits held out to him by the soldiers. The man in front of Paul asked, "What is that?"

"Lamb stew," the sailor replied.

It appeared to be a milky white liquid with bits and pieces of meat floating around in it. The aroma wasn't at all bad, though, and so the men, Paul and Tony included, hesitantly took some and walked toward the end of the table. At the end of the lamb stew tables, there were still more tables containing ham and cheese and roast beef sandwiches.

Paul asked, "Do you have any coffee?"

"Tea we got. Do you want a cuppa tea, mate?"

Tony interjected, "Tea is not my cup of tea."

"Then how about some milk then?" Paul asked.

"Soldier, you'll see some real milk when this bloody war is over and when you have returned home," the sailor retorted.

Paul sighed. "I guess it's back to the candy bars."

Tony grunted in agreement.

They found two empty seats and tried the lamb stew. After sitting, they gingerly took a few tastes of the lamb stew.

Tony made a face. "If they served this garbage in a restaurant in Brooklyn, they would be shut down in a minute."

Paul tried a taste. It had the same effect on him.

They decided by mutual consent that the sandwiches were more appealing and stuffed a few into their pockets. They then got into the line of men leaving the room and walked by a group of four steaming vats. The first one was filled with hot soapy water, the next with boiling clear water, the third with what they were told was a boiling disinfectant, and the fourth with clear saltwater. Each man in turn dipped his mess gear into each of the four vats and then proceeded toward the passageway.

Just before the doorway, there was a large canvas bag bulging at the sides, hung from a heavy steel frame. This was obviously the Lyster bag, which allegedly held drinking water. They filled their canteens, and Paul took an experimental sip. He made a terrible face and could hardly bring himself to swallow it.

"This stuff is filled with chlorine," he gasped. "This is awful."

Tony muttered, "I don't need any more convincing." They moved back to the first vat and dumped the contents of their canteen cups into that and then repeated the process of cleaning their cups.

Even though they had taken some sandwiches, based on the disappointing food they had been exposed to, they stopped in at the quartermaster's room next door to the galley. Each of them took two D rations and two K rations. They figured this should at least hold them over, and they could always get more if necessary.

Tony said, "I like the English. They are a great people and very brave. But if this is an example of their cooking, they'd better take lessons somewheres else!"

A few of the men grunted their agreement.

Paul hauled out his stash of Hershey bars, and Tony brought out his Baby Ruth bars. This time they prudently broke the bars into pieces and shared them with their bunkmates.

Lieutenants Brooks and Thomas returned.

"How was your meal?" Lieutenant Thomas asked.

"The pits," one of the men replied sullenly.

"Can we light up down here?" another asked.

Lieutenant Brooks held out a cardboard packet of English cigarettes.

"Anyone want to trade a Wild Woodbine for a Chesterfield or Lucky Strike?"

Tony pulled a pack of Chesterfields out of his duffel bag.

"Here, Lieutenant. Help yourself," he said, holding out the pack.

"I'll just take one," the lieutenant replied, taking a Chesterfield and putting a Wild Woodbine in Tony's hand.

They all solemnly lit up. This was going to be a long voyage after all.

"This is kind of mild," Tony commented, puffing on the English cigarette.

"You're just being charitable, lad," the English officer replied. "Your bloody Red Cross will keep you supplied with American cigarettes, so don't you have any worries about that. If you continue to smoke our English cigarettes, you'll get used to them after a while. We have ships' stores, which is equivalent to your PX, or our English army canteens or NAAFIs on the same deck as your mess hall, on both the port and starboard sides of the ship. Every other deck has them, and you can buy candy, cigarettes, and shaving stuff there. They have mostly English products, so you will have to learn to adapt to what your English cousins put up with. Consider yourselves very lucky to be here. On some of the other decks, the men have to sleep in shifts. You have it made in the shade here, soldiers."

A short time later, most of the men hit the sack and were asleep in no time. Tony and Paul followed this example, and soon they too were in a deep sleep brought on by the previous day's exhausting activities.

Early the next morning, Paul nearly rolled out of his bunk when the ship lurched violently. First the front part of the ship went way up and then down; this was followed by the port side dipping down at a steep angle and coming up to level, and then the starboard side followed in this same form of activity. Since he was already awake, Paul decided to go down to the latrine and wash up. When he returned, Tony and the rest of the men in the cabin were in various stages of awakening.

"What time is it?" Tony asked groggily.

"6:00 a.m." Paul replied. "I'm going to go up on deck and see what's going on."

"Wait a bit and I'll go with you," Tony replied. "I could go for a nice dish of bacon and eggs right now with some real good coffee to swallow it down with."

One of the men grumbled drowsily, "We'll probably get the same slop we got yesterday."

A few of the men joined Tony and Paul as they left to go up on A deck. When they arrived, the usual crowd of men was already out there. The seas were running rough, with whitecaps breaking over high waves as far out as one could see in all directions. The color of the water had changed from the steely gray they had seen in New York Harbor to a deep blue. One of the men turned to an English sailor reattaching some lines from a life raft to the railing.

"What y'say, buddy? Does this color of the water mean we are heading south?"

"You're right, mate. If you look carefully, you'll see some bits of seaweed around and about too."

"Does that mean we're heading for Africa or England?"

"Don't rightly know for sure, but the betting is for us to head up sometime later on to England or thereabouts."

Paul looked toward the stern of the ship and above it. Reassuringly, there was the navy blimp.

The sailor caught Paul's glance and said, "That leaves us tomorrow, and from then on, we are on our own"

"How about this life raft?" one of the men with Tony and Paul asked. "Are there enough for this many people?"

"S'God's truth, mate, I don't rightly know," he answered. "I believe there are enough life jackets to go around. This ship was built for a normal peacetime complement of five thousand people, including passengers and crew. We have lifeboats that can accommodate five thousand people. The life rafts—you just saw me fastening one up tightly—can take another three thousand. The rest of us go in the water. There's one major hitch. Here in the South Atlantic, the water is on the warm side, and floating about in a lifejacket can mean that you'll last a longer time. If we turn north, as we usually do, the water is a lot colder. In the North Atlantic, people say a bloke can last as long as twenty minutes before he freezes to death, so no fear. On a brighter note, her exact speed is top secret, but all of us know that this big lady can go well over thirty knots. Happily, we can easily outrun any sub or wolf pack lying in wait for us. If you'll notice, we are also zigzagging, which gives us a more uncomfortable ride but makes it most difficult for some Jerry sub to aim at us."

On that note, Paul and Tony decided to part company with this bearer of ill tidings and head toward the prow. About fifty feet behind the peak of the ship's bow was a barrier of bulkheads, but that did not prove too much of an obstacle.

The two of them easily climbed over the obstruction and headed toward the foremost part of the ship.

Someone called out to them, "Hey, you chaps. Better get back here. If you get washed overboard, we can't stop to pick you up!"

Tony and Paul dutifully climbed back over the bulkheads and joined the many men milling about on the deck. Some of them had motion sickness and were hanging over the side of the rail. It was the first time at sea for both Tony and Paul, and they found it exhilarating. The churning white-capped deep blue ocean waves were a beautiful sight to behold, and it held the fascinated attention of most of the men there. Since they had come out on the port side, they decided to walk back along the starboard side. They had to make their way carefully, as the ship was tossing and turning.

Paul reminded himself of going to the amusement area called Paragon Park in Nantasket Beach. One of the challenges was crossing a pair of gangways that tossed and turned up and down as well as

Looking out from the Queen Elizabeth's deck

sideways. As a child, he had learned that in order to traverse this obstacle successfully, he would have to plant his feet outward to balance himself. He laughed to himself as he did the very same thing on this vessel, noting he had indeed enjoyed good training in his childhood for just this sort of activity.

"Paulie! Paulie!" someone shouted out from the mass of men in front of him. Only his friends when he was growing up in Dorchester used that term. It had to be someone from his childhood past. He looked around eagerly.

Emanuel Puryear, his very close friend from Dorchester, came forward and clasped his hand first, and then they emotionally hugged each other briefly. Paul introduced Tony to Emanuel.

"What a coincidence!" Emanuel exclaimed. "Imagine being on the same ship!"

"What deck are you on?" Paul asked.

"Down on D deck, starboard side, toward the back of the ship."

Paul replied, "I am on the port side, D deck, toward the front part of this liner."

They both engaged in an animated conversation about what had happened to them since their childhood.

Tony, getting bored with the conversation between Paul and Emanuel, called out, "Anyone here from Jersey City?"

A couple of shouts and waving hands from the mass of men in front of them followed, and he joined them to reminisce.

Emanuel said to Paul, "I ended up going to Boston Latin School. My momma and my grandma and my pa used to say, 'You gotta work hard in school so that you can build a future for yourself!' I still remember my grandma working day and night, scrubbing floors or doing whatever she could do to earn some money to put food on the table. The rest of my family worked their fingers to the bone too, so I owe it to them to make something of myself—if I make it through this war. I remember your family and how they worked for you and your brother."

Paul recalled his father working so hard to earn a living that even during the Depression years, when he was fortunate to have a job, he would put food or coal in the houses of neighbors and family who were laid off from their jobs. He never mentioned anything about paying him back and always avoided bringing up the subject. He mused that his mother and father, like Emanuel's family, were strongly convinced that the only way to build a successful future was for Paul and Jerry to work hard to get a good education. Their schoolwork always came first.

When their favorite radio programs came on, like *Jack*

Armstrong, the All-American Boy, The Shadow, and *Don Winslow of the Navy*, they could not touch the radio dial unless their homework assignments were accounted for.

His father's brother, Uncle Lucier (Louis), and Aunt Remke (Rebecca) had brought Charlie, Paul's father, over from Russia when he was the tender age of seven.

Charlie's mother had clasped him to her tightly when he said good-bye, knowing full well that she would never see him again. A few years later, the family learned that she had been killed during a German bombing raid.

Charlie with mother and sister in Russia

Lucier and Remka had operated a haberdashery on Broadway in South Boston. This was where Charlie, Paul's father, grew up. [According to the oral history from the author, Charlie's aunt and uncle frequently invited a young parish priest over for traditional Friday night (Sabbath) dinner. He had allegedly advised Charlie at a young age not to become a prize fighter as he had wanted; and, instead, take up a trade which he did. Charlie went on to become a successful tailor and furrier. And Father Richard, the parish priest, was also successful. In later years, he became known as Richard Cardinal Cushing. *-Neil Kozol*] Lucier and Remka were of the strong opinion that good education was the only proper way a person could pick himself up by his bootstraps and move ahead in this world. They worked diligently to make a living and save whatever they could for their children's education. Consequently, their three sons—Fred, Henry, and Sammy—went to Harvard, and their daughter, Janey went to Radcliffe. The children, in turn, understanding the enormity of their parents' commitment, worked hard in grade school and high school so that each of them entered the distinguished halls of higher learning of their choice with scholarships. Yes, Paul agreed with Emanuel that their respective families understood the all-important ingredient for success.

The loudspeakers blared into action. "Attention all personnel. Line up in front of your assigned cabin for mess call."

Paul was astounded.

Emanuel spoke up. "It just can't be that time has passed so quickly. I'll try to get a hold of you before we land."

They both shook hands vigorously, and Paul returned to the port side and spotted Tony already going through the gangway to the inside port deck.

"I can see a chowhound there," he called out.

"Takes one to know one," Tony yelled turning his head slightly and grinning.

They made their way down to D deck and, after retrieving their mess kits, joined the already long, slowly moving line. As they entered the mess hall, the familiar huge urns gave off a familiar aroma.

"Don't tell me," Paul exclaimed to one of the mess personnel. "Lamb stew again!"

"You've got it right there, mate," the sailor answered.

Without even bothering to fill their mess kits, Tony and Paul fell out of line and made it back to D deck. They rummaged through their available rations, decided to get more, and walked back up to the quartermaster supply room munching on their respective candy bars.

While they were in the process of being issued more rations, the loudspeaker sounded. "Attention! Attention! Commodore Farnum speaking. As captain of this vessel, I want to report to you that our wireless operators have picked up a German submarine not too far from us signaling a wolf pack also in an uncomfortably close neighborhood, giving our precise location. We are going to change course radically and will outrun these chaps easily. Carry on."

Tony and Paul stepped out on to the deck and saw Lieutenant Brooks hurrying past them.

"Lieutenant, sir," Paul called out.

Brooks spun around and asked, "What is it, soldier?"

Paul asked, "I hate to sound dumb, sir, but just what is a wolf pack?"

"A wolf pack is a group of German submarines that operate together as a team. They have had devastating successes in torpedoing many ships in our convoys and also have a nasty habit of machine-gunning survivors in lifeboats and those swimming in the water. But with our vastly superior speed, we will easily outmaneuver and get away from these killers."

Tony thanked him for his information, and Brooks returned to his rapid pace along the deck.

"I guess we can't do anything about it but just wait it out," Tony suggested.

"A little prayer won't hurt us either," Paul suggested.

Coincidentally they spotted Chaplains Murray, Rose, and Thompson coming their way, talking to various individuals and groups of soldiers.

"Chaplains," Tony called out. "I think now is a good time to collect for the prayers that you people owe me."

They smiled and came over to greet Tony and Paul warmly.

"Happy to oblige," Father Murray answered. "Dear Father in heaven, please, in this perilous time, protect us and help us survive this dreadful ordeal."

Rabbi Rose invoked, "Dear Lord God in heaven, please help us and protect us in this terrible time of danger."

Reverend Thompson prayed, "Almighty God, Lord of the universe, we humbly beseech you to hear our prayers for deliverance from this frightening and horrific peril."

Many of the soldiers within hearing distance bowed their heads, most of them having removed their hats, and murmured their individual prayers as well. Many of them called out to the chaplains, expressing their thanks and gratitude.

The chaplains continued on their way to comfort other soldiers and sailors.

Tony murmured, "I'm afraid to go back down into our bunks. I think it's safer to stay out here on deck."

Paul readily agreed, and so they remained there, each with his own private thoughts.

Tony called out, "Paul, look up there, toward the stern. The blimp is gone!"

— 6 —

Sure enough, they had not thought earlier to look for the blimp, and there was no telling how long ago it had left. The destroyers were still in the vicinity, but as they watched, each one in turn changed course and started heading back in the opposite direction. They were now alone in the middle of the Atlantic Ocean with no company except for the German submarines who were eager to destroy them. It was more discomforting at this time than ever before. It was the reassurance of the chaplains' collective prayers that gave them some hope for survival.

Tony spoke up. "How is somebody supposed to spot the periscope of a sub in these choppy waters?"

"They would have to have a powerful set of binoculars and very good eyesight to pick out something like that," Paul agreed.

After several hours, the water started to change back to a steel-gray color, and the height of the waves had increased substantially, along with a more severe rocking of the ship. The wind picked up as well, and it grew increasingly colder.

One of the men next to Tony and Paul remarked, "Those waves must be thirty to forty feet high, I'll bet."

"We're probably heading into the North Atlantic," Tony suggested.

"If it's not, then it's a very good imitation," Paul said.

The afternoon mess call came and went. Although the wind got considerably colder, Paul and Tony had no desire to go back down to either the mess hall or their cabin.

"Attention! Attention!" the loudspeakers blared out. "This is Commodore Farnum speaking. We have outdistanced the submarines by quite a bit. To put it mildly, they are frantically radioing back and forth to each other, very distressed, because we, as they put it, have disappeared off the surface of the ocean. They don't have a clue as to where we are, and we plan to keep it that way. Stand easy now, and relax. Carry on."

"Wow," Tony exclaimed. "What a relief! I don't know about you, buddy, but I'm getting cold."

Paul, who was very chilled and starting to shiver, said, "What are we waiting for? Let's get back to that warm, luxurious stateroom of ours."

They descended the stairway more conscious than ever that they were located below the waterline. They returned to find that most of their roommates were already back—some snoozing away, and a few keeping themselves busy writing letters. Paul fished down to the bottom of his barracks bag to find a worn copy of a C. S. Forester book—*Captain Horatio Hornblower.* Very apropos, he thought. *Reading a book about the British Navy while here I am on board an English ship.* Tony occupied himself trying to compose some thoughts to his family, wondering where or when he would be able to post the letter. Paul dozed off with the book open lying on his chest and fell into a deep sleep. Tony soon followed suit.

A tremendous clanging sounded on the loudspeakers, jolting everyone out of their sleep. Lieutenant Brooks and Lieutenant Thomas entered the doorway.

"Everyone out of here now! Form up on deck A," Lieutenant Brooks called out.

"Move along now, chaps," Lieutenant Thomas added.

"What's going on?" one of the men asked drowsily.

"I think it's a some kind of attack alarm," another GI replied.

The men formed into a long, slowly moving line that made its way down the companionway to the staircase. Then it was a long, slow climb up to deck A. There was no moon, and the sky was ominously pitch black. The men squeezed their way onto the crowded deck and tried to move along in order to make way for the men following behind them. No sooner did they get positioned on a part of the deck when the loudspeaker sounded again.

"Attention! Attention! The all-clear signal has been given. A plane was flying overhead, and it has been identified as one of ours. As you were, men."

It was back to their rooms, with the hope of getting some sleep once again.

Early the next morning, Tony announced, "I'm so hungry I could eat a horse." Paul felt the same way, and so, they daringly headed for the noncoms' mess, which was strictly off limits for buck privates. As they looked in the door, one of the English mess personnel asked, "What do you need, mate?"

Tony replied, "I'm dying for a plate of scrambled eggs and bacon."

"Got your mess kit with you?" he replied.

"We'll eat it with our hands," Paul muttered.

"Wait a bit," the English sailor replied. He quickly returned with a large platter of bacon and eggs.

"Thank you, buddy" Tony said. "You saved our lives. God bless you."

Paul and Tony rushed back down the staircase with their treasure and shared it with their eager cabin-mates. The food seemed to disappear instantly.

The next morning, they went up on deck and saw two planes approaching at rapid speed.

"They're not sounding the alarm, so they must be ours," Paul observed.

Sure enough, when they got closer, they were identified as Spitfires by some of the men familiar with their outline characteristics.

They circled overhead and then turned to proceed in gradually wider arcs and started to fly off. No sooner did they start to leave than two more fighter planes approached and performed the same pattern of circling the ship in ever-widening patterns. One of the English sailors remarked, "Those blokes are Hawker Hurricanes."

One of the planes broke out of formation and flew startlingly close to the *Queen*, waggling its wings as it circled the ship, almost skimming the water. A deep-throated cheer went up from the many GIs on the various decks. Many of them waved to the pilot who was welcoming them.

The Spitfires and Hawker Hurricanes were the highly celebrated English fighters that had played a vital role in winning the Battle of Britain. The great Winston Churchill, in paying tribute to the brave airmen who struggled against overwhelming odds to defend their homeland, said, "Never in the field of human conflict was so much owed by so many to so few..."

About fifteen hours later, a group of surface craft approached them. Some identified them as British destroyers and light cruisers. They circled the ship just as their American counterparts had done when they had left New York Harbor.

The men relaxed now with this significant air and sea protection. The rest of the trip was uneventful.

Paul woke with a start. The ship was no longer rocking. It was deathly still in their tiny compartment. Paul and Tony, like the others in their room, were fully dressed and were about to run up on deck. As if reading their thoughts, Lieutenants Brooks and Thomas appeared in the doorway.

"Stay put men," Lieutenant Brooks said.

"Where are we?" one of the men asked.

"Scotland."

Lieutenant Thomas said, "We are in the Firth of Clyde and will be docking soon."

"What is the Firth of Clyde?" Paul asked.

"The River Clyde goes from the city of Glasgow to the towns of Greenock and Gourock, where it widens out into a fjord we call "Firth of Clyde," Lieutenant Brooks answered. "Our ship and her sister ship, the *Queen Mary*, were built in Glasgow, and Gourock is our home port."

"How old is this ship?" Tony asked.

"I was there when she was launched in 1938 and have served with her ever since," said Lieutenant Brooks. She was launched by Her Majesty Queen Elizabeth, along with Princesses Elizabeth and Margaret. Her completion date was set for early 1940. The war broke out, and so her maiden voyage was cancelled and she was painted gray so as to camouflage her from the German Luftwaffe bombers out looking to destroy her. She was refitted to carry troops, and after a bit of time in the Middle East and other places, she was relocated to New York. For propaganda purposes, German Information Minister Joseph Goebbels, in one of his typical outrageous lies, triumphantly announced on German Radio in 1942 that she had been torpedoed by U-boat 704 with a loss of all troops aboard. We had a good chuckle over that, y'know. Those lying blokes never came near us. There was some talk about a sub shooting some torpedoes at us on one of our missions, and we even heard an explosion near our ship at one time. It could have been that. Others say that Jerry deliberately claimed they sunk us to get our blokes at our home base to ask us if we were all right. The Germans could then locate our position if we were radioing back and forth. Our intelligence people are too smart for that. The *Queens* have no radio communications with our shore base except for emergencies."

"This lady has been around," one of the GIs said admiringly.

Lieutenant Thomas said, "We are going be docking in about a half hour, so stick to this compartment unless you have to use the latrine. Get your gear together, and be ready to leave immediately, if not sooner. If you get hungry, pull out one of the rations you were issued. Got to go now and give this poop to the other guys in this section. See you later."

With that the two lieutenants went on down the companionway to the adjacent compartments.

It seemed to take no time before the men were called out into the corridor and lined up. Thomas and Brooks checked the men against rosters they held attached to clipboards.

Tony spoke up. "You know, lieutenants, we never got to celebrate Christmas."

"Being at sea in the North Atlantic dodging submarines did not give us any leeway in properly observing this holiday," Brooks responded. "You know, we ended up doubling back and skirting Iceland in one big semicircle. If it wasn't for those bloody Jerries, we might have celebrated Christmas properly in Scotland."

The seemingly endless line started to move slowly down the corridor toward the stairway. There was no end in sight even as they ascended the two flights of stairs to B deck. The placid blue waters of the fjord lined the startlingly green grassy hills surrounding it. There seemed to be what looked like a castle on the rim of one of the hills. The great ship was moving gently in the calm waters of the fjord. A tremendous number of ships were all around them—some merchantmen and some naval warships.

A half a dozen tugboats came alongside to take them in tow and gently nudge the *Queen* alongside the enormous dock.

Looking out at this beautiful body of water, the men noticed a goodly number of merchant ships scattered about. They were attached by very long cables to what seemed to be partially filled balloons in the shapes of blimps, but not as rigidly structured. On most of them, the tail fins sagged downward, as if they were only partially filled. One of the English sailors saw the men all looking at these lazily floating gas-filled structures in curiosity and amazement. They had never seen this type of thing before and were obviously fascinated with them.

An English sailor, noticing the attention these blimps were getting, spoke up. "Those are barrage balloons, mates. They keep the Jerry dive-bombers from giving us a going over, and their fighters and bombers have to stay at a respectable altitude, where we can pop away at them with our ack-ack."

The lines continued to move slowly forward, and finally it was the turn of Paul and Tony to step onto the wide gangway leading from their ship to the steamer. There were gangways set up on several decks, and the process of debarking the soldiers proceeded smoothly. It was amazing in that when they had left New York, the ground had been a drab gray and brown, as expected in the month of December. Here the grass was very green, and although the air was chilly, the view was more spring-like in appearance.

As the men debarked onto the giant pier, they were directed toward a very long row of tables filled with huge steaming urns. A number of smiling civilian women, some of them proudly identifying themselves as Scottish, English, Irish, or Welsh, all urged the soldiers to break out their canteen cups and try a "coop a tay." There were biscuits and cookies to go along with this, and it was indeed a warm welcome to the shores of Scotland. The soldiers needed no urging, and after the food they had been given on board the ship, many of them unashamedly wolfed down the pastries and savored the piping hot tea as well. As the men were fed, they were directed farther down the pier, where they could stop for a few moments and savor these goodies. The noncoms and officers considerately gave them time to finish their rations before they were led away in groups to a column of numerous two-and-a-half-ton trucks. The headlights had been painted over except for a small narrow rectangle in the middle of the glass.

Some of the men were told by the drivers that these were called "cat's eyes" and were of some protection when driving at night.

As each truck filled, it drove off only to be replaced by an empty one. The convoy of trucks made a brief trip to the town of Gourock, identified by a large sign at the outskirts. The vehicles made their way down to the railhead, where the men were offloaded from the trucks and directed to an enormously long group of railroad cars. These were typically English, in that each compartment had a door that opened either to the outside of the car or into a narrow passageway inside the car itself. As soon as a compartment, which held six people, was filled, the loading proceeded down to the next one. When the entire car had been fully loaded with soldiers, the process began again in the following car. This continued all the way to the end of the very long train.

Paul, Tony, and the others in their little compartment had no sooner settled down in their seats than the door slid open. A three-stripe sergeant came in with multiple pages of what appeared to be rosters. He introduced himself as Sergeant Turner. He asked each man his name and serial number, found all of them on the list and checked their names off, and turned to leave.

"Where are we heading, Sergeant?" Paul asked.

"Don't rightly know," he replied. "And if I did know, I couldn't tell you. Just figure that you're heading for somewhere in the British Isles." He pointed. "Do you see those blinds on the window, men?"

The men grunted affirmatively.

"Keep those blinds down all the way, day or night," he ordered. "We are traveling under strict blackout security measures. Anyone caught raising the blind, even a little, is subject to court-martial charges, and that's no bull. Don't forget it! Another thing: if you need to use the latrine, turn right outside this door, and it is the last compartment in this car. There is a sign on the door marked 'WC.' That stands for 'water closet,' which is the English word for 'bathroom.' I'll check back with you men from time to time."

With that he left.

The men busied themselves with getting comfortable while moving their barracks bags around the little space available in front of them. A polite knock sounded on the glass of the compartment window. The door opened once again, and this time a middle-aged couple dressed in Salvation Army uniforms stepped into the small room.

"Would you Yanks like a bit of refreshments?" the woman asked.

"You bet your life, lady. Thanks," one of the men replied quickly.

The man brought in a pitcher of steaming liquid. "Hold out your canteen cups, and I'll pour you a bit of tea."

The GI's busied themselves fishing around in their barrack bags for their canteen cups. They held their cups out to the man, who poured the steaming tea from a large pitcher.

The woman offered a large tray of sandwiches.

"Do you boys want a nice snack to go with your tea?" she asked.

The men needed no urging, but one of them in between bites of food asked, "Where are you folks from? Your accent is a little different from the other people we spoke to on the dock."

"That's because the two of us come from Wales, my boy," answered the man."

When the Salvation Army people were satisfied that all the GIs in the room had had enough to satisfy them, they left, closed the door behind them, and proceeded on down the car.

"Does anyone know where we are going?" Paul asked.

"Search me," one of the other men answered.

"May as well make ourselves comfortable," Tony suggested.

Following his advice, they tried to scrunch down in the seats. The men dozed and napped fitfully and in starts. After several times of nodding off and then awakening after what seemed to be a few short moments, Paul arose and went into the narrow corridor outside their compartment. Many other GIs apparently had the same idea and were out there too. Tony joined him just a few moments later and asked, "What's up?"

"I just wanted to stretch my legs is all," Paul answered.

"This train seems to ride a lot smoother than the ones in the States," Tony observed.

"That's true," Paul replied.

They chatted a while with some of the other men standing out there. A few grabbed a smoke, while others wondered where their journey would end.

After a while, Paul and Tony decided to return to their little room, and each of them had to move some soldiers off their individual sleeping space, which was small enough to begin with. They both fell back into the routine of dozing, napping, and then awakening. This proceeded almost endlessly until at long last the train came to a halt.

Sergeant Turner slid open the door. "All right, men. This is it!" he exclaimed.

"What's doing, Sergeant?" one of the men asked.

"We have arrived at our destination, which is Taunton, England. We have about a ten-kilometer ride from here to get to our camp."

"What is a kilometer, Sarge?" someone else asked.

"It is five eighths of a mile," Turner replied. "We will be heading for the 419th repple depple, which in English means the 419th replacement depot. You'll all be reclassified and then sent out piecemeal to different outfits that need someone with your MO, or classification status. All right, get your gear together and fall out outside here and line up in single file."

The men followed his instructions, opened the outside door, and got onto the station platform. They lined up in single file to await his return. An exact repetition occurred when a column of two-and-one-half-ton trucks maneuvered alongside the station platform. The men waited patiently for Sergeant Turner to return, which he did a short time later. He called off the men's names one by one, found their names on the roster, checked them off, and directed them to a particular truck. Turner climbed into the truck Tony and Paul had boarded. The truck convoy started to move after all of the men had boarded. The journey was brief, and since it was daylight, the flaps were not down on the backs of the trucks and the men had an opportunity to enjoy the beautiful English countryside. In this area, there were large squares of land bordered by high stone walls and, in some cases, hedgerows.

They slowed down as they passed two squads of English soldiers marching very smartly along the side of the road. They were singing:

> *Bless them all, bless them all,*
> *The long and the short and the tall.*
> *Bless all the blondies and all the brunettes.*

Their truck went by before they could hear the remainder of the song.

Turner exclaimed, "Those are some guys from the British

Eighth Army who have been shipped back here from North Africa. They were in some of the roughest battles there and proved themselves many times over to be top soldiers. They are the best of the best, just as our American guys who fought there also are top soldiers. That is one of the favorite marching songs of the Eighth Army."

"Sergeant, how come we landed in Scotland and had to travel all the way down to England by train? Why didn't they dock us at Southampton or some other port in Southern England?" Tony asked.

Turner replied, "Southampton and the other ports in Southern England are well within the range of all of the German bombers and fighters, and these ports are deathtraps for any ship crazy enough to try to dock there"

The convoy pulled up to a large set of gates that was apparently on the perimeter of the camp. As they drove along the various camp streets, they observed that there were three sets of structures available. One was the characteristic two-story barracks building that was so familiar to them all. There were also Nissen huts that housed mostly administrative offices and mess halls. Finally there were many large pyramidal tents, some of which had the side flaps up, showing that there were bunks inside. These apparently also housed soldiers as well.

"I'll be doggone," Buford Clemens Rawlins said. "This here camp is the spittin' image of what we had back in the US of A."

Buford was a six-foot-five giant of a man who was soft-spoken and good-natured. He came from Savannah, Georgia, and answered to the name of "Bubba." Colin Maxwell Johnson, also from the South, had befriended him, and the two of them had endured the voyage across the Atlantic in the compartment next to Paul and Tony's. Johnson on occasion would caution the men who met Rawlins, saying, "He's a good man and a good soul, and if we go into combat, I want him covering my back. But one thing you've got to remember is just don't get him riled up. He's very scary then."

Their truck pulled up in front of a two-story barracks building. The men in their vehicle were all directed to the second floor. Everyone was totally exhausted from the long train ride, and some fell on their bunks fully clothed and were sleeping in moments.

It seemed that only five minutes had passed since they had all gone to bed, when all of the lights came on and some private first class was yelling and screaming, "All right! This is it! Up and at 'em! You're all on KP! Out of that sack!"

Paul groaned, "What's going on here? We just got here a little while ago. Give us a break."

Tony echoed his sentiments. "This is a great welcome to England."

Most of the men were moving, but Bubba, with his head hanging over the back of the bunk and his feet hanging over the front, did not stir.

The PFC noticed this and moved toward him

"I wouldn't do that, soldier," warned Johnson.

"He'd better get his butt out right now, or I'll roll him out," The PFC replied. He grabbed one of Bubba's feet and tried to turn it.

Bubba raised himself up on one elbow and asked, "What you tryin' to do with mah feet?"

The PFC did not answer but increased his efforts to turn Bubba's foot.

Bubba now was incensed and leaped to the floor. He then grabbed the startled PFC by the neck and lifted him up.

"Soldier, what you all bothering me for? Ah doan like to be bothered when ah'm sleepin'."

The PFC could only grunt in fear.

Bubba lifted the man up over his head and walked to the head of the stairs.

"Bubba, stop!" Johnson called out.

Rawlins stopped and turned slightly, blinking at Johnson.

"Set him down right now, Bubba."

Rawlins paused for a moment and set the terrified soldier down. When he saw he was free, he ran down the stairs, two at a time, and flew out of the door.

It took only several minutes before a squad of tough-looking burly MP's arrived. They charged up the stairs, and the sergeant in charge of the group asked, "Okay, what kind of a brawl is going on here?"

Tony answered, "Sergeant, there is no problem here whatsoever. We are just getting ready to report for KP; that's all there is to it."

Paul corroborated Tony's reply, and the Sergeant looked confused for a moment and then muttered, "Get your butts downstairs now—and I mean right now!"

The men meekly complied, and in no time they were in the back of a truck that was to take them to their assigned mess hall. Not much later, the truck stopped in front of a large Nissen hut, which was apparently their destination. In the late-night gloom, with the windows blacked out, it was difficult to see. Even the process of getting off the truck was cumbersome, but all of the men made it without any mishap. They entered the mess hall and noticed a broad bank of tables with attached benches set up around the room. Off to one side, up against a wall, was an upright piano. A stocky man wearing an undershirt and fatigue pants came out of a set of swinging doors that apparently led to the kitchen. He was chewing on a cigar and seemed to be in a foul mood.

"We're not ready for you yet. Sit down and I'll call you and assign jobs when I come back," he snarled.

Tony spoke up. "Paul, why don't you give us a few songs on that piano?"

Paul, in order to relieve the boredom, and being annoyed with having been hurried out of bed in the middle of the night, only to be told to sit and wait, readily agreed.

First he played some of his favorite classics, and he then segued into a few popular Hispanic songs. From there, at the request of some of the men, he moved to "Stardust,"

"Blue Champagne," "You Made Me Love You," and then into some deep-down boogie-woogie.

The fat man came charging out of the kitchen, chewing vigorously on his cigar. He pointed to Paul.

"You there, Private—that's going to be your job: playing the piano. Don't get up and leave until I tell you to. Keep playing!"

With that, he turned to the rest of the group. "Follow me."

They all disappeared behind the doors to the kitchen, while Paul followed his instructions to keep playing. He had a large repertoire, and it looked as if he were about to exhaust the entire group of selections when the men returned with mops and pails. One group started to clean the floors, while others were put to work cleaning the tables and benches. It was a number of hours before all of the men had finished their assigned tasks, and now they were all not only exhausted but hungry as well. Johnson turned to the man who was apparently the mess sergeant and asked, "How about giving us a break, Sergeant? Can we have something to eat?"

"All right," he replied. "You don't have your mess kits with you, so grab a metal plate in the kitchen with a knife and fork and get some scrambled eggs. You can pick up a coffee mug on the same table as the plates so you can have some coffee too."

When Paul saw that the men had finished their chores and were heading back into the kitchen, he followed them. They did as they were told and picked up a metal plate and a mug and headed for a steam tray containing what looked to be scrambled eggs. The eggs were very watery and cold. The coffee was consistent and also very watery and cold. It was difficult to get this food down, but the men had no choice.

Tony spoke his thoughts. "I wonder what all that food was that we loaded onto some English civilian trucks in the back. Maybe these guys have a good business going on the side."

"You'd better shut up, soldier, or you'll end up in the guardhouse!" the burly man yelled out.

"What was that all about?" Paul asked Tony.

"Later," Tony whispered.

After they got on the truck, Tony explained that when the men got into the kitchen, some of them had been assigned to various jobs inside, such as peeling potatoes and unpacking crates of dehydrated foods. He and a few others were given the task of carrying out huge cartons of bacon and other meats to a waiting truck parked behind the mess hall. The English civilians who directed the unloading referred to their vehicle as a "lorry" and did not in any way appear to be connected with the armed forces. A lieutenant, who was obviously the mess lieutenant, and the foul-tempered soldier who was identified as the mess sergeant, supervised. After the men had completed their job and were ordered back into the kitchen, Tony glanced over his shoulder and saw one of the civilians hand a wad of bills to the mess lieutenant.

"That absolutely stinks!" Paul exclaimed.

"We've got to do something about this," Tony answered, "but who do we go to with this?"

They returned to their barracks and hurried inside as a heavy rainfall hit them suddenly. It seemed that they had been in their bunks a very short time when, once again, whistles blew, and the lights turned on and the men were ordered to line up for chow. There was some frantic searching in their barracks bags, with some locating them and others not having time, before they were hustled outside into a soaking rain. This time there was no truck to take them to the mess hall, and the men marched in the miserable soaking cold rain. After they arrived in the vicinity of their destination, they were told to stay in formation.

"Does this happen very often, soldier?" an older-looking man with a raincoat over his shoulders asked. He wore no badge of rank on his overseas cap, and so no one could tell whether he was an enlisted man or an officer. No one in their group had seen this man before, but they assumed he was a new arrival.

"We just got here, buddy," Tony answered, "but this looks real bad from what I can see." He then related the incident of the men having to load the civilian truck with lots of food supplies and the mess lieutenant taking a large wad of bills from one of the civilians.

"That's just what we thought," the older man said.

"What are you, some kind of cop?" Paul asked.

"You might call us that," the man replied. "My name is Neylon, by the way."

The men had been standing out in the soaking rain for more than a half an hour, and the misery of the cold, damp soaking storm became worse with every minute. Finally, at long last, the line started to move, and shuffling along, they finally entered the mess hall, grateful to be in the warm interior of the building. A number of long tables had been set up, with large metal trays holding the food. Many of the men held out their mess kits expectantly, only to find the same cold, watery scrambled eggs being dished out that the KP crew had suffered with.

Neylon held out his mess kit, and a soldier slopped out a small ladleful. Neylon stopped. "Is this what you call food, soldier?" he asked.

The mess sergeant came over. "What the hell is wrong with you?" he barked.

"Are you the mess sergeant?" Neylon asked.

"What's it to you, Private?" the reply shot back.

Neylon threw off his raincoat from around his shoulders, and there on his epaulets was a set of silver eagles.

"Attention!" someone yelled.

"You are under arrest, Sergeant!" Neylon shouted.

At that same time, a dozen MPs rushed in the door to secure the room.

The mess sergeant picked up a meat cleaver menacingly and advanced toward Colonel Neylon.

"No one's gonna lock me up." snarled the sergeant.

Bubba who was standing beside Paul, acting faster than even the MPs could, shot his right hand out over the table, grabbed the sergeant by the neck, and yanked him off the floor. His left hand, clenched in a fist, smashed down on top of the sergeant's head. The sergeant's eyes turned upward, and he sagged toward the floor as he lost consciousness.

Colonel Neylon held his hand out to Bubba. "Thank you, son."

"Glad to oblige, suh," Bubba answered.

"My name is John Christopher Neylon, Colonel, CID," Neylon said. "We are with the Criminal Investigation Department of the Inspector General's office. As a result of many complaints that we have received for the past several months, we have conducted an intense investigation that involved us and the English police as well. We found that not only the mess sergeant and mess lieutenant were involved, but the Colonel running this camp was in on it too. They have been in cahoots with a gang of English gangsters who have been paying large amounts of money for the food and in turn selling it for even bigger amounts of money on the black market. Sorry it took so long, but we had to get signed depositions from the complainants, and some of them were afraid to give testimony for fear of retribution. You new arrivals were lucky. You just had to put up with this for a little while. As we speak, the colonel, lieutenant, and other military personnel who were implicated are being put under arrest. You can count on the fact that the army will not tolerate this kind of activity These men will also have additional charges leveled against them for their unacceptable treatment of the men in their command."

He then turned to Bubba, Paul, Tony, and Colin, who clustered about him. "You men have been especially helpful and impress me as being really on the ball. What kind of outfit are you hoping to be assigned to?"

Bubba was the first to speak up. "Suh, with respect, ah'd like to get into some kind of MP outfit."

Paul, Tony, and Colin looked at one another and shrugged in agreement.

"If it's all the same to you, sir," Tony said, "we'd like that too, sir."

He pointed to Paul and said, "We are medics, but we would be proud to serve in the same outfit as these other two men."

"Give your names and serial numbers to my adjutant here." He pointed to an MP lieutenant standing beside him. "We will locate you through personnel files and see what can be done. We are through here, men." He spun around and headed toward the door.

The four of them automatically came to attention and watched the colonel leave the building.

The very next morning, when the men stood formation for reveille, an MP sergeant approached the sergeant in command of their barracks. He handed him a roster, and the barracks sergeant called out their names.

"Martino, Anthony."

"Here, sir," Tony replied.

"Step forward," the sergeant ordered.

He then called out Paul, Bubba, and Colin, in turn. He handed each of them an envelope, which was apparently from Colonel Neylon.

"Open this and read it," he ordered.

The message was brief: "Write to me at the following address if you run into any problems that merit my attention. My address is as follows: Colonel John C. Neylon, CID, Hdqtrs, Inspector General's Office, APO 5442, England."

"Now get back to your barracks, pack up your gear, and report to the orderly room immediately if not sooner!" the sergeant ordered.

The four of them dashed into the barracks, ran up the stairs, and furiously packed away what few belongings they had previously removed from their barracks bags. They made it to the company orderly room and found the sergeant waiting for them. He handed each of them a set of mimeographed orders stating that they were transferred from the 419th replacement depot in Taunton, England, to the 456th Military Police Battalion in Manchester. Paul and Tony's orders read that they were to report to battalion headquarters, medical detachment, while Colin and Bubba's orders directed them to report to Company A. After they were handed their orders, the MP sergeant introduced himself as Sergeant Harry Woods and welcomed them to the outfit.

"We have a great group of officers and enlisted men, and our CO, Colonel Macklin, is the best CO in the US Army. Now climb on the back of the one-and-a-half-ton truck waiting outside, and let's get going." The four of them eagerly leaped up onto the back of the truck, and almost immediately, it started to move forward. They looked out at the departing camp with no regrets, although they had been there only a short time.

— 7 —

The truck had gone just a few miles down the road when they came across a British Army truck parked by the side of the road. Several English soldiers were peering under the hood and shaking their heads in obvious disgust. Sergeant Woods ordered his driver to pull over and then got out of the truck.

"What's the problem, men?" he asked.

An English lance corporal laughingly answered, "It's so bloody stupid, Sergeant. I'm almost ashamed to admit that we have run out of petrol."

An English private offered, "We were looking under the bonnet, looking for a bleeding engine problem, and there it was. We forgot to check the fuel level. What makes it more of a headache is the fact that our radio has gone daft and we can't call for help."

Sergeant Woods offered, "No problem, men. We have some extra jerricans on the back of the truck, loaded with gas. If you don't mind signing for whatever you take, putting down the name of your outfit, we can put it on your lend-lease tab."

"God bless you Yanks. You always come through in a pinch," the lance corporal replied. "My name is Bill Somersby, and if I can ever return the favor, I will be happy to oblige."

Bubba unfastened a jerrican, lifted it as one would pick up a piece of paper, and handed it to Somersby, who in turn signed the proffered form. Returning it to Sergeant Woods, he shook his hand and waved as he stepped back from the vehicle.

"Thanks again, mate," Somersby said.

Woods gave the driver a signal to proceed.

It was still very strange driving on the left-hand side of the road, but this was England, and in England, this is the way everyone drove their vehicles. After what seemed to be an interminably long ride, the men seated in the back of the truck noticed some road signs indicating that Manchester was ten kilometers from where they were.

They collectively breathed a sigh of relief, and not very much later they pulled into a compound with a large sign at the gate that read "456th Military Police Battalion." Two military police noncoms, each wearing a sidearm, waved the truck to a halt. Sergeant Woods handed the travel orders to them, which they read very carefully. They finally were satisfied that all was in order but still checked the back of the truck in order to make certain that the number of men there complied with what the travel orders indicated. They then handed the orders back to Sergeant Woods, and told the driver to proceed. The truck stopped in front of a building marked "Battalion Headquarters."

"Everybody out!" ordered Sergeant Woods.

All of the men got out of the truck and followed Sergeant Woods into the battalion orderly room. There were two desks in the room. A sergeant major was seated behind one, and a corporal was behind the other. Both men arose as Sergeant Woods and his group entered the room. Woods handed his orders to the sergeant major, who read them carefully and then turned them over to the corporal. The sergeant major, turning to the men, said, "My name is Sergeant Harrison," and he shook hands with Woods, adding, "Harry, glad to have you back."

He then handed the orders to the corporal, instructing him to record the men's names into the day log and assign them to their company and department. As their orders had indicated, Paul and Tony were to report to the medical detachment, while Colin and Bubba would go to Company A.

Sergeant Woods knocked on a door marked "Colonel John Macklin."

A short, thin man wearing lieutenant colonel insignia stepped into the room. His uniform was immaculately pressed, and he gave the impression of being a professional soldier. With a warm, friendly expression on his face, he walked up to each man in the group and shook his hand. He said, "Welcome to the 456th MP Battalion. We have a great group of men here, and it will be even better with you new recruits joining up with us. We are a tight group, and in the event any of you has a problem, personal or otherwise, I want you to come directly to me, and we will straighten it out together. Corporal Bleck, Sergeant Woods, and Sergeant Harrison will get you to your quarters. Good luck, men."

With that he spun around on his heels and returned to his office.

Sergeant Woods told Paul and Tony to follow him. They left the building area in one of several jeeps parked in front. Sergeant Harrison followed closely and got into another jeep with Bubba and Colin.

Paul and Tony noted with interest that most of the housing units consisted of four-man tents, some with the side canvases rolled up. After turning down several company streets, they came to a large pyramidal tent with a sign in front of it indicating that this was the medical detachment. Paul and Tony followed Sergeant Woods into the tent and found a tall, thin man, wearing captain's insignia putting a splint on a private's arm.

"You'll be okay now, soldier. Give it about a week on light duty, and you'll never know you strained your arm playing softball."

He patted the soldier reassuringly on the back and turned to greet the men who had just entered.

Sergeant Woods introduced Paul and Tony to Captain Wilfred Sheridan, the battalion medical officer. A caduceus emblem was on the opposite side of the collar attached to the railroad tracks—the double silver bars of a captain. He smiled warmly and shook hands with Tony and Paul.

"We're glad to have you with us. We are short on medical and surgical technicians and need more people running sick call in the morning. Sergeant Woods will show you where you will bunk, and you will report back here at 0800 for sick call. We medics don't have to stand formation or drill or any of that business—at least as long as Colonel Macklin is around. Our dental officer is up at the rec tent, so I guess you'll have to meet him tomorrow." He turned to a man who seemed to be in his mid-thirties. He was a tec 5, a pleasant sort of person who genuinely appeared pleased to meet Tony and Paul. His name was Sanford Evans, but he suggested that he be called Red. He did, in fact, have a flaming shock of red hair at the top of his head, and he seemed to be in bad need of a haircut as well.

Captain Sheridan suggested, "Evans, why don't you take these men down to the empty tent next to yours, where they will bunk. When they get settled, give them a bit of orientation about where everything is here." He then turned to Tony and Paul. "Take the rest of the day to orient yourselves. Evans will show you where the mess tent is, but you don't have to wait for chow call if you are hungry now. You can just go over and find something that will tide you over. And I'll see you tomorrow at 0800 sharp, when you can help with running sick call.

Tony and Paul followed Corporal Evans to a pyramidal four-man tent just a short distance from the dispensary. There were four cots, each with a footlocker at the foot of the bed. The floor consisted of a raised wooden platform, giving them some satisfaction that they would be off the ground. The side flaps of the tent had been rolled up and strapped into the open position so that a cold breeze wafted through, giving Paul the feeling that as soon as possible, he was going to drop the flaps and tie them down. Evans had each of them select a bunk, opened their footlockers for them, and patiently waited until they had unloaded the contents of barracks bags into their respective footlockers. He then suggested that they follow him outside. At the end of the street, there was a very large tent with a sign in front of it indicating that this was the mess hall. Across the street, an equally large tent was identified as the rec tent. Adjacent to the rec tent was an equally large tent marked "Latrine." Corporal Evans then turned to Paul and Tony and said, "Okay, men. You're on your own until sick call tomorrow." He turned around and headed back up the company street toward the dispensary.

Tony and Paul returned to their tent to continue unpacking. When they entered, they found another GI, who had apparently just arrived. He was short, on the chubby side, light complexioned, and apparently friendly. He extended his hand first to Tony and then to Paul, saying with a strong, guttural German accent, "Hello, my name is Kurt Schoenfeld."

They shook his hand in turn and introduced themselves.

After each of them had unpacked, they sat down on their respective bunks and talked about where they had been born and grown up.

Kurt was Jewish. He had been born in a small town in Germany and grew up being a proud German. After Hitler came to power, his life, even in the small town, became increasingly painful. Finally one day, a group of young Nazi thugs, in order to amuse themselves, decided to hang him from a telephone pole. Fortunately something distracted their attention, and he was able to make his escape A short time later, through the good offices of the Hebrew Immigration Aid Society (HIAS), he was able to make his way first to Spain, then to England, and finally to America, where some members of his family sponsored him. He managed to get a year of college in before he determined that he was old enough to enlist and joined the US Army. He, too, had gone through the surgical and medical technician training schools and was eager to start his work in the dispensary. Kurt was also fluent in French as well as English. Paul, who spoke High School French with some fluency, could detect Kurt's heavy German accent when he shared some comments with him in French.

The following morning, at 0730 hours sharp, the three of them reported to the dispensary. Corporal Evans greeted them and handed each a pair of Red Cross brassards.

"From here on, wear these whenever you leave your tent. They will go a long way toward keeping you from getting drafted for KP or latrine duty. Also, our dental officer, Lieutenant Saffridi, wants to meet you."

A man in his mid-thirties, wearing lieutenant's bars, stepped out of a cubicle set apart by pieces of canvas hanging from metal pipes. He was about medium height with thinning hair. He stepped forward with his right hand held out.

"I am Saffridi—that is, Lieutenant Walter Saffridi. I need a dental technician badly. I checked your MOs and see that the three of you are medical and surgical technicians. I'm willing to train whoever wants to work with me." He looked searchingly at the three of them.

Finally Kurt stepped forward. "I'm willing to give it a try, sir."

"Done," said the Lieutenant. "I'll show you the ropes, and you'll be just fine in a little while."

Kurt didn't seem to be too sure about this, and so he reluctantly followed the lieutenant into the dental area.

Corporal Evans had Tony and Paul follow him to a litter (stretcher) that was laid across two footlockers.

"This is where we hold sick call and dispense medications. I'll walk you through this time, but you follow what you know; and if there is a problem, I'll help you. Whatever you feel you cannot handle, don't hesitate to ask me or Captain Sheridan. There are some other medics here who will work on rotation with you. On the days that you are not holding sick call, if necessary, you will take our ambulance—which is not a real ambulance but a three-quarter-ton truck—to the medical depot in town and draw whatever supplies the captain or lieutenant decides to requisition. If you are not running sick call or getting supplies, you are on your own. Any questions?"

"Yes, Corporal," Paul asked. "How come we don't rate an ambulance?"

"If you can figure that out, Private, you'll know when this dad-blarsted war will be over," he replied.

Just then the tent flap opened and several GIs came in. The first one was sniffling and coughing. Tony felt his forehead and determined that the man had no fever. He gave him a small bottle of aspirin tablets and told him to take two every four hours for the next four days. He also gave him a small bottle of elixir of terpin hydrate cough syrup. He told him, almost laughing, to drink as much water as he could. Considering how rotten the medicated water tasted, this was almost a joke. Tony told him to take a spoonful of the cough syrup at night before bedtime, adding that he should report back if he had any more problems or did not seem to be getting better.

The next patient seemed to have a sprained ankle, which Paul strapped up.

One man walked in holding his hand wrapped in a bloody handkerchief.

"I guess I got a little careless trying to whittle some wood," he laughed.

Paul and Tony moved him to the head of the line. Corporal Evans took over, cleaning the wound with hydrogen peroxide, dropping some sulfanilamide powder into the wound, and closing it with several butterfly bandages.

One man seemed to be running a temperature, so Captain Sheridan took over the care of that patient.

Another patient had what seemed to be a possible fracture of his forearm. Captain Sheridan immobilized the arm and asked the patient if he needed a shot for the pain. The man declined. He then told Corporal Evans to drive the soldier to the evacuation hospital in town for an X-ray and possible further treatment. He turned to Tony and Paul and said, "One of you go with Corporal Evans so you can learn the way to the hospital." He turned to the corporal. "Evans, on the way back, drive by the medical depot and fill this requisition form." He then turned back to Tony and Paul. "When you are not on sick call, among your other duties, you are going to check our medical supplies, fill out a requisition form for Corporal Evans to check, and turn it over to me for my signature. Then whoever is available will go to the depot to draw whatever supplies we need. Who wants to go with Evans?"

Tony spoke up. "I'll go, sir."

"That's fine," Captain Sheridan replied. "Now I'll have Corporal Evans show you how to fill out a trip ticket, which has to be signed by me, as well as the requisition form. Remember: you cannot leave the base or enter here without formal orders, a leave, or a pass signed by an officer—or, for that matter, a trip ticket."

Tony watched Evans fill out the necessary forms and followed him and the injured GI out of the tent.

Paul got back to seeing sick call GIs and found the work interesting and a bit challenging at times. With Captain Sheridan to back him up, he felt secure, and the job proceeded without any problems.

Tony and Corporal Evans returned about one hour later. Evans spoke up first.

"They took a wet reading on the X-ray and found a hairline fracture. They're going to keep him there a while and fit him up to a cast. We can go pick him up tomorrow."

Tony said, "You gotta see this town. It is amazing. Here, just like everywhere else in England, everyone drives on the wrong side of the road. We stopped outside of a movie theater, which people here call a cinema. Folks coming out of the movie complained that everyone smoking in there so much makes the screen fuzzy. They're all nice and friendly and hospitable. As a matter of fact, they made me feel right at home. But the big news is we had an air raid. Some German bombers came in pretty low, and what the English told us were Hurricanes and Spitfires came out of nowheres and jumped them. Those English pilots have a lot of guts and mixed it up good with the Jerries. They shot down one bomber after another until the krauts decided to get the hell out of there."

Paul told him about the patients he had seen and what had been done for them.

The following days fell into a routine. On certain days, the men were assigned to work sick call. The other days were spent either taking inventory of their medical supplies, going into town to draw new supplies, or alternating working with the dental officer. It seemed that Lieutenant Saffridi wanted to recruit as many GIs as he could as potential dental students.

One day Paul and Tony found themselves with free time, and so they wandered over to the recreation tent. There was a small upright piano in there, as well as a juke box that was not plugged in. About a dozen soldiers lounged around on folding chairs, some of them drinking coffee that was served by two men and one woman wearing Salvation Army uniforms.

"C'mon, let's go, buddy," Tony urged. "Sit down at that piano and give us some music."

Paul needed no urging and ensconced himself at the piano, using a folding chair as a seat. He busied himself with many jazz tunes in his extensive repertoire, and he changed pace with an occasional foray into some of his favorite classical selections.

Someone yelled out, "Attention!"

Paul jumped up out of his seat, stood at attention alongside Tony, and joined the other GIs in saluting. Colonel Macklin had walked into the tent accompanied by a fairly young civilian couple. They were in about their mid-thirties as far as Paul could judge. The woman was a short, thin brunette with long hair that hung down around her shoulders. She was very pretty and had a warm smile. The man was tall and thin and had a warm, friendly smile on his face.

"At ease, men—as you were," Colonel Macklin commanded. "We're just visiting, with Lord and Lady Martindale."

Lady Martindale stepped over to Paul. "Soldier, would you please continue with that delightful music?" she asked.

"You prefer classical music, I'm sure," Paul replied.

"Oh no," she demurred. "Please play more of that wonderful jazz music, especially some boogie-woogie if you don't mind. We also love ragtime."

"Happy to oblige, ma'am," Paul replied, and he returned to the keys of the piano.

Lord Martindale, followed by Colonel Macklin, joined Lady Martindale at the side of the piano.

The colonel remarked, "Soldier, that's my kind of music too."

Paul stammered his thanks and continued to play.

Lady Martindale looked at the colonel. "Colonel Macklin,

could you do my husband and me a very big favor and allow this young man to come and visit us at our place for a fortnight or so? That is, if he doesn't mind. We have a piano there and would love to hear him continue with this delightful concert."

Macklin shrugged. "I don't see why not, young lady," he answered. Then, turning to Paul, he asked, "Is that all right with you, soldier?"

Paul thought that this would be a welcome break from the daily routine. He said, "Colonel, it would be a pleasure. But just one thing, sir."

"What's that?" Macklin asked gruffly.

"Would it be too much trouble if my buddy came along?" he asked, pointing to Tony.

"Oh please, Colonel," Lady Martindale pleaded.

Macklin looked at Tony and then back to Paul and laughed. "Sure, soldier. The both of you report to battalion headquarters, where you can pick up a pass. But before I get in trouble with my medical officer, check with him before you do anything."

"Oh, Colonel, thank you so much," Lady Martindale said with a smile directed to the colonel that would have melted a rock. She wrote something on a card and handed it to Paul. "These are directions that you can follow to get to our place," she added.

Tony and Paul flew to the dispensary. They arrived breathless, and Captain Sheridan asked, "What's the problem? The both of you look like there's an emergency brewing."

"We just want to ask you a big favor, Captain," Tony said.

Paul told the captain what had happened and asked if they could be relieved from their duties in order to visit Lord and Lady Martindale.

"Sure," the Captain agreed. "We have no problem with staffing, but I'll agree only on the condition that you pull double duty when you get back so we can give the same time off to the other men in our unit."

"Yes, sir!" Tony and Paul replied in unison.

Paul added, "That's very fair, sir."

"Just one thing?" Captain Sheridan asked. "Did either of you figure out what you would put your clothing and shaving gear in, or are you just going to stuff it in your pockets?"

Paul answered, "Sir, I was thinking about using our barracks bags."

Sheridan responded, "I have something better than that." He went to a cabinet and pulled out two small rucksacks. "We use these for carrying bandages and dressings when we are traveling somewhere. Since we are planning to be here for a while, you can borrow these."

Tony exclaimed, "These will be perfect, sir. Thank you very much."

Paul, taken aback by the kindness and generosity of the captain, mumbled his thanks and took the proffered bags.

"If this is the kind of officer we are going to work with for the rest of this war, we've got it made in the shade," Paul said as they hurried back to their tent.

The big day finally arrived. They were both clean shaven and all slicked up, and they had even borrowed some cheap cologne from Corporal Evans, who had bragged earlier that it was a copy of what the movie stars used.

As Tony and Paul picked up their passes at the battalion orderly room, Colonel Macklin stepped into the front office.

"You men behave now, and act like good representatives of the US Armed Forces. We can't have the English believing that we are uncivilized, or something like that."

"Yes, sir, and thank you, sir," Tony answered.

Paul declared, "We'll make you proud to have sent us, sir."

They made it out to the main gate and presented their passes to the two MPs at the gatehouse. The guards scanned the passes and handed them back without a word, waving them on.

Following Lady Martindale's instructions, a civilian bus would stop here every half hour on the hour. They had to wait only about ten minutes before the bus arrived. When they got on board, they asked the bus driver how much the fare was.

"Just a moment," someone shouted from the back of the bus.

An English soldier stepped forward with a broad smile on his face.

He looked very familiar, and seemed even more so when he said, "I'm one of the blokes you helped out of a proper fix not long ago. Do you remember giving us some of your petrol when we were bloomin' stuck by the side of the road?" said Lance Corporal Somersby.

"In that case, your ride is on the British Transportation System," the bus driver said firmly, and he covered the fare box with his hand.

Tony and Paul thanked him and joined Bill Somersby near his seat.

"What brings you out on one of our civvy buses?" Somersby asked.

"We are heading out to visit these people," Tony replied, and he handed over to him the written set of directions Lady Martindale had given them.

"You boys are stepping out in some real fancy places, I would say," Somersby responded. "You are about three stops from your destination. I'll ask the bus driver to let you off at the proper stop. What you are looking for is the first turning after you get off the bus."

"I don't want to sound ignorant," Paul said, "but just what is the first turning?"

"Oh, that," Somersby laughed. "That is the first road you come to while you are heading in the same direction we are now moving."

"It may take us a few years, but we will finally get the hang of your lingo," Tony commented.

Not too long later, the bus driver stopped the vehicle and turned to Tony and Paul.

"I overheard your conversation and want to let you know we have arrived at your stop."

"Thank you, sir," Paul replied, and the two of them shook hands with Somersby and the bus driver and stepped off onto the narrow pavement.

Walking along the road, they came to a side street, which also was very narrow. They decided that this fitted in with their directions and proceeded to walk, not noticing a single structure or house on either side. They came to a slight hill, and arriving at the crest, they saw a beautiful valley stretching out ahead of them, with what appeared to be a magnificent castle a little farther on down the hill. They agreed that this could not be the place that they were looking for, but at least they could be directed to their destination from there.

It really was a castle, complete with turrets and all in perfect condition. There was no moat around the structure, and for a moment Paul expected to see King Arthur charging out at them.

They approached the massive front door timidly and spotted a doorbell on the side of the door, as well as a heavy-looking brass knocker attached to the front. Wanting to take no chances, Tony rang the bell, and Paul slammed the knocker against the brass plate attached to the door.

A moment later, a bespectacled middle-aged man in shirtsleeves and wearing an apron opened it widely. He smiled when he saw

Paul and Tony, and he said, "You must be Mr. Kramer and Mr. Martino."

"That's right, sir," Tony answered.

"I am Thompson, the family butler," he said with another warm, welcoming smile.

He took their bags and said, "Please come right this way. Lord and Lady Martindale are expecting you."

They entered a large foyer with high vaulted ceilings and stepped into an enormous hall. A concert grand piano was located in the middle of the room, and the vast size of the hall made the piano look tiny and insignificant. Beautiful tapestries were hung all around this main hall.

As Tony and Paul were admiring the beauty of the structure, a little girl ran screaming past them with a little boy in hot pursuit. A teenage girl ran after them, calling out to them, "You naughty children, come back here!"

"Are those some of the Martindale children?" Paul asked.

"Oh no, sir. But then you likely were not told. Lord and Lady Martindale have arranged to take in many children who have been evacuated from London because of the blitz. Our entire staff is involved with taking care of them, and sometimes it is quite challenging." He rolled his eyes upward.

"That's very nice of them," Tony noted.

"Not only do they do this," Thompson commented, "but all offers of the government to compensate them have been politely refused. This is all done at the expense of Lord and Lady Martindale. They supply food, medical, and dental care and have hired a group of private tutors to keep the children up to date with their schoolwork. Many of the little ones come out here with sparse supplies of clothing, and here they are given more than adequate wearing apparel, as well as toys they need for fun and recreation. The children have overcome their homesickness, and since they are having such a good time, we fear that when this war is over, they will be reluctant to return home to their families.

Lord and Lady Martindale made their way down a long, curving staircase. On reaching the main floor, they welcomed Tony and Paul very warmly.

"You boys must be starved," Lady Martindale suggested.

"No ma'am," Paul objected, "but don't you people have severe rationing in effect?"

Lord Martindale interjected, "Please do not concern yourselves, since our government has seen fit to supply us with all the food we require because of our very welcome little guests. So please, let us go into the dining room and see what our cook has managed to scrape up."

They entered another large room; this one held a massive table with about thirty chairs around it. The walls appeared to be made of mahogany that had been sculpted with magnificent designs. Beautiful brocaded draperies hung from ceiling to floor. A candelabra, a light with many candles, was placed in the center of the table. It seemed to be made of solid silver.

The table silver and glassware were beautiful, and Paul assumed that they had been passed on from generation to generation.

Lady Martindale turned to Paul. "Please tell me about yourself," she inquired.

"Well, ma'am ... How do I refer to you? Do I call you Your Ladyship or what?" Paul asked.

"Call me Lillian," she replied, and please call my husband Bertram."

Paul told her about his growing up in Dorchester and how after high school he had studied for one year at an optometry school. He then related his brief experience in the army.

Lord Martindale asked the same question of Tony, who also gave a brief résumé of growing up and being educated in New Jersey.

Thompson brought a large tray into the room and deposited a small dish of salad beside each of the four of them. He also had brought a steaming kettle, and he poured tea for each of them. He said, "I hope you will excuse me, but we have to save whatever little supply of condensed milk we get for the children, so if you don't mind, we will break the English tradition of taking tea with milk."

This evoked a shy grin from Lillian and Bertram.

"Do you ever have trouble with German bombers here?" Paul asked.

"Some of them, after they drop most of their load on the cities, will fly out over the countryside and empty the remainder of their bomb load haphazardly. We have lost a few farm animals, but, thank goodness, none of our children have been hurt," Lillian replied.

"So the Germans concentrate mostly on military targets?" Tony asked.

"Please don't get the idea that they are conducting the war in a civilized, gentlemanly manner," Bertram objected. "There was a beautiful town called Coventry, and on the night of November 14 to 15, 1940, if I remember correctly, these Nazi murderers came out and subjected this town to a saturation bombing that left most of the place in ruins and many of the inhabitants dead or wounded. German bombers perpetrated this horror from dusk to dawn and smashed the heart out of this once beautiful place. Entire blocks of buildings were decimated by incendiary and high-explosive bombs, which left the world-famous fourteenth-century brownstone cathedral, except for its spire, in a jumble of stone and mortar. During the bombing, a firestorm was created that burned out most of the city center."

"There were over a thousand known dead and wounded, not counting unknown innocent civilians trapped in the pile of stone and smoking wood," he spluttered angrily. "It was a night of unrelenting terror."

Bertram then regained control of his feelings and once again returned to his usual composure.

Lillian added, with tears in her eyes, "Don't forget the terrible incendiary raid on London during the last part of December, 1940. Over fifteen hundred fires were started in the center of the city, which destroyed many churches and other historic structures. But enough of our reminiscing about these tragedies in our lives. Paul, why don't we go back to the main hall and have you give our piano, as you Americans say, a once-over?"

Paul readily agreed, and the four of them returned to the adjacent room. Paul sat down on the piano bench and ran his fingers over the keys. The tone was perfect, and it was obvious that the piano had been properly tuned on a regular basis.

Lady Martindale asked, "Would you do me a favor, please, Paul?"

"Of course, ma'am—that is, Lillian."

"Please play for us your very own favorite music. We will all enjoy what you play, I am sure."

"Well then, I'm going to start you off with some George Gershwin selections. Then we will go into a bit of Meade Lux Lewis, Louis Armstrong, Duke Wellington, Harry James, Benny Goodman, and a few others," he replied, and he started to play.

He then segued into "La Cumparcita," "Stardust," and some boogie-woogie songs.

His audience grew incrementally with each song, and when he finally looked up, the room was crowded with many children and apparently the people who were watching over them.

The applause was encouraging, and he needed no urging to continue. Finally he lowered his hands from the keyboard and looked up. "If it's all the same to you folks, I'd like to take a little break," he said apologetically.

Lord Martindale came over beside him. "Our apologies to you, Paul. You must be tired from all of that strenuous activity at the piano. Let us go back into the drawing room and have some cold drinks."

Tony and Paul made their way through the sizeable group of people, stopping to chat with some of them as they continued on.

A young woman came running into the room.

"The bloody Germans. They're flying over us, and it looks like they're getting ready to bomb and shoot at us!"

Lillian and Bertram headed for the door.

She called out in a very calm voice, "We must gather up the children and bring them down to the shelter!"

Tony and Paul followed them outside, where everyone was busy scooping up children and bringing them indoors. They followed suit.

Inside of the building, a sign over a large door near the kitchen read "Shelter." They brought the children down there, deposited them gently, and ran back to look for more. The children had obviously experienced this before, and all of them made themselves comfortable without a single whimper or complaint.

Outside, everyone ran around frantically, looking for any children who might have been missed.

Paul glanced upward. Two German fighters—he thought they were Messerschmitts—accompanied by a fighter-bomber circled overhead. One of the fighters peeled off, apparently to make a strafing run.

"Hit the dirt!" Tony called out.

Paul looked around one more time; and, not seeing any remaining children, followed Tony's call. He jumped down to the ground and stretched out, wishing that he could have dug a foxhole. The plane started machine-gunning—haphazardly, since there were no obvious targets—with the bullets striking some distance away.

Suddenly, from out of the sun, two English Spitfires came roaring down on the planes. The German fighter that was strafing blew apart. The fighter-bomber caught fire and spiraled downward, while the two English fighter planes chased after the remaining German who was trying to hightail it out of there. They all disappeared over the horizon, with the odds of the German's survival either nonexistent or very slim.

Paul picked himself up, and dusted the dirt and leaves off of himself. Tony was doing the same, and by mutual consent, they returned to the castle.

Bertram said, "Now you can understand the unrelenting savagery of these Nazis. In the first three months of raids on London, close to thirteen thousand Londoners were killed, along with one hundred twenty thousand wounded."

Paul said, "We Americans salute the courage of the British people—military and civilian alike—who not only endured the savagery of these cruel attacks but went on to beat the murdering Nazis back."

Lord and Lady Martindale expressed their appreciation for this tribute.

Paul and Tony spent the rest of their time with the Martindales in helping to feed the children, as well as telling groups of them about life in the United States and their experiences in elementary and grammar school.

More interesting and fascinating to the children was Tony and Paul telling them their own versions of fairy tales that had been related to them when they were children. Lillian insisted on writing down the addresses of Tony and Paul's parents so that she could correspond with them.

The kindness and consideration of the Martindales knew no bounds, and sadly, when it came time to leave, it was with a good deal of regret.

Lillian said to them, "You are always welcome here. Please come without any formal invitation, and in return for your helping to care for our children, you can play our piano as often as you wish, Paul. And you, Tony, can simply enjoy being our honored guest."

Tony said, "We both thank you and your husband for this wonderful visit. It was very educational and enlightening."

Paul said, "After what you told us about the brutal bombings of Coventry and London, as well as many other places, I can see why the Nazis persist in attacking a nonmilitary target such as this."

Tony asked, "Why don't you folks put a giant red cross on the roof of your castle?"

"The answer to that, my young friend," Bertram answered, "is that the Jerries would simply use it as a target."

The conversation about the aerial attacks gradually shifted to Tony and Paul and their necessity to return to camp.

"If you expect to ship out soon, we understand that you can't say anything, but in the event you do stay where you are, we would like you to come back for return visits," Lillian said.

"If we don't hear from you, we will assume you have been shipped out, as is so often the case with all of our military—English and American," Bertram added.

They formally shook hands, and then Lillian hugged Tony and Paul, and with her eyes filling with tears, she said, "God bless you."

Once again, Tony and Paul murmured their thanks and were on their way.

— 8 —

Tony and Paul arrived back at camp and, by previous agreement, beat a hasty path to Colonel Macklin's office at battalion headquarters. Corporal Evans was lounging in a chair and greeted them when they stepped into the office.

"Colonel Macklin is tied up in a meeting, and his orderly had to step out for a minute. You two have a problem?" Evans asked.

"Why no, corporal, we just wanted to thank the colonel and all of you people who were involved with letting us get out on our pass," Tony replied.

"I'll pass it on to the colonel, but you guys better hightail it back to the dispensary. We just got a notice that our outfit will go on full alert in twenty-four hours. That means we will be shipping out very soon. Captain Sheridan will need all the help he can get to pack up our dispensary gear and be ready when we bail out of here!"

They double-timed it back to the dispensary, and saw a harried Captain Sheridan in the front office handing some equipment to Private Kurt Schoenfeld.

He glanced up and said, "Glad to see you back. I had no idea that we were going on alert so soon. Battalion headquarters is sending out recall notices to all men on leave to hurry up back so we can start getting all of our material and equipment packed up.

As long as you're here, you can give Schoenfeld a hand. The rest of our medical detachment are being rounded up now."

Tony and Paul immediately got to work assisting Kurt, who was packing heavy equipment into a large metal case. When they finished, Kurt indicated that they would have to put this onto a two-and-a-half-ton truck parked outside. Tony and Paul got on opposite ends of the case, while Kurt grabbed the middle area. They struggled to get the heavy case off the floor and then struggled further just getting it out of the dispensary doorway. A jeep going by came to a screeching halt, and Bubba jumped out. Seeing their plight, he grabbed both sides of the case and said, "You skinny young fellers just leave this to me." He effortlessly carried his burden to the truck, as directed by Kurt.

Captain Sheridan, following the men out of the door, saw Bubba performing his good deed.

"What outfit you in, son?" Sheridan asked.

"Didn't mean to cause no ruckus, sir," Bubba answered, putting down his burden and saluting. "Ah'm in Company A, suh."

"Soldier, if you have no serious objections with this, I'm going to ask your company commander if I can moonlight requisition you for a few days," Sheridan said. "We sure can use your help."

"Ah'm mighty glad to oblige, suh" Bubba replied, saluting again. "These h'yre fellas are mah buddies." He then picked up his burden easily and deposited it onto the back of the waiting truck. "Suh," Bubba added, "Ah have to return this h'yre vehicle after I pick up our company mail at battalion headquarters."

"You go right ahead, soldier, and in the meantime, I'll call your CO and clear it for you to come back," Sheridan replied.

The very next day, as Corporal Evans had announced, the battalion went on full alert. Everyone busied himself packing up his own gear, as well as the departmental equipment and supplies.

Two days later, a convoy of two-and-one-half-ton trucks rolled onto the grounds. The trucks then split up, with a number going down each company street and the remainder parking outside the medical detachment and battalion headquarters. Corporal "Red" Evans, Kurt Schoenfeld, Tony, and Paul, along with Bubba, did a heroic job storing all of the medical detachment gear on the trucks in a remarkably short time. Captain Sheridan and Lieutenant Saffridi pitched right in with the enlisted men, making the task even easier.

Paul and Tony regretted that there was no way to communicate with Lord and Lady Martindale but knew that they would understand the vagaries of military people being constantly on the move.

Their reliable three-quarter-ton truck was parked outside the dispensary, designated as their battalion ambulance. In spite of the equipment stored in the back, Paul, Tony, Kurt, and the rest of the medical enlisted staff were able to find a spot for themselves there, and they even squeezed in the bulging barracks bags that each of them carried, loaded with all of their possessions.

The convoy started to move slowly. As it left the camp grounds, it picked up speed slowly and steadily until at last they were moving at a good clip. Several hours later, the convoy stopped, allowing the men to get out of their cramped quarters and move around. A jeep with the supply sergeant aboard drove up to each truck and unloaded several K rations for each GI. The convoy then continued on, going through a series of towns and villages. The civilians they passed all waved to them, and more than a few shouted words of encouragement. The trip seemed endless until they reached a seaside area and began pulling into a dockside location.

Tony said, "This is it, men!"

Paul joined in. "We're probably going to invade France now, I'll bet!"

Kurt rejoined, "No way that this can happen now. You would have seen a lot of planes heading out toward France. We've got to be going somewhere else."

A series of large vessels were tied up at a group of docks. Almost as soon as the men got off their trucks, they were directed to board these boats. The men, coming aboard, walked up a wide gangplank, while the stern of the ship had massive doors that opened to accommodate the trucks that drove on board.

A group of British Army trucks also pulled into the dockside area. As the medical detachment was lined up in preparation to get on the vessel, the British Army personnel were marched into formation alongside them.

"Hello, you chaps," Lance Corporal Somersby called out.

Sure enough, he was standing there with the soldiers in his unit, awaiting orders to board.

"Bill," Tony called out.

Paul and Tony left their place in line to walk over and greet Somersby.

"You lads know where you are going?" Somersby asked.

"We don't have a clue," answered Paul.

"These are the Northern Ireland ferries, and we are about to head out on the Irish Sea and go over the briny to Northern Ireland.," Bill offered. "When you get on this ship, be sure to locate a place for yourself out on the deck."

"Why is that?" Paul asked.

"This bloody Irish Sea is wilder than the North Atlantic at its worst. You'll have a better chance of not getting sick by staying out on deck and filling your belly with any food you can get your hands on. By the way, if you don't have enough, we have plenty with us, so we can share whatever we have with you blokes," Bill answered.

"Thanks, Bill, but we have plenty to go around. And thanks for the tip," Paul replied.

Kurt called out to them, "Our line is moving now, so get back here!"

Tony and Paul returned to their places, and as they did, they saw Bill's line start to advance as well.

As they came on board, an American army sergeant, as well as a British sergeant, were alternately directing the men either into the hold or onto the deck. Tony and Paul were directed to the hold but pretended they did not hear the sergeant and made their way onto the deck. Kurt followed suit and quickly joined them. The sergeant saw the trio go out on the deck but shrugged his shoulders. There were just too many men coming up to go after them.

Somersby greeted them and bade the three of them to join him at a spot they had ensconced for themselves in the center of the forward deck.

"Grab whatever is fastened to the deck and wrap an arm around it. This will brace you when we get out to sea," Bill cautioned.

The men did as they were told, and each of the group found a place he could anchor himself to. Other GIs and English soldiers were doing the same thing, Paul noted.

They compared notes on their respective rations and came to the conclusion that while they were all adequate, none of them would fit the bill as gourmet fare.

It seemed to take very little time for the ferry to be packed with vehicles and troops. The lines that held the vessel to the dock were cast off, and the engines roared to life. The ferry turned and headed out to the middle of the inlet that sheltered the ships and boats. As soon as they started to move at a good clip, another ferry headed in toward the dock space they had vacated. The water of the inlet was calm, and so far the passengers felt little motion.

Just as they approached the opening of the inlet, two Spitfire planes, skimming just barely over the masts of the ships, roared over, heading out to sea. A moment later, two American fighter planes, just as low, raced in toward the harbor. The sight of these planes flying cover for them was very comforting indeed. As soon as the ferry left the inlet, the waters changed drastically. The waves became very choppy, and the ferry started to toss and turn with each large wave it encountered.

"Better get used to this," Bill cautioned. "We're in for this and a lot more before we reach port."

The ferries moved in an uneven line with a sizeable distance separating each vessel. As they sailed along, a destroyer flying the English flag cut across their wake, churning through the wild waves. A second destroyer, distinguished as an American vessel flying the Stars and Stripes, moved in an opposite direction. Some lighter vessels, identified by one of the English soldiers as corvettes, were also sailing at high speed in and around the convoy of ferries. This, too, was reassuring for the military passengers.

Paul remarked, "We're as safe as babies in our mother's arms."

Bill retorted, "Don't feel so smug, Yank. The Jerries have sent their fighter-bombers after this kind of convoy many times. If they don't get us, their E-boats may torpedo us. And talk about torpedoes—there's always the bloody submarines. The Nazis are very busy blokes around these waters."

"What is an E-boat?" Paul asked.

"I understand that it is some kind of high-speed motor torpedo boat that can outrun our ferries," Bill answered. "They carry torpedoes that have sent a number of our ships to the bottom. They also have a nasty habit of machine-gunning survivors in the water. The subs are well known for doing that too."

"I can see that we may be in for a rough trip," Paul suggested nervously. "How come they didn't hand out life jackets to us when we came aboard?"

Bill answered, "Look around you." Both sides of the deck were lined with large wooden lockers labeled "Life Jackets." He added, "In case of an attack, we are supposed to put these vests on—if they'll do us any good. If we have to go into the water, which is so killing cold here, we won't last very long if we're not picked up quickly. Wearing the bloody things is just a waste of time."

As their ferry proceeded farther and farther from land, the waters became rougher and wilder. Whoever was steering the ship kept it going back and forth in a zigzag pattern so as to spoil the aim of any attacking submarine. The waves at this point had to be close to thirty or forty feet high. The vessels bounced around like tiny corks, and as Bill predicted, there was a steady flow of men rushing to the railing in misery, hanging over the side, many of them retching. By following Bill's advice, they all remained in good shape, and they were grateful to their mentor.

A cold wind blew in on them, prompting some to scramble in to their duffel bags for warmer clothing. After a while, some of the personnel on deck, feeling chilled, opted to go below to the cramped and crowded, but warmer, facilities rather than put up with the icy blasts of the sea. Little by little, the crowd on the deck started to thin out; but, Paul, Tony, and Kurt chose to stay with Bill and his group of buddies. Some of the English soldiers called each other "mate," but they were all equally friendly with the Americans.

Bubba appeared on deck, making his way toward Paul, Tony, and Kurt. Just then a GI decided to head in the opposite direction to the hold. A wild gust of wind and a sharp turn of the ship made him lose his balance, and he started to fall headlong toward the railing. Bubba easily caught him with one arm, scooped him off the deck, and deposited him in front of Bill.

"Ah cain't take the doggone stuffy air down there," he complained. "Kin ah join you folks h'yere?" he asked.

"Make yourself at home," Paul welcomed.

The GI who had nearly gone over the side turned to him to express his thanks.

"T'waren't nuthin'," Bubba replied.

They all got back to trying to endure the cold and the bouncing around of their ship. Some thought about home and their loved ones. Others were thinking about what lay ahead for them.

At long last, one of the men near the railing called out, "I just spotted land!"

Bill said, "That's got to be our port in Northern Ireland. It won't be long before we're ashore."

As they entered the little harbor, they saw a steady procession of ferries approach the dock. One by one, they unloaded their respective cargos and moved out in order to make room for the next vessel.

Within a very short time, it was their turn to dock, and the offloading process proceeded very smoothly and efficiently. Tony and Paul said their good-byes to Bill and some of his group. Bubba hightailed it back inside to join his unit.

Once ashore, Paul and Tony spotted their three-quarter-ton truck and joined some of the other men in the medical detachment on the back of the vehicle. A long line of battalion vehicles moved out of the dock area and on into the countryside. One of the men spotted a sign that read, "Londonderry," and following the direction of the arrow on the sign, the convoy raced into the outskirts of the city. British and American military police were stationed at key intersections and waved them through while holding up civilian traffic. At the speed they were traveling, it did not take them long to traverse Londonderry, and then they were off again into the countryside. Paul saw a sign that read "Limavady," and without any pause, the convoy rushed through the little town. Just at the end of the village was a large military encampment, and the trucks all pulled into the main gate. There were a series of Nissen huts arranged in neat rows as far as one could see. The vehicles for the medical detachment drove to a street, and the lead truck stopped at the end while all of the others came to a halt behind it. A large Nissen hut in the center of the roadway was designated by a sign indicating that it was the medical detachment headquarters as well as the battalion dispensary. All of the medical personnel, including the commissioned officers, pitched in to unload the vehicles.

"I could sure use Bubba right now," Tony uttered, and Paul grunted in agreement.

Captain Macklin, Lieutenant Saffridi, and Corporal "Red" Evans were already at work setting up equipment and storing away supplies.

Tony and Paul were joined by Kurt, who arrived a little later, and they all got involved in the task at hand.

While they were all intensely busy, Sergeant Woods entered the dispensary.

"I just was handed this set of orders from battalion headquarters. The sergeant major says that this is hot off the mimeograph machine."

Woods handed the orders to Captain Sheridan, who read them out loud.

"It says here, 'From Colonel John Macklin to commanders, Company A, B, C, D, quartermaster, mess, and medical dispensary. The 456th Military Police Battalion is hereby placed on special orders to receive combat training from units of the British Army, Commandos, and Royal Marines.' The training will start at 0700 tomorrow, and all personnel will report in front of battalion headquarters at 0630, with the exception of medical, mess, and quartermaster personnel. Chow will be at 0530."

Woods then spun around. "I've got to get going, sir," he said to Captain Sheridan, and with that he left the room.

Captain Sheridan spoke up. "The Nissen hut next to us will be the barracks for all of you enlisted personnel. When we finish unpacking, you can go over there and get settled. Lieutenant Saffridi and I are scheduled to bunk in the officers' quarters, but I am going to settle in here in case any emergency comes up." He pointed to a cot in the adjoining room.

Paul, Tony, Kurt, and "Red" Evans hurried to finish their work and then went next door to a spacious Nissen hut. Some of the other men of the medical detachment were already there, unpacking their clothing and gear. Tony, Paul, Kurt, and Red followed the example of the other men in selecting a bunk and unpacking their gear into packing cases, similar to footlockers, at the foot of each bed. Corporal Evans set up a duty roster determining who would hold sick call with Captain Sheridan and who would assist Lieutenant Saffridi. It listed which days and hours each would be on duty.

Evans announced that six-hour passes to go into town would be issued the next afternoon to those who were not on duty. That would be a welcome change from army life—getting into the village of Limavady and seeing what the locals were like.

The next afternoon, Paul was able to receive a pass along with Red, and so they ambled down to the gate, presented their passes to the MPs there, and proceeded to walk the relatively short distance to Limavady. As they approached the square, the first thing Paul noticed was a bookstore. A large sign in the window proclaimed that all books were on sale. Both men ambled in and were greeted by an elderly gentleman smoking a curved meerschaum pipe. Paul jokingly exclaimed, "Mr. Sherlock Holmes, as I live and breathe!"

The older man chuckled and asked, "Can I interest you gentlemen in some books?"

Evans replied, "I'll bet you don't have any Westerns."

"As a matter of fact, I do," he replied, walking over to a shelf and pointing to a cluster of books at the end. "They are very popular here, and we are constantly reordering them."

Red and Paul walked over to the shelf and perused the titles. Several of the books were by Max Brand, prompting Paul to reach over and take a copy of *Destry Rides Again*. He had enjoyed reading it a number of years earlier and felt it would be enjoyable to read again.

Red selected a book with the title *Cheyenne Autumn*, another Max Brand Book, exclaiming, "I can't understand how someone from Boston would be interested in Western stories!"

"There are a lot of people from New England who like cowboy stories," Paul replied. "Look how many people here enjoy them. By the way, when we finish, we can swap the books."

"Great idea," Red responded.

Paul and Red both took out some of the bills in English money they had been issued earlier and offered them to the proprietor. Neither one had figured out the intricacies of the English monetary system, but this man looked honest enough to leave their money in his hands.

The gentleman counted out the proper bills for Paul and for Red and handed them back their change in English coins.

They left the store satisfied and headed for the center of town.

There was a small water fountain surrounded by a concrete wall. They both sat down wondering what to do next.

A white-haired elderly woman approached them.

"Are you boys Yanks?" she asked.

"That we are, ma'am," Red responded.

"And where might you two lads be coming from?" she asked.

"I'm from the Boston area in Massachusetts, and my friend here is from LaPlata in Maryland, which is somewhat south of

Washington, DC," Paul answered. "My apologies, ma'am, for not introducing ourselves. My name is Paul, and his name is Sanford, but he likes to be called Red."

She smiled and said, "Me name is Bridget O'Reilly. Many years ago, we came north here from Erin, which is in southern Ireland, so that my late husband could find work. He passed away several years ago, and since we don't have any family here or in the South, I have chosen to stay where I am. The people here all treat me well, and many drop in from time to time just to make sure I am in good health. Let me ask you boys, do either of you play whist? I understand it is like the game of bridge."

Red answered, "I'm sorry; I am not familiar with that, ma'am. I seem to have heard somewhere that it is like bridge."

"That's exactly right, me boy. Could you and your friend take the time to visit a lonely old lady sometimes and maybe play whist?" Bridget asked.

"I understand that it takes four people to play this game," Red suggested. "What if we try to get two more buddies to come sometime and try this game?"

"That would be wonderful. I am going to celebrate my eightieth birthday this coming Friday. It would make me happy to have someone help me celebrate this event in me life," Bridget responded.

"We can't promise you, but when we get back to camp, we will ask our commanding officer if we could come back this Friday," Paul answered.

"I bake some mighty delicious cookies, boys. So if you can come, bring your appetites with you," Bridget ventured.

When they arrived back in camp, they sought out Captain Sheridan with their request.

"Evans," Captain Sheridan said, "you are in charge of scheduling. Assuming you and Kramer want to go, find two more willing GIs who are not on the duty roster, and I'll sign the passes."

The following Friday night, Paul, Red, Tony, and Kurt, each of them armed with a six-hour pass, left the camp gates and, following Bridget's directions, found her little cottage. The four of them crowded into her front parlor. Each, in turn, wished her a happy birthday. Paul, seeing an upright piano in the parlor, sat down and played "Happy Birthday to You" while they all enthusiastically joined in singing the melody—off tune but enthusiastically. They presented her with a can of condensed milk, a bag of sugar, and a slice of cake they had managed to get from the mess sergeant.

Bridget's reaction was immediate. Tears rolled down her eyes.

"Me heart is overflowing, you dear boys," she sobbed. "I have something for you besides the cake." She went into the dining room and brought out a large platter filled with delicious-looking cookies. "What with our wartime rationing, I don't have too much to work with, but this is the best I could do. Help yourselves, you dear boys," she said. "Now I'm going to put the kettle on and brew us up a nice coop a tay."

After her chores were completed, Bridget sat them down at a bridge table. She then brought out a deck of cards, dealt them out, and at first instructed them how to play a hand with the cards dealt face up. Following that, it didn't take them very long to understand and appreciate the game. In a short time they were playing enthusiastically while Bridget cheered them on from the sidelines.

"Paul," Tony said, "why don't you take a break and play us some songs on the piano, and we can have the pleasure of Bridget's company while we play—but I insist that she be my partner."

Paul willingly gave up his seat to a protesting Bridget and started to play a few tunes he thought she would enjoy. First there was "Danny Boy," and then followed "When Irish Eyes are Smiling." He sang his own off-key accompaniment. Then he played "The Wearing of the Green."

Bridget jumped up, horrified. "You mustn't play that! The Brits will arrest you, child. It is against the law to play that tune or to sing it."

Paul smiled at her. "Don't forget, dear lady, that we are Americans and are not restricted by that stupid law."

All of a sudden, there came a rapping at one of the windows.

Bridget clasped her hands to her heart and said, "Dear Lord, we are in trouble now for certain."

Red went to the window to find one of the villagers rapping again on the window, calling out, "Let's hear it again, Yank."

Bridget went to the door and invited in the young man, who was followed by several others. They all joined in a song fest in honor of Bridget's birthday.

She was thrilled, and in appreciation, she asked the boys for their parents' names and addresses. She planned to write each and every one of them and tell them what wonderful sons they had.

On the way back to camp, they made a solemn pact to try to visit Bridget as many Friday nights as they could manage. And so it was that every Friday night, four men from the medical detachment made their way to Bridget's little cottage. Sometimes the group included Tony, Paul, Kurt, and Red. When they were on duty, some of the other men in their group were persuaded and cajoled into making a visit to the sweet old lady.

Once when Paul was visiting, he said to Bridget, "May I ask you a question that puzzles me? I do not want to be rude or impertinent, so please bear with me, if I may."

"Of course, dear boy, go right ahead and ask me whatever you want," she replied.

"I was in England for just a short amount of time, and all

of the English people I have come in contact with are decent, honorable, God-fearing people. Now that we have had a chance to meet a few Irish people, we have the very same impression. How can it be that these two groups of such fine people have been involved in this tragic conflict?" Paul asked.

"The answer is very complex, child, and is not easy. I believe that there are small groups of firebrands on both sides who go at each other's throats with the result that many innocent people suffer. The more sensible people on each side have difficulty controlling those who want to act in a radical manner. As a person from Ireland, I am very touched that an American would be so concerned. Bless you, my child."

Back at camp, the combat training continued, with occasional presentations by British Army medics to the people in the American medical units. All of the dispensary personnel paid careful attention to what was said by veterans of the African and Italian Campaigns. Some of them had been on hit-and-run raids on selected target areas in France and Norway.

One evening on the way back to Camp, after a pleasant visit with Bridget, Red suggested that they stop at a local pub and get a glass of beer. "They call it 'arf and arf' or some such thing and generally serve it at room temperature. They think you are nuts if you ask for your beer to be served cold," Red commented, and he added, "You can even play their favorite game—darts."

The place that they stopped at was on a different side of town, and it was not the typical type of pub they had seen. Tony observed, "This joint looks like a real bucket of blood."

It was true. It was a rough-looking place with some shady-looking characters sitting around. Interspersed among them were some American paratroopers, US Army, British Army, and British Navy personnel located in various parts of the very smoky room.

As soon as they entered, Bubba walked over to greet them. "Come on, y'all. I have room at my table," he said enthusiastically.

Tony, Paul, Red, and Kurt followed him to a table, but there didn't seem to be enough chairs. Without hesitation, Bubba lifted two chairs from a table and two more from a different table. Because of his size, no one challenged him or voiced any objection.

As soon as they were seated, they gave their orders to a barmaid, and within a short time, everyone had a beer in front of him and was happily drinking away.

Two paratroopers got into an argument over something that no one could figure out, and within seconds they began to pummel each other.

Paul spoke up. "They are disgracing the highly respected uniform of the paratroopers, going at it like that."

Bubba answered, "Y'all are right theya. I'm ashamed to have two men wearing an American paratrooper's uniform acting like that."

With that he got up on his feet, walked over to them, and attempted to lecture and scold them like a schoolmarm. They paid no attention to him and kept swinging viciously at each other. In frustration he picked each of them up by the scruff of the neck and pleaded with them to stop embarrassing him and the other Americans present.

They simply continued flailing away at one another, and in desperation, while holding them off the floor, he knocked their heads together. Both of their heads rolled semi-lifelessly as each of them lost consciousness. He then put his arms around their waists, carried them to two empty chairs, propped them up, and continued lecturing the semiconscious combatants. One of the other paratroopers in the room came over, picked up a glass of water, and poured the contents on the faces of the now recovering men. He turned to Bubba. "Thanks, buddy. I've got it under control now."

Bubba, with a look of satisfaction on his face, returned to his group and went on as if nothing had happened.

Five minutes later, a group of town MPs rushed into the pub.

"What's going on?" one of them asked.

"We got a call that there was a brawl going on in here," a second one said.

Tony and Paul looked at them innocently. Paul looked one of the MPs directly in the eye and said, "You men must have been told to go to the wrong place. Everything is nice and quiet in here."

Some of the paratroopers agreed with Paul, backed up by emphatic statements from other US and British military and naval personnel. The MPs slowly withdrew, and normal conversation returned to all parts of the room.

A short time later, they were all notified that in seventy-two hours they were to report at 0800 in class A uniform to the parade ground, which was located at the outskirts of the camp. A military review was going to be held for all Allied military and naval personnel. The men assumed that their training program would be officially over very soon.

"This is it," Tony commented.

Paul agreed. "We'll be placed on alert soon after this and shipped God knows where."

Red cautioned, "One of us had better try to get into town and let Bridget know."

As it turned out, Tony and Paul, fortunately, were each issued a six-hour pass.

They rushed over to Bridget's house, and as soon as they entered all out of breath, she knew immediately what was happening.

"Dear Lord," she sobbed, "I'll be going to church and praying for you boys. I just felt it in my old bones that something like this was about to happen. But then, I promise you, I will write to your mothers and tell them what fine young men they have and how well you all look. I joost feel that you are all part of me family. Me heart is breaking, dear, sweet boys. Now get along with you before I start blubbering and make a fool of meself."

Paul and Tony both hugged her and kissed her and sadly made their way back to camp.

The next morning, right after reveille and chow, the entire battalion marched in formation to the outskirts of the camp to a large parade ground. This had formerly been a soccer field but was taken over by the military. US Army, Navy, and Marine units were there, along with elements of the British Army and Royal Marines. At first the formation remained in place, but as the men waited, some got impatient, slipped out of their places, and moved on to greet buddies in other groups. Apparently the civilians living in the adjoining villages and towns had been invited, and crowds of them thronged around the perimeter and in the viewing stands.

Kurt said, "The sight of this soccer field brings back some frightening memories. In Germany I and some other Jewish kids were being hidden and moved from town to town by good Germans who did not hold with the Nazi philosophy. The ultimate goal of these decent people was to get us to a safe place like Switzerland or Spain."

"One day we stopped for a rest on the outskirts of a forest bordering what looked like a soccer field, just like this. All of a sudden, a crowd of what we were told were Jewish men, women, and children were herded onto the field by SS troopers all carrying weapons that were pointed at the poor souls. The pitiful group of people were struggling to carry their belongings. We were told later on that these people had been ordered by the SS to leave their homes immediately and to take with them only what they could cram into a small bag. When they got to the field, they were ordered to leave their belongings on the ground and were told that these would follow them later on. The SS told these prisoners that they were going to be taken to a labor camp. They were then marched to a railroad siding not far away and crammed into cattle cars with no windows. The doors were slammed shut and sealed, and ultimately they would take this pitiful group of men, women, children, and some infants to a death camp—something the Germans referred to politely as a concentration camp." With that his eyes filled with tears and he could not continue.

Tony and Paul put their arms on his shoulders to comfort him, but the stark horror of this memory would not leave Kurt.

Suddenly some whistles blew, and a few of the noncoms came up to the ranks and began to bark out orders.

Red, as a member of the noncoms, called out, "This is it, men! Line up!"

They all got into formation and could see that several military bands had come onto the field. The first was a US Army band, and it struck up "The Caissons Go Rolling Along." A color guard marched in front of them, and the battalion GIs were instructed to follow closely behind them. "Forward march!" was called out, and their unit stepped in perfect formation. Some of the men began to sing,

> *Over hill, over dale,*
> *as we hit the dusty trail,*
> *and the caissons go rolling along.*

As they marched by the reviewing stand, the men heard Colonel Macklin roar out, "Eyes right!"

All of their eyes snapped toward the reviewing stand, and

Colonel Macklin smartly saluted. The officers there just as smartly returned the salute.

As they marched back to their starting point, they halted, and more units moved in beside them. They found themselves alongside Bill's group. When he recognized Paul and Tony, he stepped over to them and said, "You chaps will enjoy this!"

A marching band of pipers came onto the field and started playing as all of the English military units, including Bill's, marched off to fall in behind. Bill had to run in order to catch up with his group as they moved out.

Red said, "I have been told that when these guys go into combat, they play those pipes just as they are doing now."

Paul looked at the large throng of civilians and remembered how as a child growing up in Dorchester, at the time of the High Holidays, crowds like this would congregate on the streets in the vicinity of the synagogues and temples. Local police would cordon off a number of the streets near the Jewish places of worship in order to allow people to safely walk there. At some of the larger temples with well-known cantors officiating at the services, many enthusiastic people would gather near the open doors just to catch some of the melodies and songs of the prayer service.

Paul was snapped out of his reverie by a shout of "Attention!" Their unit was then marched off the field, accompanied by many cheers and shouts of encouragement from the watching civilians.

The next day, the battalion was put on alert, which prompted a flurry of activity in packing up gear and equipment.

Two days later, they were on board their motor convoy, heading for the coast. Once they boarded the ferry, following the earlier tips given them by Bill, most of the medical detachment headed for the upper deck and fortified themselves with some of the rations they carried. Each of them located a satisfactory secure spot beside which they could brace themselves for the expected rough trip ahead of them.

Leaving the harbor was disarmingly smooth, but as soon as they left the shelter of the bay, ominously heavy waves started to crash onto the decks and toss the boat from side to side. They had no sooner gotten out of sight of land than the ship's alarm went off. A series of deafening blasts came from of the ship's horns located adjacent to the smokestack.

Coincidental with this, a very loud cracking noise sounded from somewhere behind them, and a large plume of water flew up just in front of the prow of the vessel. The ship heeled wildly to port, and another crack sounded, this time creating another plume of water on their starboard side, but alarmingly closer. Someone called out, "It's a sub!" All eyes turned to the starboard side of their ship, and sure enough, about a half a mile away, a submarine had surfaced, and men on the deck were manning a deck gun, pointing it directly at them.

Rushing at top speed between the sub and their ferry, a British destroyer sped wildly toward the sub with all guns blazing and hammering away. First the deck gun was hit, and it disappeared over the side in a massive explosion. Then a large hole blew out at the base of the conning tower, and still another huge explosion tore a gaping hole in the deck of the sub, just at the waterline. It apparently was taking on large amounts of seawater, and shortly thereafter, the stern of the sub came out of the water, turning almost vertical, and gradually started to sink into the water. German sailors frantically jumped overboard—at least those who were able to make it out of the rapidly sinking vessel. The destroyer ceased firing and put out two lifeboats, apparently to pick up survivors. It maintained a good level of speed and kept back quite a distance from the sub.

Another destroyer, flying the Stars and Stripes, charged

up and moved quickly to circle the ferry while monitoring the surrounding area for any other enemy vessels that might be in their vicinity. Suddenly its guns started to fire at a target that seemed to be over the horizon. What appeared to be a line of surf started rapidly moving toward them, while the destroyer's shells fell right in the dead center of this target zone.

"That's got to be an E-boat!" one of the British sailors exclaimed.

Two torpedoes, one closely following the other, crossed their wake and kept moving away from them.

"A miss is as good as a mile," Tony snickered—with little enthusiasm.

Suddenly a huge explosion occurred in the center of the areas the destroyer was firing at.

"Scratch one E-boat!" someone exclaimed.

Bill and some of his buddies came up on deck and joined the medical detachment group. "We came up to see what the racket was all about. It appears that you lads have just had your first baptism of fire. Welcome to the war!" He grinned.

"How do you Jewish guys like being baptized?" Red jokingly asked.

Kurt rejoined, "We can call this body of water a ritual bath—something we Jews have been using for centuries."

"I respect any religious ritual, but to tell you the truth, I would prefer the enjoyment and excitement of a John Wayne movie," Paul observed.

As they settled back, more or less in comfort, now understanding better the significant protection they were being given by the British and American destroyers, talk turned to other things.

Paul turned to Kurt and asked, "How did you manage to get to the States from Nazi Germany?"

"It was because of a number of dedicated brave people in

Germany, France, and Spain—Jews and Christians alike—who, at the risk of their own lives, helped me and many other lucky souls to escape. When I finally made it to England, the people were all very warm and welcoming and encouraged me to stay there. Since I had family in the States, I chose, with their great help, to go to your beautiful land of America.

"And there is one more thing you should know. When I was in Spain, with a family who sheltered me as well as a number of others, they told me that they had heard on their shortwave radio about a series of mass executions the Nazis had inflicted on Jews, Gypsies, Poles, Russians, and many others. A short time after they told me this, they used their precious radio to tune in on the Vatican, and we heard the pope broadcast, 'The horror and inexcusable excesses committed on a helpless and homeless people have been established by the unimpeachable testimony of eyewitnesses.' Those brave words are firmly ingrained into my mind and helped give me the strength to go on; I'll never forget them!" At this point, tears streamed down his face.

Bill turned to Kurt.

"Thanks for the compliment about the Brits, Yank. I accept this on behalf of all of my countrymen. Now that you are in the US Army, you really are a Yank."

They all continued to spend the rest of the voyage on deck, reminiscing about their civilian lives before the war. Apart from the numerous seasick men rushing to the railings, the remainder of the cruise was uneventful.

— 9 —

They arrived at a location in southern England close to the English Channel; or, so they determined from their surroundings. The area was a desolate-looking place that had been cleared of trees and shrubbery as far as they could see. Huge rolls of barbed wire went out from a large double wooden gate that was twelve feet high and about forty feet across. A dozen MPs, armed with Thompson submachine guns guarded the entrance and carefully checked the papers of each vehicle as it stopped. The trucks drove for several miles until they no longer could see the gate and then stopped, one column alongside the other, until the entire battalion of vehicles was all in one general area. The men were ordered to dismount and were directed to the vast open ground around the trucks. They were then told to put their barracks bags down on the ground and to sit down. The order was given to "light up if you want," and many of the men reached for their ever-present pack of cigarettes to begin puffing away and wondering what they were doing in this godforsaken place that looked so barren.

Colonel Macklin, accompanied by several of his staff officers, appeared.

"All right men," he called out in a loud voice. "If you can't hear everything I say, your company commanders will repeat the information to you. This is it! We are in a camp called a concentration location." He laughed. "This is not what the Germans call a concentration camp. Our next stop is somewhere in France or Germany. We have not been told that or when we are going. Any letters you write can only have the notation 'Somewhere in England.' Your letters are going to be heavily censored, so don't even try to hint about what is going on. Our battalion headquarters will be a pyramidal tent that will be identified by a sign in front of it. Each company headquarters will also have a pyramidal tent, the same going for the medical battalion, quartermaster, and mess. Unit commanders will assign men to dig latrines in their area. Each of you has a shelter half in your barracks bag. You will buddy up with a man in your unit and, using the shelter halves, assemble them and make yourselves a pup tent. Tomorrow you will be ordered when called by your noncoms, to report to the quartermaster tent for new additional supplies.

"You will draw K and C rations, gas-impregnated clothing, and a new gas mask that is an improved version of the one you have been lugging around since before you left the US of A. Also several more items. The weather here is miserably cold and damp. You will also draw several extra blankets, and believe it or not, we are going to be one of the first units to get issued the new army combat boots. No one leaves this place under any circumstances, especially in an emergency. Final briefing will be at the time of our embarkation. Our mess lieutenant and mess sergeant, even though we are only authorized to draw C and K rations, may use some illegal procedures—I didn't say it—to draw class A rations from the supply dump not far from here, but I can't promise you anything. It all depends on them finding a suitable forger who can doctor up the requisition forms. Any questions, ask your NCOs. Now get busy!"

With that he left. Everybody got busy unloading their trucks and setting up the headquarters tents as directed by their noncoms.

Tony nudged Paul. "Guess we'll buddy up. Okay?"

"Sure," Paul replied. "Looks like this is really it."

For the better part of a week, the men worked diligently from dawn to dusk, setting up the larger pyramidal headquarters tents for the battalion and company headquarters, dispensary, quartermaster, motor pool, and mess. Finally, when all had been completed, the men were given a little time to sack out and catch up on their sleep. When everything settled down to a routine—including mandatory close-order drill; calisthenics, including the hated push-ups; and double-timing—everyone breathed a collective sigh of relief.

One morning as the medical detachment reported for duty in the newly assembled medical dispensary, Captain Sheridan called out, "Kramer, take the truck down to the motor pool and have them do whatever it is they are supposed to. I think they have to work on the exhaust system. Martino, you do the same with our jeep."

Paul and Tony went outside the tent to their respective vehicles.

"Tony," Paul called out, "where is the motor pool?"

I don't know, buddy, so let's drive up to the gate and ask the MPs there."

When they arrived at their destination, there were only two armed MPs there, talking to a third. The third MP turned around, and Paul and Tony saw it was Bubba.

"What you fellers need?" Bubba asked.

"We've got to find the motor pool." Tony replied.

"Y'all cain't miss it" was Bubba's response. He pointed along the perimeter of the fence. "It's just a mite down there, 'bout a half mile. Whah doan ah just jine you?"

"Sure," Paul answered. "Jump aboard."

They returned to their jeep and truck and found an area filled with all sorts of vehicles. This had to be the motor pool. After signing a series of papers and in return getting receipts for the vehicles, they were told that the medical detachment would be notified when the truck and jeep would be ready.

"What do you have to do to this truck and jeep?" Tony asked a grease-covered noncom.

"We've got to waterproof these things here so that when you are landing and go into the water, as we have been told you will, you won't get stuck and have to swim ashore"

"How do you do this?" Paul queried.

"We have to waterproof critical engine parts and make air hoses that will be clamped to the body, near the front door, so that the carburetor and exhaust pipe can breathe. You already have cat's eye blackout lights, so you are all set there."

Paul, Tony, and Bubba started to trudge back toward the medical dispensary. The three of them, following the dress code adopted by most of the personnel, were dressed very casually with no neckties. It just so happened that the three of them had chosen to wear their wool knit caps, which were very effective in taking the pressure of the helmet liner straps off their heads. It was a popular clothing item among the GIs, because it was sensible apparel along with fatigues, trousers and field jackets. On account of the cold, damp weather pervading in Southern England at the time, Paul had even chosen to wear a scarf as well. Bubba had, as was his habit, neglected to button all of his shirt buttons, and his T-shirted beer belly was popping out.

As they trudged along, chattering aimlessly and hardly paying attention to what was on the road, they suddenly heard a loud, high-pitched voice scream out, "What in God's name do you poor excuses for men represent?"

Startled, the three of them saw an older man, wearing no

badge of rank, dressed immaculately. There was a sharp crease to his trousers, and his belt buckle and boots were polished like mirrors. The man's face was red with rage and anger.

"Who do you think you are, walking around dressed like a bunch of blasted sad sacks of garbage?" he raged. He then pointed to their heads. "What in hell is that thing you're wearing?"

They were all wearing the wool knit cap they had been issued by the Quartermaster. This cap came in handy when donning the helmet liner and then the helmet on top of it. Without the wool knit cap, the helmet liner straps cut fiercely into one's head.

The men as did most of the G.I.'s had gotten into the habit of wearing the wool knit cap rather than the fatigue cap or the dressy overseas cap.

"Who is this old creep?" Tony asked Paul and Bubba in a loud voice.

"I don't know," Paul replied, "but I think he must have escaped from some nuthouse."

Bubba objected, "Ah don't rahtly know about showing disrespect for this h'yere elderly gentleman."

"Elderly!" the older man shrieked. "I could whip all of your butts with one arm tied behind my back!"

Paul nudged Tony hard in the ribs and moaned, "Look at what he is wearing!" He pointed to what appeared to be two pearl-handled revolvers attached to the man's waist.

General George Patton's reputation for being mercurial as well as a stickler for good military dress codes was all too well known.

Bubba yelled, "Attinshun!"

The three of them stood stiffly at attention, not even daring to breathe.

The man approached them, put his snarling face right in front of first Bubba, then Tony, and finally Paul. The three miscreants were standing so firmly at attention that, one by one, they started to shake and tremble.

The general, who could not control himself, slapped his leg and laughed helplessly. "Officially I am not here, you understand?" the general shouted. "You men get back to your outfit and make up your minds to dress like real soldiers. It's going to take real soldiers to whip those murdering Nazi scum. You're going to grab them by the nose and kick them in the rear end all the way to Berlin! You got that, you pitiful sad sacks?"

"Yes, sir!" they all answered, still standing at attention and repeatedly saluting him.

"At least you men know how to salute like soldiers! Now, dismissed!" he yelled at them, trying to maintain a stern attitude.

The three of them broke into a run to escape Patton's rage, not bothering to look back, but they heard him roaring with laughter as they raced back for the safety of the dispensary.

"Captain Sheridan won't believe this," Tony huffed.

When they got within sight of the medical dispensary tent, they all recognized a familiar figure. It was Chaplain Thompson.

"You certainly are a welcome sight, Chaplain," Paul said.

"The very same goes for the three of you," Reverend Thompson replied. "We—that is, the three of us chaplains—are doing a circuit of the camps here in Southern England. I should say that I am proud to be in the company of Father Murray and Rabbi Rose. They are inside, getting Father Murray's sprained ankle attended to by Captain Sheridan."

Paul, Tony, and Bubba needed no further urging to go into the large pyramidal tent, where they saw Captain Sheridan finishing up a neat job of strapping Father Murray's left ankle.

"Well look who came in to visit," Rabbi Rose called out.

Captain Sheridan looked up from his handiwork, as did Father Murray. There were warm greetings all around.

"You must have been filled in by Reverend Thompson," Father Murray said. "We are trying to set up services for as many men that we can reach in this division. Colonel Macklin has generously offered the use of your battalion recreation tent for this." Spotting Paul, he added, "It will be appreciated if you can help us with our services, Private Kramer. We have come equipped with a small field-type pump organ, and we are sure you will do yourself proud with this. We just came from battalion headquarters, where they are busy cranking out news of our schedules on their mimeograph machines. Colonel Macklin has been most cooperative and helpful. Sorry we can't make it every week, but because we have many other units in this camp as well as additional camps to go to, we will simply have to try to do the best we can."

"I'll be glad to oblige, Chaplains," Paul replied.

Bubba spoke up, directing his remarks to Captain Sheridan. "Suh, y'all will nevah evah giss who jist reamed ouwah butts out—'scuse me suhs—but royally."

Captain Sheridan smiled and said, "I have been alerted that General Patton is in the area, making an unannounced tour of the camp. The general has insisted on not allowing any ranking officers to accompany him on his personal tour of the facility. His not wearing any badge of rank is because he is making an unsuccessful attempt at remaining incognito. Apparently you met Old Blood and Guts in person. That's something you can tell your grandchildren about if you live through this rotten war. He's supposed to be in charge of some other army or something, but who knows, we may meet up with this general again. People say that he is the best combat general in the US Army. By the way, was he wearing his usual shoulder holster, packing a pearl-handled revolver, or was he wearing his other pair of pearl-handled revolvers, attached to his belt?"

"Suh," Bubba said, saluting Captain Sheridan, "This hyere

Ginarel was packin' two pistols, but beggin' the captain's permission, suh, ah have to git back to mah outfit, with your permission, suh. But raht now, ah would follow that man over a cliff." He turned and saluted Captains Murray and Rose. They, along with Captain Sheridan, smartly returned his salute.

"Get back to your outfit, Bubba, and thanks for helping Kramer and Martino find the motor pool." Sheridan returned the salute and returned to checking Father Murray's ankle, giving him some encouraging words about the prognosis of the injury.

Paul and Tony bid their good-byes to all three chaplains and decided to explore the recreation tent that had been referred to as the future location of all three religious services. It was not far from battalion headquarters, and it was enormous. It reminded them of a huge circus tent. It was filled with simple wooden benches. On one side of the large entrance was a battered upright piano. In the center was a large wooden table on which was sitting what seemed to be just an ordinary radio. It was attached to a wire that went through the ceiling, apparently connected to the power source distributed throughout the camp. The most incredible music emanated from the radio and caught their rapt attention. There did not seem to be an announcer for this station; there was simply fabulous music played for their pleasure and enjoyment. It must have been an English radio station, for the first several songs were decidedly British. The great Vera Lynn sang her incomparable "We'll Meet Again," the words so beautifully and clearly enunciated by Ms. Lynn:

> We'll meet again
> Don't know where
> Don't know when
> But I know we'll meet again some sunny day.

And on it went, followed by a fantastic instrumental.

Then Vera Lynn sang another song so very popular in England:

There'll be bluebirds over
the white cliffs of Dover
Tomorrow, just you wait and see.

And she continued this song to the end. Another song that had originally been popular with the German Afrika Korps and then became popular with the opposing English troops, "Lili Marlene," was sung in English. "Underneath the lantern by the barrack gate" got their rapt attention. The next song by Vaughn Monroe was "When the Lights Go On Again (All Over the World)." This was highly popular in both the United States and Britain. The amazing tunes continued, each more enjoyable than the last. There was Bing Crosby singing "I'll Be Seeing You," followed by his immensely popular rendition of "White Christmas." This was followed by "In the Mood," played by Glenn Miller and his great orchestra. The Andrews Sisters singing "Boogie Woogie Bugle Boy" came through loud and clear. The great Frank Sinatra sang several of his lilting melodies, such as "Dream," "Put Your Dreams Away," and " Night and Day." There followed the great music of Tommy and Jimmy Dorsey, Duke Ellington, Louis Armstrong, Bennie Goodman, Dizzy Gillespie, Harry James, and Charlie Parker, along with such great vocalists as Helen O'Connell, Dinah Shore, Kate Smith, Sarah Vaughan, Billie Holiday, Tex Beneke, Marion Hutton, Ray and Bob Eberly, and a host of others.

As they were listening to the song "Tangerine," a couple of MPs came into the tent, wanting to know why the volume on the radio was turned up so high. As soon as they heard the music, they too sat down to listen to the myriad of great songs and instrumentals. Realizing how late it was getting, Paul and Tony left to the refrain of "Don't Sit Under the Apple Tree" and made up their minds to tell their buddies about this incredible radio station.

The battalion headquarters orderly met them outside of the tent and told them to return to the motor pool and pick up their vehicles immediately, if not sooner. They readily complied with their orders.

Just a few days later, as evening approached, Paul and Tony were preparing their pup tent so that they could retire for the evening.

Paul said, "I think I'll read a while before I hit the sack," and he picked up his book while stretching out on the grass outside of the tent in order to get what little remained of the failing daylight.

Tony went on with his housekeeping efforts in the tent; and then, following Paul's example, took his book out to read a while before falling asleep.

Two civilian cars painted an olive drab color circled the area of pup tents Paul and Tony were ensconced in. The door of the front vehicle opened, and Colonel Macklin jumped out of the front seat. A lieutenant, followed by a brigadier general, left the backseat, followed by none other than the great General Dwight Eisenhower. The second car emptied out, also occupied by high-ranking officers.

General Ike, as he was fondly called by his men, approached Paul and Tony. They did not need to have anyone call out "Attention!" They stood at attention and gave the general a smart salute. In the process of doing this, each of them had to transfer his own book from his right hand to his left hand in order to properly render the salute.

General Eisenhower returned the salute and approached Paul and Tony. He looked at Paul and asked, "What's your name, soldier, and where are you from?"

"Paul Kramer, sir, and I come from a suburb of Boston, Mass, called Dorchester."

"I'm familiar with Boston, but not with Dorchester," the general replied, and glancing down at the book Paul was holding, he asked, "What are you reading, son?"

"It's a Western by Max Brand, sir, called *Destry Rides Again*," Paul replied.

Ike broke out in his famous grin. "Why, Max Brand is my favorite author, soldier, and I have a copy of *Destry* next to my cot," the general responded.

"Begging the general's pardon, sir," Tony said, "I also have a Max Brand Western here." He held it out for the general to see.

"Well, we three soldiers have a lot in common then," the general suggested.

"We have to get moving on sir," a bird colonel interrupted, prompting Ike to turn back to Paul and Tony and say, "Good luck, men, and nice talking to you." He then moved on.

"Getting to meet two top generals just a few days apart—that is the cat's meow," Tony chortled.

"This is really something to tell our grandchildren about— that is, if we make it," Paul replied. "Wow!"

A few days later, late on a Friday afternoon, Chaplain Rose drove up to the recreation tent in a jeep. Paul, Tony, and Kurt, who also volunteered, met him and helped unload the field organ and prayer books, and set everything up. Paul played a number of selections during the service, which was appreciated by the men attending as well as the rabbi. Following the service, they gathered up all of the chaplain's materials and reloaded them back on to the jeep. The three of them repeated the same procedure the following Saturday afternoon for the Catholic services and the following Sunday morning for the Protestant services. The three of them were warmly thanked by all three chaplains, and so they felt a strong sense of satisfaction with what they had done.

The cold, damp, windy rain that hit them endlessly seemed to deteriorate for a while and then got even worse. The men were talking about when the invasion would occur.

"There's no way we can pull this off in this weather," one GI observed.

Most agreed with them, but a few wondered if it would not be best, assuming the Germans felt the same way, to go ahead regardless of the weather.

Just a few days later, close to 9:00 p.m., before hitting the sack, Paul, Tony, and some others walked by the recreation tent. There was always a good chance that they would get to hear some great music on the radio. As usual, at 9:00 p.m., three short tones played, followed by a long tone. This was the Morse code signal for victory. Then a voice came on saying, "This is the BBC." The news items were covered, and the war seemed to be progressing slowly, but nevertheless steadily, toward ultimate victory, which still seemed to be a depressingly long way off. Then followed a series of coded messages, such as "Uncle Percival's cat has a toothache. Schoolmarm Millicent is taking a fortnight holiday in Surrey." These coded messages went directly to the heroic members of the French Resistance, who were setting up operations throughout France to prepare the way for the invasion. This evening the messages were "I am looking for four leaf clovers ... The tomatoes should be picked. ... The dice are on the table ... It is hot in Suez ... The children are bored on Sundays." Then the second line of a Verlaine couplet: "Pierce my heart with a dull languor." Much later in the war, many of the men would find out that this was the key signal to the French Resistance that the invasion would commence imminently, and that it initiated carefully laid plans for demolitions in support of the invasion.

Tony and Paul, bored with these announcements and disappointed that the usual musical program was not following, had gone into their pup tent. They were going to try to get some sleep, and as always, they fought a losing battle with trying to stay warm and dry. A tremendous roaring sound woke them, and the very earth started to tremble.

"I think we're having an earthquake," Tony said nervously.

They rushed out of the tent and noted that the loud roar seemed to be coming from the heavily overcast sky.

Moments later they saw countless black outlines of planes, most of them flying at low levels, all heading out over the English Channel in the direction of France. There were alternate black-and-white stripes painted on the wings and fuselages with no other identification marks.

"Whoever they are, they are going in the right direction," Paul uttered apprehensively.

Some were bombers, and some were fighter planes. Some flew at low levels, and some were at a much higher altitude. From a distance they seemed to be flying wing tip to wing tip, but as they got closer, it was clear even through the darkness that they were farther apart than that. They all had the same mysterious black-and-white stripes on their wings, and they were all flying toward the European Continent.

"This is it!" Paul uttered.

"Today is June 6, isn't it?" Tony asked.

"You've got it right there," Paul responded.

Kurt joined them. "How come we are not on our way too?" he asked.

"We'll be going soon; just you wait and see," Tony replied.

As it got lighter and there was no call for alert, some of the men, including Tony and Paul, walked over to the recreation tent. The radio was blaring out an announcement from the BBC: "Early this morning, members of the Allied Armed Forces began landing on the shores of Europe. These landings will be followed by many others at various locations, and it is expected that these landings will be the first steps in liberating the European Continent from the tyranny of the Nazi Axis."

"There's not many details theyah," Bubba complained.

"I guess they can't give away our strategy at this early stage," Tony suggested.

"I'm going to keep my toothbrush handy in case we have to start moving like right away," Paul commented.

"Y'all heeyah take a gander at mah new weapon," Bubba said, holding out a rifle that was considerably smaller than the M-1 Garand he usually carried with him. "This heeyah is what they call ah carbeen. It sure is a sweet rahfle. Every man Jack in mah outfit has been issued one. Jist in tahm for the invasion."

Some of the medics crowded around, admiring the new weapon.

When they returned to duty, they tried to question Captain Sheridan about what was going on. "I'm just as much in the dark as you are, men. As soon as we get any word, official or not, I promise I'll pass it on to you."

They settled back in to their usual routine, while expecting, almost minute by minute, to be put on alert.

A few days later, Captain Sheridan told Paul and Tony to once again bring their ambulance and jeep back to the motor pool. According to the latest orders, brackets were to be fastened onto all vehicles that could accommodate five-gallon jerricans. These five-gallon containers would be filled with gasoline to keep their trucks and jeeps going. As Paul brought the truck to a stop at the motor pool, followed by Tony in the jeep, a familiar voice called out, "Hi, Paulie."

Sure enough, it was Manny Puryear, Paul's childhood friend.

"What are you doing here, Manny?"

"I had to bring my deuce-and-a-half in for service," Emanuel replied.

"Deuce-and-a-half," Paul replied. "Is that what they call a two-and-a-half-ton truck?"

"Yes, that and Jimmies—we also call them Jimmies for 'GM.' That's exactly right, Paulie. We also drive ten-ton tractor trailers, also equipped to carry lots of jerricans and ammunition."

"Are you part of the First Division?" Paul asked.

"This is a huge camp, my friend," Manny said. "There are many different units here. I have been put into an outfit just starting to be formed up, called the Red Ball Express. From what I've seen, all of our enlisted men are Negroes, as are most of our noncoms and officers. We are going to go to France sometime soon, we hear, and our job is going to be to move all kinds of supplies and deliver them up to the front lines and keep them coming. We have been training very hard for the past several months," Manny added.

"I'm a medic in an MP battalion, Paul said, "and we're also heading over there sometime soon. Maybe we'll catch up with each other."

"I hope so," Manny replied, "and I hope we both make it back when this war is over."

"Amen to that," Paul responded.

"Why are they putting these brackets on our trucks and jeeps?" Tony asked.

"You probably have already heard that we have to carry a lot of jerricans," Manny responded. "Supplying all of our vehicles with gasoline may decide the course of the war."

"Why are they so stuck on fitting us for jerrican brackets, and just what are they?" Tony asked.

"Back when we were fighting in Africa, Rommel's army

finally surrendered, and we captured huge stocks of the German gas cans. At first we called the new American jerricans "Americans." The name never made it, and after that it was always called the jerrican."

They then talked about the folks back home, with Manny wistfully longing for some of Paul's mother's chocolate chip cookies, and Paul salivating when he thought about Manny's mother's barbecue brisket. They lost track of time until the motor pool sergeant came over to tell them that their trucks were ready. They reluctantly bade good-bye to each other, and each headed back to his own outfit.

It had to be about a week after D-day, in the early hours of the morning, when a tremendous racket of anti-aircraft fire erupted around the outside of the camp, with some shooting coming from inside the grounds as well. Many of the men were awakened, including Tony and Paul, who rushed outside their tent and looked upward to see what the guns were firing at.

Searchlights had caught what seemed to be a small airplane with short, stubby wings and no cockpit, flying along at a good clip. It did not seem to have any propeller, and what appeared to be faint flames came out of the back of the tube-like body. It emitted a *brrrp, brrp* sound as it flew almost overhead. When it was almost out of sight, the engine cut out, and whatever it was went into a steep dive and crashed in a huge ball of flame.

"What in God's name was that?" asked Tony.

"I heard mention of something called a buzz bomb, or what the Germans call a V-1 rocket," answered Paul.

"Then that's got to be it!" Tony replied. "That bloody thing is really scary. It can drop out of the sky anywheres!"

When they got back to the dispensary, there was animated talk about the V-1 weapon.

"It doesn't make any sense," Paul exclaimed. "Since the engine seems to cut out at any given time, this is not a strategic weapon; it looks like Hitler has dreamed up some kind of terror weapon. If that jerk thinks he is going to scare any of us, and especially the English civilians, he's got another thing coming."

Over the next several days, the V-1s came at unexpected times of the day and night. The Allied defenses had quickly developed a strategy for dealing with them. Some fighter planes got to shoot them down, while others were brought down by anti-aircraft fire. Unfortunately there were still some, apparently, that got through.

It had to be just two weeks after D-day when, early in the morning, before reveille, the alert came through. Everyone got busy packing gear and equipment in the early morning darkness. With the ruling that no lights could be on, no one could make his task easier by using a flashlight. As dawn started to arrive, most of the packing was finished. The men were lined up, ready to get on their assigned trucks.

The convoy made its way out of the camp and down a long, winding road toward the water. A lonely old woman standing at the side of the road waved her handkerchief to them and broke down into tears as the trucks slowly moved by her.

"Good luck, you boys. May God bless you." she called out.

As they neared the dock area, more and more civilians had made their way to the edge of the road and shouted out words of encouragement to them.

Landing craft of all sizes and shapes crowded the dock area, which was closed off to the civilians. Many of them were landing craft infantry vessels. This type of vessel was the one that the medical detachment, as well as many men of the battalion, were directed to board. The weather was still windy, cool, and damp, and the water even at the dock area was choppy.

"Looks like we're in for another bumpy trip," someone commented.

Each landing craft, or at least most of them, had a barrage balloon attached to the stern by a long steel cable. The balloon itself was not always fully inflated, and some of them sagged downward to the rear. These were apparently designed to keep German fighters and bombers at a reasonable distance from them, where Allied fighters could defend the vessels.

As soon as one landing craft was loaded, it pulled away from the docks, followed by another and another. The landing craft the medical detachment was on had a loudspeaker system that played a familiar tune just as the vessel pulled out into the harbor waters.

> There'll be bluebirds over
> the white cliffs of Dover
> Tomorrow, just you wait and see.

Some of the men joined in singing the words, but Paul refrained. He figured that with his terrible voice, he would end up being thrown overboard by offended GIs.

As they proceeded out into the English Channel proper, as far as the eye could see, there were vessels of all types. Most of them were landing craft, but some were destroyers, corvettes, and even what appeared to be cruisers or battleships. Flights of Allied fighter planes flew overhead and circled the craft also.

Most of the men were in deep thought about what lay ahead, and many of them reached for their pocket Bibles so that they could offer up prayers of their own. The vessels proceeded toward France, bouncing around on the rough, wild waves of the English Channel.

They were heading for the fire of Normandy and beyond—to the war!

—Part III—

The Combat Soldier

— 10 —

The harbor was filled with blacked-out ships of all kinds, including the small landing craft upon which the men of the medical detachment were traveling. Paul, Tony, and their buddies noted that even at anchor in the harbor, their assigned craft was slapping the cold, forbidding-looking choppy water. They looked through the gloom with envy at the men lining the decks of the larger, sturdier-looking vessels. Those lucky guys would have a much smoother voyage. As they weighed anchor and started to move, they were hit by huge waves that smashed over one side and poured off the other. Their landing craft was small in comparison to the other, much larger, landing craft, all of which were attached to barrage balloons.

The ships moved across the channel, and as they proceeded, they were joined by more vessels from all sides. They were preceded by minesweepers, coast guard cutters, motor launches, battleships, cruisers, sloops, corvettes, PT boats, and destroyers. There were also fast-attack transports, ocean liners, freighters, hospital ships, tugboats, and of course the various landing craft, large and small. Looking out at this vast armada, Paul imagined what it must have been like on D-day, when the waters would have been even more crowded.

On their relatively tiny vessel, noncommissioned American

naval personnel passed among them handing out small brochures labeled "Conversational French Made Easy." Looking through these illustrated manuals took the minds of many of the GIs off the rough trip they were enduring.

"Now we know for sure where we are heading," one GI said.

"Where did you think you were going? To Tahiti maybe?" another asked.

"Say Paul," Tony said, "you speak that lingo pretty good from what I remember. How do you say 'Give me a kiss?'"

Paul replied, "If you get that close to a French girl who can put up with you, it's 'Voulez vous embrassez moi?'"

Somebody else spoke to Paul. "Never mind this stupid book. How do you say 'Where is the bathroom?'"

Tony replied, "The answer is 'Latrine!'"

Paul said, "Never mind. It is 'Où es le Lavabo? or 'Où se trouvent les toilettes? '"

This was followed by some laughter, and the conversation turned to something else.

"So," somebody yelled, "we're going to France. But are we going to Normandy or Pas-de-Calais? Latrine rumor has it that Normandy was just a trick and the real landings are going to be in Pas-de-Calais. Besides, everyone says that Patton is heading up a big army group that's going in there."

Somebody else called out, "Want to take some bets, anybody?"

Some music had been playing on loudspeakers positioned throughout the craft, and suddenly there was a click. The music stopped. Several moments of silence ensued, and then a gravelly voice came on.

"Now hear this. Now hear this. When we are ready to go over the side into our beach landing craft, hand your duffel bag to the sailor standing at the rail. You will pick them up on the beach and then follow the directions of the beachmaster to your assembly point. Unbuckle your pack straps." That was something else to think about besides the constant rolling and bouncing of their little vessel.

As the convoy moved farther out into the English Channel, the effect of the waves was far more severe. The ships were rocking wildly, and it felt as bad as crossing the Irish Sea to Northern Ireland, or worse. Even the mighty *Queen Elizabeth* in the wild waters of the winter North Atlantic did not toss and turn like this.

When the ship had been tied up in port, the waves had imparted an unceasing motion to the craft that made many men sick even before the lines were cast off. Now far more men were rushing to the side of the ship to miserably retch out whatever remained in their stomachs. Still others ran inside to the latrines, only to find them stopped up. The smell of diesel oil, backed-up latrines, and vomit pervaded the ship.

Tony, Paul, and a few others in the medical detachment were either too excited about what was going on or were fortified against the pervading seasickness, having forced themselves to eat before boarding.

"These guys are going to be in such rough shape when we land that they won't be able to do their jobs," Kurt commented.

Paul stuffed another Hershey bar into his mouth and got back to reading the French conversation manual.

Tony said with a laugh, "Enough of that studying. Let's stroll around the deck of this great ocean liner."

Paul put the booklet into his pocket and got up.

They noticed that as small as the ship was, there were four anti-aircraft gun tubs in the forward part of the ship, port and starboard, and two others near the stern. Each of them contained twin forty-millimeter anti-aircraft guns. Surprisingly they were not manned by American personnel but by British sailors. Each of them wore what seemed to be a warm flannel coat fastened by long leather loops rather than buttons and buttonholes. The coats also had hoods attached as well, which made a lot of sense for men continually exposed to the elements in the cold English Channel.

"How's it going, mate?" Paul asked one of the English sailors.

"Right now I'd rather be in Piccadilly Circus having at some fish and chips. They wrap them in newspaper, don't you know, 'cause it makes them taste better that way."

"I'll take a Coney Island hot dog," Tony replied.

"These French people sure know how to cook," Paul added. "If we make it to shore without getting croaked, we'll have to try some of their cooking. And from what I hear, their pastries are out of sight."

"Talking about food is a good way to get our mind off this bleedin' war," the English sailor rejoined. "Your General Eisenhower is quite the military leader. Of course, we have Monty, y'know, but when word's gone around that the Yank and British generals and admirals are having a go at it, Ike steps in and smoothes things out."

"I can believe that," Paul replied. "He sure is a great general!"

Tony joined in. "You can say that again. Better yet, he even likes some of my favorite books!"

The sailor, not understanding what he meant, and somewhat perplexed, shook his head. "As a matter of fact, from what I've heard, the whole blinkin' family is top-drawer."

"What do you mean by that?" Paul asked.

"Well, I was reading the *London Times* recently, and there was a great story about Ike's brother Milton," the sailor replied. "It seems that a short time ago, Milton—who was president of some university from Pennsylvania, I believe—happened to be in Washington, DC. He was at a cocktail party there run by a wealthy old lady you blokes might call a dowager. She said to Milton, 'You must come from a very nice family, young man. You have an important job here, and your brother Ike is leading our troops abroad, and I understand that you have another brother who is a banker. What a pity it is that you are Jewish!' Milton Eisenhower looked her in the eye, sighed unhappily, and replied, 'Ah, Madam, what a pity that we are not!'"

"Say, that's a great story," Tony exclaimed.

"Well, mate, it was in the *London Times*, so it's got to be the bleedin' truth!"

Someone near them yelled out, "There's land ahead!"

Sure enough, very low to the horizon was a dark area that could have been either land or a low-hanging cloud formation. As they got closer, from their position it appeared to be a beach several miles long set between steep cliffs. Actually it stretched over six miles, with the western third of the beach backed by a ten-foot-high seawall. The entire beach was overlooked by cliffs one hundred feet high. There was a line of low hills ahead. This, as they were told, was Omaha Beach.

Doesn't look too rough from here," one GI exclaimed.

"Wait till we get inside the range of their guns," someone else cautioned.

The loudspeakers blared to life with the announcement "Now hear this. Now hear this. Companies A, able; B, baker; quartermaster; and medical detachment report to the right side of the railing facing the front of the ship. Companies C, Charlie; D, dog; mess; and motor pool, report to the left side of the railing facing the front. The right and left are for you landlubbers who don't know starboard from port."

This got a little laugh from some of the GIs, and they slowly started to move toward their embarkation stations.

Tony reminded Paul, "Remember to unbuckle the straps to your pack, medical bags, and gas mask, and be sure to take off your helmet and buckle it on your belt."

Paul replied, "Thanks, buddy. I was just thinking about doing that."

Looking around, Paul saw that other men were doing the very same thing. Sailors took the men's barracks bags and dropped them over the side into another landing craft, this one larger than the one designated for the troops.

Paul, Tony, and the rest of the medical detachment, including Captain Sheridan and Lieutenant Saffridi, moved toward their designated spot beside the railing. They passed the anti-aircraft gun tub where the English sailor Paul and Tony had recently befriended stood. The sailor noticed that all of the members of the medical detachment were wearing Red Cross brassards and had red crosses painted on their helmets.

"If I were you mates, I would get rid of those Red Cross insignias right now. They make too good of a target for the Nazi murderers."

"Wait a minute, sailor," Captain Sheridan objected. "We respect the Geneva Convention, and hopefully so do they."

"Begging your pardon, sir, the sailor replied, "I was on one of the first boats to bring in some Canadian soldiers on D-day. I think it was Gold Beach or Juno Beach. Whatever it was, the Germans captured fifteen of them and shot them right on the spot, just for being prisoners of war. I don't want to sound impertinent, Captain, but that doesn't sound very Geneva Convention–like."

Captain Sheridan said, "We'll have to take our chances for now and leave them on."

On the deck of the troop landing craft, a large rope ladder on each side of the vessel was spread across the railing and down the entire side of the ship. Looking over the rail down toward the water line, one could see a smaller troop landing craft slightly in front of the one being loaded with barracks bags, also tied up alongside their ship. It was bobbing alarmingly up and down and rapidly swinging in toward their ship and then just as swiftly moving away from the side.

On the deck, two noncoms were stationed at each end of the rope ladder. One of them said, "Okay, men. I want two of you at a time to go over the side facing our ship. Make sure your gear is unbuckled and you take off your helmet. It can be hooked up to your belt. When you get about halfway down, stop and turn your head toward the craft you are heading for. The sailor in that boat will give you instructions about going the rest of the way."

The men proceeded as directed. Paul and Tony noticed that when the GIs were about halfway down, the chief bosun's mate— or so he was called by some of the other men—told the men to stop. He then directed the GIs on the ladder to take two more steps and then called out in a foghorn voice, "Listen to me. When I say 'Jump,' you jump, and you'll land in the boat."

When it was Paul's turn, he noted that Tony had preceded him and was already in the little craft, waving to him. He followed all of the instructions he had been given and proceeded halfway down until he was told to stop. The sailor then yelled out "Jump!" Out of the corner of his eye, Paul noted with apprehension that the two boats were at the farthest point apart, but he did as he was told, closed his eyes, and jumped. "God help me," he murmured to himself, and he landed in the middle of a space made empty for him by the other men in the landing craft. He realized that if he had jumped when the boats were closest together, he would have ended up in the water by the time he got down to water level. It did not take long for the little boat to be filled. A noncom leaned over the side and called out, "Away all boats!"

The sailor at the controls gunned the throttle, and it sped away from the larger vessel. The craft turned in a huge circle, followed by the boat that had been loaded on the opposite side. What had been tossing and turning before became even more violent, and the majority of the passengers were leaning over the side, retching miserably. The anti-seasickness pills were not even making a dent in the number of victims who succumbed to motion sickness. The circling continued until all of the landing craft were full, and then they maneuvered into a line, side by side, and approached the beach. The small landing craft looked as if they might overturn at times but continued on a steady course.

As they got nearer to the shore, they slowed down and proceeded more gradually. The sailor turned around to his passengers and called out, "You should have seen this place on D-day. We had to get the men landed much farther from shore because of the heavy fire from the beach. Some of those poor blokes sunk right to the bottom, and others cleared away from their backpacks and managed to wallow in—that is, those who were not hit by gunfire and shelling."

Off to the right, the GIs noticed that the artificial harbors that Winston Churchill had envisioned were being used to offload trucks and armored vehicles.

The boats bumped on the sand close to the shore, and the ramps were lowered. The men, grateful to be away from the churning waters, took their first shaky steps on the shores of Normandy. Paul thought, "This is free France. Vive La France!"

Suddenly the group of men landing ashore, as if on command, came to a sudden halt, although no word was spoken. The entire length of the beach, as far as their eyes could see, was covered with pyramids of dead bodies. They were in mattress covers, but there was no mistaking what the contents were. The mounds of corpses were arranged in neat rows. Some of the GIs knelt and prayed. Others prayed while standing with their heads bowed. Still others saluted their fallen comrades. All of the GIs were stricken with grief and horror as the impact of this sight ground itself indelibly into their respective memories.

"This is just part of the price we had to pay for liberating this land." one of the men muttered.

Another joined in. "Only God knows how many bodies were left on the beach on D-day and the days after that."

A major who identified himself as the beachmaster ordered, "All right there. Get into a column of two's and move up this beach to the trail that starts at the foot of the hill. Then you'll move into single file going up that slope. Stick to the middle of the trail, because there are still live mines out there alongside the trail."

Several noncoms directed them up the beach to the beginning of the fairly narrow trail. Here they were ordered to dovetail into a single column and urged to keep moving up the steep hill. Signs, both in English and German, were posted on either side of the pathway. The German signs had skulls and crossbones on them, as well as the caption "Achtung Minen." The English signs proclaimed "Mines cleared to ditches."

As Tony and Paul followed in the file of men, Tony tripped over a small root sticking up out of the sand. Paul instinctively reached out to grab him, but another person stepped in and caught Tony in mid-fall. Paul noticed that the sleeve of the man's jacket had a black stripe on it, which signified to him that this person was a general.

"Attention!" Paul called out.

"At ease," the man replied. "Keep moving, men." He held on to Tony's arm. "Are you all right, soldier?"

"Yes, sir, thank you, sir," Tony replied, saluting.

The general returned the salute and said, "It's good you didn't fall into the ditch there, son. There's all kinds of nasty mines in those ditches. We don't need any more casualties here. Lord knows we have had enough."

Paul, who had remained at Tony's side, saluted the general and asked, "Begging your pardon, sir, what is your name, sir?"

"I am General J. Lawton Collins, and now that you are both in good shape, I suggest you carry on."

They both saluted General Collins, and Tony murmured, "Thanks again, sir." They then rejoined the seemingly endless column proceeding up the slope.

It took a while to reach the top, and then the line moved into a gently sloping valley. The men were ordered to spread out along the perimeter of the area and told to "smoke if you wish." Some sat down, and others stretched out their feet, grateful to be on dry land—especially the ones who had been miserable in the throes of seasickness.

Colonel Macklin walked to the center of the grassy floor of the little valley. "Welcome to France, men. We are going to wait until all of our vehicles and supplies are offloaded, and then we move right up to the lines. Check your ration supplies and see to it that you have enough to eat for a few days. If not, the quartermaster is setting up just over this ridge, and you can draw whatever food or clothing or blankets you need."

Just then a familiar figure cut across the front row of the men. Paul and Tony looked in amazement at the tall figure sporting what appeared to be two ivory-handled revolvers and wearing a shiny helmet that sported his stars.

He paused for a moment and glowered at Tony and Paul.

"Don't I know you two from somewhere?" he growled.

They stuttered and stammered in confusion.

He moved to the side of Colonel Macklin, who said, "This fine officer needs no introduction" and turned to General Patton.

General Patton looked around the gathering of the soldiers. "You have just seen a sight I do not and will not abide anymore! I do not want to see any more dead American soldiers. I just want to see dead German soldiers. I want to see plenty of dead German soldiers, and sometime soon, we are going to join up in killing this rotten enemy and go all the way to Berlin, where I personally am going to shoot that maniac paperhanging son of a b...h" ————"

Tony turned to Paul. "I guess it's our day to see some generals."

General Patton looked at him and shrieked out, "What's that, soldier? You got something more important to say?"

The general paused for a moment, half expecting a reply, and then turned back to Colonel Macklin and said, "You may dismiss your men."

Colonel Macklin saluted General Patton and then turned back to address the troops. "Before I dismiss you, I have some people I want you to hear out. The first is Chaplain Thompson, who is a congregational minister.

Reverend Thompson stepped forward. "Men," he called out, "I would like those of you who wish to join me in prayer. We who are about to go into combat can now pray, each in his own manner. Those who wish to do so, please stand up and join hands."

Every man stood up and joined hands.

The chaplain continued. "Dear God, Master of the Universe, please hear our prayers. We ask you to give us the courage and determination needed to help us stop the wholesale slaughter and help free all of the poor souls who are suffering at the hands of our murdering foe. Dear God in heaven, we ask that you be merciful unto us and watch over us. Here in our place of worship in this wild wood—our church in the wild wood, our temple in the wild wood, our synagogue in the wild wood, our mosque in the wild wood—we beseech you to grant us your divine mercy. Amen."

The men, some silent and some joining in the amens, all sat down again.

Colonel Macklin moved to the front again and said, "There are two officers here who I want you to listen to."

A lieutenant colonel and a major stepped in to take a position at Colonel Macklin's side. The major spoke first.

"Men, we need a volunteer for a very critical assignment. We need to know if there is anyone here who speaks passable French."

One of the men in the back called out, pointing to Paul, "This guy speaks French. He was teaching some of us on board ship."

Bubba, who was standing next to the man, shoved him with such strength that the man fell over. Bubba complained, "What you gitten mah friend into hyah? In this man's army, you don't volunteer for nothin'."

The deed was done, however, and the colonel approached Paul.

"You speak French, soldier?" he asked.

"What's this about, sir?" Paul asked.

Author in uniform wearing insignia of Private

"You come along with us, and we will tell you along the way," the colonel replied.

Paul looked at Colonel Macklin questioningly.

Macklin in turn addressed the major. "What authority do you possess to step in and appropriate one of my men?" he asked.

The lieutenant colonel took out a wallet and opened it. "We are with the CIC, Counter Intelligence Corps, and we have the authority of the commanding general to requisition any personnel we deem necessary to fulfill our mission," he said in a flat monotone. "By order of the commanding general, I outrank any unit commander."

Colonel Macklin said angrily, "I protest your moonlight requisitioning of one of my men, and I will make this protest in writing and send it through channels to division headquarters."

Captain Sheridan, who had been standing nearby, stepped forward and just as vehemently announced in a loud voice, "I also take issue with your taking away one of my men. He is one of the best people I have in my medical detachment. When we get into combat, any casualties we may suffer will be drastically affected by his loss. This will be your responsibility and on your head. I plan to register an urgent complaint about this and send this on to division headquarters."

"I welcome you both to do that. With my respect, this shows how much you care about your men, and I commend the two of you for it."

"Never mind you soft-soaping me, Colonel," Macklin grumbled. "I still think this whole thing stinks!"

The major stepped forward. "I don't think it is appropriate to argue in front of the men, sirs."

Macklin, Sheridan, and their opponents silently agreed.

The major turned to Paul. "Come along, soldier."

Tony asked, "Where are you taking him? I want to know."

"That's none of your business, Private," the major tersely replied.

Paul got up, shrugged, and shook hands with Tony. Turning to Colonel Macklin and Captain Sheridan, he said, "Thank you all for trying. If I can make it through this, I hope you'll see my ugly face sooner than you expect."

He then followed the two officers, walking single file along a trail that went east of where they were. They came to a pyramidal tent that had no sign in front of it but was guarded by two military policemen Paul had never seen before. Each had a Thompson submachine gun strapped around his chest and carried a holstered Colt .45 pistol on his hip, attached to a web belt. As far as Paul could determine, the MPs were not from his battalion.

When they entered, one soldier was laboriously typing on

an aging Underwood machine. A small table supporting the typewriter also had a large stack of papers on one side. Another GI was laboriously cranking out something on a mimeograph machine.

The major turned to face Paul. "You are needed to go on an intelligence-gathering mission that is of great importance to the war effort."

Paul, sensing some possible danger into which he was about to be thrust, said, "With respect, sirs, I don't remember volunteering for this."

"You have just volunteered, soldier," said the lieutenant colonel, who continued. "You are going to be assigned to a group of French Resistance fighters who will guide you behind enemy lines. Your mission there is to find out which military units are opposing us in this sector and get this information back to us. We also need to know about tank units—if possible, approximately the number of tanks, antitank weapons, and other vehicles, the locations of any of their fuel dumps, as well as the identification of any SS units that may be in this area."

The colonel added, "We realize that if you are strongly opposed to doing this, we will return you to your outfit. There's just one thing. What we have planned for you to do will, we believe, help shorten the war a bit and more than likely will save American lives. We don't want you to go into this reluctantly, because then you'll hardly be of any use to us and you could possibly endanger the French Resistance fighters you'll be with."

"Do I get any written orders, sirs?" Paul asked. "And what about my uniform? Won't that stand out like a sore thumb?"

"We have taken that into account," the major replied. "You are going to take off all of your clothing, including socks, underwear, and shoes. You will also remove your dog tags, military identification card, wallet, cigarettes, matches, and any other personal items you may have. Remember: even a little V-mail[1]

letter could give you away, and so when I say all of your personal items, I mean *all!* Put everything you have into this barracks bag here. This will be returned to you when you have completed your mission. You see this pile of civilian clothing here?" He pointed to a spot on the floor. "Put these on, and pocket the French cigarettes and matches there."

He picked up a large cardboard folder, rifled through a thick batch of documents, and finally selected one, holding it out to Paul. He continued. "Just as important, and maybe more, we have identification

Examples of V Mail

---

[1] V-mail was a mechanism whereby a soldier would write a one-page letter on a designated sheet of V-mail stationery. It was turned in to his company clerk, who would then have the officer serving as a censor read it carefully. Then it was sent to a central processing area in the rear echelon, where the letter was microfilmed and sent to the major city or town of its destination. Army postal authorities there would then print up a miniature version of the letter and turn it over to local postal authorities for delivery.

papers for you. The picture, which bears a fairly decent resemblance to you, belonged to a member of the local resistance group you will be joining. In his rush to leave, he forgot these papers, which proved to be a tragic mistake. They were caught by the Gestapo and tried to fight their way out. A few got away, but unfortunately he did not make it; and after prolonged torture, he bought the farm. According to this, you are a farmer and you are twenty-two years old. You can pass for an old man of twenty-two, I believe. And by the way, here are about twenty dollars' worth of French francs." He put some bills and coins into Paul's hands.

The shoes were well worn, one of them having a hole in the sole. They did not fit very well and felt uncomfortable as soon as he put them on. The clothing was not that much better, being shabby and ill fitting. The only thing good about the clothes was that the pants and shirt apparently had been washed recently.

"Who am I supposed to get this information to? Paul asked.

"You will have to come through the lines. Give the correct password when you approach our men. Our people have already been oriented about the passwords. If you give the wrong one, chances are you'll be shot. These passwords change every day. Since you are leaving today, your password will be Mickey Mouse. Tomorrow it will be Minnie Mouse. The day after that, it will be Donald Duck; and the day following that, it will be Goofy. You then repeat the sequence until you return. When you come through the lines, ask for the intelligence tent, and give your information only to me or the major."

"You need a code name. Did you ever have a dog?"

"Yes, sir," Paul replied.

"What kind of dog was it?" the colonel inquired.

"It was a mix of many breeds. We said it was a Heinz variety dog," Paul answered.

"Your code name is Heinz, in case any one of our people asks you to identify yourself."

"Who do I ask for? What is your name, sir?" Paul asked.

"My name is not important. You just give your code name and tell the personnel who will take you to our intelligence tent that you have a report."

"What are my chances of making it back, sir?" Paul asked apprehensively.

"About as good as you'll have going into combat," the major replied. "If you are caught, you have to depend on your being able to pass as a Frenchman. Try to learn as much slang as you can as quickly as possible. Using that will help you get by. The Germans are not sophisticated enough to pick up your American accent when you speak French. Sometimes when they suspect that certain French civilians are in the French Resistance, they just shoot them anyway. Keep that in mind. If there is any danger of your being caught, take off immediately, if not sooner."

While the colonel was talking to him, Paul was busy removing his military clothing and gear, and changing into the civilian clothes.

The colonel looked at his watch and said, "Just about any minute now, our French comrade in arms will arrive here."

A few minutes later, the tent flap was pulled back by a young civilian. He turned to the colonel, saluted him in the manner of the French military, and said, "Bonjour, mon Colonel."

The colonel returned the salute and answered him in English. "Happy to see you again, Louis."

The civilian faced Paul and looked him over very carefully. He appeared to be about Paul's age.

"Tu parle en Francais? [Do you speak French?]" he asked.

"Mais certainement [But certainly]," Paul replied.

The French youth then turned to the colonel and saluted him again. In a heavy accent, he said, "We must leave now, *mon Colonel.*"

The colonel returned the salute and said, "God help you both."

The young Frenchman faced Paul and said tersely, "Alors, viens avec moi. [Come with me then.]"

Paul turned and saluted the major and the colonel. "If I don't make it back, will you both make sure my folks get my ten-thousand-dollar GI insurance?"

"Go on, there," the major replied. "Think positively," he added, opening the flap of the tent. "This man"—he pointed to one of the MPs—"will escort you back to your point of departure."

As they left the tent, Louis turned to him and said, "J'ai apportez en petite souvenir pour toi. [I have brought you a little souvenir.]"

"Q'est que c'est, un billet pour voyager al les Etas Unis? [What is it, a ticket for a trip back to the US?]" Paul asked.

Louis laughed and, in heavily French-accented English, replied, "Nothing as fancy as that, I'm afraid." He silently handed a Beretta pistol to Paul, along with an extra magazine.

"If it looks like we are going to be captured by Germans, especially SS, shoot your way out if you can. If you are captured, as you Americans say, your life won't be worth a plugged nickel. Now put the pistol in your waistband and the magazine in your pocket. Pull your shirt over the pistol so it can't be seen." Then he added in French, "Comment vous appelez vous? [What is your name?]"

Paul replied, "Je m'appele Paul. [My name is Paul.]"

Louis replied, "Nous avons un petite problem ici. Une de nos soldats s'appele Paul aussi. [We have a little problem here. One of our men is also called Paul.]" He then added in English, "We'll have to work on that when we get back."

They approached a roll of concertina wire that had been strung out. A small opening in the middle was guarded by a GI. The MP turned to them and said tersely, "This is where you take off."

"So long, soldier," Paul answered, and he followed Louis into the narrow opening of the barbed wire fence.

The familiar signs written in German were alongside the trail, and Paul was very careful to follow in Louis's footsteps.

They had walked for several miles when suddenly Louis turned back to Paul and whispered, "Fait attention. Voila les boches! [Be careful. Here are some Germans!]"

Louis dropped to the ground, and Paul followed suit.

Apparently about a dozen German soldiers were out on patrol in the very area the two of them were heading for. The Germans did not seem too concerned about finding any Americans. One of them was busy asking his buddy for a cigarette. Another was yawning and complained about not having enough sleep.

He kept muttering, "Schlaffen. [Sleep.]"

Paul took a deep breath and was afraid to make a sound by exhaling. Louis had already drawn out a Luger pistol, and while hugging the ground, he was taking aim at the first German in line. Fortunately, the patrol passed by without seeing them.

After several minutes had gone by, Louis stirred himself and got up.

Paul said, "That was a narrow escape!"

Louis replied, "They seemed to be from the 352nd Infantry Division, but I'm not sure. We'll have to confirm it when we get to our base. Get used to the narrow escapes. We will have plenty more of them."

He then muttered, "This is just the beginning. That German patrol was just outside of their lines, and from here on in, we will have to be extremely careful if we want to stay alive. Try to keep in a crouched position, and speak to me only in either hand signals or whispers. Okay, *Viens-Y*! [let's go!] Sois tres prudent! [Be very careful!]"

—11—

Paul and Louis approached a farmhouse, and as they got closer, the back door opened and a man wordlessly motioned them to enter.

Paul did not question Louis but followed his example and walked into the old-fashioned kitchen of what appeared to be a very old house. There was a large-handled pump over a stone sink, and the furnishings were spartan.

"Est-il L'Americain? [Is he the American?]" the farmer asked.

"Oui, [Yes,]" Louis replied.

"C'est necessaire pour se preparer [Let's get ready]," the farmer urged, pointing the way out a side door.

Louis strode out with Paul in tow and found an empty horse-drawn wagon.

"Take a rake and start loading this hay onto the wagon," he said, pointing to mounds of hay stacked out in the field.

Paul needed no further urging. As a child, he had loved to visit some of his parents' friends who had a farm in Taunton, Massachusetts, and he loved the work that this involved. He enthusiastically grabbed a heavy forkful of hay and loaded it onto the wagon. Louis was on the opposite side and was also loading hay onto the heavy four-wheeled conveyance. There was only one horse tied up to the front, and Paul worried about whether the poor animal could pull a heavy load. The farmer who was looking on did not seem concerned, and so Paul thought it would be prudent to avoid questioning him about this. It did not take very long for the task to be completed.

"The farmer looked at Paul. "Tu comprends Francais? [You understand French?]" he asked.

"Mais oui [But yes]," Paul replied.

"Allors, allons y [Then let's go]," he urged.

Louis positioned himself along one side of the wagon, and so Paul opted for the opposite side. The farmer got up into the seat in the front and whistled to the horse, who started ahead at a slow, ambling pace. They moved at a slow, steady pace on a dirt road and were out in the middle of the countryside before Paul realized it.

Suddenly, from behind a clump of trees, two Germans holding submachine guns pointing directly at them appeared.

"Halt!" one of the Germans barked. "Vo gehen zie? [Where are you going?]"

"Nous allons dans une ferme dans notre quartier [We are going to a farm in our neighborhood]," the farmer replied, pointing to the hay.

The second German walked up to Paul, pushing the barrel of the submachine gun against his chest. "Papieren! [Papers!]" he yelled.

Paul pulled his recently acquired ID papers from his pocket and held them out to the German. He looked them over and seemed to study the picture on them, looked back at Paul, and silently returned them to him. Paul had taken a deep breath and now was afraid to let his breath out quickly.

The German spun away and repeated the same routine with Louis and then the farmer. The two soldiers then grabbed some forks in the wagon and speared through the hay. Apparently satisfied that all was in order, they threw the forks back onto the wagon and curtly waved them on.

After they were well clear of the Germans, Paul asked Louis, "Did you notice their division patches?"

"Yes," said Paul. The farmer, who understood, said in broken English, "They are with the 352nd Infantry Division; I am sure of it."

"Well, if you are positive, I have to get this information back to my outfit," Paul said anxiously.

"We'll have to wait until nightfall and then see if we can slip back toward your lines," replied Louis. "Are you sure that this is so important?"

"This is the reason why I am here." Paul grumbled.

The three of them came to a neighbor's farm and unloaded the hay. They then turned around and went back to their point of departure. They were not stopped on their return, and so Paul figured that the Germans were either still there and didn't want to be bothered with them again or simply had moved on.

When they returned to the farmer's home, Louis suggested that they await nightfall in the barn, where they could take a brief nap and then move on in the protection of darkness.

Paul dozed off almost immediately, and it seemed just moments later that Louis was shaking his shoulder.

"Time to go." he urged.

Paul got up and cleared his head. He had dreamed about devouring a giant Howard Johnson's sundae.

They were cautiously moving back toward the American lines when someone called out, "Halt. Who goes there?"

Paul panicked. What were the passwords? Mickey Mouse, Minnie Mouse, Donald Duck, and Goofy. Today, although it was nighttime, it was still Mickey Mouse.

The voice called out menacingly, "I said halt; who goes there? Better answer or I'll open fire!"

"Mickey Mouse, Mickey Mouse," Paul called out anxiously.

"Get off your butt and answer or have your butt shot off," the voiced charged back. "Advance and be recognized!"

Paul and Louis advanced toward a sentry they could now see. The sentry yelled, "State your business!"

"We need to go to Intelligence."

An MP alongside the sentry motioned them to follow him. In no time, they had arrived at the tent, and as they entered, they noticed the colonel was not there but the major was.

Paul stated that he had definitely confirmed that the army group immediately facing the Americans in that sector of Omaha Beach was the 352nd German Infantry Division.

The major said, "I don't want to shoot you down, soldier. You did well, but this simply confirms what we had already been told. We just were not sure. Get back and see what other key information you can bring back to us!"

Paul and Louis returned back through the American lines, and in no time they were at the old farmhouse. To their surprise, not only was the farmer and his family seated around the dinner table, but an elderly robust man with a ruddy complexion and a white beard tinged with black and gray was also there.

"Le Flic!" Louis gasped.

The old man glowered at Louis, changing Paul's impression that this person could easily have passed for Santa Claus. There was nothing like Saint Nick in his demeanor.

"Le Americain? [The American?]" he queried.

"Oui," replied Louis.

He turned to Paul and said, "I speak a little English. You are here, I have been told, to gather intelligence for your unit. The latest I can give you is that the Second SS Panzer Division is coming this way. They were scheduled to be here shortly after D-day, but our Allied fighters have destroyed all of the bridges on their approach.

Our resistance fighters have slowed them down considerably by repeated acts of sabotage. We have lost a lot of men, women, and children holding these monsters back. Several British agents were actively involved in blowing up railroad bridges and setting up ambushes by their agents and French Resistance fighters. These murderers are equipped with the latest heavy tanks, and our successful ambushes have reduced their petrol supplies down to a point where they are practically no longer operational. You have to get this back to your unit without delay."

Paul turned to Louis. "Here I go again."

Since it was after midnight, he would have to change his password to "Minnie Mouse." When he returned, the Lieutenant Colonel was there. He welcomed the information and said, "Soldier, you are so good, it looks like we are going to have to keep you with us permanently."

"Sir," Paul pleaded anxiously, "I want to get back to my outfit as soon as I can."

"Just joking, soldier," the colonel replied. "Get back to your French buddies and keep getting us this vital information. Let me remind you that by doing this, you are saving a lot of American lives. And don't worry, we'll get you back soon."

When Paul arrived back at the farmhouse, Le Flic was sitting at the kitchen table, drinking some kind of hot drink.

"Coffee?" Le Flic asked.

"No thanks," Paul replied politely. He had already heard about how rough the French coffee was, as well as their cigarettes. At the very same moment, Le Flic held out a crumpled pack of French cigarettes. The brand was something like "Gauloises"; Paul could not make this out clearly, but he just as politely declined the offer.

Le Flic addressed him in English. "Our primary mission— that is, of any unit—is to disrupt communications as well as rail and road travel. This we have succeeded in doing with a good deal of success, although it has cost us heavily in casualties. I really cannot spare any of my people, but since your American intelligence officers have placed a high priority on your mission, I am going to send two of my best fighters with you. They both speak English at least well enough to communicate with you. One of them you already know."

He opened a door off the kitchen, and Louis stepped in, accompanied by a young woman. She had sharp features and wore her hair in a prim-looking bun pulled around the back of her head.

Le Flic turned to her and said, "This is Pierette."

Paul politely held his hand out to her and simply said, "Bonjour."

She nodded and turned to face Le Flic, who added, "Your intelligence people have told me that getting the following information is of the highest priority. The strategy of the Germans, whether or not to accept the fact that the Normandy invasion is the real thing, is of critical importance to our high-level Allied planners. We have learned that some high-ranking German generals believe that the First US Army group in Southern England is about to embark on an invasion of the Pas-de-Calais area. This is supposed to be under the command of your fearsome General Patton. You have to get some confirmation that this belief on the part of the Germans is still in effect. This must come from a reliable source. The wife of one of our fighters has obtained a job as a cleaning woman at a high-ranking German Army headquarters not far from Paris. Louis and Pierette will get you onto a river barge that will bring you close enough to land not too distant from her home. You will meet with her when she returns from work and get the word on the latest possible development. You will return by the same route and get this information back to your intelligence officers."

Paul shook his head. "I don't know about this. I have a problem with the idea of putting this girl at risk." He glanced at Pierette.

There was no change in her solemn expression. Louis and Le Flic laughed hilariously.

"What's so funny?" Paul asked, getting a little miffed at the idea of being the object of some kind of a stupid joke.

Louis spoke up. "Forgive us; we should have explained why Pierette was chosen."

Le Flic stepped in. "There is a tiny village known as Oradour-sur-Glane. This is where Pierette comes from. A few days after the invasion, Pierette went to visit an aunt and uncle in a town not too far away. The very next day, SS troops moved into Oradour-sur-Glane and, as a reprisal for a resistance attack on a military formation moving up to the Normandy battlefield, murdered every man, woman, and child in the village."

At this point, Pierette broke into tears and was comforted by both Louis and Le Flic.

Le Flic continued. "The Germans, as they always do prior to a mass murder, separated the men from the women and children. They brutally shoved the women and children into the church, while the men were crammed into a barn not far away. They set fire to both structures and machine-gunned the inhabitants. Six hundred forty-two villagers were put to death, including one hundred ninety schoolchildren, Pierette's mother and father, and her young sister. Ironically, the villagers had given shelter to some Jewish men, women, and children, who were also among those murdered. People spoke about finding partially eaten meals on kitchen tables, where the Nazis had rushed people helter-skelter to their doom."

"This young woman, who you call a girl, has one goal in life. That is to avenge the deaths of her beloved parents and sister. She handles a machine gun better than any of my men. As a matter of fact, she can strip down a machine gun faster than I myself can. When it comes to a firefight, she is always at the front. You are worried about protecting her? We are sending her with you to protect you, my young American friend." He laughed and then continued. "Come outside now and meet some more of our band of fighters."

They stepped out of the little farmhouse, and Paul wordlessly followed Le Flic and Louis to a small clearing not far away. There were assembled about ten or twelve men, women, and children. Le Flic introduced Paul to each one of them, who in turn solemnly shook their hands and murmured "Enchante." Le Flic stopped in front of one young man, turned to Paul, and said, "Paul, I want you to meet Paul." A very pale-complexioned youngster who appeared to be about fourteen years of age looked sadly at Paul and simply nodded his head.

Le Flic said, "We must do something about this to avoid any possible confusion." He faced the American Paul, ordered him to kneel, and pulled a German bayonet from the belt of an older man standing next to him. He lightly tapped each of Paul's shoulders and said, "I hereby dub thee Jean Paul. That is the code name you will go by from now on. Rise, Jean Paul."

Paul said, "I now feel like one of the knights of the round table."

Le Flic laughed and replied, "Don't forget that the greatest knight of all was a Frenchman by the name of Sir Lancelot. Don't let this little ceremony go to your head. I only did this to avoid confusion."

"On a more serious note, Pierette and Louis will be your guides. They will take you to a location where you can get a direct report from the person who will have the information your intelligence officers need. You will carry no weapons, and nor will they; but along the route, at locations only they know, there are secreted caches of weapons you can get to if necessary. Well then, go with them, and we wish you Godspeed. By the way, and first things first, are you hungry?"

Paul was starved, and he nodded eagerly.

"Then let's go back to the kitchen," Le Flic said, and Paul, Pierette, and Louis, needing no further urging, entered the farmhouse kitchen door. Le Flic produced a huge wheel of cheese, and he cut a generous wedge for each of them. He then took a large, round bread that smelled like cake out of the oven and cut thick, generous slices. The cheese was delicious and had a slight tang to it. The bread was equally tasty, and in no time, the trio had finished their repast.

"It is now time for you to go," Le Flic announced, and he nodded to Pierette. She got up first and headed toward the door. Louis motioned for Paul to follow and then brought up the rear. Pierette quickly moved toward a stand of trees near the farmhouse, and in no time, they were in the middle of a forest. Paul had to rush to keep up with the young woman, who seemed to be familiar with this dense wood that they were rushing through. It seemed that they had travelled several miles when they emerged close to a riverbank. They followed this for several more miles, until they came to what appeared to be a river barge. A barrel-chested, balding middle-aged man in bad need of a shave waved to Pierette. She jumped from the edge of the riverbank up to the deck, followed by Paul and Louis.

Louis faced Paul and said solemnly, "From here on, we are in serious danger. The place is thick with German patrols. If one of them challenges us, remember to keep your mouth shut. Even though you speak passable French, one of these murdering scum can pick up on any little clue, no matter how slight, that you are not what you appear to be."

"We are here because we are transporting these bales of hay to a German stable." He pointed to the bundles of hay covering the deck. "You Americans are used to mechanized equipment. The Germans, who are supposed to have a modern army, still use lots of horses for transporting carts and personnel, believe it or not."

Just at that very moment, four German privates, led by a sergeant, boarded the vessel.

"Papieren," the sergeant demanded curtly. The Germans menacingly kept their machine pistols pointed right at Paul and the French people.

Wordlessly, in turn, they handed their papers over to the sergeant, who then asked in broken French what they were doing. The barge captain pointed to the bales of hay announcing they were delivering them to the German Army stable.

"Ach, das is gut," the sergeant muttered, handing them back their papers. A German patrol boat passed slowly alongside them, and the Germans aboard the barge waved to the sergeant, who then led his men ashore.

The captain, who was introduced as Monsieur LeFevre, then got busy casting off the bow and stern lines, while Paul and the rest pitched in to help him; and, in no time they were under way. Pierette, who was apparently familiar with this barge, descended a narrow winding gangway to a series of rooms. The inside of the boat was surprisingly luxurious, with the walls and furniture being made up of exotic-looking woods—quite the opposite of what one would expect looking at the grubby exterior of the vessel.

Pierette pointed to one cot and looked at Paul, and then indicated another cot across the room for Louis. Then she disappeared forward.

"She doesn't say much." Paul observed.

"Considering the horror of the tragedy she endured, it is easy to understand how this has affected her," Louis replied.

Paul hadn't realized how tired he was, but after bothering only to take his shoes off, he plopped down on the narrow cot and in no time was fast asleep. He was awakened by a flashlight being shined in his face.

"Are all you Americans this lazy?" Pierette was asking.

He felt he had only slept for an hour or two, but Pierette told him that it was already midmorning and Louis had already had his breakfast. He got up groggily and tried to shake the sleep out of his head. The captain was at a little stove, cooking some eggs, and he pointed to a coffeepot on the stove. Paul poured himself a generous helping into a large mug. Louis warned him, "My friend, just take a little sip first. This is ersatz coffee—or fake coffee, as you might call it. We won't have real coffee until this war is over."

Paul took a little sip and was instantly grateful that he had been warned. The coffee was unbelievably bad. It didn't deserve to be called coffee, but this was only a minor part of the hardship the French people had to put up with under the terrible German occupation. Paul felt that if he just took another sip, he would gag, and so he gently put the mug down on the little table in the center of the room. However, making up for this tenfold was a platter of steaming hot croissants, which he devoured until he realized that the croissants were for the four of them. The captain, as if reading his mind, smiled and brought another platter out of the oven. There were also several long, thin breads that Louis referred to as baguettes. These were equally delicious, especially when supplemented by some of the cheese offered by Captain LeFevre.

"If you think the coffee is bad, just wait till you get a taste of the German cigarettes. They are disgusting enough to make you want to give up smoking," Louis laughed. He then got serious. "We will soon arrive, and then we will get involved with delivering our bales of hay to the German stable. This is part of the Fifteenth Panzer Grenadieren Brigade, and they have been put on alert to go to the beachheads and to try to repel the allies. However, on the direct orders of General Gerd Von Rundstedt and Hitler, they have been kept on hold. Hitler is firmly convinced that the Normandy operation is just a ploy and that the real invasion will take place at Pas-de-Calais. Von Rundstedt is either toadying to him or believes it also. Your mission is to find out if this plan is still in effect or if von Rundstedt and Hitler have changed their minds."

"How am I supposed to find this out?" Paul asked.

"The wife of Paul, who you met a little while ago, got a job as a cleaning woman at brigade headquarters. She does a lot of her work near the radio room, and since she speaks fluent German, she is in a position to find out if there has been any change in their standing orders," Louis replied. "She knows approximately when we are coming, and will, when she can, approach the barracks looking for us. She knows Pierette and me by sight, and so there will be no problem getting to speak to her. If she greets us with "Ca Va! [Everything goes well!]" we will know that the standing orders have not been changed. If her greeting is "Les choses ne vont pas bien [Things are not going well]," we will know that Hitler has changed his mind and that not only this unit but others in the Pas-de-Calais area are being sent to attack the beachheads."

"The plan you have set up makes sense," Paul mused.

"Our mission will still not be complete. Your people insist on confirmation. We have to get some of our people to tap the telephone lines going to various other military units stationed around here. Our operatives will find out what other German units are communicating to each other. This is the Paris area, or didn't you realize that you are on the outskirts of Paris?"

"I wasn't sure just where we were," Paul answered.

"In order to get confirmation," Louis reported, "we will go to a small café not far from here, and the word will be passed to us. If we are told, "C'est Vrai, C'est Vrai," that will mean that the original message, that the Germans are not moving, is confirmed. The message 'Tu est un menteur [You're a liar]' means that the message is not confirmed."

"Who is the message coming from?" Paul asked.

"We don't know," Louis responded. "The message will simply be given to us by an unknown person in that café. The message, however, will be delivered clearly enough so that we can make no mistakes."

Pierette interrupted. "Allors, allons y [Let's go already]," she said, and then she continued in English. "First things first. Let us unload the hay and deliver it to the stable. The barracks are not far from there, and we will have to look to see if our contact is around. Let's find out from her what the latest information is that she can supply us with."

Louis nodded and said to Paul, "Let's move as soon as we are moored!"

Under the expert hands of Captain LeFevre, the barge glided in toward the dock, and at the last minute, he cut the engines and hopped ashore with a line in his hand. He moored the line to a mooring post and jumped back on board and repeated the procedure with the line at the stern of the vessel.

Pierette called out, "Alors, allons y."

The three of them got busy carrying the heavy bales off the barge and depositing them on the dock. There were a lot more bales than Paul anticipated, and the work was strenuous. Pierette worked just as diligently as Paul and Louis, and in a reasonably short time, they had assembled an impressive-looking pyramid. At the far end of the dock were some large empty wagons that Paul assumed were there for this purpose. They pulled over one wagon that had two long handles in front and got to work loading it to the very top. They then brought a second wagon over and repeated the process. The third wagon was only half full when the loading task was finished.

Louis took a hold of one of the wagon handles and motioned Paul to take the other one. Pierette got behind the wagon, and she vigorously pushed it forward while Paul and Louis pulled just as strongly to get the wagon in motion at a fair speed.

Paul wondered, *How far do we have to haul this load?*

Finally they approached what seemed to be a corral of some sort, and as they moved closer, a German corporal appeared and opened a wide gate to the enclosure. He motioned them inside and pointed to a barn nearby. Apparently they were supposed to unload the hay there, and so they got busy. Since they had only one pitchfork for the three of them, the work was made even more strenuous. When the first wagon was unloaded, they returned for the second. When they were in the process of unloading the third, a female voice behind them greeted Pierette.

"Alors, jeune femme. Ca va bien?" the woman asked.

She had given them the code words that the plan to hold the German soldiers in place was still operational!

Pierette took her by the arm, and they strolled a little distance and chatted briefly. The woman then turned back and headed for the barracks.

Pierette looked around to see if anyone was within earshot. In a hushed voice, she said, "Our friend reported that she was cleaning near the communications room when the radio man rushed out holding a piece of paper and ran into the colonel's office. Leaving the door open, he dropped the paper on the desk. The colonel nearly had an apoplectic fit. The order, sent by Field Marshall Rommel, emphasized that he agreed with Hitler and von Rundstedt, and it stated that all units would be kept in place and not sent to the Normandy front. Apparently the colonel felt strongly that the strategy of "this Bavarian corporal" (meaning

Hitler), as well as Rommel and von Rundstedt, was a disaster in the making. These "idiots" were sealing the fate of the German forces in France! The Colonel howled and wailed in protest, but as a German officer, he felt compelled to follow the orders of his superiors."

The woman had calmly continued with her cleaning chores and acted as if she did not understand what was going on. At the first opportunity, she left the building in order to search for Pierette and her companions.

When she arrived at the designated spot, no one was there, and so she returned to her job. A short time later, she again left, ostensibly to have a cigarette. The colonel did not like to have the workers smoking while they were working. This time she spotted Louis and Pierette and got to relay her information.

Louis was beside himself; this was fantastic news. But now there remained the job of getting confirmation, which was just as much a priority. Just as Paul was agonizing over the long distance they would have to walk to get to the café, a hand reached out and touched his shoulder. He spun around and found that it belonged to the German sergeant who had checked their identification papers on the barge.

What does this creep want now? Paul thought.

"Je cherche pour un cafe ou il y a une chanteuse qui s'apple Edith Piaf [I am looking for a café where there is a singer by the name of Edith Piaf]," the sergeant said questioningly.

Louis spoke up enthusiastically, "Nous, voudrons fair un visit at cet cafe ce soir. Si vous voulais, vous pouvez aller avec nous ce soir, monsieur le Sergeant. ["We wish to go to the café tonight. If you wish, you may come with us.]"

"Das ist Prima [That is great]," the sergeant responded. "Ce soir at Sept heures, ici. [Tonight at seven o'clock, here.]"

"Oui entendu [Yes, until then]," Louis replied.

As soon as they were out of sight of the Germans, Pierette punched Louis on the shoulder.

"Tu est tellement fou [You are really crazy]," she sputtered.

Louis answered her in English. "If we have a German with us, there will be a much better chance for us to go there without being challenged by the Gestapo or anyone else." he remonstrated.

Paul said, "I think it is a right smart idea."

Pierette thought a bit and then seemed to accept the inevitable. She looked heavenward, as if asking for divine protection.

Paul spoke up. "Doesn't it bother you two, helping the Germans by bringing them supplies? I know it makes me feel funny!"

Louis replied patiently, "By bringing the Germans supplies, our people—and we work in shifts—have free and ready access to a German military facility. Our getting desperately needed information, such as now, is just one example of why this access is essential."

Paul nodded, understanding the method to this apparent madness.

Louis continued. *"Ecoute mon ami* [Listen, my friend], do not have any conversation with either the Germans or any French people we bump into. The French will determine from your accent right away that you are American. Who knows? They all may be with us, or some of them may be Vichy sympathizers and turn you in to the Germans. The Germans, especially their Gestapo, are too bloody efficient at picking out the least little thing that is out of place. Ta compris? [Understood?]"

Again Paul nodded in assent.

Later, at precisely 6:45 p.m., the trio was standing at the corral gate, and they waited anxiously, without any sign of the sergeant. At a little after seven, a Volkswagen, the German equivalent of the US Army jeep, pulled up alongside them.

The sergeant, sitting in the back alongside a lieutenant, spoke up. "Mon ami, Lieutenant Koffler voudrais aller at la cafe avec nous. [My friend Lieutenant Koffler wants to go to the café with us.]" He motioned for Pierette to join them in the backseat, and Louis, followed by Paul, crowded into the front with the driver.

Paul thought, *All the better protection for us.*

Louis directed the driver, and in several minutes they arrived at a nondescript two-story building with a worn sign in front indicating that this was the "Cafe Les Deux Magots."

As they walked in, they noted that tables and chairs were crowded in close together. Lieutenant Koffler led the way to one empty table and took a chair for himself. The other two were appropriated by the sergeant. Koffler waved Louis to the empty chair beside him. Pierette selected an empty adjacent table and sat down, followed by the driver and Paul. Most of the tables were filled with French civilians, but some were occupied by German military people. On a small elevated stage on the far side of the smoke-filled room, a small band was playing for the pleasure of those Germans present.

The four-piece ensemble consisted of an accordionist, a violin player, a drummer, and one man playing the clarinet. They were apparently playing a popular German tune; it was sung enthusiastically by the Nazis in the audience, some waving their beer glasses in the air, and others moving their drinks around carelessly, spilling their contents on neighbors.

The Germans thought it was great fun, and the French were not about to risk the displeasure of the Germans by objecting. The words to the song seemed to be "Du, du, likst mir in hertzen, du, du likst mir in zlnden, du, du makst mir fil smertzen," and it continued on in a spirited way.

A waiter took their drink order. The Germans all ordered beer, while Louis and Pierette ordered white wine. Paul followed their example.

When the song finally ended, conversation among many of the patrons resumed at a high pitch, resulting in a clamor of noise throughout the café. A tiny, thin woman who seemed to be less than five feet tall and had a sad expression on her face then appeared at the side of the stage.

All conversation stopped, and attention was focused on her. She was affectionately called "Little Sparrow" by her fans and admirers.

Without fanfare, she sang "La Vie en Rose" in a haunting, penetrating voice while the band muted their tones in accompanying her. Although Paul had never heard Edith Piaf sing before, he was thunderstruck by the simplicity, beauty, and eloquence of her stage-stopping presentation. She had the same effect on all in the audience, with some sitting there in open-mouthed admiration. When she finished, the entire audience stood on their feet and cheered and whistled. She then sang several more songs in her repertoire, each time followed by wildly enthusiastic applause from her admiring audience. The Germans were just as enthralled as the French, along with the sole American in the audience.

She then stepped out onto the floor and greeted individual members of the audience, some by sitting on their laps, and some by just stroking her hand alongside their faces.

She came to Koffler and sat on his lap, singing, "Qu'il est beau, qu'il est beau. [How handsome he is; how handsome he is.]." Then, stroking the side of the sergeant's face, she sang, "C'est Vrai, C'est Vrai. [It is true; it is true.]"

God almighty! Paul thought. *She is singing the coded message, indicating that the earlier information we got is confirmed! Now how do we get out of here?*

Civilians at the table behind them moved rapidly to get out of the way of four arrogant SS officers, a captain and three lieutenants, just entering, intent on appropriating a table they wanted. Ms.

Piaf paid them no heed and went on visiting each table, except
that occupied by SS men. She pointedly ignored them, but they
did not seem slighted in the least and busied themselves ordering
drinks from the hovering waiters. She returned to the stage and
disappeared behind the shabby curtains.

The SS captain turned to Paul, holding a cigarette in his hand,
apparently demanding a light. Paul clumsily fished in his pockets
for the box of French matches he had been equipped with, but
Lieutenant Koffler whipped out a cigarette lighter and ignited it
for the captain.

"Danke schoen [Thank you]," the SS captain murmured,
puffing on his cigarette.

"Bitte schoen [You're welcome]," Koffler responded.

The band went back to playing a mixture of popular French
and German tunes.

Koffler stood up, looking at his watch. The sergeant and driver
also stood up and followed him out the door. Louis looked over
at Paul and Pierette. The three of them needed no further urging,
and with Louis in the lead, they moved quickly out the door.
The Germans offered them a lift back to the corral, courtesy of
Lieutenant Koffler. As they were crowding into the Volkswagen,
Louis said, "Danke, herr Lieutenant. [Thank you, Lieutenant.]"
Koffler simply waved his hand and signaled the driver to move on.

They were dropped off almost exactly at the spot where they
had been picked up. Once again, they all thanked the lieutenant
and the sergeant for the ride.

"Well, my friend," Louis said as they watched the German
vehicle move off in the distance, "thanks to the courtesy of the
German Army, we have the information we need, and we even
got a ride back in the bargain."

Paul looked with alarm at the dock. Their barge was gone!
Just as he really started to develop some genuine anxiety, another

barge pulled up alongside them, and a man jumped off, securing the forward and stern lines. He immediately nodded to Louis and approached him, whispering a few words. Louis turned to Paul and said, "Do what I do." Pierette had apparently heard the barge man talking to Louis, and she knew the drill. Louis, followed by Paul and Pierette, leaped aboard and started to unload a cargo of cheese wheels, cases of wine, and crates of vegetables, stacking them into neat piles. After a short time, some horse-drawn carts manned by German soldiers pulled up, and the three of them wordlessly started to work alongside the Germans, loading the cargo onto the wagons. When the task was finally completed, again without any conversation, Louis, followed by Paul and Pierette, jumped back onto the barge.

As soon as he saw them safely aboard, the barge captain cast off the lines. They were on their way back to their point of departure. It was a nail-biting trip back, with several German patrol boats going by them menacingly, with their deck guns pointed at the barge. Their fears were assuaged by the barge captain, who explained that they had been inspected by these same patrol boats on the journey to the German facility.

The journey going back seemed to be shorter and to take less time, but Paul assumed it was only his imagination. When they arrived at their drop-off point, they wordlessly debarked without any conversation. Louis solemnly shook the hand of the captain, who called out "Bon Chance! [Good Luck!]"

Louis then rapidly moved into the woods, with Pierette and Paul close behind. They were traveling quickly down a path that was hardly discernible when a voice called out "Halt!"

Paul's heart sank. Here they were, so near and yet so far from their destination, the farmhouse. They soon saw a patrol of five Germans, led by a sergeant, some holding rifles and some holding machine pistols, all of which were pointed at them.

"Hanter Hoch! [Hands up!]" one of the Germans ordered.

They complied immediately.

"Papieren!" one of them demanded.

The three of them handed over their papers to the sergeant, who studied them carefully. One of the soldiers muttered something like "Schießen sie die französische hunde (Shoot the French dogs)." Paul's knowledge of Yiddish helped him understand that. Whatever it was, the Germans were matter-of-factly planning to shoot them out of hand!

Louis grabbed Paul's arm on one side and Pierette's on the other, and he dragged them down to the ground. The forest around them erupted in gunfire at the Germans, who quickly fell, either dead or mortally wounded.

Le Flic appeared, holding a smoking pistol.

"Alors, viens, vite! [Let's go quickly!]" he commanded.

Paul needed no convincing and rapidly fell into the single line of French fighters moving out of the area.

After several hours, and with Paul feeling totally exhausted, he gratefully saw the farmhouse come into sight. A civilian he had not seen before approached and asked, "Which one of you is Kramer?"

Paul held up his hand.

The man then sputtered, "Am I glad to see you! I was told not to come back without you!"

He held out his hand, saying, "I'm Lieutenant Murphy, and Colonel Gerrior ordered me to get you back immediately, if not sooner!" The password code has been changed, and you would never make it past the sentries. Let's go now, soldier!"

Paul turned to Louis, grabbed him in a bear hug, and then did the same to Pierette, who kissed him on each cheek.

"Mon cher petit Americain [My dear little American]," she murmured.

Le Flic grasped his hand and said, "Congratulations, my friend. You have accomplished your mission!"

In turn, Paul shook the hands of all of the other men, women, and children in the group. He faced them and said, "Fighters of France, you have paid dearly for every inch of your liberated land. Someday I hope your entire country will be totally free and ruled by free French people like you. Vive La France!" With that he gave them all a snappy military salute and followed Lieutenant Murphy.

They got through the American lines with no problem, and as soon as they did, Paul breathed a giant sigh of relief. "I can't wait till we get to the colonel's tent and get out of these civvy clothes. Never thought I would be so eager to get out of civilian clothes." He laughed.

Murphy smiled. "We have a slight detour we have to make before we get to Gerrior's tent." They approached a nearby jeep driven by a private first class wearing an MP brassard.

"Where are we going?" Paul asked, getting alarmed.

"Don't sweat it, soldier," Murphy replied. "You're not in trouble. Just get in!"

The jeep traveled some very rough roads, and the shaking up the occupants got was worse than being on the North Atlantic in a tiny boat. They pulled into an area with a large pyramidal tent in the center of a group of smaller tents. A command car with a trailer attached to it was parked in front of the larger tent, and Paul saw with some apprehension that the license plate sported general's stars.

Murphy got out and motioned for Paul to enter alongside him. As they entered, Paul noted that a desk was set up right at the entrance. There were light wood partitions separating the tent into various cubicles. A sergeant major sitting there looked up at them and turned to a captain alongside him who was ruffling through a sheaf of papers. Murphy came to attention and saluted the captain. "Lieutenant Murphy and Private Kramer reporting as ordered, sir." he stated to the captain.

The captain returned the salute and said, "I am Captain Lewis Bridge, aide to General Bradley. I'll let him know you are here." He disappeared inside a door behind him.

Paul, getting alarmed, sputtered, "But lieutenant, I am supposed to report to Major Helms and Colonel Gerrior!"

"You'll get to give them your report in a little while, soldier," Murphy replied.

The captain opened the door and motioned Murphy and Kramer to enter. Sitting behind a small desk was an older gentleman wearing general's stars. Right away, Paul recognized the unmistakable craggy features of General Omar Bradley. He came to attention, as did Murphy, and he noted that standing at the general's side were Major Helms and Colonel Gerrior.

"At ease," the general said softly, and then he asked, "Kramer?"

Paul took one step forward and said briskly, "Yes, sir."

"Report," ordered the general. Paul for one brief moment looked at the colonel, who nodded, and he then proceeded to give a detailed report leaving out no details, however minute.

The general listened very carefully and then said, "Well done. This information is most helpful." He turned to Major Helms and Colonel Gerrior. "Your operation turned out well. I do have another problem with protocol, however. Several weeks ago, my headquarters was invaded by an explosively wild Colonel Macklin, Captain Sheridan, and two privates. One of the privates was a huge bruiser, equally furious, who held one of my orderlies up in the air until I ordered him to let the man go. He was accompanied by a wildly sputtering skinny medic."

"It appears, according to them—and I have already sent for them—that you took one of their people—a medic by the name of Paul Kramer—without any written authorization from his commanding officers—namely this Colonel Macklin and Captain Sheridan. Is this true?"

"General, sir, this man volunteered for this mission." the colonel sputtered.

General Bradley spoke accusingly. "Colonel Macklin and Captain Sheridan, as well as the wild enlisted men who were with them, all insist that Kramer did not volunteer, and you state that he did." Turning to Paul, he snapped, "Who is lying here, soldier?"

"General, sir, neither one is lying, Sir. When I was out of hearing of Colonel Macklin and Captain Sheridan, I did volunteer without getting permission from my Commanding Officers; and, so if anyone is at fault, it is me, sir. I would follow Colonel Macklin and Captain Sheridan off a cliff, sir. They are dedicated, honorable soldiers, sir. Colonel Gerrior and Major Helms were trying to get intelligence that they deemed vital to our war effort, and so they needed a volunteer."

The general grinned and then caught himself and adopted a sterner-looking appearance. He called out, "Captain?"

The door opened, and his aide appeared.

"Are Colonel Macklin and his people here yet?"

"Yes, sir" was the reply. "They have just arrived."

"Send them in."

Colonel Macklin, Captain Sheridan, Bubba, and Tony crowded into the small room. They all came to attention.

"At ease," the general ordered.

"It seems that the mission was a success," he said, "and I am satisfied with the results. I am equally impressed with the devotion to duty as well as the loyalty each of you has demonstrated to your responsibilities as well as to the people working with you."

He turned to Colonel Macklin. "You may take your man

with you now, and in the future, think twice before you decide to invade a general's headquarters!"

He then faced Gerrior and Helms. "In the future," he directed, "You will do your recruiting of volunteers through proper channels. I want a detailed written report on Private Kramer's mission on my desk no later than 0600 tomorrow! Dismissed!"

They all came to attention, did an about-face, and filed out of the general's office.

When they got to the anteroom, Major Helms took Paul's arm, pointing to a large carton. "We brought your things here."

Paul said, "Thank you, sir."

This elicited a frown from Colonel Macklin, who growled, "Grab your gear and let's get out of here!"

—12—

They piled into a waiting jeep with Bubba in the driver's seat. Colonel Macklin sat in the front, while Captain Sheridan, Tony, and Paul positioned themselves in the back of the vehicle.

"Captain, sir," Paul asked, "how is our outfit?"

"We went right into the lines when you were grabbed by those spooks." Sheridan replied.

Colonel Macklin turned around frowning, but did not say anything.

"We took a lot of casualties while we were part of the army sweeping across this Cotentin Peninsula. Our medics worked overtime treating the wounded and evacuating the seriously hurt GIs to the rear. We are now moving into a new headache. That is the hedgerows that are like small checkerboard fields, which the French call *Le Bocage*. The borders of every pasture are lined with high earthen walls and are infested with deep-rooted trees and shrubs. You name it, we've got it. Whatever tiny openings there are in these hedgerows are covered by German machine guns and mortars. They are not satisfied with that but also string very thin piano-like wire across some openings that are attached to booby traps. Right now, we have stayed put, while our infantry has moved ahead. We are waiting for more replacements and supplies to come up. We were down to about one K ration per soldier when we were replaced by another MP outfit. Our job is to secure the villages and towns we liberate, so we now can afford to wait a little while. The infantry does not have that luxury, and small units can be taken out of the line for only a few hours; or, at the most, one day."

The jeep came to a small clearing in the woods where several truck canvases had been spread out over some piled-up jerricans and cartons. A soiled Red Cross flag was draped over the top, signaling that this was the battalion aid station. Several dozen litters lay on the group near the opening of the station.

Captain Sheridan went on. "I don't know what I would have done without our dental officer and the rest of our medics. The wounded just kept piling up on us, but we did the very best with each and every one of them."

Sheridan, Tony, and Paul exited the jeep.

Paul walked over to the side of Colonel Sheridan, saluting him, saying, "Colonel, sir, I don't know how to thank you and the rest of our people who went to bat for me." He then turned to Captain Sheridan, as well as to Tony and Bubba.

"You've got your work laid out for you, Kramer. Glad to have you back." the Colonel replied, returning the salute, and he then ordered Bubba to move on.

Tony piped up. "We still have some wounded who are waiting for our truck to get back so we can evacuate them to the rear. You can give me a hand when we load these guys onto the truck."

A short time later, their truck arrived laden with medical supplies, food, clothing, and equipment. Everyone in sight got busy unloading the materials and stacking them alongside the aid station.

"What happened to all the blankets we had, as well as the clothing and food?" Paul asked.

Tony explained, "Just about one or two days ago, we were

barreling through one of these small towns that had already been secured. There wasn't a single building standing or in one piece. Bombs and shells had ripped all of them to pieces. As we were moving down what seemed to be the main street, a pitiful group of men, women, and children lined the side of the road. They were all silent, but it was obvious they were cold and hungry. The colonel ordered our convoy to halt and had all of our supplies taken out and given to the civilians, including our medicines. That's why we are waiting to be resupplied. Now get busy and stack four of those litters on the truck."

Paul grabbed two litters, placed them crossways along the back of the truck, and then covered them with blankets. He grabbed another two and repeated the process.

Tony had already gone into the tent and he came back out with Kurt, carrying a wounded GI to the truck. They gently placed him on one of the litters and strapped him down.

Kurt looked at Paul and snorted. "Nice to have you back. Been on vacation?"

"Nuts to you too, buddy," Paul retorted, hoisting another patient onto the truck.

Kurt asked, "Did you notice anything wrong with Colonel Macklin?"

"Why?" Paul replied. "He seemed to be in a rotten mood— more than what my shenanigans would rate, come to think of it."

"He got a Dear John letter from his wife," Kurt muttered.

"What's a Dear John letter?" Paul asked.

"That's where someone's loving wife dumps him for someone else," Kurt explained. "She was a showgirl and running with a fast, wild crowd. It was bound to happen. Too bad it had to be a great guy like Macklin to get kicked in the teeth."

"Gee, I'm sorry to hear that," Paul answered, feeling very sorry for his commanding officer.

"We're going to be here just one or two days more until we get all of our replacements and supplies. Then we move back up to the lines," Kurt said. "In the meantime, some of us are going to take the colonel back to this little town a few miles from here, buy him a few drinks, and try to cheer him up. Want to come?"

"Sure I do, and what's more, I'll help spring for his drinks too," Paul replied.

After the wounded had all been attended to, Paul, noticed with some satisfaction that some were even sitting up on their stretchers. Those needing more urgent care had been safely transported back to the rear.

Tony walked into the aid station saying, "I hear you're going with some of our guys to try to lighten Macklin's bad mood. I've got the duty here. You can drink a beer for me."

"I'll stay here and cover for you, Tony, if you want to go," Paul suggested.

"No, it's okay, buddy. By the way, are you old enough to drink?"

"Cut it out," Paul objected.

Just then, a low *thrum*, *thrum* started to come from somewhere overhead.

"What's that?" Paul asked.

"It's that rotten *Bed Check Charlie* again. The Germans know where we are and send this light bomber over here every night. I think it's a Heinkel. This bum comes here to drop some bombs, strafe us, and in general make our lives miserable," Tony explained.

Paul went to open the flap of the tent but was stopped by Tony.

"Don't let any light show, because that Nazi will zero us in and we'll all go up in smoke!"

Paul eased under the tent flap so that he could see the German plane flying at a fairly high altitude. Suddenly a roar came from the treetops, and an all-black fighter plane swooped up at the

German with machine guns and cannons blazing away and blew him into flaming broken pieces.

"What in God's name was that?" Paul asked.

"That was one of our Black Widow fighters that just saved our behinds," Tony explained. "If this guy had dropped a bomb on our aid station, these wounded guys and all of us would have gone the way this German just went," Tony explained.

"Well," Paul exclaimed, "God bless our air forces."

"You can say that again, Kramer," Captain Sheridan offered as he entered the aid station.

He went from one wounded soldier to the next, carefully checking their condition, their medications, and how they were doing. He turned to Tony.

"I am prescribing some therapy for Colonel Macklin in the form of a few drinks at a café, and I understand you are coming along, Kramer," Sheridan remarked.

"Yes, sir," Paul replied.

"As soon as I finish here, follow me out to the two trucks parked outside here. We'll pick up whoever else is going along with us and the colonel and take off."

Paul nodded in assent and followed the captain around the aid station as he double-checked each wounded GI. At times, he would assist the captain in changing a bandage or dispensing some more medication. When their tasks had all been completed, Paul waved to Tony and followed Sheridan out to the two trucks waiting with motors already idling. Colonel Macklin was escorted to the front of one of the trucks, where he got in beside the driver.

"This whole thing is not necessary, and I don't want to be coddled by you guys," the colonel sputtered. Nevertheless, inwardly, he was pleased that his men showed such loyalty to and concern for him.

Paul followed Kurt into the back of the vehicle and noted that all of the men already seated on the facing benches were fully armed. Some carried rifles, others submachine guns, and a few of them sported .45-caliber pistols attached to their web belts. Most of them wore MP brassards as well.

"Say, what's with the artillery?" Paul asked no one in particular.

"We're in a combat zone, buddy, and we just don't want to get caught with our pants down by the German patrols that run around these here parts," one of the seated men answered.

"Why the MP brassards?" Kurt asked.

The same GI replied, "Town MPs sometimes are real chicken, and we don't want any of them to spoil the colonel's good time."

Captain Sheridan, sitting in the passenger's seat, rode by in an uncovered jeep that had an MP placard on the front windshield. He waved to the two trucks and they followed his vehicle down the narrow country road on the way to the village.

In the middle of the little town, there was a sign hanging in front of two very dirty windows that proclaimed the building to be Le Petit Cochon (The Little Pig).

As they entered the café, two town MPs holding a wildly struggling soldier elbowed their way out of the door, nearly bowling over Colonel Macklin. He indignantly asked, "What's going on here?"

"This flyboy was getting out of hand, sir," one of the MPs explained, "and we're going to haul him down to our calaboose and let him cool off."

"Are you a flier, son?" the colonel asked.

"You've got that right, Colonel. If you were in this general area last night, you would have seen me shoot a Jerry bomber out of the sky, sir," he replied.

"Y'all the man who got that Bed Check Charley off our back last night?" Bubba asked, moving up alongside Colonel Macklin.

"You got that right also, soldier. We just got one of them P-38

Black Widow night fighters. We fly around looking for these Germans," the flier responded.

Colonel Macklin put out his hand to the pilot but was warded off by one of the MPs.

"I'm sorry, sir, but this man is under our custody, and we are bringing him in," the soldier said almost apologetically.

The colonel looked at Bubba and snorted, "Give me your brassard!"

Turning to the town MPs, he growled, "Now if there is any question in your mind, I am an MP colonel, and I am giving you a direct order to turn this man over to my custody!"

The rest of the colonel's men crowded around, some carelessly pointing the barrels of their weapons at the pair of uneasy town MPs.

One of them snapped to attention. Bubba eased the flier over beside the colonel, who turned back to the men he had just intimidated and snapped, "Dismissed!"

They spun around and made it out of the place with as much dignity as they could muster.

The colonel took the flier by the arm, and said, "You, soldier, are a credit to our armed forces and deserve a drink—or, for that matter, several drinks. We've got to thank you good and proper for saving our necks!"

The proprietor walked over and said, "Pardon, Monsieur. I speak and understand English very well. I too want to express my thanks and those of our entire village for what this man did last night. And to you brave Americans who came here to liberate our country, I ask for the privilege of serving all of your drinks on the house, as you Yankees put it so well."

"We accept with many thanks your offer, sir, but this liquor costs you a lot of money. We are happy to accept your good wishes, but we insist, with respect, on paying you, since obviously you are not independently wealthy."

The Frenchman grabbed the colonel in his arms and kissed him on both cheeks.

"Then we will drink together, *mon ami*, and toast the liberation of La Belle France and toast the great United States of America for coming here to save us."

"Well said, my friend," The colonel replied. "Now let's get down to some serious drinking!"

All of the men around the colonel needed no further invitation and sat down, laying their weapons under the tables.

The air force man turned to Colonel Macklin and said, "Do I have a good story for you, sir."

"What's that, son?" the colonel asked.

The flier went on. "General Pete Quesada, commander of our Tactical Air Command, came out to our airbase with none other than General Eisenhower. We had just taken delivery of some P-51 Mustang fighters, and General Pete offered to take General Ike on a tour of the front. General Bradley had been very upset about it, but Ike was determined to go and overruled poor General Omar Bradley, who was very nervous and upset about this. But Ike insisted on going. We had to remove the large radio behind the pilot's seat, as well as a seventy-gallon fuel tank that had been added for extra range. General Eisenhower was crouched down behind General Quesada with his helmet scraping the canopy and enjoyed the ride of his life. We got three fighters to escort them as they flew well out over German territory. Some of my buddies estimate that it was a good fifty miles over really hostile and dangerous areas, but Ike wanted to better understand the hedgerow terrain, and he had his way. He kept pushing Pete to fly faster, but flying the commander-in-chief of all of armed forces in a very dangerous place would raise some real flak from the VIPs. Quesada said that here he had the supreme commander stuffed behind him in a single-engine airplane with no parachute over enemy territory, and no way to get him out in the event of an emergency. After a dicey landing, Ike grinned sheepishly and remarked that General Marshall would give him hell."

The owner's wife and son came out to join in the festivities. Soon after that, and a number of drinks later, the colonel was on top of one of the tables, doing his version of an Irish jig.

The front door suddenly burst open, and the two town MPs rushed in, accompanied by a red-faced MP Lieutenant.

"Colonel, sir, I am placing you under arrest for unmilitary conduct and conduct not becoming an officer!" the lieutenant shouted.

All of the men in the room retrieved their weapons, some ominously clicking bullets into their chambers.

Bubba placed his massive hulk in front of the lieutenant and saluted. "Suh, if mah cunnel wants to dance, then he's gat a raht to dance, and no one, suh is gonna stop him!" Bubba exclaimed.

Colonel Macklin, still wearing his MP brassards, got off the table and approached the lieutenant.

"My men just came off the lines and are heading back really soon. I advise you to get yourself the hell out of here before this thing gets real nasty and your commanding officer gets a serious complaint about you with a copy to General Bradley," the colonel sputtered.

The lieutenant looked around the room. Now with every weapon pointing directly at him, he decided that discretion was the better part of valor. He silently did an about-face and walked out of the café, followed by his two men.

Captain Sheridan approached Macklin.

"Colonel, sir, I think it is time for us to make a strategic retreat before these guys come back with their entire outfit. While we're at it, why don't I drive our flyboy back to his outfit before he gets into any more trouble?"

The colonel replied, slightly slurring his words, "Thank you, Captain. By golly, if you weren't a medic, I would have made you my exec!"

They all gave warm farewells to the French family and made their way out to the vehicles. The very next morning, word came down from division headquarters that they were moving up.

In no time, a convoy of all battalion vehicles lined up to take personnel, equipment, and supplies up to the front lines. They were back into hedgerow country in short order. The German snipers were having a field day shooting from their hiding places in the thick shrubbery.

As soon as the Americans began to take casualties, the litter bearers went out looking for the wounded, and oftentimes they too became casualties. The medics got busy locating the wounded and attending to them. The first job they had was to stop the bleeding; it was very challenging and difficult.

Author wearing Red Cross brassard in front of a group of tents

Pressure bandages and sometimes a butterfly bandage would do the trick. Sulfanilamide powder was poured into the wound, and the patient was then helped to take two sulfathiazole pills, after making sure he had enough water in his canteen. The hurt GI was given a half dozen or so pills to hold him over until the litter bearers picked him up. Then they instructed him, if he was conscious, to take two more every four hours, or until Captain Sheridan decided on an alternative treatment. So far the new miracle medicine penicillin had not yet reached their quartermaster supplies. Morphine was used in cases of extreme pain, and the medics had been cautioned by Captain Sheridan to carry adequate supplies, as well as the other critical medical supplies.

After attending to the wounded soldier, an emergency medical tag was filled out detailing all of the treatments. The GI's rifle, with attached bayonet, was shoved into the ground, and the EMT tag was attached to the trigger guard. In this way, when the wounded GI arrived back at the aid station, those attending him would know what treatment he had been given. Frequently, those who were unconscious on the battlefield were given plasma. This was supplied by plasma powder that was mixed with sterile water and then injected into a blood vessel in the arm. Paul noted the miraculous effects of this form of treatment. There were many times when he could not find a pulse and the wounded man did not appear to be breathing. Nevertheless, he injected the plasma serum anyway, and many times, after about a half hour or so had passed, while going by the same GI, Paul would note that the man's eyes would be open, and oftentimes he would be asking for a cigarette.

After a couple of bullets found their way dangerously close to his arm—the one with the Red Cross brassard—Tony muttered, "The hell with this! and the hell with the Geneva Convention. Those krauts are using my red cross as a target!" He angrily ripped it off.

Paul followed suit, as did Kurt, and the three of them decided to trade in their helmets marked with Red Cross emblems on them. A short time later, Paul found an intact helmet in a ditch and made sure it had no bullet or shrapnel holes in it. Kurt and Tony had also achieved the same thing. Paul picked up his old helmet and tossed it into a hedgerow. A German machine gun opened up on it immediately.

Kurt, not too far away, observed this and muttered, "You see how the Nazis respect the Geneva Convention?"

Paul decided to find a net to put over his helmet in the fashion of many of the other GIs, who also put some branches and leaves into the holes of the net to serve as a form of camouflage.

The Germans had also fiendishly run thin piano wire across the few openings in the hedgerows, which served as trip wires for mines that were buried close by. If a GI crawling through a narrow opening in the hedgerow missed seeing the wire, he would get blown up.

An even more difficult job was evacuating the wounded from the hedgerows. The litter bearers oftentimes needed help getting the wounded out of the thick underbrush. Aside from attending to the wounded, Tony, Paul, and Kurt were kept busy assisting in this job also. An abandoned farmhouse with part of the roof blown off served as their battalion aid station.

Earlier, Paul had removed the Hershey bars from a gas mask bag he had been saving and filled it with necessary gauze packs, plasma bottles, morphine, and bandages, in addition to what he had stuffed into his two medic bags.

He still ran short on supplies and had to make frequent trips back to the aid station. There he saw Captain Sheridan and Lieutenant Saffridi working frantically to help the wounded scattered around the station on litters. One problem was the fact that they kept running out of blankets and continually had to find someone who could take the time to run over to the quartermaster to get more. Another major handicap was the shortage of vehicles that could be pressed into service as ambulances.

Getting the severely wounded quickly to an evacuation hospital in the rear echelon could be a matter of life and death. On occasion, some wounded men made it back on their own to the battalion aid station, and frequently Paul, Tony, and Kurt were told to stay and assist Sheridan and Saffridi with their overwhelming tasks. The battalion did not rate an ambulance for some reason that no one could figure out. Thus any vehicle that could be spared, truck or jeep, was used. Litters were slung across the hood of a jeep or the back of a truck and secured as best as they could for the ride back to the rear. Wounded Germans were also given the same treatment that Americans received.

With Paul's fractured Yiddish, he managed to convey to wounded Germans the necessity of taking medication. "Tvai yeder feer shtoonder [Two every four hours]," he would say, referring to the sulfathiazole pills he supplied them with. He filled out the emergency medical tag, attaching it to the front of the uniform, and supplied the wounded soldier with enough pills to hold him over until his own medics got to him. Paul did this in the hope that the German medics would reciprocate with wounded Americans.

Several times, Paul crawled by a German medic, but they exchanged no conversation.

As he moved about, looking for more wounded, he was constantly reminded of the admonition by all to keep his head and his butt down. He literally ground himself into the terrain. While doing so one day, a familiar voice called out.

"Paul Kramer! Is that you?"

He turned and saw a cross on the helmet of someone he had not seen in a while. It was Chaplain Murray.

"Father Murray," he murmured. I am glad to see you, sir, but not in this godforsaken place."

"This is where I am needed, Paul," Father Murray said, speaking softly, adding, "I am also carrying some first aid equipment with me so I can minister to the men's wounds while helping them with prayers."

"Father, I am sure that your prayers are far more powerful than whatever treatments I can supply. But to tell you the truth, I am very nervous with your being in this hot spot," Paul answered. "But if I catch a bullet, I will need you to help me with your prayers."

"You just stay in one piece, Paul, and keep up the good work," Father Murray urged.

Paul spotted a pair of legs sticking out of a hedgerow and crawled just as quickly as he could toward the victim.

Just then a German artillery barrage opened up, and Paul heard the sound of a huge explosion and felt himself being blown up into the air. It was a very weird sensation, and although he felt no pain, he lost consciousness. He opened his eyes for what seemed to be a short time later. He was lying in a bunk, and Father Murray was leaning over him, asking anxiously, "Paul, are you awake? Do you know who I am?"

"Father, for a minute I thought I had died and was trying to get into heaven. You were trying to intercede with Saint Peter, but you were not doing so well in my case," Paul answered.

Chaplain Murray smiled and said, "You are in an evacuation hospital, and I came with you to make sure you are all right."

As he spoke, a corporal walked by, stopping at each bed and reading the notation at the foot of the bed. He stopped in front of Paul, read the notation, and dropped a medal on Paul' s hand, which was outstretched.

Paul asked, "What's this, soldier?"

"That's a Purple Heart," the corporal replied, "and you'll get your written commendation just as soon as I finish writing this up for you and the other guys who are getting one."

Paul sat up in alarm, calling out, "Just a minute there; this means that my mother is going to get a telegram telling her that I have been hurt!"

"That's right, buddy. Your next of kin gets a telegram. That's true," the corporal stated. "But that's not all."

"That is all," Paul yelled, getting very agitated. "My Mother getting that telegram, will have a heart attack or drop dead on the spot. You've got to take this back!"

Father Murray put an arm on Paul's shoulder. "Calm down there; it won't be so terrible. And as the corporal was trying to tell you, there will be benefits in store for you if you get this medal."

"Please, Father Murray, my mother told me she was taking a deep breath when I went away and could not breathe again properly until I got back. She is fanatical about my brother and me, and I just know this will kill her. Please try to help me. I am not causing any harm to the army if I don't get this medal. Besides, I don't feel any wounds on me. Just my getting blown up in the air without any wounds really makes me not qualified to receive this medal."

"The army has a policy that anyone who is hurt in combat does deserve to get this Purple Heart," Father Murray replied, trying to console Paul.

Paul took the Chaplain's arm, pleading, "Please! Help me! I don't want this medal! No way! I just want to get back to my outfit. They are shorthanded as it is. Please, get that commendation stopped and help me get back. It will be a great act of compassion and humanity if you can do that for me."

Father Murray stood up, stating, "I don't know if I can do anything, Paul, but I'll give it a college try."

Paul, with tears in his eyes, said, "Thank you, Father, for understanding my predicament."

The chaplain left and returned a short time later with a man wearing a colonel's insignia. He spoke to Paul.

"The chaplain has explained your problem and asked for my help. Like everyone else around, I have a tremendous amount of respect and admiration for this man. If you'll just sign this release form, I'll have you discharged and Father Murray can get you back to your outfit. By rights, you should understand you have suffered a severe concussion and would be a lot better off spending the next twenty-four hours in bed. But again, because the Chaplain has asked for this, I'll go along and let you go now. Personally I think you ought to have your head examined," the colonel muttered.

Fifteen minutes later, Paul was outside of the hospital, sitting contentedly in the passenger seat of the chaplain's jeep. He turned to the Chaplain.

"Father Murray, I can't thank you enough. I'll never forget this. I don't want to bother you with any more requests, but can you keep me in your prayers?"

Father Murray smiled. "Maybe the colonel was right. But you know your mother, and maybe we did save her from a terrible trauma and possibly a terrible aftermath as well. If you really feel up to it, we're going to head back right now."

"Father, I never felt more up to anything than I do right now in getting back, and to sound like a broken record, thanks again and many more times," Paul said.

They clambered into the padre's jeep and headed back to the battalion. Paul asked if he could be dropped off at the battalion aid station, and Father Murray thought that was a good idea so that he could explain to Captain Sheridan what had happened. As they entered the aid station, Colonel Macklin was in the process of arguing with Captain Sheridan, and judging by his angry demeanor, he was not getting the best of the verbal duel. Colonel Macklin had sprained his ankle, which Captain Sheridan had determined by a careful examination, but he still wanted a confirming X-ray. The colonel refused to go to the evacuation hospital. He had settled for an Ace bandage, applied by a luckless Kurt. This was of no use to the sputtering colonel, who claimed he couldn't walk a single inch with that rag on his ankle. Captain Sheridan looked up in desperation just as Paul and the chaplain entered.

"Kramer," the captain called out. "Are you okay now?"

"Yes, sir," Paul answered.

"You know that basket weave you use on sprained ankles?" Sheridan asked.

Paul nodded in agreement.

"Put one on the colonel's sore ankle and see if you can get him walking with that," the captain ordered.

Paul turned to the colonel. "Colonel, sir, I'll do the best I can, but I can't give you any guarantees it will work," he said hoarsely.

"I'll try anything that will help me walk and stay the hell out of that blasted hospital!" the colonel growled.

Paul got Kurt to help him lift the colonel on to a stretcher lying across two footlockers just as Tony entered holding a wounded soldier. As soon as Tony had deposited the soldier carefully and gently onto another litter, he came over to Paul's side.

"You all right?" Tony asked anxiously.

"I'm just fine," Paul reassured him, and with that the colonel looked at Paul.

"Can you do this soldier?" Macklin asked.

"Yes, sir," Paul responded, and he proceeded to roll up the colonel's trouser leg on the side of the affected ankle and removed the combat boot and sock. He procured a double-edged razor and shaved the leg from midcalf downward. He then got a bottle of tincture of benzoin, soaked a cotton swab in it, and then applied it liberally to the skin of the affected leg from midcalf all the way down to the toes. Paul then got several rolls of half-inch adhesive tape and, with the adhesive side outward, carefully measured lengths of the tape he would need, both horizontal and vertical, and attached their ends to the edge of the stretcher. The colonel seemed fascinated with the procedure, as was Father Murray, who had silently observed all that had gone on earlier.

The colonel asked, "What is this contraption going to do, soldier?"

"It's going to help you walk, sir—that is, I hope," Paul answered.

Paul then dexterously applied first one vertical strip and then a horizontal strip of adhesive tape, interweaving them and making them tight enough to secure the ankle but not too tight to endanger circulation. All the while, he was silently thanking the instructors from Fort Benjamin Harrison Surgical Technician School. At long last, the job was completed, and Paul asked the colonel to put his foot down gently, offering him the use of a crutch to help him.

The colonel pushed the crutch away, and stepped down gingerly on his affected foot. "I'll be blasted!" he yelled. "I can walk!"

Paul urged, "Please go easy, sir."

The colonel looked at Paul seriously and extended his right hand.

"Thank you, soldier. That is, Private ...Private who?"

"Kramer, sir," Paul replied.

Colonel Macklin turned to Captain Sheridan.

"How come this man Kramer is a buck private?"

"He actually got promoted to a PFC some time back, sir, but never got around to sewing on his stripe. He has asked repeatedly not to be promoted. I saw from his record that he turned down being sent to officer candidate preparatory school. He has some hang-up about not wanting to order men around who are older than him."

"Being promoted is not up to the individual soldier. It is a military fact of life. I want this man promoted, and I want to see his new badge of rank on his uniform immediately, if not sooner!" Colonel Macklin fumed.

"Yes, sir," Captain Sheridan replied.

"And one more thing," the colonel growled.

"Yes, sir?" Captain Sheridan asked.

"Thanks for getting me back on my feet," Macklin said, shaking first the captain's hand and then Paul's.

The next morning, Paul was back on the front lines, seeking out wounded and treating them.

— 13 —

There was no letup in the fighting—no time off on weekends. The war dragged on twenty-four hours a day every day. Paul had to fight off sleep by drinking a lot of black coffee whenever he could manage it. The coffee made from the chemically treated water in the Lyster bags was horrible in taste, but that was all there was. Some smart aleck ninety-day wonder (a brand-new second lieutenant) came up from the rear echelon with a supply of mysterious pills he went about trying to distribute to the men. He first urged Captain Sheridan to give them out. The captain swung his foot upward violently, trying to hit the lieutenant in the rear end, hastening his departure out of the aid station with a colorful array of curses.

"You are not going to pump my men up with Benzedrine or whatever the hell you have there! Beat it!" Captain Sheridan called after him.

The pills the man was trying to distribute were designed to keep a person awake, but the captain felt that taking them over a prolonged period of time could have serious side effects.

"Somebody find Bubba and have him get this bum out of here!" the captain called out.

"I am a Second Lieutenant, that is a commissioned officer,

and you will treat me with respect," the lieutenant grumped, peering back through the entrance.

"If you are not out of my sight immediately, if not sooner, I will forget I am a medical officer, pick up any weapon I have, and show you how much respect you deserve. Now bail out!"

The lieutenant thought that prudence was the better part of valor and made his way quickly out of the area. This was none too soon, because Bubba was bearing down on him with a mean look on his face, and the man barely escaped.

Finally, the battalion was pulled out of the line to wait for more supplies and replacements. Early one morning, Paul checked into the tent that was now used as the aid station. Captain Sheridan called him over.

"Kramer," he said, "you got drafted for another mission."

"Captain, sir, they are not sending me behind the lines again, are they?" he asked nervously.

"No such problem," Sheridan responded. "An English supply ship bringing essential materials to the British troops around Caen was sunk by a mine. They have requested that we send a motor convoy with the essential supplies they need to hold them over until they can get another ship to them. Our battalion is sending a group of MP's to guard the convoy. Colonel Macklin asked me if I could spare you for a few days, since you speak French so well. He has a Michelin road map of some kind, and with your ability to speak the lingo, he believes the convoy will have a better chance of getting through without any problems."

"I guess I am volunteering for this job, Captain," Paul suggested sarcastically.

"Well, when you get right down to it, if you don't want to go, you don't have to." Captain Sheridan commented.

"The bottom line, Captain, is that I would never turn you or

Colonel Macklin down—that is, as long as you can do without me here," Paul replied.

"We have a few days before we go back onto the line, so don't dillydally, and get back to us pronto when you have delivered the goods."

Paul made his way to the pyramidal tent that housed battalion headquarters. Colonel Macklin was at the tent flap, looking outside, as Paul made his way toward him.

Paul saluted him.

"You okay with this, Kramer?" the colonel asked, returning the salute.

"Yes, sir," Paul replied. "The captain has already filled me in, and I am reporting for duty, sir."

"We have a couple of two-and-a-half-ton trucks that will take you and the rest of our group to the convoy, which is loading up at a quartermaster dump right now. Take this map with you and get there as fast as you can, and get back just as quickly."

He handed Paul the map along with two cartons of Chesterfield cigarettes.

"If your lingo can't ease your way through all the roadblocks you will run into, maybe a few packs here and there of these cigarettes will keep you going. We are scheduled to receive our supplies and replacements soon, and when that happens, we go back up to the front." the colonel explained. "Captain Sheridan will be pacing until he gets you back. Understand?"

Paul saluted him and answered, "Yes, sir." Meanwhile, he realized that he had not thought to bring anything with him that he needed, such as a toothbrush, razor, or rations.

What the heck, he thought, *I'll mooch some rations from the convoy GIs and wash up with some water in my helmet.* He could do without his toothbrush for a couple of days, but he was going to miss his candy bars.

Two trucks were parked not far from the tent, and already some GIs wearing MP brassards were climbing into the backs of them. Paul noticed that each one carried side arms and a few carried carbines, while some others were armed with Thompson submachine guns.

One of them spotted him and yelled out, "Move your butt there, soldier! Climb aboard!"

Paul clambered into the back of the truck and found a space on a bench he could squeeze onto.

It did not take long before they reached the truck convoy. There had to be at least twenty trucks. The very lead vehicle had a swivel-mounted set of twin .30-caliber machine guns mounted on the front passenger side. The last truck in the convoy was similarly equipped. When the MPs disembarked, following prearranged instructions, they fanned out, with one or two going to each truck. Paul waited for just a moment as a jeep drove up with a second lieutenant in the front passenger seat.

"You the interpreter?" he asked Paul.

"That's right, sir," Paul replied, saluting him.

The lieutenant returned the salute and then asked, "What's that you're carrying?"

"A Michelin road map, sir, and a few cartons of cigarettes."

"Good thinking," the lieutenant replied. "By the way, my name is Connors—Jack Connors."

"Pleased to meet you, sir. My name is Paul Kramer. That is, currently, Tec 5 Kramer, sir."

"Get in the back of the jeep, Kramer. Before we take off, I want you to go over the map with me, and we'll figure the best way to get to our destination, which is Caen. That is where the British and Canadian troops are, and there are several French units as well. We have to deliver these supplies to the English quartermaster at Caen."

"We've got to have one hell of a lot of supplies in these trucks, sir," Paul ventured.

"This is just a fraction of what they need. Some of our brass wanted to divert the Red Ball Express bringing supplies up to our front lines, but higher-ranking brass nixed that deal," Connors explained.

Paul got into the back of the jeep and unfolded the large map. He located approximately where they were.

Lieutenant Connors got into the front of the jeep and then turned around to look at the map. He put his finger on a spot between St. Lo and Isigny and said, "I figure we are just about here."

"I think you're right, sir," Paul agreed.

"By the way," Connors asked, "How come you're not wearing MP brassards?"

"That's because I'm a medic, sir, but I was encouraged to volunteer for this job," Paul explained.

"I guess we are sort of fracturing the Geneva Convention, but to hell with that anyway. The Germans are not strong on the Geneva Convention either. I want you to head us for Colleville-sur-Mer, then to Bayeux, over to Mouene, and then to Caen—that is, if you can figure any roads that are open and will get us to those places."

"Somewheres near Caen, we have to cross the Orne river," Paul said. "But I hear the English troops captured the bridge intact, so we won't have to swim across."

"I don't think we'll have any problems with the American, French, or British troops," Connors commented. "The French Resistance may take us for a German convoy and open up on us. That, Kramer, is where you come in. The British soldiers came in on Gold and Sword Beaches, with Juno Beach between them being taken by Canadian troops. They have French Army units scattered between them as well. These beach areas are the ones that we are headed for first on the way to Caen" he said while pointing his finger on the map."

"I'm ready whenever you are, sir," Paul said.

Connors held out his left arm, bent the hand at the elbow, and then jerked it up and down several times. That was a signal for the convoy to take off, and they started to move, slowly at first, on the narrow two-lane road, which was still pockmarked by bomb and shell holes.

They had gone several miles when they came to a small town that was marked by some broken signs as Isigny. As they approached over the crest of a small hill, they saw a Sherman tank at the side of the road, which swung its turret around so that its huge gun was pointed directly at them. A few armed military police came out from behind the tank, and one of them called, "Get out of that vehicle and approach and be recognized."

The soldiers were all holding submachine guns, and they were pointed directly at Paul and Lieutenant Connors. They approached the MPs holding their hands in the air, so as not to provoke any nervous reaction from the MPs or the soldiers manning the tank.

"I'm going to reach inside my field jacket and take out my orders," Connors said.

"Your hand comes out with anything more than papers and I'll blow your head off," one of the MPs said threateningly.

Connors brought out his orders and handed them to one of the GIs.

Both of them scanned the documents carefully and handed them back to Connors. They then stepped back and waved the convoy on.

Once more the convoy proceeded slowly through the thoroughly bombed and shelled ruins of the town of Isigny and headed east. Paul carefully studied his road map and was satisfied that they were moving in the right direction.

They then traveled approximately ten miles before the convoy approached the town of Trevieres. This time, going through the center of the town, two civilians, armed with rifles that they held casually pointing toward the ground, approached the lead jeep. One of them held his hand up in the air and called out, "Halt!"

The jeep stopped, and the civilians, both men, approached the vehicle.

"Avez vous des papiers? [Do you have papers?]" one of them asked.

Connors and Kramer left the jeep to walk toward the civilians. As they did, on either side of the roadway, about twenty or thirty armed men and women appeared, all pointing weapons at them.

"Don't you recognize an old friend, mon cher Louis?" Paul asked.

"Jean Paul, c'est toi!" [Jean Paul, it is you!]" Louis called out in total amazement.

"Please, my good friend, speak English so that my lieutenant can understand you," Paul requested. "We are taking a convoy of supplies to the English troops over in the Caen area."

"You will likely run into a lot more resistance fighters along the way," said Louis. "Why don't you let me come with you, if that is all right with your officer?"

Connors thought about it and finally said, "It might not be such a bad idea, Kramer. Why don't you throw our friends some packs of cigs?"

Paul pulled four packs of Chesterfields out of the carton and handed them to Louis. He in turn called some of his fighters over to carefully distribute the contents of the packs, one cigarette at a time.

"I know these are not Gauloises or Wild Woodbines, but I think your buddies will enjoy them," Paul laughed.

Gauloises was a French brand of cigarettes that were too strong for Paul's taste. The Wild Woodbines were an English variety of smokes that just were too bland for him.

A man and woman approached the jeep. It was Le Flic and Pierette. Le Flic asked Paul, "Are you old enough to smoke cigarettes, my young friend?"

"I already feel like an old man," Paul answered, smiling.

Pierette gave one of her very rare smiles and nodded to Paul.

Connors looked at Paul and said, "To tell you the truth, I'd a lot rather have this good-looking gal come with us than this buddy of yours."

"I think she is a lot tougher than any of these men you see here—in fact, a lot tougher—but I think we should go with this guy Louis, and we ought to get going now, sir," Paul suggested.

Connors nodded in agreement and headed for the jeep with Paul and Louis in tow.

It turned out that it was a good move to have Louis come with them. They ran into several roadblocks manned by French Resistance forces. Sometimes it was the FFI and sometimes it was the Maquis. These groups, at least from Paul's observations, were always at odds with one another, sometimes to the point of approaching armed conflict. Louis, besides being a resourceful fighter, was a master at diplomacy, telling each group with as much sincerity as he could muster that he and the Americans with him were sympathetic to their side.

The long trip involved going through many checkpoints manned by heavily armed Americans and here Lieutenant Connors took over. The orders he carried with him left no doubt in anyone's mind about the validity of his mission or the top brass who endorsed it.

They finally reached a roadblock manned by Canadian soldiers, who greeted them in a warm, friendly manner after nonchalantly but carefully checking out their papers and the contents of the trucks. Realizing these supplies were being brought to help them, first the Canadians and then the British soldiers enthusiastically welcomed them. They were now in the British sector, and shortly thereafter they located the British supply center, where the trucks were to be unloaded. Paul and Lieutenant Connors stood by the jeep, waiting for all of the supplies to be taken off and stored in the depot.

A lieutenant accompanied by a sergeant major approached Paul and Jack. Both of them saluted Jack, who returned the salute. Paul saluted the British officer.

He extended his hand to Jack.

"My name is Middleton—Lieutenant Percival Middleton. And this chap is Sergeant Major Andrew Collingwood."

"Hi, I'm Lieutenant Jack Connors, and this is Corporal Paul Kramer," Jack replied.

"Pleased to meet you both, and thank you and your chaps for going through what must have been a challenging trip to get here. Your greatly needed supplies are being unloaded—hastily, I hope—by my men," Middleton said.

"Sir," Paul said, "I had a friend of mine with the British 50th Infantry Division. Would there be any chance that his unit is in this area?"

"They came in on Gold Beach," Sergeant Collingwood answered. "They, like us, have their hands full. These bloody Germans are fanatical and tough."

"Guess I'll have to wait and see my friend after the war, maybe," Paul answered wistfully, thinking about Bill Somersby.

"While we're at it, Sergeant, just a minute," Paul said, and he ran back to the jeep. He came back with what remained of the cartons of cigarettes, and Louis accompanied him.

Collingwood exclaimed, "Blimey, some genuine American smokes! These will be very welcome here."

Paul introduced Louis, who reached over for a pack of cigarettes asking, "My good friends and allies would not deny me the pleasure of sharing some smokes, would you?"

They all had a good laugh. Andrew looked at Paul and said, "What say, mate? How would you like to join us for a coop a tay?"

"What's he talking about, Kramer?" Connors asked.

"He wants us to have a cup of tea with him," Paul replied.

"I'm going to teach you Yanks and our French friend here how to brew up a proper pot a tay," Andrew said

"When we were in the middle of a real hot spot and bullets were flying all around, this chap Collingwood has calmly gone about brewing up some tea for his mates," Middleton observed.

Andrew came up with a large tin open on one end which he nearly filled with water. Then he placed the tin over an open fire and waited for the water come to a boil. Carefully, as if he were performing some kind of surgical procedure, he introduced tea leaves into the boiling water, steeping them one at a time until they were fully saturated with the boiling water, which now turned to a dark brown color. Middleton, who had disappeared for a few moments, rejoined the group, juggling as many canteen cups as he could handle.

"I apologize, chaps," he said, "the war has temporarily closed down our milk rations, so we will have to drink the tea black—or straight, as you Yanks call it."

"That's the way I like it," Paul responded.

They no sooner had squatted down on the ground in a circle than one of the British soldiers came running up.

"Jerry's trying to break through just south of us," he announced.

Middleton and Collingwood both got up. Percival calmly remarked, "You chaps enjoy the refreshments. We've got to go off and teach Jerry a nasty lesson. It's not proper to interrupt an Englishman when he is sitting down to take tea."

Paul, Louis, and Jack bade them a hasty good-bye and muttered their thanks for their refreshments. They then returned to the vehicles to check on the progress of the unloading process. It was practically finished, and in no time they were back in the jeep, with the convoy moving rapidly toward their original point of departure.

At the first roadblock they came to, they were waved to a halt by one of the MPs manning the outpost.

"Something wrong here, soldier?" Connors asked.

"We have a company of Germans led by a colonel who want to surrender only to an officer, Sir. We can't handle any prisoners here, Lieutenant. Can you take these guys in your trucks back to your own outfit?"

Jack looked at Paul and then over to Louis, who remarked eagerly, "Let me take these prisoners with me to my people, *mon lieutenant*. They will know what to do with them."

"I know, Louis, and I understand what these murderers have done to you and your countrymen. I just can't do that. I'll take his surrender and bring them back with us. We have enough armed MPs of our own to guard them in our convoy."

He turned to the MP manning the roadblock.

"Where is this colonel?" he asked.

A German colonel strode up to him haughtily.

"Are you an officer?" he demanded in perfect English.

Jack nodded.

"You are supposed to salute a superior officer." the colonel demanded.

"I don't see anything in you lousy murdering scum that makes you superior to anything. Besides, I have a member of the French Resistance with me who would just love to take you and your men back to his fighters," Jack replied.

"I'll have your impertinence reported," the colonel huffed, and his face turned very scarlet.

"Tell your men to put their weapons on the ground and to raise their arms high in the air," he ordered. "By the way, where is your weapon?"

The colonel pulled a Luger pistol out of his holster and held it butt first toward Jack.

Jack turned around to the convoy personnel, some of whom had debarked to see what the delay was. He called out, "Are any of you men Jewish?"

Paul spoke up. "I am, sir."

"Then take this man's surrender and take his weapon, Paul."

The colonel turned apoplectic.

"Surrender to a common soldier, and what's worse, to a Jew?" he screamed.

Jack said, "Then I have no alternative but to turn you over to the French Resistance. They have been waiting a long time for payback."

The colonel fell silent and handed his weapon to Paul.

The firm look on Jack's face convinced the German that further argument was futile.

"What am I supposed to do with this weapon, lieutenant?" Paul asked. "I'm a medic."

"If you come up against their SS or any other murdering rats who make a habit of killing prisoners or wounded GIs on the battlefield, you'll know what to do with it," Jack replied. "Some of my buddies were shot after they surrendered, and I'll never forget that."

Paul, without any further objections, slipped the gun inside his belt.

The colonel stood there and then hesitantly asked, "Herr Lieutenant, Do you want me to get in the jeep with you?"

"No. You will go back to the first truck and ride in the back with some of your men."

"This is against the Geneva Convention! I'll report this to the International Red Cross!" The colonel thundered. "This is humiliating!"

Louis spoke up. "You rotten *Boche* pig! How many of my people have you tortured and murdered? They would gladly have been humiliated instead of being killed," Louis thundered. "My intelligence people, who are very good by the way, have reported about your murdering people by the millions in your concentration camps—Jews, and all the others who don't seem to fit in with your master race ideas. Wouldn't any of them have eagerly traded some embarrassment instead of being brutally tortured and murdered?"

Jack turned to the colonel and muttered tersely, "You'd better get your butt into the back of that truck, or I'll change my mind!"

The colonel then sullenly walked back to the first truck, muttering, "The story about concentration camps is just Jew propaganda."

He then got into the back of the first truck, where he snarled for his men to get out of the way until he was confronted by a burly MP who shoved a rifle barrel in his face and ordered him to get on the floor and shut up.

They then proceeded without further incident, stopping periodically for roadblock checks.

Paul asked, "Lieutenant, could we go back by way of my outfit, sir? I am sure that my colonel would like to question this colonel and his men or turn them over to counterintelligence. Maybe they can supply some useful information."

Jack answered, "I think that is a good idea. A truck depot is no place to unload some unexpected prisoners."

They stopped the convoy some time before they returned to battalion headquarters to let Louis off.

"Thanks, buddy," Paul said to him, shaking his hand.

"You have been a great help to us, soldier, and I'm calling you a soldier because you deserve that honor," Jack said to Louis. "You are a brave soldier of France."

Louis turned to the both of them with a broad smile on his face. "I'll never forget what you Americans have done to help liberate my *Belle France*."

He then turned, giving them a smart French Army salute, and was on his way.

The journey back seemed to be a lot quicker than when they started out.

When they arrived at battalion headquarters, Jack ordered the colonel off the truck. He and Paul escorted him into the front room, where their colonel was giving some papers to his battalion clerk.

The German colonel snapped to attention, clicking his heels and holding his right arm out stiffly.

"None of that Nazi crap," Colonel Macklin snapped angrily. He then stifled his revulsion for this prisoner and asked, "How come a high-ranking officer and armed soldiers voluntarily surrendered?"

"Das Krieg ist Kaput." [The war is finished.]," The German spluttered, adding in English, "I asked many times to be able to pull my men back to better lines of defense, and each time, I was given direct orders not to. It is insane to waste good men just because officers in the rear echelon decide to sacrifice us needlessly. It was inevitable that we would be wiped out to the last man. I asked for people who wanted to join me in surrender to come along. The others we have left behind to carry on this stupid war and be annihilated. Besides, we would rather surrender to you Amis or Brits than those rotten Russkies."

"Yeah," Colonel Macklin replied, "you and your pals would prefer to spend the rest of the war in a prisoner of war camp where you'll get a place to keep warm and be given three good meals a day. In fact, you'll eat a hell of a lot better than my men and I do." He then turned to Jack. "Lieutenant, order the rest of the prisoners off the trucks. My men will put them under guard while I send for counterintelligence people to interrogate them. In the meantime, I want to commend you for having the good sense to bring these prisoners here."

"It was Kramer's idea, sir, but I agreed with him," Jack answered. He came to attention and saluted Macklin, who returned the salute. He then left with the German colonel in tow.

Paul started to leave also, but Macklin called him back.

When Jack and the German were out of earshot, Colonel Macklin said, "I have big news for you. We have been attached to the Third Army and are waiting for orders at any time to move up to the lines. Get back to the aid station, and give them a hand in packing up their gear. And by the way, Kramer, you have done a good job. I've just got to keep you out of sight of these spooks when they come to get our prisoners."

Paul saluted him and spun around to get back to his duties as a medic. This war surely had made for some strange and crazy turns.

The entire medical detachment was busy frantically packing up their supplies and materials, and they welcomed Paul when he came into sight.

Tony was the first to remark, "Good to have you back, you character. Now give us a hand."

Captain Sheridan came over to shake Paul's hand. "Thanks, soldier. I appreciate your help."

Lieutenant Saffridi smiled and said, "Welcome back, Kramer."

The others either nodded or smiled at him.

"Rumors are flying fast and furious around here," Captain Sheridan said, "but the only thing I know is that we are going to be with the Third Army, whatever that means."

"It probably means that we have seen enough combat and are going to be sent back to England and tell them all war stories." Kurt suggested.

Lieutenant Saffridi laughed. "That's as good a latrine rumor as I've heard in a long time. But who knows; maybe that's true."

Red Evans laughed. "If that's believable to you, I have some swampland in Florida I can sell to you dirt cheap."

"That's all a lot of garbage," spouted Sergeant Woods. "I just got back from scouting out the location we are heading for in the vicinity of St. Lo. Our planes started bombing and plastering the Germans when the rotten weather let up a little bit. Some of the bombs hit our guys, who were farther forward than our people thought they were. Guess who came charging up first in a command car with the siren going off like a fire engine? None other than General George Patton!"

"I thought he was back in England," Captain Sheridan argued.

"It was none other than his nibs, the general, I swear; only he wasn't in his usual spit-and-polish uniform. He was wearing a single pistol in a shoulder holster, with no brightly polished helmet or uniform. He was yelling like a banshee how great it was to be back in the war. He is the new commanding officer of the Third Army, I heard some officers say, only it was supposed to be hush-hush."

"I'll bet it was a big boost in morale for the guys to see him," Paul offered.

"Are you kidding?" Woods asked. "He had a bigger cheering section than the Brooklyn Dodgers have at Ebbets Field. Everyone was yelling and screaming for him, and he just ate it up."

"Okay now. We don't want to keep our CO waiting, do we?" Captain Sheridan asked.

In short order, they finished the job and joined the rest of the battalion in a huge convoy that pulled out of their camp area and headed for St. Lo.

— 14 —

The convoy pulled into a staging area northwest of Saint Lo. The entire region was a madhouse of frenzied activity. Huge trucks hauling enormous trailers supporting tanks and tank destroyers were heading for the front lines just a short distance from them. Other trailers, heading to the rear, were filled with German prisoners of war who were packed together like sardines, glumly looking over the French countryside that they had been dominating for the past several years.

Several sergeants moved around to each truck in the battalion convoy, ordering the men to disembark and to match their individual shelter half with a buddy so that they could set up a pup tent. They were cautioned that they were on alert and had to be ready to move out at a moment's notice. The unit had rushed here headlong only to be told to wait. It was the same old army routine of hurry up and wait. But that was the way it had to be.

Colonel Macklin called a meeting of the battalion officers at a large pyramidal tent designated to serve as battalion headquarters. Captain Sheridan and Lieutenant Saffridi headed for the meeting, while the enlisted men in the medical company started to make themselves at home—temporarily, at least.

Paul reached into his barracks bag, which still retained the putrid odor of the chemically treated clothing each GI had been issued prior to embarking for Normandy. This was a precaution against the Germans using chemical weapons against the allies. When the higher-ranking officers determined that, because the German air force was so depleted, there was no likely chance of the Germans using such nasty things as mustard gas and other such life-threatening weapons, permission had been given to discard the gas masks as well as the smelly clothing. The soldiers happily complied. Paul had for a long time been using his gas mask bag to store Hershey bars and extra medical dressings and bandages. On the eve of D-day, the sight of a sky filled with Allied planes heading by the thousands in the direction of France convinced Paul, along with many others, that there was no way that the Germans could attempt to use poison gas.

Captain Sheridan returned to the trucks storing the medical detachment's gear and equipment. He gathered all of his men around and said, "This is it! The head honchos say that we are going to join an operation that could have the war won by Christmas!"

There was an understandable cluster of favorable comments from all of the GIs listening. As if to punctuate his remarks, the sky filled with Allied bombers and fighters, all heading in the direction of the German lines. A short time later, there was the sound of tremendous explosions coming from that area.

Captain Sheridan took a moment to look up at the planes and then went on. "At least that's what the brass thinks. General Bradley's forces have punched a hole into the German lines south of Saint Lo. General "Lightning Joe" Collins, with his armor, followed up and pushed through a penetration right at the peak of the opening that Bradley's units made. The Germans are scattering and trying to avoid being trapped. Meanwhile, a lot of them are surrendering on the spot. There is a latrine rumor that an entire division surrendered to a jeep carrying American war correspondents; but, that has still to be confirmed. General Bradley has made the Third Army operational under General Patton and is turning him loose."

"We are now attached to the Third Army and have to get our gear together and catch up with our Third Army spearheads. General Patton is tearing around the countryside, sometimes in a jeep and sometimes in a command car. Whatever vehicle he is using, he has it equipped with a siren and has the bloody thing going full blast all the time. That has to be a sight worth seeing. So pack up your gear, men, and return to your designated vehicle. We are moving to a forward area where we will be issued more supplies to renew our stocks of rations, medical supplies, ammo, and the like. We are ordered to get moving immediately, if not sooner, so let's move it!"

The medical detachment personnel eagerly followed Captain Sheridan's orders and scrambled to load their gear and equipment, and finally themselves, onto their trucks. They noted that the rest of the battalion was hustling to do the same. In no time the convoy was on the move again. After a relatively short trip, the convoy arrived at the scheduled destination, which was a very large field rimmed by trees and shrubs. Some sporadic firing was going on at the far end of the field, but apparently no one gave this much attention. The story circulating was that some of the infantry was still mopping up the few remaining holdout enemy forces in this spot.

The trucks spread out in a U formation, and the men started unloading their equipment. Just as the medical detachment was in the process of setting up a temporary aid station in a pyramidal tent, two two-and-a-half-ton trucks pulled in. They were not from their battalion; that was made obvious when the back flap of one vehicle opened up and it contained two Salvation Army people—a man and a woman, both middle-aged—who were trying to manipulate a huge steaming cauldron of coffee to the back of the tailgate. Some of the men rushed over to help these older people, who had to be in their midforties. A generous supply of donuts was also forthcoming, which also was happily greeted by the GIs.

"Help yourselves, boys," the woman called out with a warm smile on her face.

The second truck contained a field piano that looked like a miniature spinet, which required some work to get down from the back of the truck and onto the ground. Peering around the piano was a beautiful young lady who looked as if she were no more than sixteen years old. Bubba was the first to spot her, and he ran up to the tailgate of her truck, holding out his hands.

"Jess jump raht hyah, honey," he called out to her.

The young woman had long dark-blond hair that curled around her shoulders, giving her a delicate feminine look. Her beautiful smile lightened up the drab-looking countryside around them, which had been pockmarked by bombs and shells. She wore a pretty flowered silk dress that turned every man's thoughts to the girls back home.

"This is what we are fighting for," Tony called out.

She laughed and squealed to Bubba, "Here ah come, big boy."

She leaped off the tailgate and landed neatly in Bubba's outstretched arms.

"Y'all talk southern," Bubba exclaimed.

"That's because ah come from the South—and mahty proud of it too," she replied. "Ah'm from Tennessee, if that's what y'all call the South."

"That sure is, honey," Bubba replied. "Wal now, y'all sure are mah kind of gal." He spotted Colonel Macklin making his way up to them, and so he spun around, muttering, "Scuse me, ma'am," and gave the colonel a smart salute.

Addressing the colonel, the young lady said, "Mah name is

Dinah Shore, Colonel, suh, but ah would appreciate your calling me Dinah. And if y'all'l let me, ah'll sing some songs for you and your boys."

The colonel looked into her eyes and melted. He responded, "We are happy to have you here to entertain us, but I must point out that there has been some gunfire in this location, and it might be dangerous for you to be standing up here and singing for us."

"That there don't worry me one single bit, and if y'all will let the men spread out here in front of me, ah'll get to work," she answered. "There's just one thing ah would like to request, suh."

"Name it, Dinah," the colonel replied.

"Ah would like to have the enlisted men setting in the front and the officers in the rear, if that is all right with you, Colonel, darling," she answered.

Macklin turned beet red and, with a silly grin on his face, turned to face the sizeable group of gaping officers and enlisted men who had gathered around him and Dinah.

"You heard the girl," he ordered. "Get moving!"

In accordance with Dinah's request, the enlisted men sat down in the field directly in front of her and around her, while the officers took up positions behind them.

A short, skinny man in an army uniform, wearing a USO patch, managed to position the little piano, with the help of several GIs, right next to Dinah. He then produced a wooden barrel from the back of the truck that was to serve as his piano stool.

After positioning the barrel a comfortable position from the piano, he sat down and looked expectantly up at Dinah.

The man and woman with the Salvation Army moved quickly to serve all of the men coffee, donuts, and even napkins, which to Paul seemed the height of luxury. The coffee was delicious and totally foreign to the army version.

Dinah swirled around in her pretty party dress, and the

men were grateful that she had chosen to be dressed in civvies. She turned to her accompanist and gave him a brief nod, which signaled the start of the entertainment.

Much to the delight of her audience, she sang, "Dinah," "Yes My Darling Daughter," "Blues in the Night," "Shoo Fly Pie," "Buttons and Bows," "Dear Hearts and Gentle People," and "It's So Nice to Have a Man around the House." She exuded a happy type of optimism and genuine southern charm. When she finished the set, she put her hand over her mouth and flung it outwards, blowing a kiss to her delighted audience. All of the soldiers stood up whistling, clapping, whooping, hollering, and stamping their feet in enthusiastic appreciation. Strangely, the intermittent firing that had been going on before she started had come to an abrupt stop when she started to sing.

"Either our guys did a good job of mopping up, or maybe the Germans are enjoying her just as much as we are," observed Tony.

"Ahm gonna take a little break and the get back to mah singing before you know it," she promised.

Dinah chose to walk among the men, chatting with them about where they were from and asking if she could take an address or phone number to get in touch with a special person back home, saying she would contact them just as soon as she returned stateside. A number of the men took her up on her offer, and some time later on, there was many a surprised loved one of a GI who received a phone call or a very caring note from none other than Dinah Shore.

She approached Tony and Paul, who were sitting together in the second row of GIs. Her genuinely sincere smile was so compelling and gorgeous that she could easily have melted a rock with it.

"What's your name, soldier?" she asked, looking at Paul.

"Paul Kramer, ma'am, and I want to thank you for your

wonderful singing. I just want to know what a nice Jewish girl like you is doing in a place like this?" he replied.

She giggled and then said in a serious tone of voice, "Ahm jess delahted and honored to be here with you boys, and if ah kin bring a smidgen of happiness into your lives, even if it is for just a few moments, then I feel worthwhile."

Tony spoke up. "Like all of us, I'm just worried about your being up so close to the front lines."

"You sound like someone's mother." she observed.

"Call me an Italian mother," Tony laughed.

"Do you two boys want me to write to someone for you or call them when I get back?" she asked.

"There is one thing you can do for me," Paul replied, holding up a napkin. "Would you mind giving me an autograph, please?"

She laughed and took the napkin, holding it to her lips so as to leave a lipstick imprint on it.

"Do you want the autograph addressed to you, Paul?" she asked.

"If it's all the same to you, I would appreciate your signing it for my kid brother Jerry, who is also one of your devoted fans," Paul replied.

Dinah wrote on the napkin, "With love to Jerry from Dinah Shore."

She then turned to Tony and asked, "What can I do for you, soldier?"

"I hope the Good Lord will bless you and protect you for what you are doing here," he murmured.

"She leaned over and kissed the side of his face, saying, "Thank you, sweetheart, for those kind words."

She moved on to Kurt, who asked, "Is Dinah Shore your real name?"

"Why no," she responded. "I was born as Fannye Rose Shore.

When I was on a radio show in Nashville, my theme song was the Ethel Waters melody "Dinah." And so I changed my name to Dinah Shore."

When she was about halfway through the group of men, she stopped and returned to the piano and her accompanist.

"Ah want to explain to y'all that I sang on the radio before singing for Xavier Cugat as a guest vocalist. Then my big break happened when I became a regular on the Eddie Cantor radio show. And now, boys, it's time to get back to some more musical selections."

She then sang some more of her popular tunes of the time, including, "I'll Walk Alone," "Smoke Gets in Your Eyes," "Now I Know," and many others. When she completed this set, she went to the men she had not yet spoken to, and she continued until she had visited the very last person. She returned to her position by the piano to receive a tumultuous ovation that was even more enthusiastic than the previous one.

She announced sadly that it was time for her to leave. Many of the men clustered around the back of the truck, each of them clamoring for an opportunity to lift her back onto the tailgate. Bubba elbowed his way forward and insisted on being her knight in shining armor. As he was lifting her, she leaned over and kissed him on the side of his face. The piano, accompanist, and barrel followed her on board, and she turned to face all of the men, blowing a kiss to them. A few of the grizzled veterans and rookies unashamedly had tears in their eyes as they waved a loving farewell to her. They also fervently thanked the Salvation Army crew for their hospitality as well. The majority of the men looked on longingly as the truck carrying Dinah and her crew, along with the Salvation Army truck, made their way down the road, taking them back to the rear echelon.

The next morning, at daybreak, the battalion convoy moved

again and caught up with an infantry unit liberating a small town. The villagers streamed out of their houses holding flowers and bottles of wine.

"Vive Les Americains!" [Long live the Americans!]" they shouted and screamed hysterically.

People were dancing in the streets, and many were crying tears of joy and thanksgiving. The cruel occupation and oppression by the Nazi regime was over, and now they were free to get on with their lives in a normal fashion.

Colonel Macklin and his staff sent select units of the battalion out in the town to locate men and women loyal to the Free French. They would be helpful in organizing the town administrators, as well as identifying the Vichy people who had allied themselves with the Germans. In short order, the villagers determined who were to be their administrators, including the mayor, members of the police and fire departments, school personnel, and others. This was done so swiftly that some of the Americans felt that this had been planned a long time ago.

Now that the town was secured, the battalion moved on to the next area being cleared. Some of the farmhouses were spread out, and various men were assigned to check each one out in order to ensure that no holdout Germans were lurking around.

Paul went along with a group of men who were heading toward one particular farmhouse when suddenly they were attacked by mortar fire. A farmer who had been out plowing his fields got hit and dropped like a stone on to the ground. Paul raced to his side and saw that the Frenchman had a nasty scalp wound. As he tried to staunch the flow of blood and clean up the nasty looking gash, a girl about eighteen years old ran to their side. She saw the man lying on the ground and started to scream hysterically.

"Mon pere. Il is est mort! [My father. He is dead!]" she screamed.

Paul snapped without even looking her way, "Il n'est pas mort. Va't'en. Je suis occupe pour guerrir lui." [He's not dead. Scram! I am busy trying to heal him.]"

She kept wailing and moaning, rocking back and forth on her knees.

"What a giant pain in the neck you are!" he snarled.

Tony came up and asked, "You need any help, buddy?"

"I've put some sulfanilamide powder into the wound and attached a loose dressing because I'm afraid he might have a skull fracture," Paul replied. "See if you can get me a vehicle and get this guy evacuated to a hospital in the rear for some skull X-rays."

The girl, who had gotten control of herself, said to Paul in perfect English, "If you are going to send my father to a hospital, I am going with him."

"Like fun you are," Paul retorted. "We don't transport unwounded civilians in combat."

"You are now, *monsieur le soldat*, because I am not letting you take my father unless I go with him!" she snapped. "And if he dies, it will be your fault."

"Get off my back, lady, and go with him and don't bother me anymore," Paul replied with anger and frustration in his voice. "And don't call me *monsieur le soldat!* If you want to talk to me, call me Jean Paul."

Kurt and Tony pulled up in the battalion ambulance, which was the one-and-a-half-ton truck they used for this purpose. Both of them jumped out of the vehicle and helped Paul secure the man, who was starting to regain consciousness, to a stretcher. They then gently and carefully loaded him on to the back of the truck and secured the litter. The girl quickly jumped onto the back of the vehicle and snapped at Paul, "If you ever talk to me again, my name is Claudette." She looked at Paul with venom in her eyes.

"What's this?" Kurt asked.

"Don't even argue with this nutcase," Paul advised. "Just let her go with her father while he is checked out."

"She may be a wacko," Tony noted, "but she sure is one good-looking broad."

For the first time, Paul looked at her. She was indeed a very pretty girl, in spite of her face being contorted with fear and worry about her father.

"I may have been a little rough on you, Claudette. I'm sure your dad will be okay," Paul ventured.

She looked up from her father momentarily and said, "I forgot to thank you for treating him."

Tony called out from the front of the truck, "Enough of this talk; we're taking off!"

He put the truck in gear, and the vehicle moved off.

Later that afternoon, Paul saw Tony and Kurt pull up, and he ambled over to them, asking, "What happened?"

"They X-rayed him and checked him over good. He just got a big smack in the head from a piece of shrapnel, and an ugly scalp wound to go with it," Tony explained.

"The doctors said that whoever took care of him did a good job," Kurt offered.

"The doctors said that aside from having a concussion, a giant headache for a few days, and being a little dizzy for a while, he will be as good as new soon," Tony said. "We dropped him and his feisty daughter over at his place and just got back." He sighed wistfully. "She sure is one great looker, though."

Paul, relieved that the man was recovering, went on with his work. There were many scattered homes and farms in the area. For the next several days, the men of the battalion were intensely occupied with their task of making sure that the entire area was cleared of enemy soldiers. As they swung back in a huge semicircle, Paul thought that the surroundings looked familiar.

A familiar voice called out to him, "Monsiuer Jean Paul. Mon pere. Il va bien!" [Mr. Jean Paul, my father is doing well!]". It was Claudette, but this time she was calling out in a more subdued, pleasant voice. She went on to say, "I never got a chance to thank you and your friends for what you did to help my father. Besides, my mother and father both want to thank you. Please come back to the house with me now so that they can express their thanks."

"Sorry, young lady," Paul murmured, "we are kind of tied up right now."

"Then come for dinner tonight, and please bring your two friends who took us to the hospital," she pleaded. "Our place is right there." she pointed to a large farmhouse with a huge barn adjacent to it. "My father is much better now, and he gets around well, thanks to you Americans."

"I have to get permission from my commanding officer," Paul explained. "I can't promise you, but if we can make it, we will come over. What time do you want us there?"

"We eat dinner late, generally between seven and eight o'clock. Whatever time you get there will be fine with us."

When Paul returned to the battalion aid station, he related his story to Captain Sheridan, who smiled, commenting, "It will be a good break from those C rations, and especially the K rations, for you three. We are enjoying a temporary lull with the number of wounded we have. Go tell your buddies, and enjoy yourselves, but try to bring us back a taste of something good. If you go, it will only be right if you bring them something. Don't bring a French farmer wine. I am sure he has that over his head, and besides, where would we find any wine? Go down to the mess sergeant and ask him if you can moonlight requisition some goodies, like some meat, condensed milk, and bread. Maybe a few of your candy bars will make a hit too."

Tony and Kurt were never happier.

Kurt asked, "You going to part with some of your candy bars?"

"I guess I have to," Paul replied. "Let's head for the mess tent and see what we can scrounge up."

The mess sergeant said, "I'd better stay on the good side of you medics. Never can tell when I will need one. Let's see that we can part with."

He loaded Tony, Paul, and Kurt up with some food essentials that he felt were in good supply.

The trio, struggling with their burdens, made their way past a couple of heckling guards at the perimeter.

"Do you call that lend-lease, soldier?" one of them hooted.

Tony snarled something back that was unintelligible.

At long last they completed the relatively short journey to their destination. Paul knocked on the door hesitantly. The aroma of delicious cooking and baking pastries assaulted their nostrils even through the closed door.

"I'm drooling already," Paul noted.

A perspiring gray-haired, heavyset middle-aged woman opened the door expectantly. She looked at them with tears in her eyes and, without saying a word, grabbed each of them in turn and kissed them on both cheeks.

"Merci, merci, merci, mille fois [thank you, thank you, thank you a thousand times]," she murmured, and she started to weep out of happiness.

"This is my mother, Pierette Langevin," Claudette offered.

Paul put his bundles down on a table in the hall, followed by Tony and Kurt. Mme. Langevin peered at each article they had brought, and again, sighing with gratitude, she hugged them. She was like a child discovering toys on Christmas morning.

"Encore, merci, milles fois pour tous les choses que vous avez apportez ici. Mais, ce n'etait pas necessaire. Vous Americains sont tous tres gentils et tres genereux. [Again, thank you a thousand times for the things you have brought here. But it was not necessary. You Americans are all very nice and very generous.]"

"Madame, nous sont tres heureux d'avoir l'opportunite d'etre ici avec vous, [Madame, we are very happy to have the opportunity of being here with you]," Paul replied, a bit flustered.

Claudette stepped forward and ushered the men into the kitchen, where the compelling aroma of the food and pastries was even stronger.

She said, "Gentlemen, please follow me into our *Salle a Manger* [dining room]." She nodded to their former patient, who was still wearing a bandage around his head, saying, Of course you remember my father, Henri Langevin."

The man came forward and hugged each of them and shook their hands vigorously.

"It seems to me that he is all better, judging from his grip," Tony noted.

Henri said emotionally, "Vous Americians. Vous avez sauvez nous pendant la premier guerre and maintentant vous etes ici encore un fois pour aidez dans la liberation de notre belle France. Merci monsieurs. [You Americans. You saved us during the First World War and now you are here in help in the liberation of our beautiful France. Thank you, gentlemen.]"

A cute girl who had to be no more than about twelve years old peered out from the side of Claudette, who glanced down at her and said, "This is my little sister, Solange. Like my parents, she understands English but does not speak it too well. I am going to interpret for all of you, even though you, Jean Paul, can speak French fluently. I also notice that Kurt here speaks French well, although it is with a noticeable German accent. To make life easier on everyone, I will serve as interpreter."

"That's all right with us, and thanks for the compliment," Paul responded.

The table was set up beautifully, with sparkling glasses, gleaming silverware, and two large bottles of wine at each end of the table.

"Then let's sit right down and get busy eating," Claudette urged.

The boys needed no further invitation, and as soon as they were seated, Mme. Langevin entered from her kitchen, carrying several steaming bowls of onion soup topped with cheese and some kind of pastry. Paul inhaled the appetizing aroma of the soup and hunched down low over the bowl so as not to miss a single drop. He looked sideways at Kurt and Tony, who were doing the very same thing, and chuckled to himself.

"Why do you laugh, Jean Paul?" Claudette asked.

"Because this is so incredibly delicious, my friends and I don't want to miss even a precious drop," he replied.

Claudette translated, and her parents and sister laughed appreciatively.

It started to get very warm in the room, and Tony and Kurt both asked Claudette for permission to take off their jackets. They were both wearing field jackets, which was similar to the common type of zipper jacket that was very popular back home.

Claudette insisted that they all feel right at home and asked, "Jean Paul, why don't you take your jacket off?"

Paul had been wearing fatigues that he had forgotten to change, being intensely focused on finding the right foods to bring with them. He started to unbutton the jacket and realized, much to his embarrassment, that his Luger pistol was still tucked into his waistband, under his fatigue jacket.

Flustered, he turned to Claudette and said, "I feel perfectly comfortable, and if you don't mind, I will keep it on."

"As you wish." She smiled and directed the conversation to life, as the boys could describe it, in the United States.

When the empty soup plates had been carried away by Claudette and Solange, Mme. Langevin returned with huge plates crammed with what looked like chicken and cheese-covered potatoes that apparently had been roasted.

The mouthwatering aroma emanating from the food actually got Paul to salivate. He took a large forkful of meat, chewed it, and swallowed it. He found himself torn between the appealing potatoes and the meat.

"Mme. Langevin. C'est Poulet is vraiment formidable. [Mme. Langevin, this chicken is truly terrific.]"

Claudette laughed. "That is not chicken, young man; that is rabbit!"

"Rabbit!" Paul exclaimed, horrified.

"Why, is there something wrong?" she asked anxiously.

"Why no, of course not," he expostulated. "I just think that is wildly delicious."

In his own mind, his thoughts were racing. Back home, a rabbit was a pet to be enjoyed and played with. Here it was a compelling offering at a dinner table. He forced those wicked thoughts out of his mind and put on a show of relaxed enjoyment.

Henri poured glasses of wine for everyone at the table.

He looked doubtfully over at Solange, who sipped happily away at the wine.

Claudette read his thoughts and said, "Forgive us. Here in France, we give wine to our children at an early age. We very much prefer it to water."

In spite of his guilty thoughts, Paul had no difficulty finishing the food on his plate. Tony and Kurt did justice to theirs as well.

Pierette returned with a huge bowl of salad, which she placed on the table and then proceeded to mix with a large wooden fork and ladle. As she did this, Solange poured a bottle of salad dressing onto the salad.

"Here," Claudette explained. "We generally serve the salad at the end of the main course rather than the beginning—which is what you Americans do, I believe."

Tony said, "Lady, with these fabulous dishes you gals are serving up, just keep them coming—in any order, but just please, keep them coming."

Everyone at the table got a good laugh out of that remark.

No sooner were the salad plates cleared away than the women returned with dishes of pastries topped with butter cream and whipped cream.

"This is a rum baba," Claudette explained. "You are all thin, and so you don't have to worry about getting fat when you eat it. I can't have any, because if I gain weight, I will get fired."

"What kind of a job is that, where you get fired for gaining weight?" Kurt asked.

"I am a dancer at the Folies Bergère in Paris. I came here for a brief vacation and was caught up in the invasion. My parents insist that I stay with them until Paris is liberated," Claudette explained. "If you boys ever get to Paris, I insist that you come to the Folies. Go to the box office and tell them that you are there to see Claudette Langevin and give them your names. I promise you, you will be given the best seats in the house."

"Wow!" Tony exclaimed. "That would really be something."

Paul sighed, "If we don't croak before then, I would love to go there."

"My fiancé is still with the French Foreign Legion. He has never seen me in this show. I hope he will get there too," Claudette murmured hopefully.

Mme. Langevin scolded the two girls, reminding them that they had forgotten some chores in the barn and at the chicken coop. They quickly left the room, and it fell to Paul to do the translating for Monsieur and Mme. Langevin, as well as for Tony.

Kurt could understand the gist of the conversation in French.

Suddenly they heard screaming coming from the outside of the house. Paul, Tony and Kurt, followed by the Langevins, rushed outside.

Two soldiers were outside the chicken coop, one holding Solange, and the other unsuccessfully trying to grab Claudette.

"What are you characters up to?" Tony asked.

"We just wanted to pick up a few eggs and a chicken or two," one of the soldiers answered in a surly voice.

"Take your hand off the girl or you'll pull back a bloody stump," Paul said through gritted teeth.

The man let go of her, complaining, "We just thought we would help ourselves to a little something. Don't see no harm in that."

"Claudette," Paul said softly, "why don't you take your sister and your parents back into the house."

She needed no further convincing and was so frightened she was shaking. She turned to Paul. "Ils sont bêtes. Viens avec nous dans la maison. [They are beastly. Come into the house with us.]"

"We'll be there in just a minute. You go on ahead," Kurt answered.

As soon as the door closed, Paul unbuttoned his jacket all the way, and as it opened, the butt of the Luger came into view.

"Now just a minute there. You guys ain't gonna give us no trouble, are you?" one of the men expostulated.

"What outfit you guys from?" Tony asked.

"We're war correspondents," one of the men answered. "Get out of our hair, or we'll write something bad about you. There's nothing wrong about taking some of this frog stuff."

"If I pull this gun, I'll give you both a new belly button, so get the hell out of here now!" Paul snarled.

The men looked expectantly at Tony and Kurt, one of them saying, "You going to let this character kill us?"

"You'd better get out of here while the going is good," Tony warned. "This guy enjoys knocking off people, and he hasn't killed anyone for a few hours. You two better get the hell out of here now, because he looks like he is starting to get nervous."

A look for fear and apprehension came over the two correspondents.

One of them looked at the other and said, "This guy's not kidding; let's get the hell out of here!"

Tony, Paul, and Kurt waited until the men were out of sight. Paul buttoned up his jacket, and they returned to the house.

As they returned to the dining room, Paul addressed the Langevins. "Dear Friends, please accept our profound apologies for the animals you saw outside. I hope and pray that no American solider would behave like that. They were not soldiers but people who write for newspapers, dressed in American uniforms. On the other hand, it could have been soldiers that acted like that also, but I promise you that if there are people like that, they are very few and far between. If these two had been soldiers, they would have been court-martialed."

"We wouldn't want anyone to receive severe punishment just for trying to take a few eggs or a chicken," Claudette remonstrated.

Paul answered, "I want you to translate this for me. These two people who frightened you are also Americans. And for that I apologize. I just want you and your sister and parents to know that the majority of us are decent God-fearing people. We come from multiple religious and racial backgrounds and grow up being taught to respect everyone. Please explain that to them, Claudette."

Tony and Paul walked over to Solange, Claudette, and their

parents to shake their hands solemnly while Kurt kissed the hands of each of the women.

The Langevins in turn embraced Paul, Tony, and Kurt.

"Now that that is over, please let us give you something to bring back with you," Claudette said.

Mme. Langevin had wrapped up several pastries, and she handed a package to each of the boys.

"My mother wants you boys to enjoy these souvenirs of your visit with us," Claudette explained.

Paul thought to himself, *These goodies are for Captain Sheridan, but I won't tell these people that. I don't want to hurt their feelings.*

As if reading Paul's thoughts, Tony commented, "We will enjoy these delicious reminders of our delicious visit with you wonderful people. We may even let some of our buddies watch us while we devour all this."

As he did this, he looked Paul straight in the eye so as to preclude any thoughts Paul might have had of sharing this treasure with anyone.

It was as if, for a brief and precious moment in time, the three of them had been taken out of the horror, agony, dirt, and grime of the fighting and enjoyed a peaceful, sublime, and pleasurable few moments with a very warm and welcoming French family.

—15—

The Germans were in headlong retreat for the most part, but in some instances they stopped and put up fierce resistance. The battalion was moving ahead slowly but surely when they came under mortar and shell attack. The shelling was so intense that Paul, who had been out in a field looking for casualties, jumped into a deep shell hole for cover. This was better than digging a foxhole. A short time later, a GI came tumbling down into the same hole, narrowly missing Paul. The soldier looked at Paul and then hunkered down to wait out the end of the attack. It seemed to go on endlessly, and finally the soldier looked at Paul and pulled out his prayer book.

"This'll probably help us more than anything else," he murmured hopefully.

"That's the truth, buddy," Paul replied.

After studying his prayer book for a while, he looked up at Paul and asked, "Aren't you going to do the same thing?"

Paul pulled his own prayer book out of his breast pocket, and as he did, the soldier asked, "Do you mind if I look at yours?"

Paul handed it over to him. This was one of two prayer books he had been issued by Chaplain Rose a long time ago in basic training. In combat he always kept this book in his left breast pocket. The front cover read "Prayer Book for Jews in the Armed

Forces of the United States." His second book, "Readings from the Holy Jewish Scriptures," was in his right breast pocket. He felt, somewhat foolishly, that these would help deflect a bullet aimed for his chest.

The GI took Paul's prayer book and skimmed through the pages. He said, "You know, these must have been copied from my own book of prayers."

"I think you've got it backward there, buddy, but that's all right. A lot of our prayers are the same," Paul responded.

The young man looked intensely at Paul's forehead.

"What's the matter?" Paul asked. "Do I have some dirt or mud on my forehead?" He pushed his helmet back slightly.

"You don't have any," the man said in an astonished voice.

"I don't have any what?" Paul asked in exasperation.

"You don't have any horns," the man answered, looking again at Paul's forehead incredulously.

"I don't have any horns?" Paul screamed out. "What in the hell is the matter with you? Are you some kind of nut?"

"I was brought up in a small town in Pennsylvania where there were no Jews. I was brought up believing that all Jews had horns," the man answered sheepishly.

"If I knew you any better," Paul replied acidly, "I would drop my pants and show you that I don't have a tail either."

The soldier handed Paul's prayer book back to him and said, "My name is Andrew Waldon. You'll have to forgive me, but that's the way I was raised. I guess we all pray in the same way."

Paul held up his prayer book and said, "I can't understand that in this modern day and age of 1944, people can still believe in such nonsense."

"Well, I sure got straightened out," Andrew replied.

The shelling died down and stopped altogether, and wordlessly, the two of them went on their separate ways, with Paul still shaking his head in disbelief.

When he returned to the battalion aid station, he thankfully found it intact, but Captain Sheridan was frantic.

"Colonel Macklin has been captured by a German patrol," he spluttered. "The battalion exec and some men are putting together a plan to free him, and they are looking for your buddy Schoenfeld."

"You mean Kurt?" Paul answered. "I think I saw a glimpse of him on my way here. I'll go out and get him for you."

Just at that moment, Kurt entered, followed by two heavily armed MPs, Corporal Evans, the colonel's clerk, and the new battalion exec., Major Grant. The last exec had been seriously wounded and sent off to the rear echelon.

Major Grant turned to Captain Sheridan. "I have to moonlight requisition this here enlisted man." He pointed to Kurt. "We have a plan to spring our colonel. A German patrol came across him while he was checking out the front lines and grabbed him up after killing his jeep driver."

Captain Sheridan turned to Kurt, asking, "Are you okay with this, Schoenfeld?"

Kurt responded, "I'll do anything to free our colonel, sir."

Grant went on. "The Germans, who are holding Colonel Macklin, I believe, are regular infantry and not SS. If they were SS, he would be dead already. Based on what the men who have gotten close to the location believe, he is still alive. They have him in a little barn about two miles from here. There are about eleven or twelve men posted as guards outside, and four or five inside. Now then, Schoenfeld, our intelligence friends who are always nearby"—he glanced at Kramer, who rolled his eyes upward—"have taken a high-ranking officer, a colonel in the 453rd Panzergrenadieren Regiment, prisoner. He claims he was sent out to gather intelligence on our operation's plans. We are using his uniform, complete with Iron Cross and other decorations, Luger, holster, and belt, along with a full magazine, for our good kraut, Schoenfeld, who is going to wear it. We are using the German colonel's orders, which are intact, for getting Schoenfeld into that barn. Anyone have any questions? Schoenfeld will make a convincing German officer, and he will bring one of our men in as his prisoner. We really want the man we designate as Schoenfeld's prisoner to be able to speak French and have Schoenfeld identify him as a Free French fighter. We also can fix up a GI uniform with a cross of Lorraine patch. That will get those krauts' attention."

Looking directly at Paul, he then asked, "Are you willing to volunteer to be Schoenfeld's French prisoner?"

"Yes, sir," Paul answered without hesitation.

Grant continued on. "Good then. The Germans are desperate to get intelligence about the plans of our units. We have plenty of our own men who want to go on this mission. Since the entire battalion has volunteered to a man, we have plenty of men. First we are going to take out the guards around the building, one by one. This has to be done quietly so that the Germans inside the barn won't hear anything. Then, Schoenfeld, from outside the barn, will pound on the door and order the Germans to let him in with his 'prisoner.' Schoenfeld will have his Luger drawn and pointed at Kramer. As soon as he enters the room where they have Colonel Macklin, Schoenfeld will move behind our Colonel and shoot any Germans standing near him. At that very moment, Kramer will drop to the floor, and our men on the outside, hearing the shooting, will knock the door down and charge in. Bubba insists on leading that charge."

Grant's aide produced the German uniform for Kurt, and Evans handed over an army-issued field jacket that had been slightly altered to include the cross of Lorraine patch.

When Kurt and Paul were fully dressed in their disguises, Grant ordered them out of the aid station, where it seemed the entire battalion was waiting for them. They spread out as they usually did in combat until they came to within sight of the target. The rest of the men faded into the woods in the vicinity of the structure, while Kurt grabbed Paul by the neck, drew his Luger pistol, pointing it at him loosely, and yelled out, "Raus! Raus! [Out! Out!]"

One of the German guards rushed over with his machine pistol pointed directly at Kurt's stomach.

"Achtung! Vas ist los? [Attention! What's going on?]"

The muzzle of the machine pistol never wavered until the soldier spotted the badges of rank on Kurt's uniform.

He lowered the muzzle of the gun, snapped to attention, and saluted Kurt smartly.

Kurt snapped out, "Ich habe eine Franzoizischen Gefeangene. [I have a French prisoner.]"

The soldier replied meekly, "Herr Oberst, Bitte, Komen zie mit. Bitte. [Colonel, please, come with me.]"

The guard waved off two more German soldiers, who, hearing the ruckus, had begun to approach. He then escorted Kurt and Paul to the door of the barn. He then hammered on the door and shouted out, "Achtung. Richter hier. Offend das Tur! [Attention. Richter here. Open the door!]"

The door opened just a crack, so that the inhabitant inside could identify the soldier along with Kurt and Paul.

Kurt entered the barn still dragging Paul by the neck. As he entered the room, he spotted Colonel Macklin in the center of the barn, bound to a chair and guarded by a German standing next to him. Colonel Macklin showed no sign of recognizing Kurt and Paul. Two more Germans were near the door.

Kurt repeated his earlier message. "Ich habe eine Franzoizischen Gefangene. [I have a French prisoner.]"

The soldier standing next to Macklin held his hand out to Kurt and asked, "Papieren, bitte? [Papers, please?]"

The two soldiers near the door held Paul back alongside them.

Kurt walked over behind Colonel Macklin, reached into his coat, produced the orders, and handed them over to the German guarding Colonel Macklin.

The soldier took the papers and read them intently. While he was deeply involved with his task, Kurt muttered, pulling his Luger out and pointing it at the man's forehead, "Das ist fur mein Mutter [That is for my mother]," and he shot him between the eyes.

Instantaneously, he swung the pistol around to the Germans at the door, who were both moving the muzzles of their weapons upward.

Paul did as he was told and dropped to the floor, lying as flat as he possibly could.

Kurt shot one German in the right ear and the other in the left eye. The effect was the same; they both dropped like stones.

"Das ist fur mein Vater, und das ist fur die ganz millionen du hast mord behegen. [That is for my Father, and that is for all of the millions you have murdered.]"

Colonel Macklin called out, "And that is retribution!"

At that moment, the door smashed open with Bubba in the lead, and the Americans poured into the room.

Grant helped Paul get to his feet, muttering, "Thank God for the training we all got from the British commandos and our own rangers! This went off without a hitch!"

Everyone crowded around Colonel Macklin. Bubba asked with concern, "Y'all okay, Cunnel?"

"Thanks, boys. I'm fine but a little confused. It looks like our entire outfit took a time-out from the war to come and set me free."

"Colonel, sir," Grant replied, "without you, sir, this bloody war wouldn't be the same to us."

Macklin looked over at Kurt and Paul, saying with a gleam in his eye. "Having Medics participate in this operation could make the International Red Cross scream bloody murder. What the hell, you all saved my neck, and I'm mighty grateful."

He looked at Paul with a smile on his face, adding,

"You seem to make a habit of being out of uniform, Kramer, but thanks again for risking your life for me and all of you here."

"It was our pleasure, sir," Paul replied, a bit embarrassed by the colonel's attention.

"Now let's get back to our outfit and get back into this war!" the colonel exclaimed.

Grant addressed Colonel Macklin. "Of course, sir, we'll have to put this on our morning report. I'll tone it down a bit so it won't look too dramatic."

A chicken captain up at division headquarters wanted to start an official inquiry as to how medics were involved in a firefight. His superior read the riot act to him and told him to withdraw his memorandum or face demotion and be shipped back to the States. The report of the battalion freeing Colonel Macklin made its way still higher up. It was reported that General Patton himself read about this with pride and exclaimed, "I would like to personally decorate every son of a b****h ——— in that outfit. If we had more combat troops like that, this glorious war would be over much quicker!"

A few days later, division headquarters wrote a letter of commendation to the entire battalion, and awarded them a Special Unit Citation. It was rumored that the general himself had ordered that the battalion be decorated.

Up at the front lines, a vital German counterattack was beaten back with severe losses to the enemy. The Germans started pulling back with many of their units in total disorder. General Patton had ordered one of his divisions to move toward Le Mans.

Paul's battalion had spread out into the countryside looking for Germans who might be lurking in some of the farmhouses on the outskirts of Le Mans.

Paul and Kurt had been tapped to interpret for the GIs as they came to each home in their search for enemy soldiers. Because the Germans frequently used the Red Cross brassards as a target, neither Kurt nor Paul wore them. Each of them, however, in violation of the Geneva Convention, carried a weapon. Paul positioned his Luger inside the belt of his pants, and Kurt had his in a holster on his belt. Since each of them wore a field jacket, both weapons were concealed.

No one questioned what the medics were doing. The Germans had established a set of ground rules when they enthusiastically and frequently murdered Allied prisoners, including French, British, Canadian, and, of course, American soldiers.

The tragedy of Oradour-sur-Glane, a small French village where the Germans had murdered every man, woman, and child, was still on Paul's mind as he approached a farmhouse in the company of a well-armed MP. Paul rapped on the front door, which opened very slightly, and an obviously frightened young woman peered out at him.

"S'il vous plait, ce n'est pas necessaire d'avoir peure, jeune femme. Nous sommes Americains [Please, young lady, it is not necessary to be afraid. We are Americans]," Paul spoke reassuringly.

She opened the door a little further and said in perfect English, "Forgive me. We have lived so long under threat of death from the Germans that I forgot my manners. My name is Christine DuMonde. Please enter my house."

Christine was a petite, very pretty blonde with deep blue eyes, and she appeared to be in her midthirties.

As Paul entered the hallway, two small children suddenly came out of an inside room, ran over to Christine, and, clinging to her knees, peered up at him fearfully. The small boy was about seven years old, and his younger sister was about five. They would not let go of their tight grip on the young woman's knees.

Paul automatically reached into the pocket of his field jacket and pulled out a Hershey bar. He held it out to them and said, "Je m'appele Jean Paul. Tu voudrais avoir de chocolat, cher petits gosses? [My names is Jean Paul. Would you dear little kids like some chocolate?]"

The both looked questioningly up at Christine. Paul noted that whereas Christine was very fair, the children were both dark complexioned. Christine smiled and nodded her assent, and they eagerly held their little hands out. Paul handed them the entire bar, looking at them quizzically.

Christine put her arms around the children protectively and explained. "Several years ago, some priests and nuns brought these children to us, as they had done countless numbers of times with other people in the neighborhood. They are Jewish, and the Germans were desperately anxious to find any of them so they could cart them off to their concentration camps to be gassed. If the Germans caught any of the clergy seeking shelter for these children, they shot them on the spot. Tragically, this happened all too often. But the priests and nuns kept doing this, and in the process, they saved many Jewish children from being murdered. The French families who took these children in did so at the risk of their own lives, which also were forfeit when they were discovered by the Germans. For the most part, we have kept

Raoul and Lillian, poor little children, hidden below a trap door in our *Lavabo* [bathroom]. Maybe you Americans can help us return them to their families, although we are willing to keep them with us as long as necessary."

Paul replied, "Please write their full names down for me, and I'll see what I can do."

A short time later, the Americans liberated Le Mans. Paul was among the GIs entering the city. As he neared the center of town, he noticed a small sign on the door of a nearby building that read, "H.I.A.S." This stood for "Hebrew Immigration Aid Society."

He knocked on the door and entered a small office where a gray-haired middle-aged woman sitting behind a desk looked up at him and smiled. She asked, "May I help you, monsieur?"

Paul reached into the inside of his shirt and pulled out the chain around his neck holding his Mezzuzah.

"Je suis Juif [I am Jewish]," he said softly. "Je m'appele Jean Paul. [My name is Jean Paul.]"

"Je comprends [I understand]," the woman replied, and then, in English, she went on. "My name is Sarah Schaffer, and I still cannot believe that I have made it through this war without the Germans finding me and sending me off to a concentration camp. Can I help you with anything?"

Paul related the story of how he had found Raoul and Lillian, and he handed her the piece of paper Christine had given him.

Sarah, again speaking in perfect English, said, "This has happened many times. Many of the brave Catholic clergy, at great risk to themselves, brought Jewish children out to French families and asked them to hide the children for the duration of this terrible war. These many brave French people enthusiastically took part in this dangerous work. Too often they, along with the priests and nuns in this operation who were caught by the Germans, were murdered. We will never forget the bravery and self-sacrifice of these courageous people. Our organization is now working very hard in many cases such as this to reunite these children with their families. We will do the best we can—rest assured. Until then, let me bid you *Shalom Aleichem*."

"Aleichem Shalom," Paul replied, and he went out the door, desperately hoping and praying that these children would be reunited with their loved ones.

As he stepped out onto the sidewalk, he nearly collided with another GI. He wore an MP brassard and a web belt to which was attached a holster containing a Colt .45 pistol. He was tall and dark complexioned, with aquiline features, and he looked at Paul quizzically, asking, "What kind of place is this? Is this where a Jewish person can get some help?"

"What kind of help do you need, soldier?" Paul replied.

"I have a major problem, and our chaplain is at another battalion, and headquarters can't seem to locate him," the soldier replied.

"Why don't you come in here and let us talk it over," Paul suggested.

The soldier wordlessly followed Paul into the little room he had just left.

Paul said to him, "Let me introduce you to Sarah Schaffer. She is in charge of this office."

"Hi, my name is Hyman Fishtine." The soldier held his hand out first to Sarah and then to Paul, adding, "but my friends call me Hy."

By way of explanation, Paul turned to Sarah and said, "This guy has a problem and can't seem to locate our Jewish chaplain."

Sarah smiled and said, "I am in no way near to being a chaplain, but please tell us your problem, and perhaps we can help you."

"I believe I am in your outfit," Hy said, turning to Paul. "I've seen you near our medical detachment. Aren't you one of our medics?"

"Sure I am," Paul responded. "But you must be new to our outfit."

"I just got here a month ago from a repple depple," Hy answered. "That's where it started. And I can't really call it a problem, since I met the most wonderful girl in my life here. It was a little before the breakout, and we were helping the infantry mop up, searching for stray Germans. We were checking out an area, and I heard a scream. A girl trying to lead a horse-drawn hay wagon was being attacked by a German. He wanted to take the horse and wagon away from her, and believe me, she was putting up a good fight. He tried to put an end to it by drawing his pistol and tried to get a bead on her.

"That's when I hopped over a small fence and tangled with him. This guy was as strong as a bull, so I pulled out my weapon and put a bullet into his leg. Boy, they say a forty-five will take a man down, and they sure have that straight. Some other GIs heard the shot and came running over. They took the German prisoner with them, and there I was, all alone with the most beautiful girl I have ever seen. Lucky for me, she spoke good enough English, so I understood that when she threw her arms around me and hugged and kissed me, thanking me for saving her life, it was just that. Her name is Chantal, and she is eighteen years old, just like me. She insisted on bringing me back to her home to meet her parents. Although I really wasn't supposed to, I went with her. If she had told me to jump, I would have asked her, 'How high?'

"Her mother and father were nice people up till the time her father asked me what church I belonged to. As soon as I told him I was Jewish, he spun around and walked out of the room. Her mother was very embarrassed and apologized, though I couldn't understand everything she said, since most of it was in French.

The 'sorry' part I got. Then I decided it was best to leave and started to walk out. Chantal grabbed my hand and insisted that I promise to see her again. She then laid a kiss on me that made me forget the war and all our troubles. I was hooked. I thought about her every waking minute of the day and night. I went to my CO and told him my story, and whenever he could, he gave me a little time off so I could visit her. I never went back into the house again, but I would wait for her to look out one of the windows, which she was always doing. When she spotted me, she would fly out the door, and we would spend a few precious minutes together holding hands and thinking and dreaming about what life would be like if we were together all the time."

Paul interjected, "How did you solve the problem of our being on the move?"

"Our company commander was very understanding and continued to let me take off whenever he could. In that way I got to see Chantal, even if it was just for a little bit of time."

Sarah asked, "Do you love this girl?"

"More than I know," Hy answered. "I never knew that being in love would put your mind in another dimension. I told my CO, Captain Butterfield, that I wanted to marry the girl. He answered that this was a very serious situation and insisted that I tell my story to Colonel Macklin."

"The colonel was very sympathetic and understanding up until the time he asked me how old I was. Then he tried a lecture on puppy love and all that garbage. He brought in the Jewish chaplain, who seemed to be on my side but insisted on writing a letter to my parents. The chaplain just received a letter back that my father announced that he is sitting shivah for me. He has officially declared me dead." And with that he started to sob.

Sarah put an arm around his shoulder to comfort him and said, "If you are determined to get married and your commanding officer will not grant you permission, I will find a town official to conduct a civil marriage ceremony for you and your young lady."

"It's not what I wanted," Hy muttered. "I wanted my parents' blessing for the one time in my life that I am positively sure about something. Now my father has declared me dead, and her father has told her that if she marries me, she must leave the house and never come back again! To make matters worse, our Jewish chaplain was ordered to report to another outfit."

Paul spoke up. "I'll try to locate the chaplain and talk to him. Maybe he can get somewheres with your girlfriend's father."

"I don't know about this," Hy answered. "I'm at the end of my rope."

The next morning, the battalion went back onto the front lines. At one minute past eight o'clock in the morning, Hy stepped on a land mine and was killed instantly.

A few days later, Paul got permission to go to Chantal's home to deliver the sad news.

Chantal came to the door, and Paul explained that he had met Hy and understood how deeply Hy felt about her. And then, as gently as he could, he explained that, tragically, Hy had been killed.

She moaned, fainted dead away, and collapsed onto the floor. Paul tried desperately to revive her and was joined by her frightened parents.

When at long last she regained consciousness, she glared at her father with unforgiving hatred in her eyes. She told him that he was to blame for her not being able to marry the love of her life. She said she would leave and her father and mother would never see her again.

Paul desperately tried to intercede, explaining in French that they had all been victims of the times. He begged Chantal not to carry out her threat, but her lips were firmly set in anger and fury, and there was no way he could change her mind.

Back at his outfit, the retreat of the Germans, thanks in large part to General Patton's brilliance as a combat commander, was turning into a rout. The terrible war ground on.

— 16 —

As Paul entered the large pyramidal tent that temporarily served as the battalion aid station, he was met by Captain Sheridan, who spoke tersely. "We—that is you, Schoenfeld, Lieutenant Saffridi, and myself—have been ordered to report to battalion headquarters immediately, if not sooner!"

"What's going on, sir?" Paul asked apprehensively.

"The colonel has called for a meeting of all battalion officers. Something important is brewing, and I guess we are going to be involved," Sheridan replied.

The foursome quickly made their way to battalion headquarters. This consisted of four large pyramidal tents that had been clustered together. The front area of the tent had a portable set of panels that delineated the office for the battalion clerk and the executive officer. A separate office was a functioning communications center. The main office, to which the group was directed, held the office of Colonel Macklin. As they entered, they all came to attention and saluted.

All of the company commanders were present, but besides them, Paul was astonished to see two familiar people standing alongside the desk of Colonel Macklin. They were out of his recent past—namely, Lieutenant Colonel Gerrior and Major Helms.

They had sent Paul on his well-remembered journey behind the German lines to work with the French Resistance.

"Now just a minute, Colonel, sir!" Captain Sheridan sputtered. "I'm not going to allow these spooks to take any of my men again!"

"Hush up there, Sheridan," Macklin soothed. "These people are here to fill us in on a big operation that our entire battalion is going to be in the middle of. First let me say that since we have landed in France, we have gone into each newly liberated town, city, and village to secure them, or at least to work with other military police units. Now we are going to help secure a city by the name of Paris. To spell out what is involved, I am going to turn this orientation session over to Colonel Gerrior and Major Helms. Now, this battle plan has been formulated and directed by Generals Eisenhower and Bradley, so pay careful attention!"

Colonel Gerrior made his way in front of Colonel Macklin's desk, commenting, "I am going to start from the beginning, so hang in there with me. This is going to take awhile."

"General LeClerc, along with General DeGaulle and other high-ranking French officers, are in command of the French Armed Forces on both sides of the front lines. Helms and I have been with General LeClerc's men behind the German lines. We were working closely with some officers on LeClerc's staff— namely a Major Roger Gallois and (Henri Tanguy aka) Colonel Rol. We were right in the heart of Paris, and it seemed that the French Resistance was already starting to fight the Germans, anticipating that we would liberate Paris soon. We were at a covered stadium for bicycle races called the Velodrome D'Hiver. One of the French Resistance fighters started to cry. He explained that he was Jewish. Here, in 1942, right after a visit by the infamous Adolph Eichmann, French policemen started rounding up about thirteen thousand French Jews, including some four thousand children."

"Even the Nazis were willing to spare the children, but the Vichy French police who participated in this event insisted on including the children. They were all transported to this stadium, and most of them knew what was in store for them. About one hundred committed suicide, and all of the rest were sent to death camps, where the vast majority were brutally murdered. But this soldier emphasized that in stark contrast, the French Resistance, along with the French civilians who worked closely with them, were responsible for saving countless lives of Allied pilots who parachuted to safety from planes that had been shot down. In addition to this, they had been very actively involved with hiding Jewish men, women, and children from the Nazis. Needless to say, when these same French civilians and Resistance fighters were caught in the midst of saving whoever they could, they were shot or hanged immediately by the Germans. This is part of the reason why many French people are so emotional about the situation in Paris."

"Now, the French Resistance, especially under the command of General LeClerc, is determined not to wait an instant longer and liberate their cherished city of Paris without any delay. What the Resistance people do not know, and what we have tried to explain, is that it was General Eisenhower's plan to bypass Paris temporarily and let Patton go on with his wild charge, which would at least take him and his armed forces to the Rhine River in a very short time. If vital supplies, and especially gasoline, are diverted to supply a battle force to enter Paris, the momentum of Patton's charge would be stopped cold."

"The French cannot fathom any reason for further delay. They want Paris freed as soon as possible, and all other plans, according to them, are of secondary importance. Another major headache is the fact that there are two major factions in the Resistance—namely the Communists and the Regular Resistance, who have frequently bucked up against each other, coming dangerously close to an armed showdown on many occasions."

Gerrior took a deep breath and then went on. "Another major element here is the Germans. Major General Dietrich von Choltitz was appointed to be the commander of the German Army in Paris by Adolph Hitler. Overheard by several French Resistance people, Choltitz told his staff that he had met with Hitler shortly after the unsuccessful assassination attempt on Hitler's life. Choltitz reported that Hitler had been bathed in perspiration, trembling all over, with saliva drooling out of his mouth. The desk on which Hitler was leaning shook with him as he screamed at Choltitz, 'You are going to Paris and will totally destroy it. There must be nothing left standing when the Wehrmacht leaves—no church, no artistic monuments—and you will cut off the city's water supply so that the ruined city will be prey to epidemics. Do you understand?'"

"Choltitz confessed that he became convinced then and there that Hitler was mad, and for the first time in his military career, he questioned his own determination to carry out an order. This feeling is what permitted him to later on arrange a truce with the French Resistance in the effort to avoid an all-out battle. Gallois reported the beginning of the uprising to Bradley's headquarters. This was conveyed to General Eisenhower, who concluded that there no alternative but to go into Paris in order to avoid a general massacre."

"General Eisenhower stated that his hand was forced and then decided to give General LeClerc the honor of leading the liberating Allied Forces into the city. Under his orders, General Bradley met with General LeClerc and gave him the momentous news."

Colonel Macklin said, "General Eisenhower has ordered the American Fourth Division to be brought in to support

General LeClerc's forces. We are temporarily assigned to the Fourth Division, but since we have some personnel already identified who are fluent in French"—he nodded at Paul and Kurt—"your battalion will proceed with General LeClerc's forces, now advancing on the city. We have a primary mission of dual importance: the first is to help secure Paris from any Germans or German sympathizers. The second is to keep the regular Free French Resistance and the Communist resistance groups from starting a new war."

He nodded to Paul and Kurt, adding, "Since you men speak French fluently, if you even get a hint of an imminent break or fight between the French Resistance forces, you will report this to me immediately. We have many more French-speaking GI's who have recently joined our outfit, and they will be working with you people."

The battalion wasted no time packing up their gear, and in a very short time, they reported to General LeClerc's Second Armored Division, which was scheduled to lead the advance.

Before the liberating Allied forces moved on Paris, brave French people hung the tricolor flag of France from their balconies. Many times, German patrols going by would open fire on these symbols of their avowed enemies. Some serious fighting broke out between German and Free French Forces, and a temporary truce was arranged by Swedish Consul General Nordling and General Dietrich von Choltitz. The truce broke down almost as soon as it was started.

The drive for Paris started just before dawn on August 23, just as a drowning downpour of rain soaked everyone. General Bradley had also taken the precaution of placing General Hodges in charge of overall supervision of the operation and had given direct control to V Corp commander General Gerow. General

DeGaulle left his headquarters at Le Mans and set up his control center on the doorstep of Paris— Château de Rambouillet.

On August 24, with good weather returning, General LeClerc sent out three columns: one going west, one going straight toward the center of Paris, and the other setting up to strike Paris from the south. As the units proceeded into the city of Paris itself, throngs of civilians and eager French Resistance fighters celebrated their cherished liberation. When the French civilians spotted the fleur-de-lis emblem on the tanks of the French Second Armored division and realized that French soldiers were leading the way, they went absolutely wild! People were alternately screaming and crying. They inundated the soldiers with wine and champagne. They kissed them and hugged them, and this enthusiasm carried on to the American units following up and supporting the French forces. People were taken out of hospitals so that they could see this magnificent sight. The elderly were carried out so that they, too, could view this incredible event. Babies and children were also held aloft to see a sight that they would never forget.

The wild rush of civilians actually, to the dismay of the French and American soldiers, slowed them down and interfered with their attempt to root out any remaining German soldiers. Intermittent fighting and shooting was going on until German tanks were taken out by American tanks. This was followed by two French officers going to General von Choltitz's headquarters, calling for his surrender. The general formally surrendered to Colonel Rol and to General LeClerc.

Following this, General DeGaulle made a very emotional speech in which he thundered, "Paris, Paris outraged, Paris broken, Paris martyred, but Paris liberated! Liberated by people, with the help of the whole of France; that is to say of the France which fights, the true France, eternal France."

It was announced by the joint Allied armed forces that a

victory parade would be held and that all military units who had participated in the liberation of Paris would participate.

Paul, as part of his military police battalion, found himself lined up with his buddies in their assigned position on the magnificent Champs Élysées. Since they were not in combat, some of the medics sheepishly put their red cross brassards on. The battalion was positioned behind a unit of the French Foreign Legion.

The crowd of spectators was enormous, and from somewhere in the crowd Paul heard a voice calling out, "Jean Paul, Jean Paul, I am here!"

A lot of hoots and whistles emerged from the admiring GIs as a beautiful girl emerged from the crowd and headed straight for Paul. It was Claudette—a face from out of his past.

"How is your father feeling now?" he asked. "I remember he had a nasty head wound that I patched up."

"Thanks to you, he is fine," she replied. "My fiancé is in the French Foreign Legion, and I thought he might be in this group of soldiers positioned in front of you. Sadly to say, he is not here, and so I will go on pining for my *petit Legionnaire*."

"What are you doing in Paris?" Paul asked.

"The Folies Bergère, although they have shut down for several months, contacted me and told me to report for rehearsals for a new show they are planning. Can you take a few moments to have an aperitif with me?" she asked with a winning smile.

At this moment, Tony, who had been standing alongside Paul and listening to this conversation, interjected, "I'll go with you, baby, if this lug is too dumb to enjoy your company."

Paul looked questioningly at Captain Sheridan.

"Go ahead, but catch up to us immediately, if not sooner," Sheridan said with a grin.

Tony yelled, "I guess that means me too," and needing no

further encouragement, he grabbed Claudette's hand and made his way to the broad sidewalk lining the boulevard, with Paul in close pursuit.

They ran down about one mile in advance of what they assumed would be the start of the parade and seated themselves at one of the tables of a sidewalk café.

Claudette ordered for the three of them, and when Paul reached into his wallet to pay the waiter, the man answered, "Cher Soldat Americain [Dear American soldier], for today, everything for our brave fighting men is, as you say, on the house."

Tony and Paul thanked the waiter enthusiastically but still insisted on giving him a tip, which he accepted reluctantly.

A few moments later, the parade started, and since the trio had moved up quite a bit, the crowd lining the parade route here was substantially thinner. As the legionnaires moved past, Claudette jumped to her feet and applauded and threw kisses to the soldiers. They answered her with a lot of enthusiastic shouts and cheers.

The military police battalion approached, following the legionnaire unit. Paul and Tony jumped up while Claudette continued with her enthusiastic cheers.

As the battalion moved forward and passed Paul, Tony, and Claudette, Colonel Macklin, in the lead called out, "Eyes right!"

The entire battalion, as one man, turned their eyes on the trio and saluted.

Paul and Tony enthusiastically returned the salute.

After the battalion passed by, Paul said, "We had better get going now and catch up with our outfit."

"I understand, Jean Paul. Please go ahead, but first I have to do something." She grabbed Paul by the arms and planted a kiss on each cheek.

Tony spluttered, "What am I, chopped liver?"

Claudette shrugged her shoulders and embraced Tony in the

same way, pleading, "Please, if you both can, come and see me at the Folies."

Tony grabbed Paul by the arm and pulled him on the run back toward their outfit. Finally they made it and rejoined the battalion.

When the parade was completed, Colonel Macklin kept the men in formation and marched them down a few streets to a group of buildings that had formerly served as a barracks, called a *Kaserne* by the Germans.

The colonel and his battalion officers directed each company as well as the medical detachment to their various assigned buildings, floors, and rooms. The previous occupants had apparently lived like pigs, and the GIs had to work very diligently to clean up the area and make it livable.

Captain Sheridan addressed his men. "We are being transferred back to our original outfit in the Third Army. The French Resistance, particularly, the FFI [French Forces of the Interior] and the French Army units, have done such a good job in securing the city, we can now move on. We have to wait for orders, and so we will camp out here until we get the word to take off. Hit the sack and try to get some rest, because the word is that we are going back up to the front lines."

The very next morning, before dawn broke, the battalion convoy moved out.

Even at that time there were still some revelers on the streets, celebrating their liberation.

As the trucks rolled by, people called out, "Vive L'Amerique! Vive LaFrance! Vive Le Liberation! [Long live America, Long live France, Long live the Liberation!]"

They soon left the outskirts of Paris and quickly caught up with the forward elements of General Patton's Third Army. They had just taken Verdun, and since another military police battalion was there to help secure the area, they moved on with the infantry and tank units, fighting their way into the center of Soissons.

Right at that spot, the leading tank halted while the tank commander checked his maps in order to orient himself. Just at that moment, a very pretty girl carrying a bottle of champagne jumped up onto the lead tank and rapped on the hatch. The commander opened the hatch and was shocked to see a lovely blonde young lady holding out the champagne to him and asking in perfect English, "How about a drink, soldier?"

He looked at her and then at his watch, answering solemnly, "Sorry, lady, it's not five o'clock yet."

Then he chuckled and took the proffered bottle.

Just at that time, the mayor of Soissons, along with a delegation, approached the tank column and attempted, while struggling in broken English, to convey that they wanted to address the unit commander.

Colonel Macklin was called to meet with this group and asked to bring a translator with him. The colonel, in turn, ordered Captain Sheridan to send Paul to help the colonel understand what the French people wanted to talk about.

The mayor, or at least the man who appeared to be the mayor, was wearing a huge gold chain about his neck held in place by a red, white, and blue ribbon to which was attached a massive gold medal. In order to avoid any confusion, he introduced himself as the mayor of Soissons. Standing next to him was a very attractive young woman, who Paul took to be the mayor's daughter. She put her hand on the mayor's arm, whispering to him, and so he paused in his painful efforts to speak fractured English.

She said, in perfect English, "My name is Chantal Marie Duval. I am the wife of this gentleman, Monsieur Carlos Henri Duval, the honorable mayor of Soissons. We bid you welcome to our city and thank you for freeing us from the cruel tyranny of the Nazi yoke."

The colonel gallantly took her hand and kissed it, saying, "We are privileged and honored to meet you, madame, and your husband, and this fine group of people with you."

The mayor expressed, by way of his wife, his wish to invite the colonel, the officers of his staff, and the translator (Paul) to a dinner that evening celebrating the liberation of Soissons.

Colonel Macklin replied that he was delighted and honored by the invitation, and that since the battalion would have to be in Soissons for a while to make certain there were no more German troops lurking about, they would be pleased to attend.

At this point, Paul spoke up, feeling uncomfortable about attending a function with all of the officers.

"Colonel, sir, since you seem to be getting along so well in communicating with these folks, may I be excused?"

Before the colonel could answer, Chantal interjected, "If you don't mind, monsieur, I think it would be a good idea for you to accompany the American group. Some of our French people sitting near you may want to talk to you as well, if you don't mind. By the way, what is your name?"

"I am called Jean Paul, Madame," Paul responded.

"Of course he doesn't mind, do you Kramer?" the colonel snorted.

"Yes, sir" was all Paul could come up with.

"Then that is all settled then," Chantal replied, smiling right at Paul. "We are meeting at our town hall right across the street. Please arrive about 8:00 p.m., and we will look forward to the pleasure of your company."

The battalion officers left to move into a former German Army barracks in the near vicinity. The men got busy unloading the trucks, and the medical detachment found themselves to be assigned to a very comfortable set of quarters. While they were offloading the vehicles carrying the medical detachment equipment, Tony and Kurt both playfully punched Paul.

"What kind of buddy gets a fancy dinner invitation and forgets about his pals?" Tony asked.

Kurt grumbled, "I can translate French just as good as you."

"I tried to get out of it myself," Paul argued lamely.

"Yeah, fat chance," Tony snapped. "Since you have such great pull with the colonel, how about wangling us an invite too?"

"I'll try," answered Paul, frustrated.

"Forget it," Kurt said. "We're just giving you a hard time."

"I'll probably be sitting next to some old geezer and fall asleep out of boredom," Paul replied.

As previously instructed, he reported to battalion headquarters later that day.

Colonel Macklin nodded to him, and Paul asked shyly, "Sir, is there any chance that two of my buddies could take my place since the mayor's wife speaks English so well and you won't need a translator?"

"Knock it off, Kramer," the colonel retorted. "Besides, it was the mayor's wife who asked you to attend, although I can't see why."

That ended the brief conversation, and Paul, as bidden, silently followed his commander out to the colonel's command car. A few other jeeps were lined up behind them, and the company commanders, including Captain Sheridan and Lieutenant Saffridi, boarded these vehicles.

The small convoy left when all were aboard and headed in the direction of the town hall. It took very little time for them to arrive.

A huge U-shaped table was set up in the middle of a large and ornate reception room. Mayor Carlos beckoned to the colonel to sit beside him at the head of the table.

Chantal walked over and took Paul by the arm, saying, "Now please don't be uncomfortable or shy, Jean Paul. If you don't mind, you are going to be sitting next to me." She smiled winningly.

He apprehensively accompanied Chantal to their assigned seats, feeling somewhat leery about sitting so close to the mayor and colonel.

A waiter poured some wine in Paul's glass and then waited, looking at him. Paul was puzzled.

"Take a little drink and then look at the waiter and nod," Chantal suggested.

He followed her instructions, and the waiter happily poured a little more wine into his glass and moved on. Paul's experience with wine had been limited to drinking the sweet Passover wine his zadie had made. Zadie had given generous quantities of his wine to neighbors, family, and friends alike. The wine Paul had just tasted was not sweet at all, but it was nevertheless delightful.

Mayor Carlos stood up, holding out his wine glass, saying in his broken English, "I wish to toast the brave American soldiers who have liberated our beloved Soissons."

Colonel Macklin responded with "We salute the brave men, women, and children of France, many of whom have fought and given their lives to free your country of the Nazi invaders."

The Americans and French then got busy with the job at hand of drinking the wine and eating a delicious meal.

"How old are you, Jean Paul?" Chantal asked.

"Nineteen," he answered.

"Are you engaged, or do you have any special girlfriend at home?"

"I date a few girls, but no one special as yet."

"What do you do on a date in America, Jean Paul?"

"We usually go—that is, a group of guys go—over to a girl's house where there are a bunch of her girlfriends. We play records, and some of us dance, and that is just about it."

"Have you had any chance to meet a nice French girl yet?"

"We've been on the move ever since we landed in Normandy. I did meet one very pretty girl, but she is engaged."

"Then you haven't even had the chance to hold a French girl's hand or even kiss her?"

"Tragically, not yet," Paul answered.

"Then if you want, Jean Paul, in the interest of Franco-American friendship, you may take me by the hand and kiss me if you like," she said as she took him by the hand.

Paul really wanted to impress Chantal with his knowledge of French slang. In Normandy, he had found that the slang expression for kiss was *"Baiser."*

He looked her in the eye and said solemnly, "Madame, it would be an infinite and exquisite pleasure to *Baiser Vous.*"

She quickly pulled her hand away and giggled.

Mayor Carlos stood up and asked loudly, "What did you say, soldier?"

The colonel jumped up and snarled at Paul, "If you said anything to insult this woman, I'll have you shot at sunrise!"

Paul, horrified, stood up and stammered, "Madame, if I said anything offensive, I deeply and humbly apologize."

The entire group of French men and women in attendance burst into laughter. Mayor Carlos stepped out from behind his chair and walked over to Paul, smiling and laughing. "Monsieur, I congratulate you on your superb taste."

Colonel Macklin moved next to Paul and growled, "Tell me what you said, Kramer!"

"My dear Colonel," Chantal interjected, "Jean Paul has made an understandable error in interpreting his slang expressions. In Normandy, the slang word for 'kiss' is indeed 'Baiser.' Here in Soissons, the term means 'to make love.' He did no wrong, and we French are, if you will permit, a bit more broad-minded than you

Americans, and we take no offense in an innocent mistake such as this. Please, dear Colonel, do not be offended or angry with him."

"How can I refuse such a beautiful lady?" the colonel gallantly replied. He spun around and went back to his seat.

Paul was mortified nonetheless, and Chantal sensed it.

She diplomatically changed the subject, and everything went on as if nothing had happened. From that time on, however, Paul would be forever branded as the soldier who had propositioned the mayor's wife.

When Paul and his companions returned to their barracks, there was big news.

The railroad marshalling yards on the outskirts of Soissons were to be used as a supply depot principally for ammunition and fuel. From there, Red Ball Express drivers would unload this hazardous material from the boxcars and onto their trucks and deliver the cargo right up to the front lines. Some MPs from the battalion had already been ordered to patrol the railroad yards, while others were still working at securing the town.

The next morning was clear and bright, and sick call did not take very long. It consisted principally of a few GIs who had head colds. The treatment for this was routine—two aspirin every four hours and bed rest. Those GIs who had coughs were given elixir of terpin hydrate with codeine. Understandably, many of the men claimed they had a cough just to enjoy the alcohol-like results of drinking this great syrup.

Following sick call, several of the medics stepped outside to enjoy the sunshine.

At that very instant, what looked like a Piper Cub airplane flew very low over the town, and the German markings on the wings were evident. It dipped even lower and then went straight for the railroad yards. Not a shot was fired.

Tony yelled, "Why doesn't someone throw a rock at it?"

His call was unheeded. The plane tilted to one side, and the pilot threw a stick of incendiary bombs out of the window. This cluster landed right near one of the boxcars, which quickly started to burn. He dropped a few more, and wherever they landed, they ignited into a fierce ball of flames that immediately attached itself to the nearest boxcar. In no time, the entire railroad yard was a mass of flames, and then the boxcars started exploding, one at a time. In a few instances, several blew up together.

A messenger from battalion headquarters rushed into the dispensary. "We got most of our men out of there," he said, almost out of breath, "but two of our guys are in the basement of the terminal building, and there is no way they will come out. Can some of you medics help us with them? You'd better bring a flashlight with you. The cellar where they are holed up is pitch black."

Paul and Kurt stepped forward. Kurt grabbed a flashlight and attached it to his belt. They looked at each other wordlessly and proceeded at a run toward the railroad station.

Each time a railroad car, or a cluster of them, blew up in a massive explosion, the very ground shook as if an earthquake were occurring. It was hard for them to maintain their footing.

Just outside of the terminal stood a long line of two-and-a-half-ton trucks. It was apparently a group from the Red Ball Express. Men were running frantically to the railroad cars that had not yet caught fire or exploded and were offloading the supplies and equipment, including explosives, ammunition, and gasoline. Paul thought briefly, *Could Manny be here?* but he was pulled back to the present moment by Kurt, who yanked at his arm, pointing to the station itself.

The scene could have been lifted from a depiction of what hell looks like. Massive explosions and plumes of fire and smoke inundated the entire area. The main building had been destroyed, and just the shattered shell of a few walls remained.

In the heavy smoke, it was difficult to find the entrance to the station, and it was still more difficult to find the opening to the basement. After a few wrong attempts, they finally located the concrete stairs haltingly descending into the dark basement. Kurt unhooked his flashlight from his belt and shone it around, catching in his beam one soldier, crouched in a corner, holding his hands over his head.

He ran over to the GI and tried to get the man to stand up, but the poor soldier was frozen with terror. Kurt clamped an armlock on him and literally dragged the shivering person to the foot of the stairs.

Paul took the flashlight from Kurt and searched the rest of the basement. Some wooden crates appeared to move, and he found the other soldier cowering under the crates, also understandably frozen with fear. No wonder the MPs had been unable to get these men out.

"How'd you like a cigarette, buddy?" Paul asked, holding out a pack of Chesterfields. A hand snaked out from under a crate, reaching for the smokes.

"No, come on out and I'll give you my whole pack," Paul suggested. Every time there was an explosion, more masonry ominously fell around them. The soldier then appeared, still holding his hand out. Paul waved the pack of cigarettes under the man's nose, and as he reached for it, Paul grabbed his arm and pulled him to the foot of the stairs. Kurt by now had almost reached the top of the flight, never relaxing his grip on the GI he was clutching.

More medics were waiting for them as they emerged from the basement and helped to move them quickly away from the station.

"You two weren't that crazy to go into that building that was blowing up?" a familiar voice asked. It was Emanuel Puryear. Paul and Manny just held each other tightly for a moment, neither being able to speak.

Finally, when he was able to bring himself to say something, Paul asked, "You're not one of those crazy guys unloading those burning trucks that keep blowing up?"

"That's my job, Paul," Manny answered soberly.

"And I just did my job too, buddy," Paul responded.

One of the sergeants alongside the trucks called out, "Let's go, Puryear!"

Manny turned to face Paul, saying, "You take care of yourself."

Paul answered, "Likewise, my good friend."

With that, Manny returned to his group, and Paul spun around to find Captain Sheridan standing next to him, his face red with anger, muttering, "Going into that building was one thing. Going down into that basement while the whole place was blowing up was really harebrained!"

"We didn't have a choice, sir, and besides, everything turned out all right," Kurt remonstrated.

"Meanwhile I was wondering if I would have to write letters to your families telling them that you were killed in action!" Sheridan argued back. "You thought you could get these people out without knowing how bad the situation really was or bothering to see how bad it was!"

"I know, sir, but there didn't seem to be any time for thinking about it when we went after those men," Kurt replied.

Tony appeared next to the captain, muttering tersely, "I'll bet you guys are going to get a Section Eight."

Captain Sheridan then faced Kurt and Paul, sputtering, I'm putting you two in for a Bronze Star, although I should be taking this man's advice and recommending you two for a Section Eight."

"Thank you, sir." Paul and Kurt replied in unison.

"I already have cut the orders, and they are being sent out to division headquarters on one of our jeeps, which is also bringing back two broken typewriters for replacement.

A few hours later, the jeep moved out of the battalion headquarters area and onto the main street. Ten miles down the road, the jeep hit a land mine, not only killing the two occupants but totally destroying all of the contents of the vehicle as well.

—17—

Battalion headquarters received a general order from Supreme Headquarters Allied Expeditionary Force (SHAEF). Per directions from General Eisenhower, it stated that because of the approaching Jewish Holidays of Rosh Hashanah and Yom Kippur (the Jewish observation of the Jewish new year), all unit commanders would facilitate transportation of Jewish soldiers to a Jewish place of worship whenever possible. (The message listed a number of cities and towns where services would be held.)

The medical detachment, like all companies of the battalion, received a copy of this order. Paul read this with interest, noting that the city of Le Mans was listed. He longed to get back there and find out what had happened to the Jewish children they had found on the outskirts of Le Mans. He had reported this to the HIAS office that was just in the process of opening immediately after Le Mans was liberated.

What was the name of the woman I spoke to? He wondered. *I must be getting senile.* He laughed to himself. Then it came to him. She was Sarah Schaffer. He wondered whether or not she had been successful in relocating the children's family. He turned to Captain Sheridan, who quietly said, "I'm reading your thoughts, Kramer. Of course you can go to services."

"But sir, I don't want to go to just any place for services. I want to go to Le Mans," Paul said nervously.

"If Le Mans is on that list, it's fine with me. First things first, though. Colonel Macklin has sent out a memo to me ordering that you report to him right away. If this doesn't interfere with what he wants you for, I'm okay with it. So get going now!"

Paul reported to battalion headquarters, and as soon as he gave his name to the battalion clerk, he found himself ushered into Colonel Macklin's office. Macklin got up from his cluttered desk and came around to shake hands with him. Paul, already standing at attention, having saluted first, was a bit nonplussed at this informal gesture.

The colonel said, "At ease, Kramer. Have a seat. Smoke if you want."

Paul sat down and anxiously looked at the colonel, asking, "Is there a problem, sir?"

"There certainly is a major snafu. A trainload of supplies carrying mostly heavy winter weather gear for our front-line GIs has disappeared. In this warm weather we now have, it's hard to imagine that in just a few months we are going to be fighting an even tougher war in very cold winter weather. The train, carrying eight cars filled with winter weather gear, was checked into a major railroad yard in Paris. A few days later, the outfit that was supposed to receive these supplies complained that they hadn't received the shipment. CID [Criminal Investigation Department] has checked into it, and from what they can surmise, some pretty slick French black-marketers, likely working in cahoots with crooked GIs, stole these supplies. They're probably raking in a pretty penny—or, better stated, hundreds of thousands of dollars—on the black market."

"CID has sent a confidential memorandum to all unit commanders in this area, alerting them to this emergency. They are asking for help in sending a fluent French-speaking GI to help them zero in on these crooks. On account of what these rotten swindlers have done, many front-line GIs are going to freeze their collective asses off. This is a hush-hush operation and the person who volunteers"—at this point he chuckled—"will have to get security clearance from either the CIC or the CID. I know what you have already done, Kramer, and I am extremely grateful for your getting critical intelligence for us back in Normandy. You fill the bill on all counts. First, you speak French fluently; and second, you already have a high-priority clearance with CIC. Of course, you can say no, and I will respect that, unless CIC announces that they are unsuccessful in getting someone with those qualifications. Then I'll have to order you to go. CIC expects another train carrying critical front-line food and clothing supplies to arrive in Paris in about another ten days or two weeks. Maybe sooner. If you agree, I will alert Captain Sheridan of this, but I'm just telling him that you are on a special mission that is hush-hush. What do you have to say?"

Paul answered, "As a GI, I am ticked off and would like to get the bastards—excuse me, sir—who are ripping us off. I may be one of those poor soldiers up on the front lines freezing my butt off."

"I want to ask you a question, Colonel. I have already asked Captain Sheridan for permission to attend Jewish religious services, which start in a few days. If this interferes with your plans for me, sir, I will be happy to forget about it. The services I was hoping to get to in Le Mans to observe the Jewish New Year start in a couple of days. I wanted to check and see if a couple of Jewish kids I had found there hiding out with a French family had been reunited with their family."

"When does this holiday start, and how long is it?" Macklin asked.

Paul replied, "It starts in a couple of days, sir, and it is an eight-day holiday. In a grossly inaccurate interpretation from a not-too-religious Jew, it is the Jewish New Year. This ends with the most solemn day, called Yom Kippur, on which observant Jews fast for twenty-five hours. While interspersed with many different prayers, they confess their sins of omission and commission to God. Jewish people believe that this is the time when God decides who is to live and who is to die, and many other things, including the fact that their fate is sealed at that time by God's decision."

Macklin responded, "Like I said, the train is expected in ten days to two weeks or sooner. I can have orders cut sending you to Le Mans for the first day's service, and from there you will have to report to CID headquarters in Paris. Motor pools in all districts have vehicles being sent to Paris, so you should have no problems getting transportation there. I can't give you any more time, because it is not possible until we get a line on exactly when the train will arrive. If you agree to volunteer, I will contact CID and notify them to expect you, and I hope your efforts will be successful in nailing these crooked sons of bitches."

"Colonel, sir," Paul answered emotionally, "You and the other battalion officers, especially Captain Macklin, have consistently treated me and the rest of our men like we were members of your collective family. If I wasn't planning to go back to school after the war, I would re-up. I certainly will gladly volunteer for this job, sir."

"Then it's all settled," Macklin answered. "I'll have our battalion clerk cut orders to that effect and send word to Captain Sheridan. Now remember: this is highly confidential. You can't breathe a word of this to anyone! When you write your V-mail letters, be very careful not to mention what you are about to do."

Paul got up and saluted, saying, "Yes, sir, Colonel. Thank you, Colonel, sir!"

The colonel snapped back a salute wordlessly.

When Paul returned to the dispensary, Tony met him as he entered.

"What's going on, buddy?"

"The colonel just wanted me to explain what this Jewish New Year is all about," Paul replied.

Captain Sheridan said, "I just received word from Colonel Macklin, who called me on the field phone and briefed me. Your orders will be generated at battalion headquarters, giving you permission to get to Le Mans and attend services."

Kurt addressed Captain Sheridan, noting, "I'll be happy to stay right here in Soissons, if that's all right with you, sir."

Sheridan simply nodded, and he appeared to be in deep thought.

Tony said, "I want to convert just for this holiday, Captain."

"Knock it off there, soldier," Sheridan laughingly replied. He then added, "Kramer, when you receive your leave papers at battalion headquarters, go down to the motor pool and find out from them about getting a ride to Le Mans."

Paul waited impatiently until he couldn't stand it any longer and went back to battalion headquarters. The battalion clerk indicated that the orders weren't quite ready yet, and so he went outside for a brief period, paced nervously, and then reentered. The orders had been made up in multiple copies, a single copy of which he was to carry on his person. If he was stopped and asked for his papers, this would keep him out of a military police guardhouse.

Paul read the papers with interest. The wording was in typical army gobbledygook and gave no information other than that he was to be transferred temporarily to the army base in Le Mans. From there he was to report to the unit he had been directed to verbally by Colonel Macklin, in Paris. He immediately rushed down to the motor pool and asked the sergeant in charge if any trips were scheduled for the Le Mans vicinity.

"I've got a two and a half leaving in about an hour or so for Orleans. That is just about one hundred miles or so due east of Le Mans. We can drop you off at the motor pool there, and you should be able to hook up with a trip heading to Le Mans."

Bubba poked his nose around the entrance door and greeted Paul, asking, "How's mah favorite medic doin'?"

"I'm heading out to Orleans, I guess. How are you doing, my good buddy?"

"Ah'm gonna be on the same vehicle ah guess. Ah'm gonna pick up some new mimeograph equipment and supplies there, so ah suspect you and me are gonna be travelin' buddies," Bubba replied enthusiastically.

They both went their separate ways, each to pack up his own duffel bag of changes of clothes, shaving equipment, and some personal items. Paul still hoarded and maintained a supply of Hershey bars.

At the appointed time, Bubba and Paul both climbed onto the back of their designated truck, and in a short time they were on their way.

Bubba turned to Paul and asked, "What brings you to Orleans?"

"I'm just on the way to Le Mans, and I hope to pick up a ride from Orleans to Le Mans if I can," Paul answered.

"Good buddy, if y'all want to go to Le Mans, why don't ah convince this h'yre driver to do jiss that?"

"Thanks, Bubba, but I'll be just fine. I'm sure I won't have trouble getting a lift to Le Mans from Orleans."

The bouncing and rocking of the truck lulled Paul into a deep sleep. In what seemed to be no time, he was awakened by

Bubba shaking his shoulder and exclaiming, "Kramer, buddy, we's hyah!"

Paul opened his eyes and saw that they were indeed at a motor pool, presuming it was their destination in Orleans.

Bubba jumped off and started talking earnestly to a staff sergeant, who was likely in charge of the motor pool. He approached Paul, who was still sitting drowsily in the back of the truck, stating, "We have a truck scheduled to leave for Normandy by way of Le Mans in about an hour. You the one who wants to get to Le Mans?"

"Yes, Sergeant. Just put me in the right direction and I'll be aboard in no time," Paul answered eagerly.

The sergeant pointed to a truck parked alongside the one he was still occupying. "This vehicle leaves in about thirty minutes, so you can get off and stretch your legs for the trip, which should take about another couple of hours."

Bubba was already hard at work arranging for several heavy mimeograph machines and pieces of equipment to be loaded aboard his truck. He good-naturedly shrugged aside some struggling GIs attempting to load the heavy containers of equipment onto the back of the truck. Singlehandedly, he lifted a huge carton and eased it on to the tailgate.

The sergeant said, pointing to a tall, thin young man who had his head under the hood of the vehicle, "By the way, this is Corporal O'Malley, who is going to be driving your truck."

O'Malley, hearing his name, stepped away from the vehicle. He wiped his hands with a cloth he pulled from his back pocket and held his hand out to Paul. "Pleased to meet you, soldier. We may leave even earlier than the sergeant thinks if I can finish getting this beat-up old thing in running order."

Paul shook his hand, answering, "There's no emergency here, buddy, so take your time."

In what seemed a very short time, O'Malley slammed the hood shut and turned to Paul. "There's nothing like a little bit of American ingenuity to fix a stubborn engine."

The motor purred smoothly, and they were off and running.

Just two hours later on the dot, they pulled into the main square of Le Mans. Sergeant O'Malley bade Paul good-bye and was off, heading for his destination in Normandy.

Paul tried to remember where the HIAS office was and took a little time to get his bearings. Sure enough, it was still there, and after locating it without too much difficulty, he hesitantly approached the door and opened it.

Sarah Schaffer arose from behind her desk and greeted him cheerfully, "Why it's Paul Kramer, isn't it?"

"In the flesh. I want to wish you a *Goot Yontif* [good holiday]."

"L'Shonah tovah Tikosayvo [A beautiful holiday]," she replied. She then said sadly, "You must be here about the children."

"Yes," Paul answered anxiously.

"So far we haven't had any luck in locating either parent, but we are still searching," Sarah responded.

"I'm going to the services that the army has set up for us. Since it is Erev Rosh Hashanah [the evening of the start of Rosh Hashanah], I am planning to get to the services the army has arranged before sundown. Would you like to attend with me?" Paul asked.

Sarah answered, "The American forces have posted bulletins all over town inviting Jewish French civilians to participate. I would love to go. Just let me get this place straightened out a little bit. We don't plan to shut the office down just because of the holiday. We have too many lost and displaced people we are trying to help. Just say a little extra prayer for our efforts."

Paul waited patiently while Sarah put the office in order. When they left, she explained that the synagogue, or what remained of it, was a short distance away. For the past several weeks, the townspeople of Le Mans had watched the army come in and try to turn this structure once again into a house of worship. It was a major job of cleanup and restoration. When the Germans invaded the town, they stripped the building of any semblance of it being a religious domicile. The sacred scrolls of the Torah (scripture) were ripped and burned, along with prayer books and prayer shawls. The benches had been overturned, and some enthusiastic Nazis had even tried to chisel out the Stars of David on the stone structure. They had given this job up when their destructive attention was focused in still other directions. The Germans decided to use this place as a storage facility, and later on, toward the end of their occupation, they abandoned it in a state of total disrepair.

The structure was close to the town square, and Paul noted that a crowd had already arrived and was milling around the front entrance, eager to participate in this momentous event. Some of the people there were French civilians, like Sarah, who miraculously had survived the horrible nightmare of German occupation, persecution, and organized murder. As Paul and Sarah entered the temple, they were met at the door by three soldiers. One held out a yarmulke to Paul. He thanked the man but declined the offer, preferring to wear his army cap. A second GI offered a tallith (prayer shawl), which Paul accepted, murmuring a word of thanks. The other soldier handed Sarah and Paul each a *Mahzor* (A prayer book designated for the observation of Rosh Hashanah and Yom Kippur). Sarah pulled a scarf from her pocket and put it on.

Some of the benches that had been salvageable were in place, interspersed with an odd assortment of metal and wooden chairs. By mutual consent they chose a pair of empty chairs on an aisle near the back of the synagogue. They noted that a makeshift bimah [a raised platform in a synagogue from which the Torah is read] had been set up in the middle of the room. Two soldiers stepped onto the bimah. One was a sergeant, and the other, wearing captain's bars and a chaplain's insignia, prepared to start the service.

The sergeant, who was obviously the designated cantor, recited the opening psalm.

He signaled for the congregation to rise and chanted the words of the opening prayer. Everyone was then seated, and the rabbi delivered the first benediction. To Paul, the service was significantly beautiful and interestingly identical to the ones he had participated in back home as a youngster with his family. Although the service lasted an hour and a half, it seemed to end much too soon.

As they left, Sarah turned to Paul and asked, "What time do you plan to be here for the morning service?"

"I have to get back to my outfit," Paul lied, and instantly he felt guilty about not telling Sarah the truth, but he was honor bound to maintain secrecy about his mission assignment. He continued, "I'll do the best I can to get back for Yom Kippur Kol Nidre services."

He escorted her back to the HIAS office and shook her hand. She in turn kissed him on the cheek and said in a quiet voice, "Please God, may you come back safely."

Paul spun around and headed for a sign that pointed to the area motor pool. He had just begun to move when a military police jeep pulled up. One of the MPs said, "Soldier, let's take a look at your papers."

He pulled the orders he had received from Colonel Macklin and handed them over.

After reading the documents carefully, this same MP said, "You must be looking for transportation to get you to Paris."

"Yes, sergeant; I was trying to locate the motor pool," Paul answered.

"Jump in the back and we'll get your there pronto," the man answered.

In a matter of minutes, the jeep pulled into the motor pool area, which was a beehive of frenzied activity. Work lights were hung up all over the area, and so it was brightly illuminated. The MP located the lieutenant in charge of the facility and spoke to him briefly.

"I can get you to Paris, soldier," said the lieutenant. "We have a reconditioned command car that was requested by one of the brass in Paris. I'm just waiting for the driver to report, and you can go with him."

"Thank you, sir," Paul replied as he saluted.

"You're welcome, solider. Just remember not to salute any officers when you get into a combat area. It points them out to the German snipers as ready targets."

In a reasonably short time, the driver reported and Paul was on his way to Paris.

When the command car stopped at the checkpoint just outside of the city, Paul awakened. He had fallen asleep despite all the bouncing around of the vehicle on the rough road. The driver handed his papers over to one of the military police manning the post. After scanning the documents, he turned to Paul with his hand outstretched. Paul in turn gave the MP his orders.

"CID headquarters is just four miles down this main street. It is plainly marked," the soldier commented.

The driver let Paul off just in front of the CID Headquarters Building.

Two more military police were on guard in front, and once again Paul was asked for his papers. The man who took them looked at them carefully and said, "You have to report to room

301, which is on the third floor. Captain Broome's office is where you are headed."

"Thanks," Paul replied, and he bounded up the stairs two at a time.

A clerk in a tiny, cramped waiting room, seated behind a small metal desk, greeted him and, after reading his papers, bade him to take one of the few seats.

About ten minutes later, a tall, thin commissioned officer opened an inner door, took Paul's papers from his clerk, and beckoned Paul to enter.

Paul walked into the room and came to attention, saluting.

The captain returned the salute and said, "My name is Broome—Captain Theodore Broome. We have been expecting you, and in fact, a few more GIs are supposed to show up today or tomorrow to complete our team. The train has not arrived yet, but I will fill you in on some of the details of your assignment. When it does arrive, you and the rest of the men in our special group will go into action."

"The American and French crooks are working in cahoots with each other. First they will bribe some of the French train men who operate the switch engines to unhook a selected number of the boxcars containing the goods they want to steal. Then they have the cars moved off to a rail siding, where they hire whoever they can find to unload the goods and pack them onto some waiting civilian trucks. They warn the men that if they talk about this, they are liable to be arrested for working this shady deal. We have made sure that every one of the people you are going to work with is fluent in French. Sometimes the GIs who are grabbed to unload the cargo are recruited by French railroad workers, most of whom only speak French. Other times it is the crooked GIs who are grabbing any spare soldiers in the area. They're pretty stupid about it, though, since a few of the GIs who hired on did, in fact, report this to the local town MPs. These dummies figured that whoever worked the job would be too scared to talk to any security people. When the train does come in, we will send you and your group down to the railroad yards and have you hang around there. It is very likely that these crooked characters will hire you, and once they do, we want you to proceed with their instructions to follow the cars that are being moved to the siding. As soon as they tell you to start to unload, light a cigarette, and that will be the signal for us to move in. Do you understand?"

Paul nodded affirmatively.

"Now, check with my company clerk, Sergeant Evans, and he will take you to your assigned barracks in the basement of this building. Evans will assign you to a bunk where you can stow your gear and will show you the location of our mess hall. He will also issue you a set of orders assigning you to this headquarters and giving you a four-hour pass. You can use this pass every day that we don't need you, starting today. Check with my office tomorrow morning at 0800 hours. If we don't have any word that the arrival of this train is due tomorrow, you can take off again for four hours. My clerk also has some papers for you to sign stating that you will never divulge what you are doing here, at least for the duration. See you tomorrow."

Paul saluted, spun around, and retreated to Sergeant Evans's office. He signed the papers he was handed without even bothering to read them. He then handed them back to Evans, who in turn gave Paul his new set of orders.

The basement was clean and surprisingly dry, and they entered a large room that contained twenty single bunks. Most of them were occupied, as evidenced by gear that was either on or at the foot of the bunk. Paul stowed his duffel bag at the foot of an empty bunk and then took off at a run. He wanted to get to the Folies Bergère, as he had faithfully promised Claudette. The

French civilians and gendarmes he stopped for directions were still enthralled with their newly delivered liberation. Most of the French enthusiastically gave him detailed instructions. Some even offered to go there with him. Others simply threw their arms around him and hugged him. Much to his embarrassment, he even got a few kisses thrown in for good measure.

He approached the box office and asked politely to see Mademoiselle Claudette. The middle-aged woman explained that the show was closed for rehearsal, but she reluctantly left her booth, closed and locked the door, and disappeared. She returned a short time later with a scrawny-looking short, bald older man. He had to be at least forty years old.

"Suivez moi [Follow me]," he called out, and he proceeded into the theater.

Paul ran after the little man, who scurried into the lobby and turned left. He opened a door at the end of the lobby and descended a flight of stairs with Paul right after him. They proceeded down a long corridor that Paul assumed ran the length of the theater and finally arrived at a set of stairs that opened up onto the stage. A number of skinny young women were running back and forth, most of them wearing very little clothing. Paul decided that if they had a little more meat on them, they would be really attractive. Claudette was at the end of the group, and she called out, "Jean Paul! Jean Paul! C'est Tu vraiment? [Is it really you?]"

"It's me okay," he uttered, "in the flesh."

"What brings you to Paris again? I thought your unit went back into combat."

"I can't get into that. I just wanted to take a minute and see how you're doing. Did you ever find your fiancé?"

"No," she replied, and she started to sob, "I haven't heard anything from him either."

"I'm sure you two will be reunited," Paul answered soothingly. "By the way, how are your parents?"

"They are fine, although they are unhappy with my job. They want me to come back home, and I want to establish my career. Maybe I can work up to a *Premiere Danseuse* [first dancer]," she responded.

Claudette turned to the little man nodding and said to Paul, "This is Charles, and he will escort you to the front row of the theater to watch our show. I have to go now because we are starting right away."

She ran off, and Charles gestured for Paul to follow him. This time he took him down a small set of steps that led directly into the theater, and although it was mostly full, there were still a few empty seats in the front row. Charles simply said, "Voila! [Here!]" and pointed to a seat that was about in the center of the first row.

Paul whispered, "Merci monsieur. [Thank you, sir.]"

Charles disappeared, and Paul sat down. The show started just a few moments later, and he was stunned. This had to be one of the most beautifully entertaining productions he had ever seen. It was unbelievable and totally enjoyable. In the final number, which culminated in a series of beautiful songs, great singing, and superb dancing, Claudette appeared in a line of girls dancing in the front row. As soon as the curtain fell, she jumped across the stairs and over to where Paul was sitting enthralled. She hugged him and said, "As soon as I finish changing out of my costume, I have an appointment with the French military prefect, who promised me he would try to help me get news of my darling legionnaire, Christophe."

Paul kissed her on the cheek, murmuring, "I hope you have success finding your *Cherie* [sweetheart]. I have to get back to my outfit. Send my best to your family. Au Revoir. [Until we meet again.]"

He turned and followed the slowly moving line of patrons up the aisle. As he did so, a GI slipped into the aisle from his seat, muttering, "You lucky dog. How in the heck did you get a girlfriend who works here? We've only been here a short time."

"She's not my girlfriend, soldier. She is engaged to another guy. I just happened to meet her back when we were in Normandy," Paul replied, and he continued moving out of the theatre. The GI gave him a look that spelled out his disbelief.

It took very little time to get back to CID headquarters. Paul headed directly for Captain Broome's office. He greeted Sergeant Evans in the outer office, whereupon Evans simply noted, "Captain Broome said to tell you when you showed up that there is no word on the new operation."

Paul then spun around and headed to his quarters to sack out.

It seemed he had been sleeping only a few minutes when Evans shook him by the shoulder, exclaiming, "Wake up, man! Captain Broome wants to see you right away."

Paul didn't even bother to wash. He just pulled on a pair of pants from his duffel bag, followed by a shirt he didn't even bother to button, and in his bare feet, he followed Evans up the stairs to Captain Broome's office.

There were several other soldiers already in the narrow, cramped office.

"We just got a report that train number 419 is on the way. What I want you to do is get down to the railroad yards now and scatter. When the train comes in, some or all of you will be approached by French or American railroad people to be hired on. They will offer you some money to help unload the cars they grab and warn you not to say anything."

One soldier interjected, "Captain, what if some of the guys hired tell the military police or other authorities? Doesn't that worry them?"

Broome replied, "These crooks are not concerned. All that can be found after the deed is done is some empty boxcars. They won't have anyone or anything they can put their hands on. I want to add that right now there is talk about the war being over by Christmas. If not, a lot of GIs are going to be in deep trouble. Many of the cars that have been robbed were loaded with heavy winter gear. French and Belgian weatherpeople inform us that their winters can be very cold and severe. An awful lot of soldiers are going to be suffering in the tough winter months that are expected. I notice some of you look like yardbirds—scruffy and sloppy. That's good. Don't get spruced up. The more you look like sad sacks, the better are your chances of being grabbed by these characters to do their dirty work for them."

"Captain, sir," Paul said, "Can I at least get my shoes on?"

"That's about it, soldier. Now move!"

A few minutes later, singly and in two's and three's, the men moved off toward the railroad yards.

Paul had no sooner arrived than someone called out to him, "Hey soldier, want to make a few extra bucks?"

"Sure," Paul replied. "I don't have to kill someone, do I?"

"Nothing like that," the man, who was a corporal, answered. He pointed to a train that had an engine number of 419. A switch engine was unhooking several cars and moving them off to a side track. "I want you to follow those cars that are being moved off. When they are stopped, someone will open the side doors, and you will get to work unloading the cargo. If you promise to keep your mouth shut, you'll get fifty bucks when you finish the job."

"How about a little more? I'm strapped, and I'm in a jam with some guys I owe money to," Paul answered.

"Sixty is as high as I'll go," the corporal answered.

"Done deal," Paul replied. "You sure I won't have trouble

finding you and getting my dough when the job is done? By the way, what do I call you?"

"My name is none of your business. I'll be standing right there while you unload, so trust me; you'll get paid."

Paul followed the slowly moving cars—four in all, he counted—as they were positioned on a siding. He moved up alongside the front car, which already had its doors open. Paul recognized some of the men he had seen in Captain Broome's office.

Two of them were already in the car, lifting crates and bringing them to the open door. As per his earlier instructions from Captain Broome, now that he was ready to begin work on unloading, he lit a cigarette. His colleagues on the boxcar and others standing near him were already smoking.

What looked like a hundred MPs rushed onto the scene, shouting, "Put your hands on your heads!"

Paul followed suit and meekly surrendered to the MPs that surrounded them. He noticed that the French and Americans who were involved with the robbery were being handcuffed and led away, including the corporal who had hired Paul. He and the men he had met at Captain Broome's office were singled out by Sergeant Evans, who was also wearing an MP brassard.

"I want these men to be questioned." Evans announced, and he motioned for them to move in a different direction. They were directed to board some jeeps and command cars.

Moments later, the convoy containing Paul and his coworkers, was sped off to Captain Broome's office.

Captain Broome, with a big smile on his face, reported, "We really hit the payload. We got not only the people working the railroad yards but also the French and American train directors. They in turn caved in and brought us to several high-ranking officers—a major and one lieutenant colonel—who were all in on this. We can't thank you enough, but we caution you not to divulge anything that happened, at least until the war is over. Your buddies are sure to ask about why you were gone, and you can make up any cockamamie story you want as long as it is not what really happened. Now report to Sergeant Evans, who will issue each of you traveling papers. In that way, you can get back to your respective outfits without any hassle from MPs who may stop you. By the way, in addition, Evans will give each of you a letter to use whenever necessary in order to expedite your return back to your home base. Basically what the letter says is that the bearer, with your name inserted, has successfully performed an outstanding task that is presently classified as highly confidential. You have rendered a most important service on behalf of your country as well as the US Army. The cooperation of the reader of this letter is requested to help and assist the bearer in his mission to return to his unit. The letter is signed by my commanding officer, Colonel Reid, and countersigned by me."

He turned to Paul and said, "Your letter is a little different. We understand that you want to return to Le Mans for religious services and then rejoin your battalion. Your letter covers that as well."

All Paul could do was murmur, "Thank you, sir." He was deeply touched.

"By the way," Broome added, "we have another soldier who wants to go to services in Le Mans with you. This is Private First Class Samuel Karp."

Paul turned to meet a PFC of average height and weight but with a shock of red hair. The man extended his hand to Paul, saying, "Sam Karp."

Paul shook the man's hand, uttering, "Paul Kramer."

Captain Broome instructed, "Follow Evans, who is now waiting for you in my outer office. He will take you all to our division motor pool and see what he can do to get you men transportation back to your destination. Thank you all again for a great job."

With that he turned to each GI and shook his hand in turn. They all moved out of the office and followed the sergeant out the door.

The motor pool commander was a first lieutenant who had obviously been briefed earlier by Captain Broome. He must have been, because he went out of this way to accommodate all of the men there. He had to do some scrambling to contact other motor pool units, but his efforts were successful. Paul and Sam were directed to a two-and-a-half-ton truck that backed up into the entrance of the motor pool garage. Each of them threw his duffel bag up over the tailgate and then clambered aboard.

The back of the truck was loaded with jerricans and spare tires, all apparently destined for the quartermaster depot at Le Mans.

"I wonder if we'll make Kol Nidre," Sam said.

Paul looked at his watch. "I think we'll just make it or even have some spare time for the afternoon service. He calculated that they might have sufficient time provided that they did not run into any unforeseen obstacles. Fortunately they made it just before the afternoon service ended. The shul was jam-packed. Paul looked around, hoping to spot Sarah. Suddenly he saw her familiar face, and standing next to her were the two little Jewish children. They were clinging to a young man in a French Army type of uniform who was wearing an FFI patch, showing that he was a member of the French Resistance. It was amazing! Paul could not believe it. Was this the children's father?

He flew to the side of Sarah, who grasped him by both arms and whispered, "Goot Yontif." Tears were streaming down from her eyes.

"Is it?" Paul couldn't finish, as he was overcome with emotion.

She nodded, and she whispered to the French soldier, who leaned around Sarah and grasped Paul's hands, speaking in broken English with a heavy French accent.

"Thank you, thank you, thank you. I cannot imagine being able to thank you enough and to give thanks to God for bringing me back together with my beloved children." He, too, was weeping out of sheer happiness.

Sarah whispered, "They are still trying to locate the mother, so far without any success."

Just then the cantor intoned the solemn words of Kol Nidre.

Paul was totally overcome with emotion, and tears blurred his vision, as the cantor sang, "Kol Nidre Vaysoray, vayacharay, [By the authority of the court on high]," and the solemn service continued.

Paul had trouble concentrating on his prayers as he kept giving thanks to God for reuniting these beautiful children with their father.

— 18 —

The division motor pool in Le Mans was a huge installation. Paul arrived there well after 8:30 p.m., and the place was bustling. All manner of trucks, jeeps, and other vehicles were constantly arriving, being repaired and reconditioned, and departing. A lieutenant, obviously one of the officers in charge of the motor pool, approached Paul, who came to attention and saluted. The officer studied the papers that Paul handed him and then said, "We'll have no problems getting you fixed up with something headed for Soissons. By the way, if you want, I can have my office cut you a travel voucher and you can use it on the French railway system that is just getting up and running. They now have trains going as far as Soissons and even a little beyond."

"If you don't mind, sir," Paul replied, "I would just as soon hitch a ride with one of your vehicles. I've got a gut feeling that I will get there quicker, and I want to rejoin my outfit as soon as I can."

"Can't you blame you there, soldier. I'll check with my dispatcher and find out when we will have something heading your way. Just wait here," the lieutenant answered.

Paul noted that row after row of army vehicles were alternately being jacked up, with mechanics sliding underneath and working diligently. Wheels were being taken off to be replaced by new ones, while various other pieces of equipment were being exchanged for apparently new ones.

The lieutenant said, "We may be able to accommodate you early in the morning. You notice we have a shop that's going twenty-four hours a day. Since our mechanics are working in eight-hour shifts around the clock, we have bunks down at the end of this room. By the way, do you have any gear with you?"

"I did leave my duffel bag outside of your dispatcher's office," Paul answered. "Is it okay to retrieve it, sir?"

"Go right ahead, and we will get you out of the sack as soon as this one-and-a-half-ton truck scheduled for Soissons is ready." He pointed at a truck that had been jacked up.

"Thank you, sir," Paul replied gratefully, and he ran off to first retrieve his gear and then find an empty cot. Once ensconced in the bunk, he fell asleep immediately.

He awakened eight hours later to multiple loud bangs and clangs. He opened one eye and saw auto mechanics busy at work on a variety of vehicles. He jumped out of his cot and ran down to the dispatcher's office. A three-stripe sergeant looked up at him and said, "I guess you're the guy heading for Soissons."

Paul sleepily nodded.

"You have to go next door to the latrine, where you can get cleaned up. Our mess hall is across the street."

"What about my truck that is going to Soissons?" Paul asked.

"We were supposed to get a part last night, but it never came in. You just have to wait it out. Hand this to the mess people when you're in for chow." The sergeant handed him a meal voucher.

"How long do you think I have to wait?" Paul asked.

"Never know," he replied, "but it will probably be soon."

As soon as Paul was finished cleaning up, he fished his mess kit out of his duffel bag and headed over to the mess hall. There he dined on watery powdered scrambled eggs, greasy home fries, and bacon that was dry and brittle. The coffee was undrinkable. He yearned for a real cup of good coffee and came to the realization that he would have to wait, like all the other GIs, for this terrible war to finish, allowing him to return home—that is, if he lived long enough.

When he returned, the sergeant nodded and said, "The part we needed came in while you were gone, and they are just finishing up installing it now. You should be ready to go in a couple of minutes."

It was more like a half an hour, but when the mechanic turned on the ignition, the motor purred smoothly.

"You'll have to ride in back, soldier," the sergeant noted. "We are sending along another one of our crew to help with the driving. He'll be up front."

Paul happily threw his duffel bag onto the back of the truck and jumped in, sitting down on one of the wooden benches on each side of the canvas-covered truck bed. In between the benches, most of the available space was filled with stenciled cartons of fatigues, combat boots, socks, underwear, and olive drab shirts and pants. There was hardly any space left for him, and no sooner was he settled down on the bench with his duffel bag tucked under his bench than the motor pool sergeant appeared and simply ordered, "Stow these somewhere."

Some GIs handed up several dozen jerricans that were apparently full, judging by their weight. Paul had difficulty finding room for them while reserving a tiny spot for himself. He carefully positioned the fuel cans as far from himself as he could, knowing all too well that a single bullet into one of them could turn the truck into a wild conflagration. He wanted to be able to have a chance of bailing out of the vehicle if this should occur.

The journey started out with a lurch out of the garage, and the driver leaned back and called out, "Sorry about that."

The truck took the main road out of Le Mans, and soon they were out in the beautiful countryside. There was a lot of military traffic on the narrow two-lane road lined by trees and ditches on either side. Some refugees still lined the sides of the road, carrying their few pitiful belongings or pushing carts that contained whatever they were able to salvage in this maelstrom of violence.

Paul tried to keep track of the towns that they went through, but he soon dozed off. Almost moments afterward, the GI sitting alongside the driver called out, "Hey there buddy, do you want a K ration or a C?"

Paul chose the K ration and opened up a can of cheese and bacon that he munched down, along with the crackers that came in the box as well. The bar of heavy concentrated chocolate he would save for later. The bouillon cubes he threw back into the box, along with the little packet that proclaimed he could make coffee with them. The soldier then handed him a canteen that had water in it that apparently came out of a chemically treated Lyster bag. The taste was horrible, but he was thirsty and managed a few swallows. The truck proceeded at a reasonable pace, although Paul wished it would go faster. About every four hours, the driver changed places with his assistant, and so their journey happily proceeded without delay.

Paul thought, *I could drive this truck, but then again, the army has its chicken regulations that require the driver to be licensed for whatever vehicle he wants to use. I have a Massachusetts driver's license, and that is it.*

Once again Paul dozed off, but he was awakened when the truck lurched and threw him off the seat. Luckily he was cushioned by his duffel bag and suffered only minor discomfort.

Their route took them through Margon and Chartres, north of Paris, and through Creil, and Compiegne. Finally, at long last, they pulled into Soissons. The truck driver followed Paul's directions and took him to the location of his 456th Military Police Battalion Headquarters. Paul slung his barracks bag over his shoulder, thanked both men, and swung around to enter the gates of the barracks. He suddenly stopped in shock. No longer was there a sign proclaiming that indeed this was the 456th. Instead, there was a sign replacing it that read, "322nd Military Police Battalion."

One of the two MPs guarding the entrance said, "What's the matter, soldier? You lost?"

"I guess that's right. When I left here, my outfit, the 456th MP Battalion, was here," Paul replied.

"Your outfit took off the day before yesterday and headed for Sedan. They left a couple of guys as a rear guard to pick up mail, orders, and whatever equipment was directed to them here. Let me see your papers first," one of the MPs said.

Paul handed him his papers and then followed his directions to the headquarters building. Sure enough, there was Sergeant Woods, sitting at a small table along with Sergeant Harrison.

Woods spoke first. "Well, well, our wandering GI has come home to roost only to find that his nest has moved away."

"What happened to our outfit, Sarge?" Paul asked. "I hear they went to Sedan."

"You got that right, Kramer," Sergeant Woods replied. "We are going to be here just one more day and then head up to Sedan. You want to bunk in with us and hitch a ride back to our outfit?"

Paul eagerly nodded and found out where he could store his duffel bag and get cleaned up.

The mess hall was serving C rations, but the cans of spaghetti and meatballs had been heated up so that they were edible and even somewhat tasty. Paul had heard a rumor that some of the C rations contained franks and beans, but he was disappointed to find that was not the case.

Woods walked into the mess hall, noted what food was

available, and said, "We're still in what is considered a combat zone, so we draw combat rations."

Paul responded, "I guess our own mess sergeant doesn't agree with the army classification of us being in a combat zone. That's why he got a hold of some class A ration slips, forged them, and has been getting us good rear-echelon food. He's got the quartermaster dump people all buffaloed."

"You've got that right, Kramer. I remember getting fed chocolate pudding when we were in the Battle of St. Lo," Woods commented.

"Whatever we get, it's still a whole lot better than the garbage rations the German troops have. They all carry around with them tins of cheese that are so smelly it will stop you in your tracks a hundred yards away," Paul noted.

They finished their meal and then wandered back to the little office Woods shared with Harrison.

It was Sergeant Harrison who said, "We have some orders that were misdirected to us here that we are waiting for, as well as some battalion mail. Once that gets in, we take off."

True to his word, the very next morning, after another meal of C rations, Paul was pleased to find that Sergeants Harrison and Woods were ready to go.

Harrison said, "Colonel Macklin insisted that we take his command car, and so we ride back in style."

Paul got into the backseat, which he shared with some mail sacks. Sergeant Woods, who opted to drive, handed several large envelopes to Harrison that obviously contained the orders that had been sent by error to Soissons. The command car was comfortable as compared to the jeeps and trucks that Paul was used to. The trip back was totally boring but uneventful.

The town of Sedan is in the Ardennes on the Meuse River. It had a population of roughly twenty thousand people and had seen a lot of heavy fighting over the years. The Germans broke through Sedan into France during World War I. In World War II, the German troops first invaded neutral Belgium and then crossed the Meuse River into Sedan. In this manner they were able to go around the loudly proclaimed impregnable French Maginot Line. This system of forts simply collected dust while General Guderian and his infamous panzers poured through Sedan and spread out all over France on their way to a crushing victory for the Nazis over the Allied forces. The battalion was ensconced in a recently vacated German barracks that still earlier had been a French barracks. The French had left intact various horse stables, which the Germans had utilized as parking areas for their tanks and other vehicles. In their haste to flee Sedan, the Germans had left several of their Volkswagens, which were the German equivalent of our jeeps. Americans, when they captured these vehicles, were generally reluctant to drive in them for fear of attracting some all-too-accurate fire from American troops in the area.

Paul asked to be dropped off at battalion headquarters, where he relayed his thanks to Colonel Macklin by way of his clerk. He then headed for the medical dispensary, where Captain Sheridan was holding sick call. The captain looked up and commented, "Well, Kramer, did you say a prayer for all of us here?"

"As a matter of fact, Captain, sir, I did. I want to thank you for letting me go to the services. It meant a great deal to me," Paul answered, and he then related the story about the two children being reunited with their father.

Captain Sheridan was very moved by this and then said, "Now I understand why you were so anxious to get to services in Le Mans. You Jewish people have a way of saying that it was destined to happen, don't you?"

"It was *Bashert*," Paul replied.

Tony came in the door and grabbed Paul by his shoulders. "Good to see you buddy," he said with emotion.

"Great to see you too," Paul answered.

"By the way, Paul, I'm in a bit of a jam, and I need your help," Tony added.

"What's the problem?" Paul asked.

"Well, when we came into this town to do our usual routine of securing the area, we found that the French Resistance people had already taken care of it. They came in with us, and they spread out quickly and checked out every single building and house in the entire town and the surrounding area. Thanks to them, we just have to settle down and relax and maintain town security. So far we have no orders to move on."

"So what's that got to do with your problem?" Paul queried.

"That's just it. Now that we have it free and easy until we get marching orders, Colonel Macklin decided he wants to run a battalion dance."

"What have you got to do with this deal?" Paul wanted to know.

"Colonel Macklin called a meeting of his company officers, including Captain Sheridan. The colonel wants someone in our outfit to contact what is best described as the French version of the local chapter of the Daughters of the American Revolution. He wants these women to be invited to chaperone their beautiful daughters to our dance party, with us supplying free transportation and refreshments. It seems that Captain Sheridan described me as a handsome Italian charmer—and I am using Captain Sheridan's words—who could convince these ladies to agree to cooperate. As a matter of fact, he told everyone that I am a ladies' man. Since when have I had the time or opportunity to be a ladies' man?"

"Never mind; it seems that you have been handed a great compliment from our esteemed captain," Paul soothed.

"Now let me tell you the best part. Captain Sheridan said that when you get back, I should twist your arm to give me a hand. You know I don't speak French, and these ladies will need an interpreter," Tony explained.

"You mean I'm drafted again?" Paul asked.

"You got that right," Tony chortled.

"Just a minute there, Kramer," Captain Sheridan said, having finished with his sick call duties. "I just suggested that you might be helpful in this job. I did not say anything about forcing you or drafting you to do this. That is all this character's idea." He pointed to Tony.

"So I bent the truth a little bit," Tony sputtered. "The truth is I'm scared to talk to these dames."

"All right already," Paul said. "I'll try to help you."

Tony eagerly added, "These ladies have a dinner every Wednesday evening. Two days from now, we will put on our cleanest uniforms and go there and see if we can even get to invite them and their fair daughters."

The following day was unusually hot, and so Paul decided to head down to the river for a swim after sick call duties were over. He took a pair of old khaki pants, and cut them off at the knees; they made a good bathing suit. He put them on under his regular fatigue trousers and asked around if anyone else wanted to join him. Paul had no takers, and so left the dispensary and headed down in the direction of the river. He had gone only one block when a female voice interrupted his thoughts.

"Are you lost soldier?"

He turned around and saw a very pretty girl who had long auburn hair that fell around her shoulders. She was wearing a pretty flowered dress that was topped off by a wide-brimmed straw hat. She was carrying a large bag under her arm.

Paul automatically held out his hand. "Jean Paul, Mademoiselle, Comment vous appelez vous? [What is your name?]"

"My name is Ghislaine, and you can speak English to me," she answered.

"It is so hot I thought I would go down to the river and cool off," Paul explained.

"That is a coincidence, because I was planning to do the same thing," she replied.

"Can I enjoy the pleasure of your company there?" Paul asked.

"But of course," she answered, laughing lightly.

"Hey Paul," came a shout behind him. It was Tony, who came running up huffing and puffing.

"You holding out on me?" Tony queried. Who is this gorgeous broad?"

Ghislaine laughed.

Paul warned, "She talks better English than you, so watch your language there! We're going swimming, so buzz off!"

"As a matter of fact, I'm going to tag along," Tony said.

"You are certainly welcome to join us," Ghislaine said.

"So there, my good buddy. I'm part of this swim team. But what am I going to do for a suit?"

"You can swim in your underwear if you want. A lot of people do that,'" she suggested.

"I can't do that," Tony said. "Maybe I'll roll my pants up and go in up to my knees."

"Whatever suits you," she laughed.

The banks of the river were filled with men, women, and children—practically all civilians.

Ghislaine reached into her bag and took out a bathing suit.

"Do they have a place here where you can change?" Paul asked anxiously.

He reminisced that when he was a little boy, his mother and

father would pack him and his brother Jerry in the car and drive to Carson Beach. This was located just south of South Boston, on the Atlantic Ocean, close enough to Dorchester to be convenient. Newspapers were fastened inside all of the windows—front, sides, and back—and first Mom, then Dad, and then he and Jerry changed into bathing suits, enjoying complete privacy. They again covered the windows when they were ready to change out of their wet suits. Rows and rows of cars alongside them used the same newspaper strategy.

"Silly boy," Ghislaine replied. "We all change on the beach."

"Not here?" Tony asked in mock horror.

"But certainly," she replied.

Tony and Paul both covered their faces with their hands, and she broke out into hysterical laughter.

"You Americans are so proper and correct and uptight. Look around you; everyone is doing the same thing."

Sure enough, up and down the riverbank people were blithely changing into their bathing suits. They all did it in such a manner that at no time was there any alarming exposure.

She too changed so quickly and skillfully in the blink of an eye that even polite American society could not be offended. She ventured down toward the river and beckoned to Paul and Tony to follow her.

The water was chilly. As a matter of fact, Paul decided, it was just like swimming in the frigid waters of Nantasket Beach on Boston's south shore. He ventured in only as far as his knees. Tony followed him cautiously and did not even make it that far.

As he came out of the water, Paul looked at Ghislaine with a look of disdain on his face.

She looked at him and said, "Tu est fache avec moi. [You are angry with me.]"

"No, I'm not mad, but I resent your saying that we Americans are uptight," he answered.

"If I have offended you, I apologize," she murmured.

"When we were in thick of fighting in Normandy, I was crawling around on the battlefield looking for wounded soldiers when I heard a rustle behind me. I turned around there and saw General Eisenhower in the flesh, crawling in the dust. 'General,' I said, 'What in God's name are you doing out here, sir?' He answered, 'I'm trying to find out if you men have enough clean underwear and dry socks.' 'General, sir,' I replied, 'You shouldn't be up here on the front lines. You could get knocked off.' 'This is part of my job too, son,' the general replied. 'General, sir,' If something happened to you, your loss would be catastrophic,' I answered, adding, 'And my apologies from a lowly GI trying to advise the person who is running this whole show.' The general flashed his famous grin and noted, 'In my opinion, soldier, no one is irreplaceable, so I'll get on with what I'm doing. And by the way, do you have enough medical supplies?' 'Yes, sir. Thank you, sir,' I answered, and I then asked, 'Are you still reading Max Brand, sir?' 'I thought you looked familiar, soldier. Now get on with your job,' he responded. My attention was diverted to a wounded GI near me, so I got on with what Uncle Sam was paying me for. Is that what you mean by saying we Americans are uptight?"

"*Cher* Jean Paul, You have my deepest apologies if I have offended you and your wonderful Americans. You all are truly and really without comparison. It's not only your incredible generals like Eisenhower, Bradley, and Patton, but you fantastic soldiers as well. You know we French have felt the brunt of the German boot on us during the Franco-Prussian war, the First World War, and now the Second. It is your American people who are liberating our country at the cost of thousands of your precious lives. We French will never forget this, I promise you," she said emotionally.

"Apology accepted," Paul and Tony both chimed in, with Tony adding, "Lady, this fantastic American chooses not to go into that water that must have come from the North Pole. If you go in swimming, you'll go without me."

"Or me," Paul added. "You must have an icebox manufacturing plant under that river somewhere."

Ghislaine stood up, drawing some admiring glances from some of the males near her, both French and American, and headed down to the shore. She didn't hesitate for an instant but dived into the water and started swimming.

"She must be an Eskimo," Tony observed.

Ghislaine returned a short time later, and Paul and Tony both fought over the opportunity to hand her a towel.

"Are you married or engaged?" Tony asked.

Tears immediately came to her eyes. She said softly, "My beloved Raoul and I were married two days before the war broke out. He was a *soldat* in the mounted cavalry. That is, he rode a horse. The Germans broke through into Belgium and then came through here. One of our first defenses was the mounted cavalry, and his battalion went charging at the German tanks. It was pitiful, and those who were not slaughtered then and there were dragged off to prisoner of war camps. I have heard from a poilu (a French infantry soldier) that he was just barely existing as a prisoner of war in one of the German camps. I don't know if I'll ever see him again."

"Hopefully this blasted war will be over soon and you'll be reunited with your husband," Paul ventured.

She wept and then gained control of herself. "I have to get back to work now," she said, and she slipped her dress on over her bathing suit, which was still wet.

"We have to meet with the Societee des Grandes Dames de la

Revolution or something like that," Paul ventured. "Do you know where they are located?"

"I know the place and the group. They are very snooty, as you Americans would say. What do you have to do with them?"

"Our colonel wants to run a dance in a couple of weeks and wants me to ask them to chaperone their daughters to our party."

"Well then don't invite me to this affair," she sniffed. "Those people consider themselves a special type of high society. Most likely they won't abide any French citizens attending who are not in their social class."

"Well these are the women I was ordered to invite," Tony replied. "But if you ask me, I don't like hobnobbing with high-society people either. I guess I am stuck with this. We are supposed to go over there tomorrow evening after chow and make our pitch."

"The building where these women meet is right near where I met you, so I suggest you follow me back there, and I will show you where it is," Ghislaine recommended.

Later, when the location was pointed out to them, Ghislaine said, "This is where I say good-bye."

Paul remarked, "I don't understand how you can go to work in a dress that is wet through the bathing suit underneath."

She laughed. "I am a seamstress and work in a back room all by myself. My *patronne*—my boss, that is—couldn't care less what I wear."

"Then au revoir to you, young lady," Paul said. "We hope and pray that your husband gets back to you soon."

"The same for me," Tony chimed in.

"Tu sais? [Do you know?]" she murmured, "Vous, tous les deux sont tres gentiles. [You, the two of you, are very nice.]"

When the trio reached the spot where they had met her, she

simply pointed to a large stone building with a neat garden set around the walkway in front of it.

She then waved good-bye and disappeared around the corner.

Tony muttered, "Too bad she isn't single."

"C'mon, Romeo," Paul answered. "Let's get back."

The following evening, the reluctant duo hesitantly made their way up the front steps of the imposing building. Just as Tony reached for the big brass knocker in the middle of the door, it swung open. An attractive middle-aged woman with mostly white hair tied in a neat bun favored them with a beautiful smile and extended her hand, saying, "Bon soir messieurs. Bienvenue a notre maison. [Good evening, sirs. Welcome to our house.]"

First Paul and then Tony shook her hand. Tony, although he didn't understand what she said, instinctively knew what the gesture of her extended hand meant and grasped it.

Paul said, "Je m'appele Jean Paul et lui s'appele Tony. [My name is Jean Paul, and his name is Tony.]"

"Enchante [Delighted]," she replied. "Je m'appele Mme. Marie Therese Dupres. Suivez moi, s'il vous plait. [My name is Mme. Marie Therese Dupres. Follow me, please.]"

She walked through a small foyer and into a large dining room with eight circular tables. There were a dozen women, mostly middle aged or older, sitting around each table. Some appetizing-looking pastries were set out on each table, as well as cups and saucers, along with impressively large teapots.

Mme. Dupres turned to Paul and said in perfect English, "Please accept my apologies. Some of us like to make you Americans work at speaking French, although we speak and understand English very well. It is a little of what you people call making fun, or better still, our way of a joke. Now we understand you two, or perhaps one of you wants to talk to us about something."

Paul and Tony both felt relieved that these ladies understood and spoke English. Paul quickly said, "*Cheres Mesdames* [Dear ladies], I am now going to turn the floor over to my friend."

Tony began speaking. "I am a little nervous at having to address a group of such beautiful and charming women, without exception."

One of the women giggled. "You Americans are more charming than we had been led to believe."

Another woman held up a cup. "We would offer you our coffee, but it is the horrible German ersatz variety, which I am sure you will find revolting. Instead, happily we have some tea and, of course, our pastries, which we hope you will like."

Paul and Tony needed no further invitation and gratefully sampled some of the delicious homemade pastries that were offered to them. After Tony managed to practically inhale several of the proffered samples, he cleared his throat and began to speak.

"With your kind permission, we want to extend an invitation to you fine ladies, to attend a dance our Colonel is running on behalf of our battalion and is dedicated to you wonderful, inspiring French people. We ask that you bring your daughters and for you to come not only as chaperones but as dancing partners for our officers and enlisted men. We will have some very nice refreshments, and our colonel has used his influence with our higher-ups to have a division band that will play the latest dance tunes. We are sure that although most of the music will be strictly modern American, you will find it interesting and entertaining. We, of course, will supply transportation for you and your invited guests. With your approval, I can come by a week from today, and then the night before the dance party, to get updated lists of how many people we can expect. We promise you that everything will be very correct and highly respectable."

Paul added, "He means to say that everything will be correct and dignified." He then slapped Tony on the back, commenting,

"You did a great job there buddy, and I couldn't have done better myself."

The ladies talked among themselves, and after a few brief moments, Mme. Dupres addressed Paul and Tony.

"Our apologies for talking among ourselves. We will be happy to be your invited guests along with our daughters and other people we decide to invite. It will probably be more convenient for you to bring your transports here, and so we will all arrange to be here at the appointed date and time. This is not a formal occasion, is it?"

Tony replied, "No Madame. Whatever apparel you folks decide to wear will be fine with us. It certainly is not a formal occasion, and all of our soldiers will be in regular uniform. I can say for the record that there is not a single soldier in our battalion who could come up with a formal dress uniform."

"Then it is all arranged, gentlemen," Mme. Dupres noted. "Now please sit down and join us in devouring some more of these pastries."

Tony and Paul needed no further urging, and they returned to their barracks completely and satisfactorily stuffed.

Captain Sheridan told them that Colonel Macklin was absolutely delighted with the arrangements they had made.

On the night of the dance, the weather was perfect. It was still on the warm side but with a soft breeze blowing enough to make it refreshing. Trucks and jeeps were parked outside the society women's building, and small ladders were supplied to help the ladies and their chaperones onto the backs of the vehicles.

A great swing band was already playing some of the Glenn Miller, Benny Goodman, and Harry James favorites in the great hall that was supplied by the town for the dance. The mess lieutenant, the mess sergeant, and their entire crew were busy covering the tables with an assortment of appealing food, delicious pastries, and other delicacies. Huge punch bowls were strategically placed around on the tables, and there was some grumbling among the men because the punch did not contain any hard liquor. Some GIs generously offered to supply quantities of cognac in order to spice up the drinks. The colonel had solemnly given his word to the ladies, however, that no liquor would be made available. The local people were used to drinking wine and beer, even at an early age. Concern was expressed about the ability of the GIs to hold their liquor without acting in a rambunctious manner.

Ghislaine, who had been invited by Tony, joined him at a corner table, and they were obviously enjoying themselves.

Paul walked over to greet Mme. Dupres, accompanied apparently by her daughter and another young woman. She introduced her daughter Giselle and her friend Marie Louise to Paul. He waved to Tony to join them. Mme. Dupres asked if they wanted to dance with the girls. Needing no further urging, Tony and Paul took the young women out on the dance floor. Both girls were great dancers, and the two couples had a wonderful time on the dance floor.

Paul then noticed Ghislaine sitting alone at her table, excused himself, and walked over to her, saying, "I think I can get the band to play a java, if you like."

"Where ever did you hear about that? The java is a country type of dance—something you Americans would call hillbilly music," she replied.

"Back in Le Mans, they were having a dance in the town square, and I learned about it. As a matter of fact, I like it," Paul responded.

"Why don't you rejoin your invited guests?" she suggested.

"Not unless you come with me," Paul replied.

She reluctantly got up and let Paul escort her back to the Dupres table, where he mumbled his introductions.

The ladies shook hands coolly and formally, and Paul realized he had made a blunder by bringing Ghislaine over to Mme. Dupres.

The band started to play an Edith Piaf favorite, and in order to warm up the frosty atmosphere, Paul invited Mme. Dupres to dance. Tony, ever the diplomat, took Ghislaine out on the dance floor. Mme. Dupres laughed and said, "Surely you don't want to dance with an old lady."

Paul replied instantly, "Madame, you are not only prettier than your lovely daughter, but you dance better than her too."

"Oh, Jean Paul, you are such a charmer," she murmured.

Colonel Macklin came by and asked to be introduced. He invited Mme. Dupres out on the dance floor, and they made a great couple, twirling around and obviously enjoying themselves.

Suddenly there was a commotion at the door. A group of women, most of them young but accompanied by an older lady, were in an intense argument with one of the society women near the door. These ladies looked somehow different from the others. For the most part, they wore heavy makeup and were dressed in a more provocative manner.

Mme. Dupres saw what was going on and stood up angrily and said, "We are not staying here one more moment!"

Colonel Macklin came running over and turned to Paul.

"What's going on here, soldier?"

Paul sputtered and tried to explain what he had no explanation for.

A few of the GIs in the corner were laughing and giggling intensely. Tony assumed they had the answer to the drama that was unfolding. He grabbed one of the men and shook him, repeating Colonel Macklin's angry question.

"What's going on here?"

It seems that this group of men thought it would be intensely funny to visit the local brothel and invite the local madame and her girls. It was the sight of these people that obviously infuriated and insulted the society women.

The colonel joined Tony, noting that he was shaking one of the men, and demanded an explanation.

He handed Tony's victim a large quantity of French francs and said, "Go give this to them, tell them you apologize for the misunderstanding, and invite them to join you and your buddies in the local café for free drinks. If you are still short on money, come back. If you don't fix this right away, you'll spend the next week in the guardhouse!"

The miscreants convinced their highly offended guests to follow them out of the hall, and once again the society women sat down at their respective tables, obviously satisfied.

The rest of the evening went well, and all of the ladies were, as scheduled, driven back to their original destination at the society building. Paul and Tony insisted on accompanying Mme. Dupres and the two girls back. They were very touched, and as they said farewell at the front door, Giselle asked, "Are either of you two *Fiancee*? [Engaged?]"

Paul and Tony made sour faces.

Then Marie Louise asked, "Then are either of you *peut etre mariee*? [Maybe married?]"

Tony laughed. "No, ladies, we are both single."

Paul added, "We are confirmed bachelors and will stay that way for a long time!"

The three women giggled, and Mme. Dupres said, "You won't remain single long if you are still in France during the time of the Festival of Saint Catherine."

"What does that mean?" Paul asked nervously.

"On that special date, all single women, young and old, wear the fanciest hats that they can either make or purchase. On that day, it is a tried and true tradition here in France that when one of these women proposes marriage to a man, he cannot refuse her."

Tony said, very apprehensively, "Ladies, our apologies, but we have to go right now!"

Paul nodded his assent, and the two of them did not even wait for a ride back but fled the scene in terror on foot.

— 19 —

The weather, almost overnight, changed drastically. One day it was comfortably warm, and the very next day a chill wind came in ominously from the north and the east. All of the men made a mad scramble to wherever they stored their clothing, searching for whatever warm clothing they had. The quartermaster was overwhelmed with requests for long underwear and extra socks. It was just a matter of time before the battalion would move on back to the front lines and away from the comfy quarters that they now used. Living indoors was a luxury that one could get used to very readily. Paul reminded himself that this would not last forever.

Almost to the day that the weather changed, Lieutenant Saffridi said to Paul, "I have a job that will interest you if you are up to it."

"What's that, sir?" Paul asked.

"Instead of your working on sick call every day, how about my teaching you to be a dental technician? It will broaden your skills and keep you from getting bored."

"I'm not bored, sir," Paul replied, "and how about clearing this with Captain Sheridan?"

"He says he has no problem with this."

"Just what does this involve, Lieutenant?" Paul asked apprehensively.

"Well, you can develop a lot of new skills as a dental tech, and it could even help you get into dental school after the war is over," Saffridi noted.

"I've got my mind set on going to optometry school, sir, but I'll be willing to give you a hand with whatever it takes."

"It will take a lot of work pumping my foot pedal drill, for one thing. You'll also be taught how to scale teeth and treat patients with gingivitis, and you'll assist in filling teeth, mixing up amalgam, administering local anesthesia, and performing extractions as well. You know I'll be doing the extractions and anesthetic injections, but you'll be doing a lot of the other dental assisting procedures. By the way, when you get discharged, you should be sure and have them put this on your separation papers. If you change your mind and decide later on you want to go to dental school, this should help you with the dental school admissions people."

Paul responded, "With respect, sir, I'll be glad to work with you, and even have this notation put on my separation papers, if I don't get croaked and make it through this war."

The lieutenant patiently taught Paul how to prepare a patient for the multiple procedures that he performed in the cramped room designated as the dental office. Some civilians had approached battalion headquarters and asked if they too could avail themselves of the army medical and dental services. Some French people complained that they had but one civilian dentist in the town and he would just as soon pull a tooth as treat it. The local physician did not inspire much confidence either. The colonel didn't take long to think about it before deciding this would be good for civilian morale. Consequently, many civilians as well as soldiers received the high level medical and dental care the men of the battalion took for granted. Paul took a little gentle heckling from some of his fellow medics, but that soon ended when one of them developed a toothache.

Captain Sheridan returned one night from a meeting of the battalion officers to report that a town MP battalion was due to move in and replace them. They would then be moved toward the battle lines somewhere in Belgium. Until they were relieved, they would have to settle back and hang in there. Some of the men started to play bridge. Paul was drafted because he knew a smattering of the game of whist. Others were taught from scratch, and soon most of them became proficient in developing strategies of bidding and playing. In addition to that, one of the men managed to scrounge two Ping-Pong tables and some rackets and balls from a rear-echelon recreation center. Men would line up, patiently waiting for a turn to play Ping-Pong. As the skill of the men progressed, they developed bridge and Ping-Pong tournaments, which were followed with great interest by many of the enlisted men and officers.

One day, Captain Sheridan came back from another officers' meeting. The expression on his face was grim.

"We've had it," he muttered. "This is it!"

"What's going on?" Tony asked.

"We have just been put on alert. We are going to move out within the next twenty-four to forty-eight hours. First, every one of you go down to the quartermaster and draw whatever extra warm clothing you can get from him. Second, don't write to anyone that you are moving out. It will be censored anyway."

"Where are we going, Captain?" Paul asked.

"We are going due east, to the country of Belgium and a town called Arlon. Orders are being cut now attaching us temporarily to the Twenty-Eighth Division, although we will not be anywhere near their headquarters. And a battalion of Town MPs are already en route to relieve us."

"I guess our easy living is over," Kurt observed.

"Back to reality," Tony chimed in.

The next few hours were frantic as they packed their individual gear, and hauled out all of the dispensary and dental equipment, and stored all of it on three two-and-a-half-ton trucks that were lined up nearby.

The villagers saw all of the activity going on and understood what was imminent. Mme. Dupres and her daughter as well as Ghislaine and many others came by to see their good friends off. Mme. Dupres dabbed some tears away and murmured, "God bless you all and keep you safe."

Ghislaine muttered, "All I keep doing is saying good bye to soldiers I'm either in love with or just plain have gotten to know as dear friends. I hate this war!"

The next morning, at 0400 hours, the battalion convoy moved out with just the tiny blackout lights showing.

After a long and uneventful trip, they arrived in Arlon. This time there was no comfortable barracks for the men to be quartered in. The medical dispensary set up a large pyramidal tent; it required a lot of work on the part of the medics to unpack and assemble all of the gear and equipment. An adjacent tent was set up for the dental clinic, and putting that in working order was also a demanding job. The men were told that for the time being, they could use their shelter halves to sleep in or they could crowd into the medical and dental tents. This was a no-brainer. It was really cold out now, and the prospect of sleeping in a pup tent—or worse, a foxhole—was something they all had difficulty adjusting to.

Hot food in the form of class A rations was no longer being served in a comfortable mess hall. It was back to the old mess kit if they were lucky enough to have decent food made available to them. Otherwise they would most likely have to make do with either C or K rations.

*Early December 1944. We had just arrived in Arlon, Belgium. After a few days,
I got a pass for a few hours to go into town and look it over. One of the first things
that came to my attention was a Photography studio, and in close proximity, was a
Barber Shop. It seemed to be a good idea to have a photograph taken for my folks. I
ran back to camp, scrimmaged through my clothes to find a decent clean shirt, and
returned to the town barber shop to get spiffed up for the photograph, which was
sent off as soon as possible. Just a short time later, the Germans mounted a major
attack, which was later referred to as the Battle of the Bulge. We found ourselves
about 15 miles (20 kilometers) from German lines, with all sorts of German
soldiers dressed up in American uniforms trying to penetrate our lines. Read on.*

Slit trenches were dug to serve as latrines. The battalion was obviously up near the front lines now. To make matters worse, the temperature plummeted. Even with the wool gloves they had managed to scrounge from the quartermaster, fingers got cold very quickly. Captain Sheridan urged the men to be careful about frostbite—especially with their feet. They were all ordered to carry extra pairs of dry socks with them. If their feet got wet, at the earliest opportunity, they were to get the wet socks off, dry their feet if possible, and put on dry socks. Cold, wet feet were a sure invitation to get frostbite.

Someone heard about a rumor that there was a vacated hospital nearby, but by the time a few of the men checked it out, they found to their disappointment that it was already occupied by another outfit.

One bitterly cold morning with imminent snow in the air, Captain Sheridan summoned Paul, Kurt, and Tony to him.

"Colonel Macklin wants several men from each company and the medical detachment to report to battalion headquarters," he said. "I don't know what's up, but he wants men who can be briefed on an intelligence situation and then report back to their units. He wants you there immediately, if not sooner!"

The trio ran to the large pyramidal tent that housed battalion headquarters. Some men from other companies had preceded them and were sitting around on the grassy floor, including Bubba. He gave them a friendly wave and patiently waited for the others to arrive. Colonel Macklin had pre-established a protocol for men not to be called to attention when he entered a room. He simply walked in from another enclosure within the tent and began to address his rapt listeners.

"We have a number of serious problems that worry me and that could affect all of you. First of all, we lack the good intelligence supplied to us by local resistance units that was readily available to us in France. The French underground and Resistance units, along with the regular French Army, were a very valuable source of accurate information about the positions of German military units. Here in Belgium, there is no organized mechanism, as far as I know, for the local resistance groups to coordinate with the Allied military. All we have been told is that we are located in what is considered to be a quiet zone of the front. There are a couple of fishy things about this that I don't like. I recently had a visit from some counterintelligence people, including a few officers some of you may remember, like Colonel Gerrior and Major Helms."

At that, Paul rolled his eyes upward.

The colonel ignored Paul's gesture and continued. "These people are getting some alarming and disturbing information that they have shared with me. Some Germans on the run out of France and into Belgium and Germany have warned the civilian population that they will be back in force and will go all the way to Paris. We have captured some prisoners who had military plans about a major operation called Wacht am Rhein [Watch on the Rhine]. This allegedly was cooked up by none other than Adolph Hitler. The reports say that the Germans expect to break through and go all the way to Antwerp.

"In addition to this, British intelligence has been highly successful in breaking the German codes and deciphering their signals. They have uncovered a scary plan for what they call Operation Greif [Operation Grasp]. They have designated a wild character by the name of Otto Skorzeny to run this operation as part of Watch on the Rhine. This is the person who rescued Benito Mussolini from his captors. He is supposed to lead a task force of English-speaking German soldiers dressed in American and British uniforms. They will be wearing dog tags taken from POWs and dead British and American soldiers. Part of their mission is to try to get behind the American lines to change signposts, cause disruption, misdirect vital traffic, and seize bridges across the Meuse River. Another scary part of their mission is to try to get through our lines in order to kill General Eisenhower."

Colonel Macklin paused only briefly, looking at each and every man assembled in front of him. "Our intelligence reports that Hitler ordered that the plan of operation be camouflaged by an elaborate cover and deception plan. All who were made aware of this plan of deception and massive attack were required to sign a pledge of secrecy. They were sternly reminded that any person who talked about this to an unauthorized individual would be shot immediately. Hitler himself, however, let this information out. Early in the fall, he met with the Japanese ambassador to Berlin, Baron Hiroshi Oshima. Hitler personally told Oshima that a new army of more than a million men was now being organized. This would be used to open up a large-scale offensive in the West. Baron Oshima asked when this would happen and got a quick reply from Hitler: 'Sometime after early November.' Oshima reported this to his government in Tokyo."

"What he and Hitler did not know was that the US intelligence services had found a means of intercepting and deciphering coded Japanese signals. This vital information was on the desks of intelligence officers in the Pentagon practically at the same time it was received in Tokyo. And so there you have it. The intelligence people have been going to all unit commanders in this general area to alert them. Some commanders are saying that this is typical of Hitler's lunatic ravings and doesn't deserve close attention. This, so far, is being left to unit commanders as to what kind of action to take. I, for one, believe that this crazy bastard is really up to something. I am taking full responsibility for taking the following action."

"Number one: You men are going to go back to your units and

fill in the rest of your command with what you were just briefed about."

"Number two: All of us are going to be spread out to every checkpoint we have and will set up even more. This means not only on the roads north, south, east, and west of us, but general areas where the terrain will permit the movement of vehicles, including everything from their tanks to their Volkswagens."

"Number three: I want all men manning the checkpoints to be armed to the teeth. There is a directive from higher authority that it is permissible to use all military personnel in the event of a serious attack. That includes everybody in this outfit from motor pool, mess personnel, and quartermaster personnel. Our medics will participate in the questioning of the drivers and passengers trying to get through our lines but will not carry any weapons."

At that point, Tony groaned, "Colonel, sir, if some of these crazy SS try to come through and get stopped, they'll surely blast their way out of there."

"My boy, that's why the rest of our men manning the checkpoint will have every one of their weapons pointing at these characters," the colonel replied. "You have to remember that some people trying to get through will be legitimate GIs."

A lieutenant from C Company asked, "Colonel, sir, if all these intelligence reports point to an imminent attack by the Germans, how come the big brass is not organizing a major defense?"

"Because we don't have verified proof that all these reports are legitimate. You have to remember that when we landed on the beach in Normandy, Hitler screamed that every one of us would be annihilated on the beach. We had to interpret his lunatic rantings as just that. If we had taken him seriously, we would all still be back in England. For now, most of our brass feel the same way about these reports until we get better proof. I'm going to now let my battalion clerk take over."

Sergeant Major Harrison passed out sheets of paper to the men representing the various units of the battalion.

The sergeant said, "These are the various roadblock and checkpoint positions we have assigned to each of your units. You will return to your people and fill them in on what you have just learned. Your unit commander will assign the specific times you are out on a roadblock. Now pay careful attention. When a vehicle approaches your position, you will order it to halt. Our MPs will surround the vehicle. One of you will go to the driver's side of the jeep or truck, and another will go to the passenger side. The others will surround the vehicle, with weapons pointing straight at the driver and passengers. Fingers will be on the trigger with the safety off. First you will ask for travel papers. Check them out very carefully and make sure they look legitimate. Don't hesitate to ask someone else's opinion if you are not sure. Then you will ask such questions that any born-and-bred-in-the-USA American will know as sure as his hand in front of his face, like, what is the name of Tom Mix's horse?, who has the best arrangement of 'Moonlight Serenade'?, who is Mickey Mouse's girlfriend?, who is Flash Gordon's girlfriend?, who is Buck Rogers' girlfriend?, what position does Babe Ruth play?, what is the capital of Illinois?, who is the father of the Katzenjammer kids?, who is Dick Tracy's sidekick?, and who is Roy Rogers's partner and girlfriend? Be inventive. Besides this, you will check their dog tags, underwear, and socks, Make sure their clothing and underclothing look like genuine GI issue. Some may be wearing their German uniforms under their American ones just to make sure they don't get shot if they are captured. Check their cigarettes and matches to make sure they are legitimately American. Listen for any slight differences in their accent. Got all that?"

Kurt raised his hand. Sergeant Harrison nodded, and Kurt warned, "Some of these guys, or all of them, may be SS. That means that they would just as soon kill you as look at you. All SS have a double lightning sign tattooed underneath their armpit. Even if they pass all of the other tests and questions, check for the tattoos."

Colonel Macklin snorted. "Hell, even I didn't know that. Good job, soldier."

Kurt blushed with embarrassment but continued to pay rapt attention to the sergeant.

The colonel added, looking at Kurt, "It might be a good idea for you to yell out in perfect German, Hande Hoch! You may catch some of these bastards off guard."

Sergeant Harrison interjected, "We hope you can remember all of this and pass it on to your buddies. Now get going! Bail out of here. Your unit commanders will assign your watch, but it looks like we will start with two hours on and six hours off, until you are told differently. Now beat it!"

Enterprising members of each unit had meanwhile been desperately searching for some structure that could at least give them temporary shelter. Lieutenant Saffridi came upon an abandoned farmhouse and barn. He immediately prevailed upon Captain Sheridan to move the battalion aid station into the farmhouse. Other members of the battalion had spread out to move into houses and their cellars. Still other GIs, using homegrown ingenuity, had used logs from fallen trees to build huts that were covered with sandbags.

Paul, Kurt, and Tony came upon their fellow medics working diligently in order to accomplish moving in to their warmer quarters. At the same time, the motor pool thought that the barn would be perfect for their location and wasted no time taking over this prime location.

Tony, acting as a spokesman, filled in Captain Sheridan on what they had learned.

Sheridan cautioned, "I told the colonel that you men are on temporary loan. If we get attacked and start taking casualties, your priority is to treat the wounded. In the meantime, we will work on the schedule you got from the meeting at battalion headquarters. I'm supposed to tell you that when you reach your assigned station, you are to dig a foxhole with the entrenching tool. Good luck to you. The ground is frozen solid, and trying to dig into it will be just like trying to dig a hole in a rock. Better, if you are attacked, find a shell hole to climb into."

The next morning, at 6:00 a.m., Tony and Paul were assigned to relieve the men preceding them at a roadblock. It was bitter cold now. Even with his gloves and two sets of socks and combat boots Paul felt this fingers and toes grow numb in a short time. Just a few trucks and jeeps came their way, and all proceeded without incident. At the end of their two-hour shift, Paul was certain he would freeze to death. Tony felt the same way. When they got back to the battalion aid station, they were grateful to be in the meager shelter the farmhouse offered. Some of the men had brought in straw to be used as beds. Kurt and some of the other medics had built a fire in the kitchen stove, and all crowded around it for warmth. Since every man was alternating in taking part in the checkpoint duties, the shifts were thankfully changed to two hours on and eight hours off.

The cold did not ease up but only got worse, and then snow started to filter down—lightly at first, and then becoming heavier. The men had never felt so miserable.

One night Paul returned to the farmhouse, shivering with cold as usual. His fingers felt numb, and his feet were wet, cold, and also numb. He sat down alongside the stove and noted that even though his double sets of socks were pulled up over the bottoms of his pants legs, the snow and ice seemed to have worked in between his socks and combat boots. The melting snow and ice had no problem with freezing his feet. The combat boots were totally ineffective, and he ruefully thought back to the railroad yards in Paris, where boxcars were filled with new insulated combat boots. Because of the black marketers, these never found their way up to this part of the front.

He pulled off his socks, found an empty spot on the floor near the stove, and stretched them out, followed by his gloves. From now on, he was determined to wear three sets of socks and two sets of gloves. Luckily his parents had sent him another scarf, and he made this into a combination of one covering his face and the other wrapped around his neck. The wool knit cap had a flap he could pull down over his ears, and for a while it worked. After a period of time went by, even his earlobes and then the rest of his ears began to get cold and numb.

Tony came bursting in, shaking off the snow and crowing exuberantly, "You guys will never believe this, but so help me, it happened. A jeep was flagged down, and who was sitting in the back but none other than General Omar Bradley? His papers were in order, and a GI started asking the usual questions. He asked the general what was the capital of Illinois. The general answered correctly that it is Springfield. This guy was certain that it was Chicago, put his gun to the head of the driver, and told him to pull over to the side. Luckily Bubba was there, who not only recognized the general but also correctly knew that the capital of Illinois is Springfield. Bubba, in his own special way, convinced the man to remove his weapon and apologized to the general. Bradley was amused by the entire incident and commented that he would rather be overcautious and urged everyone to forget the matter."

Kurt remarked, "At least our generals have a sense of humor."

All the men of the battalion had found some kind of shelter. Many of the villagers were happy to take soldiers in with them, feeling this afforded them a better measure of protection. After a few days of finding no enemy soldiers trying to break through, the colonel authorized the battalion mess personnel to set up a field kitchen. This food was a welcome change from the everyday humdrum of C and K rations.

On the roadblocks, the routine settled down to a very cold but boring duty. The men had established a code word for the interviewers to use in case of any suspicious situations. The word was "Mimi." Early one morning, it was cold and starting to get foggy. A jeep approached the checkpoint and came to a stop as directed by the armed MPs. Paul approached the driver's side, and Tony walked over to the passenger in the front seat. There was a third man in the backseat wearing sergeant's stripes. The two soldiers in the front seat were apparently buck privates. A red flag went up in Paul's mind as he saw that all three men were wearing neckties. Even the mighty General Patton could not convince men up on the front lines to wear ties. Paul asked the driver for his papers, which either seemed to be in order or were very clever forgeries. This crew were, according to the papers, supposed to report to a quartermaster unit in Antwerp. Tony asked the soldier on his side, "What is the name of Tom Mix's horse?"

"Silver," said the man in the back.

"I just reminded myself I have a date with Mimi tonight," Tony blurted out.

Five MPs ran up to the jeep, with submachine guns pointed at the heads of the three soldiers, and ordered them to get out of the vehicle.

"Strip down!" one of the MPs ordered.

"You have to be joking," the driver of the jeep replied. "It's freezing out."

"If you are who I think you are," one of the MPs answered, "you'll be roasting in hell in a very short time."

Another MP got into the jeep and drove it off while the three suspects were taking off their coats, jackets, and shirts. None of them were wearing GI underwear! The underclothes were obviously German Army issue!

An MP ordered one of the suspects to pull off his undershirt and hold his hands up in the air. Sure enough, under the man's armpit was emblazoned the double lightning tattoo of the SS.

A half-track loaded with other MPs pulled up, and they hustled the nearly naked men onto their vehicle and took off. No sooner were they out of sight than another jeep, this time carrying four apparently American soldiers, stopped at the roadblock across the way from where Tony and Paul were working. Kurt approached the jeep and then unexpectedly yelled out in German at the top of his voice, "Hande Hoch!"

This time there was no need to use the code word. The two men in the backseat threw their hands up in the air, whereupon the vehicle was immediately surrounded by armed MPs. The prisoners were driven off, most likely to the counterintelligence screening unit a short distance away. An MP, using his walkie-talkie, called battalion headquarters to report that the expected attempt to break through American lines by the Germans had already started.

Colonel Macklin already had his hands full. Ominous reports were filtering in. The Germans had started their assault with a massive artillery barrage on December 16, 1944, along a sixty-mile front. The major German assault had begun at 0530. It was reported that just before the attack, to the north, there were flashes of light as far as the eye could see, with a lot of accompanying booming. This was German artillery. The dispatches said that in addition to the heavy artillery bombardment, American troops could make out the screeching sounds of rockets, dubbed by the GIs as screaming meemies. These came from the Nebelwerfer, which was a multiple-barreled rocket launcher. Reports continued to come in to battalion headquarters. Three German armies attacked through the Ardennes across a sixty-mile front. In the northern sector, the Sixth SS Panzer Army charged at the Losheim Gap and the Elsenborn Ridge; but, ran into unexpected determined resistance, which stalled them. The Fifth Panzer Army, in the center, attacked toward Bastogne and St. Vith. In the South, the German Seventh Army tried to move toward Luxembourg.

Tiger tanks and King Tiger tanks armed with fearsome 88-millimeter guns were breaking through. There were only three ways to stop the Tiger tank. The first was an attack from the air, but with the terrible fog followed by a wild snowstorm, there was no way that anything could fly. The second was the famed 90-millimeter American tank destroyer, but unfortunately, these were very few and far between in the Ardennes area. The last resort was to use the bazooka. This was an individual antitank rocket that was fired from the shoulder. The bazooka was named for a makeshift musical instrument played by a hillbilly radio comedian named Bob Burns. The rocket-powered charge would surely bounce off the armor of these behemoths like a tennis ball, but a lucky shot at the tracks could possibly disable the monster. Just enough of an explosion to blow a small part of track off its sprocket wheels could do the job. Fortunately, the battalion quartermaster had squirreled away a sufficient quantity of these weapons.

To make matters more catastrophic, Colonel Macklin read a grim account of a German V-2 rocket crashing into a cinema in Antwerp. Many Allied servicemen were among the hundreds of people slaughtered here.

The very next day, a heartbreaking report stated that close to eighty American soldiers had been captured in the Ardennes town of Malmedy by a German SS unit. The prisoners' hands were tied behind their backs, and then they were led into an open field and murdered. Some of the men managed to get away and hide in a café. The SS surrounded the café, set it on fire, and shot the soldiers as they tried to escape the flames. This same SS unit participated in a number of other massacres, murdering approximately three hundred more American soldiers who had been taken prisoner and over a hundred Belgian civilians. The commander of this unit was SS Lieutenant Colonel Joachim Peiper, who had been decorated earlier for murdering thousands of Russians on the eastern front.

Unofficially, the word went out to all American troops in the Ardennes. No prisoners were to be taken. Polished and sophisticated Nazi diplomats went screaming to the International Red Cross for protection from the "murderous Americans." Immediate pressure was applied to the American government from many sides to stop their policy of revenge.

On December 20, more terrible news arrived. Nazi troops in the Ardennes surrounded the town of Bastogne, and several thousand American soldiers faced annihilation.

—20—

Colonel Macklin opened his tent flap, looking hopelessly up to the dark sky for some type of salvation. All he saw was a fierce snow squall driven by high winds that threatened to bring his headquarters tent down. He ordered his exec to establish battalion headquarters in a more secure structure. There were no more abandoned buildings available, but a family living in a large home was found to be agreeable to the colonel and his staff moving in with them. This was a great personal risk for them, because if the Germans captured them, they would have been shot immediately for sheltering Allied military people.

Macklin then issued a series of orders. First, all personnel, when not on patrol or manning a roadblock, were confined to quarters for security reasons. He then gave the order to move all personnel out on the line: cooks, bakers, and motor pool and mess personnel. They were equipped with weapons including the carbine, the M-1 Garand, the Browning Automatic Rifle, mortars, submachine guns, .50-caliber machine guns, and, of course, the bazooka.

Terrible snowstorms made it even worse for the defending American troops. Some German units also got bogged down in huge traffic jams. To the north, the reports said the Germans continued to run into very strong resistance from the Americans there. To the south and center, the Germans were more successful and plunged through the American lines with their infantry and tanks. There were massive breakthroughs in this area, and the German boast that they would go all the way to Antwerp and Paris did not seem so far-fetched.

The checkpoint Paul and Tony were at was close to a railroad track. A steam engine pulling a caboose went chugging by just when Paul started to shiver from the cold. An artillery shell hit the engine and blew it and the caboose off the tracks. Although Paul and Tony momentarily felt sorry for the people in the train; they finally had, at least temporarily, a source of warmth.

All of the men on checkpoint had been asked to stop at battalion headquarters and be debriefed on the results of their watch. Tony and Paul met Kurt on the way into the new abode of Colonel Macklin and his staff.

Tony complained, "Y'know? It's almost Christmastime, and we don't even have a tree to remind us of the holiday at home."

Paul asked, "What's wrong with going out and chopping down a nice pine tree?"

Tony's reply came gloomily. "'Cause when we're not on duty, we're all restricted to quarters. That's why."

Sergeant Harrison noted, "It would really cheer us up to have a tree that we can enjoy around here." He looked around cautiously and added, "Don't let the colonel know I said it."

They were all in close proximity to the colonel, but if he heard it, he did not let on.

Tony, Paul, and Kurt each related all the details of their recent experience on their roadblock duty and then left, heading back to the aid station.

"Are you thinking what I'm thinking?" Paul asked Kurt.

"Sure. Right with you, buddy," Kurt replied.

"You guys have to be out of your minds!" Tony exclaimed.

"There are Germans, many of them SS, running all around here. The both of you will end up getting killed or captured, all because of a tree!"

"It does mean a lot to you, doesn't it?" Paul asked.

"Well sure it does, but not enough for you nutcakes to risk your lives over," Tony replied.

"Look, if we run into Germans, Kurt can make out like we're Germans dressed in American uniforms. If we get stopped by Belgian or French Resistance people, I speak French well enough to convince them that we are legit," Paul remonstrated. "Just remember to keep your mouth shut!"

"You guys are out of your cotton-picking minds," Tony answered.

"If anyone asks for us, just tell them we are down at battalion headquarters still, enjoying the Belgian farmer's hospitality," Paul urged.

Kurt and Paul stopped at the quartermaster's farmhouse to try to get a saw.

"You crazy guys want a saw?" the quartermaster sergeant asked. "Maybe you can be luckier with a hatchet I lifted back in Sedan," he suggested.

Kurt took the hatchet and said, "Now I feel just like George Washington when he went after his famous cherry tree."

After swearing the sergeant to secrecy, the furtive duo made it out of the building and in a short time were in the deep woods of the Ardennes. It was starting to get dark, and they didn't dare use their flashlights. Fortunately they found a tree that looked promising, although it was a little larger than what they had in mind. They started to work, taking turns trying to chop it down. The wood was moist and stubborn and it took them a long time to get through. Finally the tree came down with a resounding crash, and just at that moment, Paul and Kurt found themselves surrounded by a dozen civilians all carrying weapons pointed straight at them.

"Est ce que vous est Francais ou Americain? [Are you French or American?]" one of the men asked cautiously.

"Nous sommes Americains [We are American]," Kurt replied.

One of the civilians poked his gun in Kurt's belly and asked belligerently, "Pourquoi que vous parlez francais avec un accent fort qui est boche? [Then why are you speaking French with a heavy German accent?]"

The group, who were apparently Belgian resistance people, started arguing vehemently among themselves. A young woman stepped forward. She seemed to be a leader of this group and was arguing with a man who had his gun poked firmly in Kurt's stomach.

"Now hold there, just a minute," Paul protested. "We have our dog tags and IDs."

She spread her hands out protectively in front of Paul and Kurt and said in perfect English, "Sure, and so do all the SS who are running around here too."

A man snarled in broken English, "It will just be as easy to kill you two Nazi murderers right now. By the way, what are you doing with that tree?"

"We wanted to bring a Christmas tree back to our outfit," Paul answered, trying to be convincing.

"Seuelement les homes fou ici oeut etre Americains, [Only the crazy men here could be Americans]," the woman responded to the group. She then turned to Paul and asked, "Who is Shirley Temple?"

"That's easy," Paul answered. "She is a beautiful, talented child movie star, and I have always been in love with her. My mother would give me cereal in a bowl with her picture on the bottom of it and tell me to make all gone, and I would see the picture of my beloved Shirley Temple."

"Only Americans could be crazy enough to try something like this," argued another civilian.

"I tell you what. Let us bring you back to our outfit. They will identify us," Kurt urged.

Just then a group of battalion MPs led by Sergeant Harrison appeared from out of nowhere and surrounded the group. Harrison muttered, "I thought about it and figured you two would surely get fouled up some way or other. I let the colonel know about it, and he sent me out to find you two whackadoos. He is foaming at the mouth and is mad. We are short-handed on account of you two foul-ups, and besides that, you disobeyed a direct order to be confined to quarters when not on duty."

The resistance group, each and every man and woman, realizing Paul and Kurt were legitimate, formally shook hands with them and faded into the woods.

Some of the MPs had to help Paul and Kurt drag the tree with them, and they finally made it back to battalion headquarters.

The colonel came to the door, his face distorted in anger. Before he could say anything, Paul blurted out, "Merry Christmas, Colonel."

Macklin melted, but his face showed mixed emotions. On the one hand, it was Christmas and these two men had gone a long way in order to help him and his men enjoy the holiday. On the other hand …

"For two Jewish soldiers to go out and risk their lives so that we could enjoy our own special Christmas tree is something special," the colonel said. "We can now celebrate this special time of year during this terrible and scary war. Although I really would like to kick your rear ends in, this is the first sign of Christmas cheer we have been able to enjoy so far."

"And Colonel, sir, I'm going to hang some of my favorite Hershey bars on the tree," Paul offered apologetically.

"And I'll throw in my extra set of gloves," Kurt added.

Macklin turned to the men and nodded for them to bring the giant tree into the room behind him. The Belgian farmer and his family were delighted and moved furniture out of the way so that they could set up the tree, the peak of which brushed the ceiling. Word spread quickly that the battalion had its very own Christmas tree, and it didn't take long for word to get out. Tony was one of the first to come in to enjoy the spectacular tree, which was already being decorated by a few of the troops as well as some of the local civilians. Whenever the men of the battalion could get a break, they came to view the tree for themselves, while some brought special ornaments and gifts to attach to the branches. Rumor had it that General Patton had been told the story about the Christmas tree. He had reputedly chuckled. One enterprising soldier tried to hang a hand grenade on it but was discouraged by the colonel himself.

Captain Sheridan was told about the incident and showed up to put in a good word for his men if necessary. Fortunately he found the colonel in a little better mood, but he prudently urged Paul and Kurt to make their way back to the aid station. The colonel turned to Sheridan and said, "The reports coming in are bad. The Germans have punched a hole in our lines that is bulging quite a ways back. As a matter of fact, our higher echelon of command is calling this the Battle of the Bulge."

—21—

The Battle of the Bulge dragged on. The ominous noise of the German Schmeisser machine gun was heard on a regular basis, mostly to the north and the east. It shot in rapid fire succession that came in short bursts and sounded like *brrruuurrrrpppp*. The Americans were taking casualties that were totally unexpected. The men had run into the problem of Germans booby-trapping houses before, all the way from Normandy. Now it was on a grand scale. In all sorts of buildings, houses, and other structures, the Nazis would turn pictures at a slant and booby trap them. It is natural to straighten a crooked picture, and when an unsuspecting GI attempted to correct the problem, he ended up either dead or critically maimed. The same was true of toilet seats. They would even booby trap dead American soldiers so that when other soldiers tried to get to their dog tags, they joined the corpses in death. The Germans had also mined the roads, and soldiers were out minesweeping every day, striving to find them. They strung heavy wire across various roads, and a vehicle driving fast with the windshield down would end up with two decapitated soldiers in the front seat. There was also an alarming increase in the number of soldiers suffering from frostbite, in spite of the warnings and efforts of Captain Sheridan and Lieutenant Saffridi. Fortunately they had a clear road back to the rear, where their casualties could be evacuated to the division and regimental hospitals.

One night, coming in off his roadblock duty, Paul was surprised and pleased to see a group of candles set up on the mantle of the fireplace in the main hall of the farmhouse. There was a large candle in the center and four on each side.

"You like?" Tony asked.

"What's with the candles?" Paul asked.

"It's your holiday, right?" Tony asked. "It's Hanukkah, isn't it? I scrounged these up in the cellar along with a few bottles of wine to help us celebrate."

"Wow, this is great," Paul replied, deeply touched. "Thanks, buddy."

Kurt walked over to Tony and said, as he shook his hand, "This is very kind and thoughtful of you."

"Never mind," Tony said. "One good turn deserves another. Besides, I didn't go scrounging in the woods and nearly getting myself knocked off to get these things."

His kind and considerate act went a long way toward helping the morale of the Jewish soldiers in the battalion.

Following that, two good things happened. First, they received replacements in sufficient numbers to make up for their losses. Because of these replacements, the Colonel was able to send small groups of men in rotation back to the rear echelon, to a regimental or divisional rest camp. This was for a precious forty-eight hours, but here they could get a hot shower, a change of uniform, and a hot meal. Sometimes they would see uniformed American Red Cross girls dispensing coffee and donuts. To the men, when these girls smiled, each was beautiful enough to be a movie star. Sometimes they could even see a movie or a USO show. All too soon, their pass expired and they had to get back in order to make room for the next few lucky GIs.

Once back at the battalion, they resumed their two hours on and eight hours off at their assigned roadblock positions.

Secondly, the number of Germans trying to fake their way through the roadblocks had decreased substantially.

Somehow the mess sergeant, in an ingenious manner, had resumed forging class A ration tickets, and so he was able to send his mess truck back to a food supply depot in the rear and draw plentiful amounts of rear-echelon food. One time he made vast amounts of chocolate pudding. He first sent his men out to the roadblock positions and saw to it that everyone pulling this duty got a mess cup full of hot, delicious chocolate pudding. After that he notified the rest of the battalion to come and get it.

One night they heard the ominous clanking of tank treads and assumed they were German. Sure enough, at first daylight, they spotted two Tiger tanks that were not moving. Some of the MPs approached cautiously, waiting for the turrets to swing around at them. Surprisingly, there was no sign of life in the these monsters.

Apparently they had run out of gas and the Germans had abandoned the tanks and run off looking for their own lines. A few enterprising GIs dropped explosive charges down the tank gun barrels and that finished the usefulness of these weapons.

Another night, Paul and Tony had just finished their spell on duty and entered the farmhouse for the welcome warmth emanating from the stove and the fireplace. Sergeant Major Harrison came barreling into the aid station boiling mad.

"I've got to calm down before I kill someone!" he muttered.

In order to get him to relax, Captain Sheridan handed him a canteen cup containing a small draft of elixir of terpin hydrate—the army cough medication laced with codeine.

"What happened?" Sheridan asked sympathetically.

"We were working our roadblock and everything was quiet. All of a sudden, a Volkswagen, driven by a German WAC [equivalent to our Women's Army Corps], came rushing up to our position. She spotted us and spun the car around a hundred eighty degrees and took off back to her lines. This gal could handle that vehicle like a racetrack driver! Since I just had my forty-five, I yelled at this guy next to me, who was armed with a carbine, to open up on her, but he just stood and stared. 'What the hell's the matter with you?' I asked. 'Why didn't you open fire?' He answered, 'Sarge, she was just too gorgeous.'"

"I figured she would report where we were, and deployed my men on either side of the road with all of their weapons primed and loaded. Sure enough, ten minutes later, a German half-track came rushing back to our position. It was loaded with black-uniformed SS. One of our men opened up on it with his bazooka and hit the thing right back of the engine, and it blew up, killing all of these characters who had been so set on killing us. I just have to calm down now and not let myself anywhere near that idiot yardbird."

Captain Sheridan just smiled and waited for the medication to take effect, and he then turned to dress the wound of an MP who had cut his hand on some barbed wire.

Two medics brought in a wounded German soldier on a litter. In full German uniform, he had boldly tried to slip around the roadblock. He was challenged but kept running, and so a GI brought him down with a bullet in his leg. Since he was dressed in German uniform, he would be sent to a POW camp and be warm and enjoy better food than the battalion was getting as a rule. Since Captain Sheridan was otherwise occupied, Lieutenant Saffridi bent over to tend to the wounded prisoner. Cursing, "Verdammt Amerikanischen Schwein Hund [Damned American pig dog]," the German pulled a bayonet out of his boot and stabbed Lieutenant Saffridi in the chest. Paul and Kurt fell on the prisoner and wrenched the bayonet away from him. Sergeant Harrison simultaneously brushed Paul and Kurt aside and shot the German right between the eyes.

"The only good Nazi is a dead one," he muttered in a fury.

Captain Sheridan ripped Saffridi's jacket and blouse apart and examined the wound.

"The good news is that it missed his heart. The bad news is that it looks like his lung is collapsed," he observed gravely. "Someone run over to battalion headquarters and get the colonel's command car. I'm going to patch him up the best I can and get an IV into him!"

Paul and Kurt ran over to battalion headquarters, and when the colonel heard about the lieutenant, he insisted on joining them on the way back to the battalion aid station.

Captain Sheridan urged, "You head back on this road due west and get to the regimental evacuation hospital. There is a surgeon there who is the best at handling chest wounds. You have to get there fast! The only thing that will save him is this rotten cold. It actually is good for a wound like this."

Paul drove, with Kurt in the back tending to the lieutenant, who was sprawled out on the backseat. Kurt had one hand holding the IV container and with the other kept supporting Saffridi so he wouldn't fall off the backseat. Paul had never driven so fast or recklessly, but a man's life was in danger! They made it to the hospital and stayed with the lieutenant until he was brought in to the surgical unit, at which time they were shooed away. The lieutenant failed to regain consciousness while they were with him. They returned to the battalion in stunned silence.

Later it was learned that Hitler had predicted that it would take General Eisenhower several days to figure out that the Ardennes fighting was a major offensive. He was wrong, as usual. General Eisenhower had immediately met with his top-ranking people and discussed ways and means of dealing with this attack.

Colonel Macklin was informed that General Ike had ordered his generals to have the Red Ball Express expedite the movement of supplies and troops to the threatened area. The information included the fact that General Eisenhower had asked General Patton how long it would take to move his forces up to the region and help relieve the surrounded American troops in Bastogne. Patton, without any of the officers at the meeting knowing this, had met earlier with his staff and ordered them to set up plans to swing his units around and head north to the stricken area. He smirked knowingly and responded that he could accomplish this within forty-eight hours, maybe sooner, as some of his units were already on the move.

General Patton ordered General Middleton to meet him in Arlon on December 20. It was reported that he had commented on the GIs in the area. "On account of these fine men, none of those ——— murdering Nazi ——— got through. If they had made it, they could have inflicted terrible damage on us in many ways." He had also indicated that part of his plan was to send the Fourth Armored Division up the road from Arlon right into Bastogne. While liberating Bastogne, he wanted to capture the key location of St. Vith in order to cut off retreating Germans.

General Patton's forces attacked on December 22 in the direction of Bastogne, and east as well. Supporting American artillery was moved in on the 23rd of December, and a complete attack was initiated early on December 24. The infantry had the assigned job of clearing the area between the Alzette River and the Arlon-Bastogne highway. Once again some units came up against their old familiar foes, the 352nd Volksgrenadier Division, not far from the Arlon-Bastogne highway.

On the morning of December 25, miraculously, the sun came out. Almost immediately, C-47 transport and supply planes, as well as throngs of fighters, left Allied bases and headed toward the

Ardennes, concentrating on helping the beleaguered Americans at Bastogne. The C-47s, looking like huge birds, swooped all over the area, dropping parachutes holding quantities of vitally needed supplies. The parachutes were orange, blue, white, yellow, and red. The fighters made vigorous attacks on German tanks and vehicles, and even personnel, with devastating results. The pilots could not hear the GIs on the ground cheering, and yelling, and screaming; but, the American troops on the ground vented their happiness and appreciation to see their good buddies in the air corps coming to their rescue. Ground troops coming from the south and west, including General Patton's forces, swept in. Bastogne was liberated, and the Germans went tumbling back to their fatherland.

While the Americans were charging at the Germans in the center of the front, to the north General Bernard Law Montgomery swung his British, Canadian, Czechoslovakian, Polish, and other Allied troops into action against the Germans. To the south, where the city of Strasbourg had been on the verge of being beleaguered by the Nazis, the French forces bravely charged at the Germans .

The French considered Strasbourg symbolically to be the capital of Alsace and Lorraine. These were the two provinces the Germans had taken from the French in the periods from 1870 to1918, as well as 1940 to late 1944. Equally important to every patriotic Frenchman is that fact that in 1792, "La Marseillaise," the French national anthem, was composed in Strasbourg.

The battalion was relieved and sent back to the rear echelon for R & R. They were assigned to a rest camp, where they would continue to receive replacements and stock up on their supplies and equipment. The men were housed in a set of barracks-like buildings and had the chance to have a hot shower and eat good food on a regular basis. It was like heaven. The men had gotten used to putting some water into a helmet and washing and shaving with it. Access to hot water was an unbelievable luxury.

The rest camp had a recreation building that housed lots of great things that they could enjoy. There were a number of pool tables and Ping-Pong tables. In addition, there was an upright piano that was in tune and in good shape.

A large jukebox in one corner of the large main room played all the latest tunes. Paul spent a lot of time at the piano, as well as sharpening up his skills at the pool table. Tony was very sharp at playing pool, and he handily sunk all of the balls into pockets

The Author at the piano

with seemingly little or no effort. Kurt, who was already highly skilled at Ping-Pong, quickly became the battalion champion, since he easily beat all the many challengers who came along. At night, tables were set out for bridge and poker games. Bridge tournaments were organized, and the men quickly learned to relax and enjoy this kind of activity. Frequently, Salvation Army and Red Cross trucks would pull in to treat the men to coffee and doughnuts. The chow in the mess hall was surprisingly good and reminiscent of what Paul had enjoyed earlier at Fort Benjamin Harrison.

At this time, a replacement for Lieutenant Saffridi arrived—First Lieutenant Danny Sullivan. He had a reserved but friendly personality and was quick to establish trust and confidence with the men. He sought out Paul and said, "Captain Sheridan told me that you doubled up on your medic duties by working with Lieutenant Saffridi. If you don't mind, I would appreciate your doing me the same favor." He held out his hand to Paul. "By the way, I like to be called Sully."

"You know, Lieutenant—Sully, that is," Paul replied, shaking Sullivan's hand, "You could have pulled rank on me and ordered me to do the same thing."

"I know," Sully answered, "but I would really like to have a happy camper working with me rather than someone who is ticked at being forced to do something he doesn't want to do."

"Please remember, Lieutenant: in combat, my first responsibility is helping the wounded," Paul cautioned.

"I know that, Kramer, and it is my first responsibility to help treat the wounded in combat also," Sully noted, smiling.

Sully got along great with all of the men and fitted very readily into the job as battalion dental officer.

One night, at the recreation hall, Tony and Paul decided to write to the folks back home. There were plenty of V-mail sheets available. Soldiers would write a letter on the V-mail sheet and turn it in to their commanding officer, who in turn would pass it on to the officer serving as the battalion censor.

Once the letter was considered satisfactory or had been censored properly, it was sent on to a rear-echelon unit, where it was microfilmed. The microfilm was then sent, along with many others collected from all over the European theatre of operations, back to the United States. Here the microfilmed letters were processed once more, magnified to a readable size, and delivered to the addressee.

Paul wrote,

> December 31, 1944
> Somewhere in France

Dear Mom, Dad, and Jerry:

I am fine and hope you are all the same. We are in a rest area now and enjoying it to the hilt. Playing a lot of Ping-Pong and bridge.

The food is very good, but not exactly what you can produce in the kitchen, Ma. We have had several USO shows come in, and the entertainers are great. They all knock themselves out to give a fantastic performance, and we appreciate them. The people running this place have come up with some good movies also, and so we are far from being bored. The Red Cross and Salvation Army are doing a wonderful job here too. They even write letters for some of the guys and keep us supplied with coffee and cigarettes. That's all for now. Love to everyone.

Your loving son and brother,

Paul

The battalion mail caught up with them, and Captain Sheridan received a letter from Lieutenant Saffridi, which he gladly shared with one and all. Saffridi was in a hospital in England and was waiting to be sent back to the States for more treatment. On the one hand, he was lucky to be alive, but on the other hand, he apparently had a long series of treatments ahead of him. On the whole, he was upbeat and looking forward to returning to the States and seeing all of his family and close friends.

Colonel Macklin received confidential news that General Patton's Third Army was attacking in the direction of Coblenz and Remagen.

Somewhere in France

General Hodges's First Army was moving toward it's assigned target of Coblenz and Remagen, where it would link up with the Third Army. General Montgomery's Twenty-First Army Group was advancing toward the Ruhr. The Sixth Army Group in the South was moving toward the Saar and flanking Strasbourg. Major General J. Lawton Collins, heading the Seventh Corps, was one of the most imaginative, aggressive senior commanders in the US Army. He never lost an opportunity to confront the enemy, using brilliant strategy and consistently forging ahead.

The morning after Paul had sent out his V-mail, the 456th Military Police Battalion received orders to rejoin the Seventh Corps, First Division, units of General Collins.

Colonel Macklin received reports that stated the Generals of the First Army—including Hodges, Collins, and Ridgway—were preparing a massive continuing assault on the German forces facing them. General Patton had signaled that he proposed to move on the southeastern corner of the Bulge. General Collins was set to move his Seventh Corps east to attack the base of the Bulge from Malmedy.

Malmedy was the location of the notorious mass murder of American prisoners of war by Nazi SS troops. This had occurred at the time of the Battle of the Bulge, and no American GIs in the entire area would ever forget the horror of that terrible tragedy.

General Bradley was planning a Third Army drive eastwards from Bastogne and a First Army drive toward St. Vith. The battalion convoy moved into a village southeast of Malmedy and set to work to stabilize the area. Troops fanned out, searching the recently vacated area for Germans who were moving back in an organized manner. It was not a rout, and unfortunately the battalion started talking casualties. The Germans were still a force to be reckoned with. The medical detachment set up shop in an abandoned German Kaserne, and the men didn't even have time to unpack their medical gear before the first wounded troops started to arrive.

The battalion was again ordered to move on and joined General Patton's Third Army, Third Corps, which was moving northeastward, linked up with General Collins's First Army, Seventh Corps, in the town of Houffalize. It was intensely cold, and there were deep snowdrifts that crippled the movement of these two army units. The German troops facing them were forced to retreat toward the German frontier. In Houffalize, once again, the battalion set up their cleanup and security operations.

The medical detachment happily found an abandoned building, in which they set up their battalion aid station. Enterprising members of the medical unit found ways of getting a fireplace and stove working so that the wounded would have a better chance of recovery from shock. Broken windows were patched up with boards or whatever was handy, and they soon had a comfortable, reasonably warm shelter.

The German commanders were totally flabbergasted at the ability of American units to move so swiftly and efficiently. The determined effort of the Americans to defend major supply depots had caused a lot of harm to the Germans and was a major factor in the halting of the Germans at the time of the Battle of the Bulge. Allied aircraft, too, had played a major role in decimating the German forces. The German Luftwaffe had made an effort to put up a fight, but they were overwhelmed by Allied fighters and lost many planes and pilots.

Almost as soon as they had settled down, it was again time to move on. Allied armies linked up with French units in the Colmar pocket. American, English and French forces continued to take casualties; the German death toll was appreciably higher. The American Seventh Army initiated a drive that let them establish a foothold on the German soil beyond the Saar River. General

Patton's forces took Trier and moved fifteen miles inside the German border. His Third Army started a major attack, linked up with the First Army south of Remagen. The Ninth Armored Division of the First Army grabbed the Remagen bridge (before it could be destroyed by the retreating Germans) and established a bridgehead beyond the Rhine River. There were fortifications on the east band of the Rhine river from Karlsruhe to Switzerland

As the American forces probed deeper and deeper into Germany, the battalion moved along with them. The Third Army began to exploit its position on the east side of the Rhine and seized a bridge across the Main River in Frankfurt. Once again the First and Third Armies linked up, near Wiesbaden. General de Lattre's French First Army crossed the Rhine River near Speyer and headed for Stuttgart. American forces completed a spectacular double envelopment at Lippstadt just west of Paderborn. All of German Army Group B, along with its Fifth Panzer and Fifteenth Armies and part of their Army Group H's First Parachute Army, were caught and sealed in this trap. The Americans cut the German pocket in two and shortly thereafter took more than three hundred twenty-five thousand German prisoners.

The Fourth Armored Division, with the battalion in nearby formation, was moving northeastward near the town of Gotha when the GIs advancing cautiously approached a camp named Ohrdruf. This was a subcamp of a still larger death camp called Buchenwald. The nightmare of what the men saw was far beyond the horror of what they had seen in combat. As the soldiers proceeded into this camp, they were surrounded by the pathetic sight of skeletal, emaciated prisoners, most of whom were dead; the majority of the pathetic survivors were dying. There were gallows all over the area, as well as the rest of the killing tools that the Nazis were so efficient at using.

The pathetic survivors that still had sufficient strength to communicate explained that at the drop of a hat, for no apparent reason, the German guards would decide to hang some inmates. On occasion, as if to make an excuse for what they were doing, the Nazis would mutter "Jude." Division photographers were brought in to record the grisly sights. Captain Sheridan and other medical officers cautioned the men against feeding the inmates, because eating a lot of food—especially the rich concentrated chocolate bars in their rations—would surely kill the poor souls. The medics fanned out to tend to any inmate they could find who showed even a tiny spark of life.

Tony and Paul lifted one skeletal inmate onto a stretcher. He looked at Tony and asked feebly, "Du bist a yid? [Are you a Jew?]"

Paul pulled out his mezuzah and held it in front of him, wordlessly.

The man clasped his hands together and sobbed, "A Danken Gott. [Thanks be to God]."

The pathetic sight of the tiny children, living and dead, as well as the other inmates, was more than many tough, grizzled American soldiers could bear.

General Eisenhower, when he heard about this, arranged to tour this death camp along with Generals Patton and Bradley. When General Patton viewed the piles of dead bodies all over the area, as well as the pathetic survivors, he reacted the same way many other American soldiers did and became violently ill. He had to be helped away from the camp.

General Eisenhower's face turned white, and he turned to the Americans gathered around him, as well as those survivors of this horror within hearing.

He looked grim as he said, "Fifty years from now, people will come out of the woodwork and claim that this never happened. A second point I want to make is that many people ask what we Americans are fighting for. This is what we are fighting against!"

In a cable to the head of the joint chiefs of staff, General George C. Marshall, noted in part, "The visual evidence and the verbal testimony of starvation, cruelty, and bestiality were so overpowering as to leave me a bit sick. I made the visit deliberately in order to be in a position to give firsthand evidence of these things if ever, in the future, there develops a tendency to charge these allegations merely as 'propaganda.'"

General Eisenhower gave orders that all GIs within a radius of reasonable commuting distance be brought to this infamous place. In this way, they could see for themselves the devastating heartbreaking tragedy that had unfolded here. Most of the GIs assumed that if there was one horrific death camp here, there had to be many more scattered throughout Nazi-held territory. The assumption was proven correct too many more times.

Many of the American soldiers wept openly and unashamedly. Paul was one of them, and he tried vainly to blink away the tears so that he could see what he was doing in a desperate effort to save as many of the poor souls that he possibly could. An entire medical team was sent in to take over the critical humanitarian effort to save as many lives as possible.

As the war went on, many of the Allied troops liberated more and more concentration camps. The enormous number of them was staggering. The Russians on their front reported similar incidents. Unfortunately, the majority of the victims were already dead before the liberating troops arrived to free them.

The abundance of gas chambers and crematorium ovens was a common denominator in just about all of these camps. Survivors reported that live victims were frequently hurled into the ovens.

The Allied troops continued to move into Germany from the north, south, east, and west. New German planes began to appear in the skies—planes that did not have propellers. They were apparently called jets. Despite their great speed, Allied aircraft had no difficulty in maintaining air superiority. One day, crossing the Reichsautobahnen (a German superhighway), units of the battalion stopped a Mercedes-Benz Grosser. This was a seven-passenger limousine that was armed like a tank and could achieve a speed of about 170 kilometers per hour (105 mph). A grumpy SS colonel leaped out of the spacious rear seat, wanting to find out what was holding him up. Facing an abundance of rifles, submachine guns, and pistols pointing directly at him, he clicked his heels and held his hands up, muttering, "Kamerad, Ich gebe auf. [Comrad, I surrender]." Colonel Macklin, who was nearby, strode up to the German and held his hand out. The German prisoner handed his Luger pistol over to him and then was directed to join a group of other German prisoners of war on the wide grassy median strip. They were part of a huge column of German prisoners of war being herded back to the rear.

Colonel Macklin called out in a loud clear voice, "I hereby appropriate this here vehicle as a prize of war." He then turned and looked his battalion over and signaled to his driver to approach, saying, "From now on, you dump that blasted command car of mine and drive me around in this here slick set of wheels."

His driver was only too happy to oblige.

With the colonel happily ensconced in the Mercedes, the battalion advanced along the highway.

Troops of the First Army and Ninth Army accompanied by the battalion advanced on the Elbe River. The Ninth Army, as per previous orders, halted at the Elbe, and the First Army at the Mulde, with orders to await the advancing Russian soldiers from the East. Patrols sent out by the First and Ninth Armies made contact with the forward troops of the Russian Army. As they made contact, requests came back for soldiers who could communicate in Russian or French. Immediately Paul and Kurt were sent forward, with Kurt protesting, "I never volunteered for this job."

Paul simply resigned himself to his fate. As they approached the small group of Russians and Americans, there was something like a stiff formality going on between the two Allied groups. Paul approached with his hand out, hoping he could remember some of the Russian words his Father Charlie had taught him. He held his hand out gingerly and said, "Kak Vee Pooshavayateer? [How are you?]"

A Russian soldier wearing a fur hat with earflaps and a red star emblazoned on the front grabbed Paul, gushing, "Orchin Charashor. [I am doing great]" Panyemyetyer Par Russki? [Do you speak Russian?]"

Paul responded, "Nyet. Ni panyemyetyer Par Russki, Tovarisch, Spasebo, Dar Svedanya. [No, I do not speak Russian, comrade. Thank you, good-bye.]"

For a moment, there was a stunned silence, and then Paul desperately initiated the conversation with a limited vocabulary of down-and-dirty swear words that he was striving to remember. At that point, all of the Russians in his immediate vicinity tried to grab Paul, pushing him and hugging him, some even kissing him. Here was a man after their own thinking. The rest of the Americans, pleasantly surprised at the overwhelming display of affection directed to one of their own, simply watched and enjoyed what was going on. The Russians tried to shower Paul with their vile-tasting cigarettes, vodka, and battle medals. Just a short time later, the intelligence units scrounged up some Russian-speaking GIs and Kurt and Paul were allowed to return to the battalion.

Kurt said, "If I had spoken one word, and the Russkies picked up my heavy German accent, I would have been dead meat!"

As the American troops moved farther into Germany, the battalion received orders to establish their location in the recently liberated city of Karlsruhe. Actually they were told that Durlach, which is a suburb of Karlsruhe, was their destination. This was up in a hilly area of one part of Karlsruhe and had been set apart as a cluster of homes for prominent Nazis and their families. The battalion MPs had fanned out in this entire area, gone to these homes, and ordered the Nazis and their families to clear out within twenty-four hours. The soldiers who heard about this approved. Several cautioned that if portions of the liberal press ever found out about this, there would be a lot of hand-wringing, and charges of cruelty would erupt.

And the war went on.

—22—

The medical battalion moved into a beautiful, imposing two-story home that bore signs of having been recently vacated. The dental office was set up in an alcove, while the dispensary was established in a glass-enclosed room that might have served as an indoor greenhouse. There was plenty of light in there, and Captain Sheridan was pleased that he would have a well-illuminated medical facility. The men were busy for some days unpacking crates of instruments, equipment, and medical supplies. There was more than sufficient space for all of the medical personnel, and the men congratulated themselves on having such comfortable quarters. Some of the local German men were hired to help unload the battalion trucks, including the four companies', motor pool's, and quartermaster's supplies. As one of the civilian Germans was trying to move a heavy crate off a truck bed, it slipped onto his arm, cutting a wide, deep gash. The man screamed in pain and immediately was brought to the dispensary. Captain Sheridan found that the man could speak reasonably good English and reassured him that he would be fine.

"My name is Heinrich," the man grated out despite his pain. "You are very kind to help me in this way."

Captain Sheridan nodded, administered a shot of morphine, cleaned and dressed the wound, applied some sulfanilamide powder, and then sutured it. He gave Heinrich some sulfathiazole tablets and instructed him on how to take them. Following that, he offered to have some GIs help him back to his home, cautioning that he wanted to see him in two days to determine how the wound was healing. Heinrich was aghast. He started to stammer his thanks and then blurted out, "They were wrong! Totally wrong!"

Captain Sheridan asked, "Please tell me what was wrong. Did I do anything wrong?"

"You did nothing wrong, herr Kapitän," Heinrich murmured. "The Nazi officials warned us that when you Yanks came here, you would slaughter all of the men and rape all of the women. Instead, you don't know me or anything about me, and you treat me with a lot of kindness. Thank you. Thank you. Thank you."

Captain Sheridan responded, "This is how we Americans treat everyone. This is our way of life."

Heinrich assured the captain he could make it home and thanked him even more profusely. The very next day, he returned to the door of the dispensary, and Paul asked him anxiously, "Are you having some problems?"

Heinrich turned around and was followed by a portly woman, who looked at Paul shyly.

Paul urged, "Please come in."

Heinrich said, "My Frau, my wife. She does not speak your language so well. She has a bad pain in her tooth. Can you help her?"

Lieutenant Sullivan, who was nearby, heard the conversation and bade her to have a seat in the dental chair that was all set up. He turned to Paul and said, "Get her a bib, and let's take a look at her problem."

After a few moments, he said, "She has a rather deep and extensive cavity, but we can fix that in a jiffy." After a few well-placed shots of novocaine, the cavity was cleaned out and packed with amalgam. Sully gave the grateful woman some painkillers, and she and Heinrich made it their business to thank every medic they could find in the dispensary.

It wasn't long after that, when the word spread about the wonderful American doctor and dentist, that an increasing number of the local inhabitants began to come to the dispensary for medical care. One of the MPs who reported for sick call asked, "What's going on here? Why are we giving the Germans such good treatment?"

Captain Sheridan answered, "We treat English, French, and Belgian civilians, concentration camp survivors, Allied soldiers, and German prisoners of war. I believe that our job is to help and heal people no matter who they are. We are just doing what we have been doing since we were formed up in England."

One day there was not too much activity in the dispensary, so Paul decided to explore the rest of the house. On the second floor, there was a wide wooden staircase going up into the nearly empty attic.

A few suitcases were on the floor, and there were several photo albums scattered around. Paul picked up an album and opened it, half expecting to see photos of family celebrations, outings, picnics, and the like. To his horrific surprise, there was photo after photo of people being hanged. In many cases the men, women, and children depicted here were wearing a Star of David, indicating that they were Jewish. Some had been hanged from telephone poles. Others apparently were forced to stand on small ladders that ultimately were kicked out from under the victims. The majority of the pictures showed not only smiling German troops but accompanying civilians as well, all of them apparently enjoying the grisly pursuit of murder. One of them appeared in many of the photos, happily posing for the camera. Paul had to assume that he was likely the head of the household of the building they had appropriated. He apprehensively reached for the other albums and found that they, too, were filled with revolting echoes of the earlier pictures. He was absolutely shocked. Here was evidence of an unquestionable nature showing organized mass murder. He tucked them under his arm, walked slowly down the stairs, and silently handed them over to Captain Sheridan. All of the officers and enlisted men studied the album contents in shocked and horrified silence.

Captain Sheridan spoke softly. "If any one of you feels a little guilty about dumping the Nazis out of their homes, take another look at this!"

The very next day, when more German civilians came in for medical and dental care, Sully angrily pushed several open albums to them and snarled, "Look!"

Tony asked, "How many of you were involved with this?"

Every one of them acted startled and expressed surprise and horror at what they saw. One of the them muttered, "We had no idea!" Another swore that he knew nothing about this.

"Then didn't you ever wonder what happened to the Jewish people who surely lived in this community?" Paul asked.

One of the men said, "We were told that some of them were resettled in Palestine and others were sent to labor and rehabilitation camps. I swear on the lives of my children!"

Captain Sheridan responded, "The people who told you this nonsense—are they the same ones who told you that we would murder you men and rape all of your women?"

The man looked sheepishly downward and said, "We believed them. We believed what they said about the Jews. We never questioned them, because to do so would have meant certain imprisonment or death if we were accused of being traitors."

"By the way, herr Kapitän," one of the villagers noted, "I see the burgermeister's (mayor's) secretary in a lot of the photographs. He and his family used to live in this very house."

"We gathered that," Captain Sheridan replied. "Those Nazi murderers have a lot to answer for."

The civilians all beat a hasty retreat, and the albums were sent on to battalion headquarters. Colonel Macklin flew into a rage when he saw the heartbreaking pictures, and he then had them forwarded to the division intelligence unit.

A few days later, Colonel Macklin received an order of the day from General Eisenhower that read in part, "The Jewish holiday of Passover will be here in a short time. All unit commanders will expedite the attendance of Jewish personnel to the following areas so that they may observe this important holiday." The order listed a number of cities and towns in their immediate area, including Karlsruhe.

Paul and Kurt discussed attending the Passover observation, and while they were in conversation, Tony piped up.

"By the way, that order doesn't say that anyone else cannot go. That Passover thing is where Jesus Christ was at the Last Supper. I'm going to sign up with you guys."

"We'll let you come, but only if you permit a slight change to part of your anatomy," Kurt commented.

"We'll be glad to have you come," said Paul, "and for starters, I'll try to explain to you what is going on at the seder, or the Passover ritual. Mind you, I'm no rabbi or Hebrew scholar, but I learned everything I know about this in a little synagogue called Congregation Beth Jacob, at the top of the hill on Middleton Street, where I lived. An elderly man—our *Shamas* [caretaker], Mr. Levine—taught us about the Hebrew Bible, Jewish prayer guidelines, and lots of other things. He was really old—in his fifties or sixties—wore thick glasses, and smoked Camel cigarettes all the time, lighting one from another."

As some of the other men in the dispensary sat down near Paul, Tony, and Kurt, Paul noted, "The real story of Passover is the story of the Jewish people's search for freedom. It is the story of how God freed the early Israelites from slavery. In the Bible, Exodus 13:8—I know it well because every year I studied this—it is written, 'And thou shalt tell thy son in that day, saying: "It is because of that which the Lord did for me when I came forth out of Egypt."'"

Paul paused for a moment, took a deep breath, and went on. "This really started when Joseph was brought to the land of Egypt. Skipping a lot further in this story, we get to Moses. He had run away from Egypt because he killed an Egyptian beating an Israelite. He was in exile in the land of Midian, where he had settled and married, and tended the sheep of his father-in-law. One day, as Moses was alone with his sheep at the edge of the desert, he came across a burning bush. The voice of God spoke to him from the burning bush, telling him he must return to Egypt to free his people from slavery. Moses returned to Egypt and appeared before Pharaoh. Speaking in the name of God, Moses demanded that Pharaoh free the Israelite slaves. Pharaoh was contemptuous of Moses's demand and made the work of the Israelite slaves even harder. They begged God to help them. Suddenly plagues descended upon the land of Egypt, and with each plague the Egyptians suffered terribly. Pharaoh promised to free the slaves if the plagues disappeared."

"When the plague was lifted, he broke his promise. He commanded that every Israelite firstborn be killed. The angel of death flew over Egypt, and every Egyptian firstborn child died, including Pharaoh's own son. Moses was called before the distraught Pharaoh and told to take his people out of Egypt. After Moses and his people left, Pharaoh had a change of heart and came after them with all of his military forces. Moses, who had brought his people through the desert to the banks of the Red Sea, saw the Egyptian armies coming at them, intent on murdering all of their former slaves. A miracle occurred when the waters of the Red Sea parted and Moses had his people follow him to cross in safety. When the Israelites all reached the opposite bank, they looked back to see their opponents drown in the returning crashing waves. For forty years, Moses and his followers traveled until they reached Canaan, the land God had promised them, beyond the River Jordan. On Mount Sinai, God gave the Ten Commandments to Moses, and in Canaan the Israelites began a new life."

Corporal Red Evans said, "This is what I learned from my Bible in church."

"Jews and Christians share the Bible together—the Jews with the Old Testament and the Christians with the New Testament. Our biblical traditions, in many instances, are one and the same," Paul replied. "Passover, also called Pesach, is observed by Jewish people the world over. They observe this holiday on two successive nights at a combined meal and religious observation of the plight of the Jews in Egypt and their salvation. These observances are called seders, and for Jews everywhere, this is called the time of deliverance. It is also called the Feast of Unleavened Bread. The flat bread matzo is what the Israelites had to eat when they fled Egypt in a hurry. There was no time to prepare the dough properly, and the bread that was baked in the desert sun was made without leaven. This was the bread of slaves fleeing oppression."

"Pesach was also the spring festival of the soil. The holiday was celebrated as the beginning of the agricultural year. The holiday was celebrated by the harvesting of the barley. It was one of three pilgrimage festivals during which all Israelites traveled to Jerusalem to thank God for His blessings."

"That was most interesting and enlightening," noted Captain Sheridan, who had quietly joined them. "Someone has to stay here and mind the store, but it's fine with me if you men want to go.

There are two scheduled evenings for the holiday observation. I see that you call them seders. You men decide on your own which one you want to attend, and sign up for it. I suggest you all go to the same one."

Tony said, "Thanks, Captain. I appreciate it. We'll do exactly as you say."

Paul ventured, "Captain, I can't tell you what this means to be able to attend one of these events. As a kid growing up, we traditionally went to my grandmother's house, where delicious food was in abundance. My grandmother and my mom had the same philosophy. If twenty unexpected people dropped in for a meal, there would always be enough. I used to think both Mom and Grandma had elastic cooking pots."

Corporal Evans spoke up. "We didn't have one of them there Jewish meals to attend, but my folks and grandparents had the same philosophy about plentiful meals at Christmas and Easter."

A short time later, the quartet of Paul, Tony, Kurt, and Red joined several other GIs heading for the Passover celebration. The little convoy of several two-and-a-half-ton trucks took but a relatively short time to arrive at their destination. This was a huge gymnasium, and it was filled from wall to wall with metal tables and benches. At each place setting, there was a Passover Haggadah, which is a book of the Passover observance. Within its pages are the story of the Exodus from Egypt as well as anecdotes, prayers and hymns of praise, and songs for children. There were small cups in front of each place setting that held what looked like the traditional wine that is served at a seder. The GIs found out later that grape juice had been substituted for the wine that is traditionally served, but no one cared.

There were also a number of women in attendance—women serving in the Women's Army Corps and the Army Nurse Corps.

Huge tureens of soup were brought to the tables by a multitude of German prisoners of war. The German military had designed a land mine that was covered by a metal bowl to protect the mechanism and keep it from going off until they wanted it to. These very same metal mine covers had been scrubbed clean and sanitized in boiling water until they were fit to be used as soup bowls.

Prior to the start of the ceremony, General Collins stood up at a microphone and said, "I have been selected to welcome you to these proceedings and want to greet all of my fellow soldiers here. It is a privilege for me to serve in this capacity. Many of you have come through combat with me, while others have served in different parts of the front."

The general paused for a moment and then said emotionally, looking around at the German prisoners of war who were bringing food to the tables, "I think it is fitting and correct that those who were so bent on destroying you are now serving you." He picked up a soup bowl. "It is even more significant that one of the very instruments designed for your destruction is now being used to nourish you."

Every American man and woman in the enormous hall rose to enthusiastically cheer the general. The applause went on for so long a time that it took a lot of effort to get the audience to quiet down and be reseated.

The main course of the meal was chicken, and it was a welcome break from typical army chow. Kurt and Paul explained the significance of each part of the service to Tony and Red.

The Passover service was conducted by a Jewish chaplain and a cantor.

All too soon, the seder was over and they were once more in the trucks heading back to Durlach.

When they returned to the dispensary, a grim-faced Captain Sheridan met them at the door.

"We have bad troubles here. It happened like in an instant. A GI went out for a walk one night and never came back. He was found the next morning, lying dead in a gutter. Attached to his chest was a scrawled note that read, 'Death to all Americans.' And it was signed, 'The Werewolves of the Third Reich.'"

"Colonel Macklin restricted all personnel to our base, but one dumb guy from Charley Company went out anyway. He got ambushed by a couple of knife-wielding civilians but managed to fight them off. He got back here all cut up, and fortunately we were able to stabilize him and ship him off to our general hospital in Karlsruhe."

"Wow, that's bad news, Captain," Paul replied.

"Why don't we try to find these guys and go after them?" Tony asked.

"We reported this to division headquarters, and they sent some intelligence people here to talk with us," Captain Sheridan answered. "They are recruiting volunteers to go out in teams to try to catch these murdering rats."

"I want to volunteer right now," Kurt said.

Tony, Paul, and Red joined in asking to volunteer.

"Thanks, but the colonel is flooded with names of guys who want to get involved in this operation," Sheridan replied. "I will send a note to him, though, asking him to add your names to the list."

"How does this operation work, Captain?" Red asked.

"We park a jeep at the top of a hill with several MPs armed to the teeth. This happens after sundown, and the lights of the jeep are shut off. They send one of our men out on the sidewalk, ahead of them about twenty feet. As the decoy moves farther on, they let up on the brakes and coast slowly behind him, keeping at a respectable distance. We have caught a few of these Werewolves and even brought in some live prisoners. Our intelligence people are grilling them but are getting no results. We are dealing with fanatic murderers who see it as their solemn duty to destroy as many of us as they can," Sheridan explained.

German civilians, for a time, were prohibited from coming onto the base. After a short time, the attacks ceased, and so once more the civilians were allowed to return. Once again, Germans returned to the dispensary for the medical and dental care they valued so highly.

One day Kurt was treating a teenager who told him his sister had a serious problem. She desperately needed medical care but could not get to the dispensary, because she either had broken her ankle or sprained it badly. The young man said his sister was fifteen years old, just one year younger than him. She also believed the Nazi propaganda that the Americans were out to kill as many Germans as they could. No matter what he said to change her mind, she was too terrified to be brought to the American battalion, but she was suffering terribly in the meantime. He begged Kurt to come with him to see his sister and help her.

Captain Sheridan stepped in.

"I will not allow one of my men to put himself at risk to treat some stupid girl!" he objected, adding, "These werewolves might ambush you."

Heinrich had come in to determine how his wound was healing. He interjected, "Herr Kapitän, I give you my word of honor as an honorable German that no harm will come to any of you Americans who come to treat this girl. I will go with you to where this young man lives with his sister."

Captain Sheridan replied, "There is no way I will allow any of my men to do this unless you agree to my following terms. We will have an armored car filled with our military police go with you and my medics into whatever abode this stupid girl is living at. If she needs X-rays or treatment for a broken ankle, she will have to go with my soldiers to a US Army hospital. If she has just a sprain, they can treat her on the spot. If anything irregular happens, like your Werewolves attacking, my men will wipe you all out!"

Paul spoke up. "Please, Captain, let me go with Kurt. Our helping another German will just improve our relations with them."

Sully joined in. "Remember: there is a military edict against fraternizing with the Germans, but I guess this comes under the category of medical help. I guess, though, that if this is legitimate, it will go a long way toward instilling trust and acceptance by the civilian population."

Captain Sheridan responded, "I will discuss this with Colonel Macklin, and if he agrees, I want Bubba to be in charge of the team to treat this idiot girl."

Kurt said, "Thanks, Captain. With Bubba in charge of this operation, we are in perfect hands."

A short time later, Bubba and two MPs joined Paul and Kurt in the command car with the teenager and Heinrich. Paul and Kurt had put together a kit of materials they could use to treat a sprained ankle, if that turned out to be what it really was. A jeep loaded with MPs armed to the teeth followed them.

The little convoy made its way out of Durlach and down into one of the other suburbs of Karlsruhe. While they were en route to their destination, Bubba turned to the teenager and asked, "What's your name, son?"

"My name is Walther," the youngster replied.

"Y'all listen to me good now. If y'all are planning to ambush us or some other kind of mischief, first thing is Ah'll wring youah neck clean off, like ah used to do to chickens back home." Then he turned to Heinrich, glaring, and said, "An y'all gonna be next, mista!"

Both Germans objected vociferously that they were innocent and that their mission was really legitimate.

The two cars, at Walther's direction, pulled up in front of a four-story building, part of which had been shattered by a bomb blast. Bubba, holding a submachine gun, followed Walther, while Paul, Kurt, and Heinrich brought up the rear. The MPs in the jeep all got out and positioned themselves near the front door. They had to climb four flights of stairs. Now Paul realized that getting this girl down the stairs would be challenging.

Walther opened the door, and they all filed into a rather small apartment. Walther quickly made his way through the foyer and living room and turned into one of the two bedrooms that occupied the place. A teenage girl, likely sixteen years old, lay on the bed. She had a very pretty face and long, dark hair that curled around her shoulders, and she was on the plump side.

As soon as she spotted the Americans—especially the scary sight of Bubba wielding his submachine gun—she panicked and jumped up in alarm.

Kurt, speaking to her softly in German, reassured her and explained that they were there to help her.

Kurt then translated as Heinrich added to the reassuring words the girl had just received. Heinrich told the girl about how the Americans were sincerely and genuinely helping the German civilians and stressed that whatever they had been told about the Americans was a flat-out lie. He told her that they had all been deceived by the propaganda of the Third Reich and that the Americans were truly and legitimately their friends.

Paul stepped forward and asked, "Can you speak English?"

"Yes, I can, but I told my brother and our friends that I cannot. I was afraid," the girl answered.

"What is your name?" he asked.

"Birgitta," she replied.

"What happened to your leg?" Paul asked.

"I fell down during a bombing raid, running for my home, and I am sure I twisted my ankle."

"Can you move your foot at all?" Kurt asked.

"Yes," she replied, grimacing while she showed them that she had some limited but painful movement of her leg. Checking the leg and ankle carefully, Paul and Kurt concluded that most likely she suffered from a severely sprained ankle.

Paul got some towels out of the bathroom, and they alternately applied hot and cold soaks to the affected area. After about fifteen minutes of this, they proceeded with their work. Kurt shaved her leg from the knee down to the foot, and following this, Paul applied generous quantities of tincture of benzoin. He then positioned a series of adhesive strips on the bed. As he had done so many times earlier, he fastened first one vertical strip to the girl's leg, and then a horizontal strip, firmly but not too tight. This created a basket weave pattern of adhesive strips. Paul wasn't even completely finished when Birgitta announced in stunned surprise, "It feels better already!"

When the job was completed, they had her stand on her feet, which she was able to do, and walk gingerly along the side of the bed.

"I don't know how to thank you," she murmured shyly.

"Well, for one thing, you can tell your friends and neighbors that the Americans are really here to help them," Paul replied.

"We have been lied to and duped," she said in astonishment.

"I feel sorry for her boyfriend," Walther said. "She argued with him about going to the Americans for help, and he swore to her that he was positive that the Yanks were just as murderous as the English, French, and Russians. She was half ready to dump him, as you Americans say, after their last fight about this."

"Let me tell you another thing," Kurt added, "You have been treated not only by Americans but by two Americans who just happen to be Jewish!"

To emphasize the point, Paul pulled out his mezuzah that hung around his neck, from his shirt.

She flung her hand to her mouth in astonishment, murmuring, "And you would help a German after the persecution your fellow Jews endured from our people?"

"Our American way of life and our religion teach that all human life is precious," Kurt answered proudly as a fairly new American citizen.

She looked at Paul and then Kurt and said, "In another life, I could have been dating one of you."

"Forget it," Paul snorted. "You're much too young for the likes of me. I'm twenty, and I don't mess with sixteen-year-olds. By the way, we don't make house calls usually, so drop by in a week or two and let us remove the tape."

Bubba looked at them and said, "Eff you boys are finished, let's skeedaddle out ah hyah raht now."

"Okay, Bubba," Paul replied, and he followed him out of the room with Kurt, Heinrich, and Walther moving quickly after them while Birgitta called out, "Thank you, thank you, thank you. We were wrong! Terribly wrong!"

When they were heading back for Durlach, Walther asked hesitantly, "Can I tell you something if you won't get very angry with me?"

"Go ahead," Paul urged. "I promise we won't be upset with you."

"You may very well be when I tell you," Walther said hesitantly. "Birgitta's boyfriend belongs to the Hitlerjugend [Hitler Youth]."

"I believe that most German teenagers belong to that," Kurt offered.

"Yes, but you don't understand," Walther remonstrated. "I believe that he is also a member of the Werewolves!"

"If this guy has American blood on his hands, Ah want his ass!" Bubba exclaimed.

"Us too," Paul replied for him and Kurt. "Where can we get our hands on this guy?"

"He lives in a place that is unknown—to me at least. He comes and goes to see Birgitta, but lately she has really become disenchanted with him."

"Are you two aware that the Werewolves are murdering Americans?" Kurt asked Heinrich and Walther.

"No, we have been told that they are simply organized to protect us from the Americans who are out to maim, kill, and rape our women," Walther replied.

"We are honor bound to tell all of our neighbors and acquaintances about how well we have been treated by the Americans," Heinrich emphasized. "We don't want any part of those crazy fanatics!"

Within the period of less than a week, all reports of attacks on Americans ceased—not only in Durlach but also in the entire city of Karlsruhe.

A short time later, Colonel Macklin visited the dispensary.

"How can we help you, sir?" Captain Sheridan asked.

"Two of your men, according to our intelligence sources, were instrumental in stopping the Werewolf attacks in their area." He spotted Paul and Kurt and held his hand out to them. "I want to thank you for what you did in helping save American lives. Men, I have already given Bubba and the other MPs who went with you a three-day pass out of appreciation for what they did working with you. The least I can do is the same for you two. I know you can't go very far in three days, but for you two, I'm going to give you a little bonus." He smiled and handed over a set of keys to Paul. "You can take my Mercedes with you, which will extend the radius of your three-day pass. That's the car with a hood as long as a railroad car!"

"Wow, Colonel, sir. You have to be kidding," Paul expostulated.

"No kidding, and I brought along your papers," Sheridan added. "Unless you have any objections," he noted, turning to Captain Macklin. "I am pleased to see these men get some recognition for what they did, sir, and I am going to ask for one more little favor."

"What's that ?" Colonel Macklin asked.

Sheridan pointed to Tony. "He and these other two are like the three musketeers. They hang out together and work very well as an important part of our medical team. Can I wangle a three-day pass for him too?"

"Whatever you want, Captain," Macklin replied.

Tony jumped up in the air, clicked his heels, and yelled, "Wowee!"

"Get yourselves busy and pack up whatever you need for three days and take off," Colonel Sheridan ordered. "Bubba and his buddies have already left, going sightseeing and God knows what else. So get going."

— 23 —

April 12, 1945, brought devastating news to the battalion It was as if they had been struck with a bomb. President Franklin Delano Roosevelt was dead. He had been at his thermal resort in Warms Springs, Georgia, where he was apparently felled by a massive stroke.

This great hero to many millions of Americans, a man who had fought for civil rights and who was a champion of all minorities and the downtrodden throughout the entire world, was forever gone.

Paul turned to Kurt with tears in his eyes and asked, "Do you want to say the Kaddish [the Jewish prayer for the dead] with me?"

Kurt silently put on his cap, and together the two of them recited the Kaddish for their beloved president.

Paul thought, *There is a double tragedy here. First is the one of our great loss. The second is that President Roosevelt did not live to see the great victory that he strived so diligently to achieve.*

Tony waited a moment and then asked, "How about snapping out of this and getting to see this vehicle the Colonel is offering us?"

The trio left their quarters and headed for the battalion motor pool, where the huge Mercedes-Benz Grosser was housed, handily close to the dispensary. When they entered, they were astounded at the sight of this incredible motor car. The four-door open car had a hood that seemed to be as long as a railroad car. The building that housed it was a garage formerly used by the Wehrmacht, and all of the battalion vehicles were accommodated here. This was the location for all battalion vehicle repair work, replacement of parts, and maintenance, and the storage of all of the battalion vehicles was done here.

The battalion motor pool master sergeant, Henry Waterston, who was in charge of the facility, greeted them. "The colonel told me to expect you," he said. "Let me just check your papers."

The trio fumbled through their pockets to locate the precious documents .

Apparently satisfied, the sergeant nodded toward the car. "She's all yours. The key is in the ignition."

They needed no further invitation, with Kurt and Tony momentarily holding back to allow Paul into the driver's seat. Tony got in front alongside Paul, and Kurt ensconced himself in the wide, spacious backseat.

"Where are we heading?" Tony asked.

"I don't know. I'd really like to get down to the University of Heidelberg, just to see if it is still standing," Paul replied.

"I'd like to see Salzburg in Austria again. They have the most incredible pastry shops that even beat what they have in Vienna," Kurt ventured.

"I'm just along for the ride, so whatever you say sounds good to me," Tony remarked.

It was not too difficult to find their way to the German superhighway called the Autobahn. This highway, with a wide grass strip in the middle, meandered from Northern Germany all the way down to Austria. Rumor had it that there was no speed limit, and Paul was really anxious to open up the car and really see what it would do. It handled like a truck but gave a most comfortable ride.

As they headed south, the roadway turned into a series of hills and valleys, reminding Paul of the trips the Kramer family had taken out of Mattapan Square to Route 138 heading south toward the little town of Sharon. Sharon was a tiny community nestled in the hills some twenty-five miles southwest of Boston. During the hot summer months, his dad would manage to get two weeks off from work, and Mom, Dad, Jerry, and he would leave the steamy environs of Dorchester to escape the humidity and head for an area that was the highest elevation in Eastern Massachusetts. Just as one reached the outer limits of Sharon, the air would change noticeably for the better, being decidedly cooler and cleaner. The abundance of many pine trees and other foliage contributed to the clean air that was a haven for many people who suffered from lung and bronchial problems.

A number of Jewish hotels were located at the shores of a beautiful lake, called Lake Massapoag. They competed with one another in serving mouthwatering foods traditionally favored by many Eastern European Jewish immigrants. Their hotel was called the Highland Manor and was a spot where working-class people could afford to spend a few days or a few weeks away from the stifling heat of the city. The rooms were small and cramped, but the food was excellent. Many times, Paul would take Jerry down the hill to the lake, where the hotel rowboat awaited. They would row around the bend to the waters of the magnificent luxury resort called Sunset Lodge. Only the well-to-do could afford to stay here, and Jerry and Paul would look longingly at the beautiful structure set up atop a hill overlooking the lake. Each and every day was precious, and the time spent swimming in the cool, refreshing waters of the lake was an experience none of them ever forgot. On other occasions, when the family went to Nantasket Beach, a small peninsula just south of Boston jutting out into the Atlantic ocean, swimming was a different experience.

Most of the time, the water was so cold that just getting out in the water up to one's knees was a real challenge. The severe cold would turn one's feet totally numb.

"Where are we going, buddy?" Kurt asked, snapping Paul out of his reverie.

"I'd like to stop off at Heidelberg University, which is not far from here," Paul answered.

"What's with this Heidelberg?" Tony asked.

"I just want to make sure it is still standing," Paul replied.

"You're the driver," Tony responded.

A short time later, they pulled off the highway and onto the grounds of the magnificent Heidelberg University.

Two middle-aged men ran up toward the car with fear and apprehension on their faces. They had noticed the three American soldiers in the car, and they wondered what these GIs were up to.

Paul stopped the car alongside them and asked, "Do you speak English?"

"Yes, I do," replied one of them. He was short and thin and had graying hair that was almost white in some places.

The other was almost the total opposite. He was tall and portly and sported a handlebar mustache.

"We just came here to make sure you are all right," Paul ventured.

"Verrückter Amerikaner [Crazy American.]"

Kurt angrily replied, "Ich bin ein Deutscher. [I am a German]."

"Ach so," the shorter man answered. "I apologize for my colleague's rudeness. It just seems strange that Americans who have been so anxious to destroy us have to see if our academic institution has survived."

"You've got it wrong, mister," Tony offered. " We are not here to destroy you. We just wanted to get rid of the murdering Nazi bastards running this country."

"You are correct," the man replied softly. "My name is Heinrich Baumgartner, and I am a professor of philosophy. My friend's name is Alex Von Targer."

Von Targer ventured forward, clicking his heels together and holding out his right hand, and bowed.

"We don't go for that Nazi bullshit about heel clicking and bowing," Tony angrily exploded.

"Meine Herren [Gentlemen]," Baumgartner explained, "that is an old German custom that has nothing to do with the Nazis who appropriated it. It is simply showing you the respect that you deserve. We are amazed that American soldiers are interested in the survival of one of our cherished academic institutions." He then turned to Kurt for approval.

"Ja, das ist korrekt [Yes, that is right]," Kurt responded.

The campus was even more beautiful than Paul had imagined. Heinrich and Alex showed all the points of interest to the Americans.

Tony looked at Paul, asking, "You got that out of your system?"

Paul turned around, nodding wistfully. "This was fantastic," he uttered, and he then put the car into gear, waving good-bye to the Germans, and drove back to the Autobahn.

They made it down to Salzburg, Austria, where Paul stopped the car at one of the many pastry shops that abounded in that beautiful city.

"Before you pig out, guys, we gotta bring some of this stuff back to our outfit," Tony ventured. Paul and Kurt nodded in assent.

Standing before the showcases heaped with mouthwatering pastries of every kind, they focused on the chocolate buttercream delicacies topped with heavy layers of chocolate.

Their attention was turned by other fascinating varieties of pastries beyond their imagination. They filled three heaping bags with the goodies before deciding what samples they would take to snack on during their trip back.

They paid the incredulous girl behind the counter. After they made several trips back to the car, loading it up with all of the goodies they could find, they decided that they had bought enough.

"I don't think you'll find anything like that back home," Tony ventured.

The trip back to Durlach took less time than they thought it would, principally because Paul had the gas pedal practically down to the floor.

The pastries were carefully divided and distributed so that those who wanted some could at least have a miniscule taste of the delicious and never-to-be-forgotten goodies.

Work went back to the same routine; and, as usual, Paul divided his time between being a technician in the dental office to helping run sick call in the dispensary.

News that the war (The War in Europe) was over came as no surprise to anyone. Most of the men started to prepare themselves for the news that they would be sent to the Pacific to finish the war with the Japanese. That was not to be. The outfit had spent so much time in combat from Normandy through to Germany, with few breaks in between, that they would remain where they were for the time being. They were informed by bulletins that came from battalion headquarters.

There was more good news. Once again because of the time the battalion had spent in combat and because of their excellent record of achievement during the war, selected personnel would be sent to Switzerland on a special ten-day pass. Several different tours were available. According to Captain Sheridan and Colonel Macklin, both of whom had been there, the best tour would be the one including Geneva, Montreux, and Basel. A total of three tours were available, and those who were interested in going were to leave their names at battalion headquarters. Some of the men put in for all three, but Paul simply asked for the tour that his trusted advisors had recommended. Names would be posted for the first group selected; and, in time, on a well-planned rotation, practically everyone from the battalion would have a chance to visit Switzerland.

Every day, men eagerly crowded around the battalion headquarters bulletin board. Finally, at long last, names of the first group selected were posted. Paul was pleased and surprised to see his name listed. Following the paragraph listing the names, there was included a set of strict regulations required of them. Under no circumstances could any GI bring a weapon of any kind with him. Food products of all kinds were also banned. Paul didn't care. The only food he would be inclined to take with him would be a Hershey bar, and he knew there would be no problem finding great chocolate in Switzerland. Besides, his brother Jerry's thirteenth birthday and Bar Mitzvah had just been celebrated in December. His being in combat had prevented him from engaging in the luxury of getting a gift for his brother. Maybe now, in Switzerland, he could get Jerry a nice watch. He hoped that, since he had no time to spend any of his money accumulated while in combat, he would have enough funds to get gifts for Jerry, Mom and Dad.

The announcement also detailed the date and time of their departure. It specified the gear they could take with them, which included a duffel bag to store changes of clothes and underwear, shaving utensils, toothpaste and toothbrushes, and whatever else he could cram into it. The communication additionally reminded all of the men who were going that they represented the United States of America and consequently were expected to be on their best behavior.

The only regret Paul had was that only Red Evans and he had been included from the medical detachment on the posted list. He was assured by the battalion clerk, repeatedly, that the remainder of his buddies in the medical detachment would have an opportunity to go at a later time.

On the appointed day, Paul woke at four in the morning. He was so excited about the trip that he couldn't sleep anymore. He steeled himself to stay in his cot until about 5:00 a.m. and then moved around quietly so as not to wake his buddies. The latrine was totally devoid of people, and it was almost a luxury to brush his teeth and shave in total solitude. He then carefully checked the contents of his duffel bag to make sure he did not forget anything important. His travel papers and vouchers were carefully stored in the front breast pocket of his wrinkled dress uniform, which he located after a frantic search of his gear. Paul agonized over what shoes to wear. He had only a pair of beat-up combat boots and an old pair of GI shoes. He settled for the shoes, making sure again that he had enough socks, underwear, and handkerchiefs. After gathering up all his gear, he left the dispensary.

As Paul walked down the street toward battalion headquarters, he saw Corporal Evans emerge from the structure. He too carried a heavily packed duffel bag over his right shoulder.

"I'm glad I have another medic to go with me in case I get hurt carrying this darn blasted bag." Evans muttered.

They saw a small convoy of three two-and-a-half-ton trucks lined up farther down the street. Sergeant Woods, wearing his MP brassard, held a clipboard with a roster on it. He nodded to the men and checked off their names. Several men were already seated on the benches in the back of the first truck, and Woods motioned Paul and Evans to join them. "We still are a little early, so just relax there." Woods suggested.

Within a half an hour, the following two trucks were loaded

and the little convoy started to move. They drove slowly out of the battalion area and onto the main street.

A short time later, they arrived at the Karlsruhe Railroad Station and were herded onto the back two cars of a waiting train. Paul noted that the men assigned to his group were all located in the very last car. The train was of the typical European style, in which each car was composed of individual compartments reached by a narrow corridor. Sergeant Woods led the way, slid open the door of a vacant compartment, and motioned for Evans and Paul to enter. He sat beside Evans, and in the opposite seat, Paul made himself comfortable.

A short time after they boarded, the train started slowly to move out of the station and gradually picked up speed. It seemed that they were heading south and west, which made sense since they were heading for Switzerland.

The countryside was very picturesque, and most of the small talk was subdued, since the trio spent a good deal of the time looking out of the wide window.

After what seemed to be a long time, the train finally came to a stop at what appeared to be the border crossing. The train was moved to a side track, and a small engine came along, unhooked the last car, and moved it to a train on another track. Two people entered the compartment. One was a civilian, and the other was attired in what appeared

On the train to Switzerland

to be in a police uniform. The civilian said, in surprisingly good English, "May I see your papers please?"

Paul had been thinking he would have to use his French-speaking skills to communicate with the Swiss. Was he ever wrong!

The police officer took the papers one at a time, scrutinized them carefully, and turned them over to the civilian, who said apologetically, "We are sorry for the inconvenience. A number of Nazi war criminals are now trying to sneak into our country, and they are not welcome here. It is also obvious that a Nazi would have little luck trying to pass himself off as an American, but we have to be careful. By the way, my name is Henri LeCompte, and I am, as you probably guessed, with the security services."

Paul, Evans, and Woods each in turn shook his hand and then were introduced to the police officer, who was involved with stamping the bottom right corner of each of their papers. He and LeCompte left, with LeCompte saying over his shoulder, "I'll return in a bit for a little chat. We can't go anywhere until the entire train is checked."

Sure enough, a short time later, LeCompte returned, saying, "I would appreciate it if you would call me Henri."

Paul spoke up. "I am a little surprised. I always got the idea that you Swiss remained neutral but were firmly rooting for the Germans."

"Absolutely not," Henri replied. "Our intelligence found out that Hitler had a plan for invading Switzerland and taking it over as part of his design for a greater Germany. The commanding general of our Swiss Army, Henri Guisan, announced that Hitler was a murdering fanatic who was determined to conquer all of Europe with no exceptions. Swiss intelligence, of which I am a part, has supplied the Allies with countless amounts of essential and critical information. You are among friends here, gentlemen."

A short time later, the train started to move smoothly, with the men having hardly any clue they were moving at first. The scenery became more picturesque until they were swallowed by what seemed to be an endless tunnel. Finally they broke out into a startling panorama of beautiful mountains all around them while they passed endless lakes and streams on either side.

Paul turned to Henri, saying, "We did have problems with Germans trying to infiltrate our lines, especially during the Battle of the Bulge, and we understand the reason for your caution. We hope you catch any of those murdering bastards trying to get into your country and turn them over to any of our Allied forces, where justice will catch up with them."

Henri nodded and asked, "Where are you planning to visit here?"

"Geneva, Montreux, and Bern," Sergeant Woods replied.

Evans added, "I hope we picked the right tour."

"You made an excellent choice, and I am certain your trip will leave a lasting impression with all of you," Henri replied.

The train came to another tunnel, and after another protracted dark foray, they came out into a brilliantly lit station.

"We have arrived here in Geneva," Henri noted.

They wasted no time disembarking from the train and made their way upstairs to the street level.

"What hotel are you staying at?" Henri asked.

Woods answered, "The Hotel Geneva. By the way, Paul goes by his given name. The French Resistance dubbed him Jean Paul. Please call me Harry like everyone else does. This character next to me, Corporal Evans, is called Sanford or Red. He answers to both."

"That's fine," replied Henri, "By the way, I am not pressed for time and can show you to your hotel if that is agreeable with you."

Harry Woods answered, "If you don't mind waiting until I round up the men in my group, we would appreciate your kindness."

"Take as much time as you need." LeCompte responded.

They made their way to the street level of the enormous station and then turned patiently to wait for their group to form up with them. Paul noted that two other groups from their battalion were also starting to assemble.

While he was waiting, Red picked up an informational brochure about Geneva. Paul noted that the other two groups had already assembled and been checked out and were heading toward a different part of the station. Apparently they were going to a another hotel.

Harry had taken out his trusty clipboard and roster and finished checking off the names of the men assigned to their group. At his direction, they all followed Henri out of the station and on to the street.

Geneva was spectacularly beautiful. And it was so clean! The streets looked as if someone had just scrubbed them. There was not a scrap of paper or any kind of debris to be found anywhere. Not too far away, the magnificent Lake Geneva literally sparkled. A smattering of sailboats and lake steamers made the scene look like something Homer Winslow would have painted. Off in the distance, they could see the incredibly beautiful snow-covered Alps. Towering over all of the adjoining

Author traveling in Switzerland after the War ended.

mountains was the world-renowned Mont Blanc, the highest peak in Switzerland.

As the GIs walked down the wide sidewalk, they all took time to take in the beautiful scenery. They seemed to attract very little attention from the Swiss civilians walking by. Some nodded or greeted them politely and walked on. One inquisitive man, recognizing Henri, walked up to him and asked, "Est ce que les soldats sont Anglais ou Canadien? [Are these soldiers English or Canadian?]"

LeCompte chortled in English, "Hardly. These are real Americans!"

The man walked off shaking his head. LeCompte had earlier assured them that the hotel was a mere four blocks from the station. The trio decided that four blocks would be no problem to walk, but soon they realized that Henri's idea of a block was far more than they had anticipated.

"This is turning into a forced march just like what we had in basic training," Red grumbled in a quiet aside to Paul. Henri and Harry apparently didn't hear him.

Harry was busy trying to read his brochure.

"Switzerland is the legendary home of Wilhelm Tell, who is the national hero of the country," he noted.

"I learned that in school." Paul answered.

"Some people here speak German, some French, some Italian, and some Romansch," Harry said. "It depends what part of the country you are in. Most Swiss are fluent in several languages, including English, because of their excellent educational system."

At long last, they arrived at the hotel, which had a brass-and-gold overhang with a bold sign that read, "Hotel Geneve."

Harry approached the desk accompanied by Henri. When the four men manning the desk spotted LeCompte, they almost came to attention.

Henri turned to his new friends and addressed them.

"I am going to speak English so that you will have the benefit of understanding what I am saying. Not only that, but English is our second language." He then turned to the quartet behind the desk and, speaking in a brisk, clipped manner, said, "These gentlemen are members of the United States Army. Our government has invited them and many more of their comrades to come and visit our country. They are to be treated as welcomed guests, and I expect you to extend to them every courtesy and consideration. Your level of hospitality is expected to be the finest, and I will be back from time to time in order to determine how our guests are being treated by you and your staff."

The Swiss hoteliers, to a man, nodded in agreement and turned to Harry. One of them, apparently the maître d', said, "On behalf of our hotel and staff, we are most pleased to welcome you. We are expecting twenty of you, and we have five suites with double bedrooms and twin beds to accommodate you all. Our bell captain and his assistants will take your bags, and he will give each of you a key to your suite. Please follow them, and they will take you to your rooms."

LeCompte approached Paul, Harry, and Red and shook hands with each of them.

"It has been a genuine pleasure to meet you and I hope we will see each other soon again during your stay here. We all hope you will have a most pleasant visit." As he turned and left the hotel, the maître d' turned to them and said, "Gentlemen, each of you will find vouchers for your meals in your rooms. On these are noted the hours of our dining room for breakfast, lunch, and dinner. By the way, if any of you are hungry, our dining room is still serving dinner. Individual room keys will also be handed to you by your bell boy or bell captain. If you have the slightest problem or question, please do not hesitate to call me. My name is Guillaume."

"Now, if you will please follow our bell boys and bell captain to the elevators, you will be escorted to your rooms."

The group started to follow the bell captain and his staff, but Paul hung back.

"Pardon, sir," he said. "Is there any chance the dining room would be serving a chocolate cake and milk?"

"But of course, young man," Guillaume replied cheerfully.

Paul called out to Evans and Woods, "I'm going to check out some chow. I'll send my duffel bag up with you guys, See you in a little while." He held out his duffel bag to a bell boy who took it and waited alongside Evans and Woods.

Both of them nodded and walked off toward the elevators.

Paul eagerly followed the maître d' who, along the way, pointed to two large doors.

"That is our music room. If any of you are musically inclined, we have a beautiful piano in there that is hardly ever touched."

Paul was more interested in filling his stomach for the time being, but he made a mental note of this.

The dining room did not hold too many people at that time, and Paul was seated at a table close to a window looking out on the sidewalk.

Guillaume asked, "Can I bring you anything besides the chocolate cake and milk?"

"That will be fine, sir," Paul replied, relishing what was to come. "We have not had the luxury of being able to drink milk for a long time."

"What you are about to have will delight your palate," Guillaume replied. He snapped his fingers, and a waiter immediately appeared at his side, clicked his heels, and nodded.

Guillaume, in rapid-fire French that was too fast for Paul to catch, gave orders to the waiter, who once again clicked his heels and disappeared.

Guillaume said in a confidential tone, "the Austrians pride themselves on their pastry. We in Switzerland put them to shame. When it comes to anything that is chocolate, including chocolate cake, we are the masters of the culinary world. When you have finished, come by the front desk, and I will have someone escort you to your room."

Moments later, the waiter appeared with an enormous slice of chocolate cake covered by a thick chocolate frosting. He also carried a large glass that had apparently been chilled first and then filled to the rim with cold milk. Expertly, the waiter put them down in front of Paul without spilling a drop.

The first forkful of cake let him know that the cake was warm, moist, and delicious beyond his wildest dreams. He washed it down with some of the cold milk and then set about devouring the delicacy slowly, relishing every bite. Before he knew it, he was scraping the bottom of the plate. The waiter appeared, asking, "May I get you something else, monsieur?"

"No, thank you. Please give me the bill, and I will be on my way."

"Monsieur Guillaume has requested that you accept this as a token of our esteem," the waiter replied.

Paul thanked him profusely, went through his pockets, and came up with a most generous tip.

The waiter followed him all the way to the dining room doors, thanking him.

Paul returned to the front desk, where Monsieur Guillaume was standing with his arms folded and smiling, asking, "Did you enjoy your little snack?"

"To tell you the truth, I thought I had died and gone to heaven," Paul answered. "I want to thank you for your kindness and generosity."

"You sound like a gracious Swiss citizen, which is the highest compliment I can give you." Monsieur Guillaume replied.

A bell boy appeared at Paul's side and beckoned him to follow.

When Paul arrived at his room, he found Harry and Red putting their toilet articles out in the bathroom. What they had was a two-bedroom suite with a single bathroom. Each of the bedrooms had two beds. One of the beds was already occupied by someone, snoring softly, who had the covers pulled over his head.

Harry pointed to him, noting, "This guy is from Company C, and he was assigned to our room. Seems to be a good enough person, although he sure took his time in the shower. I have the other bed, and you and Red are in the other room. We are leaving you enough room in the bathroom to put your toothbrush, toothpaste, and shaving stuff. I'm going to sleep in late, so if you want to get up early and go out on the town, you are on your own. Red is inclined to be a late sleeper when he can, so he feels the same way."

Paul waited for the bathroom to be free and then took a long, hot shower. This was luxury piled on luxury. After he got out and dried himself off, he realized how tired he was from the long day's journey. The moment he got into his bed, he fell into a deep sleep.

Early the following morning, the sun streamed through the closed blinds and curtains and woke him. He got out of bed quietly, so as not to disturb the others, and took care of brushing his teeth, shaving, and getting dressed. The lobby was practically deserted, and the dining room was not open yet. He walked into the music room, closed the doors behind him, and sat down at a magnificent concert grand piano. He slowly started to go through his repertoire, choosing first all of his favorite classics. He could remember back to the times when he practiced assiduously at his baby grand piano at the family apartment in Dorchester. The only thing that was missing was the metronome that was positioned on the piano, which he used almost constantly. His reverie was interrupted by a polite cough behind him. Paul stopped playing and turned halfway around to find a young man in a chauffeur's uniform standing behind him, asking, "I beg your pardon monsieur, but madame would like to know if you could play Rachmaninoff's Piano Concerto Number Two for her ?"

Paul turned all the way around, and sitting across the room on a couch sat a little old lady dressed primly in black. She wore a black lace shawl around her head and shoulders, looked at him piercingly, and gave a hint of a smile.

"I'll do the best I can for her; that's all I can promise." Paul responded.

Paul had played the piece some time before, perhaps at a piano recital sometime in his distant past. He knew he was a little rusty with it, but did the best he could. When he finished, he segued into a host of classical and semiclassical numbers. Since the uniformed man did not interrupt any more, Paul assumed he had the lady's approval. To complete his presentation, Paul played several Gershwin numbers. When he finished, He turned around once more, and the lady beckoned him to sit by her.

As he approached, the woman asked, "Are you English or Canadian?"

"Madame, I am proud to say that I am 100 percent American!" Paul replied enthusiastically.

"I am genuinely shocked," she replied. "I was always convinced that Americans are barbarians—essentially cowboys or gangsters."

Paul stopped just in front of her.

"I assure you, madame, that I am neither a cowboy nor a gangster, although in my childhood I often dreamed of being a cowboy."

"It is difficult to believe that an American could be such a talented musician," she answered.

"Please believe me, madame, that I am strictly a mere amateur. There are countless Americans who are greatly talented professional musicians who could easily put me to shame. Besides, none of us are barbarians. We have many, many leaders in the fields of medicine, research, philosophy, science, literature, the arts, et cetera. Our academic institutions are on par with or superior to many of the prestigious universities all over the world."

"You have been hurt by my callous remarks, and for that I am sorry. I am a victim of what I have seen in the cinema. Please sit down by my side and tell me about yourself. Let us be friends," the woman murmured. "By the way, my name is Lily."

"My name is Paul," he answered. He sat down alongside her and held out his right hand.

"What is it that you want to do on your visit here?" Lily asked.

"My brother has just turned thirteen years old, and I would like to buy him a watch for his confirmation—or, as we call it, his Bar Mitzvah." Paul replied.

"Ah yes, I am familiar with that," she answered. "Do you think you have enough money for a watch here?"

"I'm hoping that they don't run into more money than I can afford," he noted.

Lily opened her pocketbook and removed a small envelope, opened it, and removed what appeared to be a business card. She wrote something on it, placed it in the little envelope, and then wrote something on the cover. She then handed this to Paul, saying, "Bring this to the Ervandine Watch Company, which is in this same block, just around the corner. You won't have to say a thing. Hand this to the person behind the counter who appears to be in charge. I am certain that you will get what you are searching for."

He took the envelope from her and put it in his right hand breast pocket so he wouldn't lose it.

Lily commented, "By now the dining room is open, and I want to ask you to join me for my usual *Petite Dejeuner* [breakfast]. My favorite is a croissant fresh out of the oven. While it is steaming hot, I slice it open and put a generous portion of butter in it to be washed down by a café au lait."

"It sounds good to me, Mme. Lily, but I respectfully ask if I can treat you." Paul ventured.

She laughed. "My husband has a standing account here, and you will turn the dining room into a turmoil if you even try to give them some money. Please let me just sign for our breakfast and enjoy the fact that my husband is treating us both."

"My thanks to you, madame. I will not only enjoy the pleasure of your company, but I will get rid of my hunger as well," Paul answered.

"I must make note of the fact that Americans are not only charming but generous as well," Lily replied. "You are making an old lady happy."

As they walked into the dining room, the headwaiter, followed by three waiters, stirred into action. They surrounded Paul and Lily and escorted them to a lovely table by the window overlooking Lake Geneva.

Lily looked up at the headwaiter and said, "I'll have my usual."

Paul piped up and said, "I'd like the same as what the lady is having."

The headwaiter gave commands, almost military style, to the waiters behind him.

In a very short time, two waiters brought separate plates holding steaming croissants, while another brought a huge silver coffee urn. Still a third brought a plate with a variety of thinly sliced cheeses on it, as well as a cup of butter.

Paul wasted no time and, ignoring the butter, placed two different slices of cheese on the croissant, which had been sliced open at the table by the headwaiter, who asked, "Is there anything else I can get you?"

Paul said, "I don't want to make a pig out of myself, but a glass of real orange juice would hit the spot right now."

The headwaiter once again barked out commands, and the two waiters who had been standing not too far away stirred into action.

Lily giggled. "This is what we call Continental style service. You get this kind of service in all of the better restaurants of Europe except for those barbarian Germans."

"I like it, I like it," Paul chortled.

Lily put a generous dollop of butter on each half of the croissant and then selected some cheese slices as a topping.

The orange juice appeared momentarily, and Paul savored the delicious taste of what he had dreamed about since he had left America. He then selected several appealing-looking slices of cheese and placed them on the open croissant.

Lily commented, "You will note that Swiss dairy farmers are the very best in the world."

Paul replied, "Madame, at the risk of sounding crass or ungrateful, I respectfully submit that American dairy farmers are truly outstanding."

"Paul, the Americans should have put you in the diplomatic service." she laughed.

Paul forced himself to eat slowly, but he delighted in every bite. The coffee, although a bit strong, was infinitely better than what the army had supplied. He completed his breakfast in just a few short moments and then looked at her.

"Madame," Paul said, "I don't know how to thank you for your generous kindness and hospitality. I hope your little note to the watch company will help and even if it does not, your heart is in the right place. Thank you so much."

Lily smiled. "It is I who must thank you for the delightful musical presentation and for your company. I do not want to be rude, but now that you are finished with your meal, why don't you go after that watch?"

Paul needed no further urging. He got up, shook Lily's hand, thanked her again, and headed back into the lobby and out onto the street.

Walking at a quick pace, he made it around the corner to the location of the Ervandine Watch Company. It was an imposing structure of white stone and large windows, and with the name emblazoned in gold lettering over the front door. Paul hesitantly opened it and stepped inside. A thin middle-aged man, slightly bald, looked at him disapprovingly through his pince-nez glasses, which he wore halfway down his nose. He looked at Paul questioningly, prompting Paul to hand him the little envelope, without saying a word. Large showcases containing all kinds of watches surrounded the periphery of the room. The man wore a morning coat with a wing collar and white bow tie. He opened the envelope and then disappeared into the back room. He returned with another man, portly and jovial looking, who was dressed in the same type of attire, and who looked at Paul with a genuine smile on his face.

"You are Monsieur Paul, I presume?" he asked, extending his right hand.

"Yes, that I am, monsieur." Paul responded.

"Madame has instructed me to be of the utmost help to you, and so I understand that this is for your younger brother. Why don't you look in these two showcases, and I will help you with your selection."

Paul murmured, "I really don't want to go over my budget, though."

"Just let us not concern ourselves with that, Monsieur Paul." the man replied.

Paul spotted one that really appealed to him. It appeared to be gold and was a really nice looking watch. He pointed to it, and the man removed it from the case.

"I assume your brother's wrist is smaller than yours?" he asked.

"Yes it is, but how much smaller I don't know," Paul answered.

"In that case, it would be prudent to send it larger than smaller. Back at your home, your brother can always have a watch repair person remove the extra links. On the other hand, finding links for a watch such as this might prove difficult." The man recommended. "By the way, I am the manager of this establishment, and my name is Lucien."

"Monsieur Lucien, I really do want this watch, but I want to make sure I can afford it."

"Dear young man, think nothing of the price. You may have it," Lucien offered.

"I just can't do that, sir. Please let me pay for it," Paul pleaded.

"Madame has insisted that you be given whatever you select, and I think you have made an excellent choice."

"This has to be a very expensive timepiece. What did this lady say in the note she sent you?" Paul asked.

"Mme. Lily is the wife of the owner of not only this establishment but all of our branches in most of the major cities of Switzerland. Please accept this with our thanks and appreciation for your patronizing us. Now, may I wrap this up for you, please?"

Paul was thunderstruck. He nodded silently, and Lucien produced a case that seemed to be worth more than a hundred dollars by itself. He then placed the watch inside the case with some thin linen-type cloths wrapped around the watch and, with a flourish, handed it to Paul. Paul thanked him, and Lucien replied, "I assume I may report to Mme. Lily that you have been pleased with this selection."

"Paul said, "I hope I will have the opportunity to thank Mme. Lily in person. If not, please convey my sincere gratitude."

Lucien shook his hand warmly and said, "Consider it done, and I hope your brother enjoys his new watch."

Paul stepped outside clutching the watch case and feeling as if he were on top of the world.

— 24 —

Paul flew back to the hotel, first to thank Mme. Lily and secondly to show off his new watch to his buddies. As soon as he entered the lobby, he ran to the dining room and looked carefully around the entire area. Disappointingly, she was not to be seen. The headwaiter was already walking toward him with an inquisitive look on his face when Paul waved as if to say, "All is fine," left the dining room, and walked toward the front desk. Guillaume, the maître d', greeted him.

"May I be of service, monsieur?"

"Yes, sir. I was hoping to see Mme. Lily," Paul replied.

"I regret to inform you that Madame and her husband left for Zurich a short time ago. They are expected to return in about a week."

"I am sorry to hear that," Paul answered. "I was hoping to have the opportunity of speaking to her in person. Unfortunately, my group is scheduled to leave here in two days."

"You are welcome to use my office if you wish to write her a note. I will be more than happy to deliver it personally with your profound regret at not being able to speak to her." Guillaume offered.

Paul thought about it, and then said, "If it's all right with you,

I would rather write the note in my room. I can think better when I am alone."

"Your wish is foremost in my consideration, monsieur." Guillaume said.

Paul took the elevator to his room and was fumbling with the key when a GI opened the door, asking, "Aren't you one of those pill pushers?"

Paul held out his right hand. "Guilty." he retorted.

"I thought you looked familiar. I was a replacement who caught up with the outfit in Germany and was assigned to Company C. My name is Len Pappas, but my dog tag says Leonidas. Your other two buddies took off, which I am about to do also."

"Paul Kramer," Paul answered, shaking his hand. "I'll see you later on."

As soon as Paul entered the suite, he headed for a desk situated in an alcove just off the living room. Conveniently, on the desk there was hotel stationery, pens, envelopes, and all that he needed. He sat down and agonized over how, with his terrible handwriting, he could convey his thoughts. He picked up a pen and decided he would print as carefully as possible and wrote,

My Dear Madame Lily,

Please accept my heartfelt thanks, first for the delight of your charming company. Although too brief, I will never ever forget the pleasure of our all-too-brief encounter. The kindness and generosity of you and your husband will always be remembered as well. The beautiful watch you gave me for my brother is beyond all of my expectations. Regretfully, I am leaving here in a short time and will not have the pleasure of speaking to you in person. So I will close by saying good-bye and may God bless you and your loved ones.

Sincerely,

Paul.

He folded up the letter, placed it in an envelope, and wrote "Madame Lily" on the front. He closed the door and did not wait for the elevator but ran down the stairs two at a time to reach the front desk. Guillaume greeted him, and Paul held out the envelope to him.

"I would be most grateful if you would personally deliver this to Mme. Lily as soon as she returns."

"But of course, monsieur." Guillaume replied.

Paul stepped out onto the broad sidewalk of the hotel and headed down to the waterfront. A number of boat tours were available. They even had one with its final destination being Montreux, which was their next destination. It was a little too pricey for Paul's budget. For a moment he wondered why the tour did not take the GIs there on the boat tour. Perhaps the logistics of moving a large group onto a lake steamer might have been a problem. For whatever reason, it had been decided that they were going to go there by train. Paul signed up for a short cruise on Lake Geneva and immediately ensconced himself on the top deck. The trip was very enjoyable, with the spectacular beauty of Lake Geneva, the city, and the surrounding Alps being a never-to-be-forgotten sight.

Hanging in the living room where I grew up, I never knew the
story behind this painting in which my father was obviously
inspired to memorialize his travels in Switzerland.
—Neil Kozol

Lake Geneva is the largest of the Alpine lakes of Switzerland. The sight of the towering and majestic peak of Mont Blanc was magnificent. As he looked around him and out onto the lake and beyond, Paul felt as if he were enveloped in a series of picture postcards, each more breathtaking and beautiful than the next.

He spent the next few days sightseeing and stretching out his money so that he would have enough for the entire trip.

All too soon, it was time to leave Geneva. The men all clustered on the train station platform, waiting for the conductors to give them the signal to board. They found out firsthand that the Swiss railroad system is one of the best in the world. The trains are punctual to the minute, and the cars are all immaculately clean and comfortable. When the conductors called out for everyone to board, by silent consensus, the foursome grabbed a compartment and settled down for the trip to Montreux.

According to the guidebooks, Montreux has an unusually mild climate and extends for close to four miles along the shores of Lake Geneva. With the towering mountains in the background, once again they found themselves in an absolutely beautiful area. It even had a castle that beckoned to visitors. Many of the Swiss considered this a resort town and took their vacations there.

Buses met them at the train station and drove them to Glion, which is a suburb of Montreux located high above the city. The views were once again spectacular on the way to their destination, the Hotel Victoria. The hotel was set in sumptuous gardens and afforded the residents with an incredible panorama of Lake Geneva below. As soon as they were settled, as usual, the men split up, each going his own way. Paul found himself walking along a street where there were several outdoor cafés. One establishment had a huge sign that advertised, "Cup of Tea, ten francs. Refill with water, no charge." Paul sat himself down at a table and, when the waiter approached, asked for a cup of tea, which was well within his budget. A portly middle-aged gentleman approached him and asked, "Do you speak English?"

"Absolutely sir. I am an American," Paul replied.

"May I join you?" the man asked, holding out his hand. " My name is Stephan Warmschield. Please call me Stephan."

"Paul Kramer," Paul responded, grasping the man's hand.

Stephan sat down and uttered a big sigh. "I am fifty-nine years old, and my doctors tell me that if I don't get rid of some of this fat, I'll have difficulty making it to sixty." His red face puffed with the exertion of getting to the table and sitting down. "I take it you are on some kind of leave." He waved to the hovering waiter and pointed to Paul's cup of tea.

"That is true, and I am enjoying every moment of visiting your delightful country," Paul answered.

"I assume you must be a student back home in the USA," Stephan offered.

"I'll have to give you points on being as perceptive as Sherlock Holmes," Paul commented, laughing.

"That is very flattering, but I had to assume someone as young as you is more than likely a student in civilian life," Stephan noted. "Let me fill you in on a little bit of information about our country. As you have probably seen, the majority of us are independent and a bit aloof. We are similar to the Scots, who are also mountain people. We, like them, are very superstitious, and we are both frugal with our money. By now you have been made familiar with the term 'alp.' This is used to refer to the range of mountains that stretches across south-central Europe. This word 'alp' has another meaning to both the Swiss and the Germans, which is the high alpine meadows. Here we pasture our cattle in the summer months. To many of us, therefore, Alps with a capital *A* refers to the mountains, and alps with a small *a* refers to the pastures. Interesting, isn't it?"

By this time Paul had finished his cup of tea, and he asked the waiter for a new cup.

Stephan held his right hand up in objection. He spoke rapidly to the waiter, who returned to fill each cup with hot water.

Paul look at his cup of water, made a wry face, and said, "I don't want to be rude, but for a mere twenty francs, we both can have a full cup of tea. As a matter of fact—and please don't be offended if you are short on cash—please let me treat you."

Stephan laughed. "It is the principle of the thing. The sign advertises that they will refill your cup with hot water for free. Take advantage of it."

"I respectfully point out that I do not want to drink a cup of hot water. For a piddling ten francs, I am willing to pay for a new cup of tea," Paul objected. "Do you have a job?"

"Of course I have a job," Stephan answered. "I am a munitions dealer and have supplied both sides during this highly profitable war for me."

"Doesn't it bother you about all of the millions of people who have been killed and countless more who have been wounded from these terrible supplies you have made available, especially to the murderous Germans?"

"I am a neutral, born and bred so. The casualties are a consequence of the stupidity of war," Stephan answered, still chortling.

Paul got up, totally exasperated, saying, "I have had enough of this conversation. If you will please excuse me, I will be on my way."

Stephan blustered, "I have offended you, and for that I am genuinely sorry. Money wise, I have enough to buy most of the cafés and hotels in Montreux and have many millions left over. My conscience does bother me, but believe me, the Allies and the Germans have insisted on dealing with me and countless others who have supplied munitions to both sides. That is not an excuse but simply an honest observation. Now please sit down; let us change the subject, and talk about other things."

Paul reluctantly sat down for a moment, trying his utmost to be polite but fighting a losing battle with his conscience. He got up again and nodded coldly to Stephan. He could not even shake his hand but simply walked away.

For the next few days, Len joined Paul, Red, and Harry in sightseeing and window shopping. Then it was time to return to the railroad station and embark on the last leg of their trip.

This was Bern, the capital of Switzerland. After disembarking from the train there, they found it to be a beautiful old city with many perfectly preserved medieval buildings, as well as colorful squares, great-looking shops, and many fountains. The town brims with character, appearing as it really is—a thirteenth-century wonderland. It happens to be the only Swiss city that has been declared a world heritage landmark. The Americans noted that the entire town appeared to have a festive air about it, and as always, the Swiss made the visiting Americans feel genuinely welcome. They were booked in an elegant hotel—the Grander Schweitz Land. It was the epitome of Old World elegance, and they found it a genuine pleasure to settle into their magnificent rooms. They spent the remaining time picking up souvenirs that would fit into their bags for friends and loved ones.

All too soon, it was time to return, and once again the men gathered in the railroad station for their trip back to Germany. Paul was surprised to see LeCompte approaching them. As usual, he was accompanied by a uniformed police officer and was going from group to group, apparently looking for them. Paul waved to him, and Red called out a greeting simultaneously as the Swiss duo approached them. Henri held out his hand and shook hands with Red, Harry, Paul, and then Len, whom they introduced.

"I simply came to wish you a bon voyage and express my hope that you enjoyed visiting our country." Henri said.

Harry noted, "You, sir, are privileged to be a citizen of a magnificently beautiful and charming country."

Red chimed in. "We had a great time here."

"We will never forget the unforgettable pleasure of being here," Paul added. "It was very kind of you to come down and see us off, and we thank you for your genuine hospitality."

Henri just grinned and said, "We Swiss are truly educated about how wonderful you Americans really are. Thank you again for coming here."

One more time they all shook hands, and then a conductor signaled that the train should be boarded.

As the train pulled out of the railroad yards, each of the men was lost in his own individual memories of the great time he had enjoyed while visiting Switzerland

The convoy pulled up in front of battalion headquarters and stopped alongside another line of trucks that were apparently getting ready to pull out. Paul no sooner jumped off the back of the truck, pulling his barracks bag with him, than he heard a familiar voice call out.

"So how was it, Kramer?" Tony yelled from a truck in the outgoing convoy.

Kurt was beside Tony, and he waved. "Welcome back."

Tony and Kurt had signed up for a different tour—one which would take them to Zurich, Lucerne, and some other location Paul didn't quite catch.

"I hope you have a great time," Paul told them, walking over to them and shaking their hands. "I had a marvelous experience and will never forget it."

He no sooner uttered these words than the vehicle carrying his friends started to move.

Paul was warmly welcomed back to the medical detachment led by Captain Sheridan and Lieutenant Sullivan. They said, almost in unison, to Paul and Red, "Are we ever glad to have you two back."

They were put to work immediately, helping to administer to sick GIs as well as civilians in the dispensary. Many of the German civilians continued to be shocked and surprised when they were cheerfully given free medical and dental care. They were even more astounded to find that two members of the medical detachment providing first-rate care to them were Jewish.

Paul divided his time between working in the dispensary and the dental office.

Shortly afterward, Tony and Kurt returned from their vacation and shared the stories of their adventures with the rest of the medical detachment.

They got back into their routine—not only of work but also their recreational pastimes of playing bridge, whist, and Ping-Pong. Kurt was the battalion champion, hands down, in Ping-Pong. He easily destroyed all of his opponents from the entire battalion. Captain Sheridan was the most astute bridge player, with Colonel Macklin being a close second. The colonel was very impatient with players who did not bid correctly and was forever scolding his uneasy partners. Whist was a game they had learned in Northern Ireland, and although it was similar in many ways to bridge, it had different strategies and required a different approach.

One month followed another, and suddenly, one day there was electrifying news. The war was over! Some new kind of weapon, one that none of them had ever heard about, called an atomic bomb, had been dropped on the cities of Hiroshima and Nagasaki. Countless numbers of Japanese people had been wiped out in a single instant. Everyone felt sorry for the poor souls who had died in the inferno. On the other hand, countless hundreds of thousands of American lives would be saved by virtue of the war being over. Millions of Asian civilians would owe their lives to the war being brought to an end.

"Maybe now we can go home." Tony chortled.

"Golden Gate in forty-eight." Kurt pessimistically predicted.

The battalion settled into a state of anxious anticipation. Would orders come through or not? Some of the men took to hanging around battalion headquarters in order to be the first to find out what was happening. Nothing happened, though.

One day in the dispensary, a young civilian presented himself to Paul with a severely cut hand. As Paul treated him, the thin, light-complexioned youth started up a conversation in perfect English.

"Our stories about you Americans were not correct," he observed.

"What do you mean?" Paul asked.

"We were told repeatedly that you Americans would murder every man and child and rape all of our women. We all totally believed that," the German answered. "By the way, my name is Wilhelm, but you can call me Willy."

"Willy, does our taking care of your people put the lie to your false propaganda?" Paul asked.

"To a certain extent. Some of us are worried that now that the war is over, your battalion will be sent back home and replaced by black soldiers," Willy noted.

"What's wrong with that?" Paul asked innocently.

"First, they are low-class people with inferior mentality. They are only good for menial labor and serving their superiors. They make for good servants and little else." Willy noted.

Paul looked at Willy, starting to lose his temper.

"That's your filthy Nazi philosophy coming out. Black people are just as intelligent as, or much more so than, their Caucasian or Asian counterparts," Paul retorted. "By the way, how does it feel to be treated by a Jew?"

"We may have made some mistakes by putting you Jews into displacement camps," Willy countered nervously.

"Those were death camps, you stupid, ignorant bastard," Paul answered. "And don't give me that Nazi herr Kapitän bullshit about your not knowing about killing millions of people, including Jews."

Willy protested, "I swear we were told that Jews and other undesirables were put into relocation camps."

"That's a lot of garbage, and you know it." Paul responded hotly.

Kurt wandered by, asking, "Maybe this guy was a member of the Wehrmacht or worse."

Paul had just about finished with his work and said, "You can leave now."

Willy said, "Thank you," bowed slightly, and left the dispensary.

Kurt noted, "This guy is a fanatical Nazi through and through. He still likes to get good care from the Americans, though."

One day, Tony came running up to the dispensary with electrifying news. The battalion had been placed on a seventy-two-hour alert. They were going to be moved to a cigarette camp in Southern France. Cigarette camps were departure camps, where military units assigned to be sent back to the United States would be assembled to wait for their transportation. They were called cigarette camps because they were designated with names like Camp Camel, Chesterfield, Lucky Strike, etc.

The seventy-two hours came and went, and then orders came through to stand down from the alert. This was shattering to the morale of everyone in the battalion, and they just went back to their regular duties.

A few weeks later, the very same thing happened again. Colonel Macklin erupted like a volcano. He told Captain Sheridan that he planned to go to the American section of Allied Headquarters and find out just what the hell was going on. He added that he would need Kurt and possibly Paul to help with whatever interpreting was needed to get through the French and Russian checkpoints. He was also taking Bubba with him, and he insisted that all personnel in his command car be armed. Captain Sheridan put up some objections but was silenced by the colonel's determination.

"We are not going to be sidetracked by some trigger-happy Russkies, and the more artillery we have, the better chance there'll be for us getting through those blasted checkpoints," Macklin uttered with a tone of finality.

The colonel's command car—including Bubba, who was driving with a submachine gun across his knees, and the colonel, who was similarly armed—pulled up in front of the dispensary. He handed some MP brassards to Paul and Kurt, who had been waiting patiently for their arrival.

"There's a couple of web belts with .45s holstered to them on the backseat, as well as some carbines. Put on the brassards and the web belts, and hold the carbines in your laps," the colonel ordered.

Paul and Kurt silently got into the backseat and did as they were told.

The trip to the Russian sector took a little while, and sure enough they were stopped at the Russian checkpoint by two heavily armed Russian soldiers. One of them approached the driver's side and motioned with his weapon for Bubba to pull the side window flap down. Bubba silently complied and then put both of his hands on the steering wheel. The colonel held out his authorization papers, but the Russian was not interested in them. He simply reached into the front seat and put his hand on the watch that Bubba was wearing. Immediately Bubba's machine gun came up and pushed on the Russian's forehead. In the backseat, Paul and Kurt also pushed the muzzles of their rifles up against the soldier's head. The other Russian soldier came over to the passenger side and leveled his weapon at the colonel.

Paul suddenly yelled out in Russian, "Tovarisch! [Comrade!]"

The Russian on the passenger side motioned with his weapon for Paul to come out of the vehicle.

Paul prudently left his weapon on the backseat, came out smiling, and said, "Kak Vee Pooshavayateer, Tovarisch? [How are you, comrade?]"

The Russian was astounded. Paul continued. "Panyemyetyer Par Russki ? [Do you understand Russian?]" He then added some deep-down colorful and filthy Russian sayings that he learned both from his father who was born in Russia and a Russian prisoner they had liberated in Ohrdruf.

The other Russian soldier put his weapon down, threw his hands around Paul, and gave him a big hug, kissing him on both cheeks.

Paul muttered, "Easy there, you big, ugly slob. If you were a good-looking broad, it would be okay; but you—forget it!"

Both Russians yelled "Okay, okay." and waved them on.

When Paul returned to the backseat, Colonel Macklin asked him, "Just what in hell did you say to those dirty Commie bastards?"

"I'm really not sure sir, but whatever it was, it seemed to work."

Kurt piped up. "I beg your pardon, sir. Those Russian people are decent and honorable and very brave. They faced the Nazi juggernaut, who invaded their land for the sake of murdering every Russian they could get their hands on. The Russians themselves were held hostage by the Communists. Most of them are God-fearing people: Catholics, Protestants, Jews, Muslims and many other religious denominations. They fought courageously and furiously for their survival."

"Soldier," Colonel Macklin replied, "it was the Commies I referred to as bastards, not the Russians."

They proceeded on until they came to a prominent four-story

stone building with a huge American flag flying from a flagpole in front of a large circular driveway.

"This must be it," Colonel Macklin muttered. "You men wait here."

He got out, mounted a large flight of stone steps, and disappeared into the building.

Not fifteen minutes went by before Colonel Macklin came out of the building cursing and swearing up a blue streak.

"Those darn-blasted cruds!"

He got into the command car still sputtering, and Paul asked him, "Colonel, sir, what's going on?"

"The dockworkers, or whatever the hell they are, in the New York shipyards have gone on strike. First it was on-again, off-again, and then they finally decided to go on strike. That's why we were put on alert and then taken off. Those dockworkers were told that thousands of GIs cannot come home until they end this strike, and their answer was to go on strike regardless."

"Cunnel, sar," Bubba interjected, "ah'll re-up for fahve years if y'all 'll let me pull guard duty on those docks."

Macklin looked at him sympathetically and calmed down.

"They are exercising their right to strike, which is part of what we have been fighting for. It's just that we are stuck here in Europe until they get off their cotton-picking asses and decide to end the strike and let us come home. The latest latrine rumor from here is that we will be put on alert in a few more days and may or may not get to be sent to a cigarette camp."

They returned by way of the French sector and were warmly greeted by the French soldiers manning the checkpoint. While their papers were being checked, one of the French soldiers made it clear that he had served as a legionnaire. The soldier who checked their papers spoke perfect English, albeit with a strong accent.

"Are you all military police, *messieurs*?" he asked.

"Well, actually, some of us are medics," Kurt said, prompting an angry glare from Colonel Sheridan.

"Attendez [Wait]," the soldier said.

"Now we are in for a headache," Colonel Macklin snarled.

The two soldiers went back to the guardhouse and returned with a French officer who was wearing a Red Cross brassard.

"Did any of you gentlemen serve as *Medecins* [medics] in combat?" he asked, again in perfect English.

Paul and Kurt held up their hands, and Colonel Macklin spluttered, "They took good care of a lot of French civilians too, I'll have you know."

"Please wait for just a moment," the French captain asked, and he then spun on his heel and made off for a group of buildings nearby.

He returned just minutes later and handed Paul and Kurt each a red, white, and blue ribbon with a caduceus on it. He saluted first them and then the colonel.

"We will never forget what you Americans have done in liberating our country and helping our people," he said solemnly. "These ribbons are what we give our medical people who have served in combat."

First Paul and then Kurt said gratefully, "Thank you, sir."

"Then let's get going!" Macklin roared.

Bubba threw the vehicle into gear, and they sped off.

A few days after they returned, the Battalion was placed on a seventy-two-hour alert. This time they were told to pack only their personal belongings. All equipment would be turned over to the battalion replacing them. The colonel spent some agonizing moments trying to figure out what to do with his prized car. The Mercedes-Benz Grosser would surely look good in his garage back home, but after being informed about the enormous amount of red tape that would be involved, in addition to prohibitive expenses in getting the car shipped, Colonel Macklin decided to turn it over to his successor. Latrine rumors flew rampant around the battalion. The majority of officers and enlisted men were positive that they would be told to stand down from the alert.

On the appointed day, within about an hour of their expected arrival, the new replacement battalion arrived. Each company of the soon-to-be-departing battalion was assigned the job of orienting their replacement personnel. Everyone was anxious to get going to their new destination in Southern France, as they thought maybe the strike was already called off and they would get to go home right away.

The battalion convoy pulled out and headed first for Metz and then Liechtenstein. This is a tiny principality having an area of about sixty miles that lies on the Rhine River.

The Grand Duchy of Luxembourg was next, where they stopped at a supply depot near the border to gas up. This is located between Belgium and Germany and covers an area of about one thousand miles. Strasbourg followed, and then they took a direct route for Southern France and did not stop until they got to Marseilles. Outside of this bustling seaport, the Americans had set up a number of embarkation camps, each being given the name of a popular cigarette. Their destination was Camp Lucky Strike, which was a vast area of mostly pyramidal tents, some pup tents, and a few Nissen huts.

The battalion was taken to a designated street on which was located a series of pyramidal tents. Happily they were assigned to these, with various companies of the battalion being assigned to some specified tents. The medical detachment enlisted men were directed to a group of such tents, while their officers, along with other battalion officers, were sent to the more comfortable Nissen huts at the foot of the street. Several other Nissen huts located near these were designated as mess halls. A large wooden building not far from the battalion location was designated as the post exchange, with an attached recreation hall. Across the street was the officers' club, which was also a large wooden building. The recreation hall, they were told, was well equipped with several pool tables, Ping-Pong tables, a piano, and a jukebox.

Red, Tony, Kurt, and Paul were assigned to a pyramidal tent that contained four bunks, and a small stove in the center. The stove had a metal pipe projecting through a roughly cut hole in the ceiling, in order to dispel the exhaust. Each bunk contained a skinny mattress and equally thin pillow, with a footlocker at the base of each bed. They all got busy unpacking their gear into the footlockers. Paul carefully checked his greatly diminished supply of Hershey bars and planned at the first opportunity to visit the PX.

When they had finished putting away their gear, by mutual consent, the four of them headed out for the PX.

Just at the entrance, Paul noticed three familiar faces emerging from the officers' club across the street. It was Father Murray, Rabbi Rose, and Reverend Thompson. It was Reverend Thompson who first spotted them and called out, "Hi, soldiers. Can you wait up a minute?"

The three of them quickly crossed over to the other side and warmly greeted Red, Kurt, Tony, and Paul.

Rabbi Rose said, "By the way, gentlemen, we have designated a corner of our Nissen hut that we can share as a chapel. We have a schedule for Saturday morning for Jewish services, Saturday afternoon for Catholic services, and Sunday morning for Protestant services. We will have notices posted on all of the bulletin boards available but wanted to tell you soldiers in person."

Reverend Thompson looked at Paul and asked, "By the way, aren't you the soldier who played the field organ for our services back in England?"

"Guilty as charged, Reverend," Paul replied.

"It just happens that we have been able to scrounge up a pump-type field organ similar to the one you played for us in England. Could you help us once again by playing for all three services ?" Reverend Thompson asked.

"Absolutely, Reverend. I guess your collective prayers had something to do with me making it to here," Paul responded.

They all entered the PX and the adjoining recreation room.

Paul immediately went to the post exchange and checked out their supply of chocolate bars. Thankfully there was a plentiful quantity; and, so Paul decided to wait a while before he stocked up again. He then entered the recreation room, where Tony convinced him to sit down and play a few tunes on the piano even though the juke box was running. After he played some popular classics, a GI pulled the plug on the juke box and a small crowd gathered around the piano.

A few WACs were part of the audience, and Paul instinctively favored their requests, maybe because they were a lot better looking than the other GIs. Rabbi Rose was one of the crowd, and Father Murray and Reverend Thompson circulated, chatting with various men and women and telling them about their planned religious services.

Kurt sidled up to a Ping-Pong table and challenged one of two men playing a game. He nudged Red, who accompanied him, and picked up a paddle in his left hand. Red noticed this right away and was amused, as he knew Kurt was right-handed and always played Ping-Pong right-handed. Kurt's opponent easily beat him and asked him if he wanted to play another game.

"And just to make it interesting," he said, "do you want to put up, say, five dollars?"

Kurt nodded reluctantly and handed a five-dollar bill to an interested onlooker to hold the money. The man held his hand out to the challenging GI, who eagerly pressed a five-dollar bill into his hand. Kurt played a little better this time, but still he was bested by his opponent.

He winked at Red and turned as if to leave the area, but Red spoke up.

"Why don't we make a new game interesting? How about putting up a twenty-dollar bill for a new game. That is, if you both are up to it?"

Kurt acted reluctant about it, but his opponent pressed him to do it.

"Are you chicken or what, soldier?" the man taunted Kurt, who reluctantly pulled a twenty-dollar bill out of his wallet and handed it over. The challenger, in a flash, handed his money over, and the game started with one slight difference. A few onlookers started to make side bets. This time Kurt switched to playing righty, and he annihilated his opponent.

As Kurt triumphantly walked away with forty dollars, Red glanced at Father Murray and Revered Thompson, who looked on in obvious disapproval. He said to them, sotto voce, "Reverend, I guarantee that a good portion of the winnings will go into the collection plate at all of the services."

The loser glared at Kurt and said menacingly, "Somehow you made a sucker out of me, but I can't prove it."

Father Murray and Reverend Thompson gently but quickly eased Red and Kurt out onto the company street. Paul, who did not realize what had happened, just continued to play the piano. Rabbi Rose saw a little of the commotion and followed the quartet outside. Out of curiosity, Paul ended his playing and also left the recreation room. All three chaplains were scolding Red and Kurt, but Paul did not want to get into the fracas. He spun around and went into the PX to replenish his supply of Hershey bars.

Days turned into weeks and weeks turned into months while

the men waited impatiently. Bridge games, poker games, playing the juke box, and just putting up with boredom were exasperating to one and all. Every so often, a rumor came through that the dockworker's strike was over and they would be alerted to go home any day. Very quickly afterward, the rumor would be quashed, along with the morale of everyone listening. Finally, one day, they did get put on actual alert. The strike was over! They were going to go home! The expected alert came through, and they all happily packed their belongings into their respective duffel bags or whatever else they could use to store their gear.

Paul stuffed a German helmet he had picked up on the battlefield, a few bayonets, a flare gun, and, of course, his trusty Luger pistol into the middle of his barracks bag. This was so anyone rummaging through his bag would be less likely to find his souvenirs. He, along with everyone else, could not believe that it was finally happening. But it was! They were all walking on cloud nine. All of them were happy beyond their wildest dreams.

—PART IV—

The Homecoming Veteran

—25—

The bustling port of Marseilles was a sight to behold. Large crews of dockworkers and longshoremen were busy loading soon-to-be departing ships and unloading those that had recently arrived. The motor convoy arrived at the dock area of their destination. The USAT *George W. Goethals* had originally been launched as the *Pascagoula* in 1942. Positioned at the dock in December of 1945, she still looked fairly new, but closer examination of her decks and gear showed that she had experienced many transatlantic crossings. She had been constructed as a troop ship and named in honor of Major General George Washington Goethals, who successfully engineered construction of the Panama Canal. Four hundred eighty-nine feet in length, she had a capacity for about two thousand people. She was nowhere in the league of the mighty *Queen Elizabeth* but looked sturdy and seaworthy just the same.

Hordes of civilians lined the dock area, hawking all kinds of goods: cigarettes, fruit, hummus, and all kinds of cooked food were for sale by eager men and women, young and old. There was an abundance of stoves of all types, most of them cooking foods that gave off a mouthwatering aroma to many. However, the heavy smoke that pervaded the complex and the greasy smell of some of the food made Paul slightly nauseated. Military police tried, to no avail, to get the civilians back behind the wire fence that lined the area. This was impossible, because as soon as some were moved back behind the fence, others mysteriously managed to get in and set up shop. Prominent signs were posted all along the huge dock emphasizing that food items of any kind were banned from being brought aboard ship. If a GI bought something to eat, it would have to be devoured before boarding the vessel.

It was somewhat ludicrous that the truck convoy had discharged its cargo of men and supplies outside of the fence. Each soldier was carefully checked off on a roster monitored by two sailors as he went through a wide gateway onto the dock. The only purpose the wire fence served was to keep the GIs out. It almost seemed as if the civilian food hawkers outnumbered the military.

As the medical detachment left their vehicle, Captain Sheridan called out, "We have been asked for some volunteers to check in medical supplies being loaded into the hold. How about it, men?" He got no response and then added, "Whoever does this will eat navy chow with naval enlisted personnel."

Practically to the man, all hands went up.

As soon as he heard the words "navy chow," Paul flung his hand up instantly, beating the others by seconds.

"All right, Kramer," said Captain Sheridan, "you have it." He then signaled for Tony to join him.

A stocky, ruddy-faced man, perhaps in his mid to late thirties, dressed in a naval uniform, appeared at Captain Sheridan's side. Sheridan introduced him to Paul and Tony as Chief Boatswain's Mate Harcourt. Harcourt sported a magnificent graying mustache that was curled up at the ends. With his jovial look and ruddy complexion, in another time and place he could have served as a great Santa Claus.

Tony and Paul nodded, and Harcourt grunted some kind of greeting. He then waited for Paul and Tony to offload their barracks bags from the truck and signaled them to follow him aboard ship. This was by way of a fairly narrow gangway onto a deck that was just above the waterline. As they went on board, the companionway seemed to be very dark. They then climbed five steep flights of metal stairs to a compartment that housed five bunks.

"Leave your gear on the deck," Harcourt said, "and don't get comfortable. Follow me. And by the way, you can call me Chief or Hack."

Paul asked, " Chief, what's the real story? How come the military doesn't get rid of all those civilians on the dock?"

"If we wanted to, we could get all of them out of here, but then their friends and relatives loading and unloading our ships could really mess us up," he replied laconically.

Harcourt then spun out of the cabin with Paul and Tony close on his heels. A few feet forward of where they were, he opened a metal door that he called a hatch. They entered a moderately large room that was filled with curious paraphernalia.

All of the walls had huge metal rods protruding out several feet. And each one had multiple clipboards attached to it. Above each rod was a large printed label. Hack stopped at a label that read "Medical Supplies," removed three clipboards, gave one each to Paul and Tony, and kept one for himself. He scooped up three pencils from a nearby table, holding one for himself and distributing the remaining two to his little crew. The clipboards each contained a stack of mimeographed papers listing individual medical supplies and their quantities.

Paul started to feel uncomfortably warm in the cabin. When Hack signaled him and Tony to follow him out on deck, he was momentarily relieved. The fresh salty air of the harbor was invigorating. Unfortunately this lasted only long enough for Hack to enter another hatch that opened onto a metal stairway.

"Let's go men," he flung over his shoulder, and he started to rapidly descend the stairway. It seemed that they would never stop as they went farther and farther down into the bowels of the ship. The lower they went, the warmer the temperature seemed to get, until it got to be downright hot and uncomfortable for Paul.

Tony remarked, "What are we going to do? Go right down to the bottom of the harbor? Are we looking for Davey Jones's locker?"

Hack did not reply. When they finally stopped, it seemed that they were just one deck above the engine room. He said, "Now we are in the hold." He led them into a huge area filled with steel shelves from ceiling to floor. The shelves were jam-packed with supplies of all kinds and neatly labeled. He stopped at a spot labeled "Medical" "Here is the drill," he said. "Each of you has a catalog of supplies you have to locate and check off. They are listed in terms of quantity also, and so you have to make sure that not only the items but also the number of cartons or boxes matches what you have on your list. When you have done that, put a check mark in the box next to the item on your list. Okay, let's get going."

It was very hot and uncomfortable in the hold, and the discomfort was only made worse by the poor lighting. Paul had been sick to his stomach earlier, apparently from the greasy, oily fumes of the cooking foods on the dock. Now the high level of heat and humidity in the hold only made him feel worse. As he tried to concentrate on locating the items he needed to check out, a harbor sea swell gently moved the ship up and then down. His stomach seemed to flip, and then he was attacked by an intense and disabling feeling of nausea.

"I think I'm going to heave!" he grated out.

Tony ran over to his side, saying, "For crying out loud, you're as white as a sheet. You look like you're going to pass out! Maybe we can get you someplace where you can lie down."

Chief took a look at him and said, "This is it. You are out of action for a while." He nodded to Tony to take Paul under one arm, while he took him under the other arm, and they led him to the compartment hatch.

"Where's the bathroom?" Paul asked.

"We call it the head. You'll find it right next to where your quarters are," Harcourt replied. "Hang on, kid."

It took the pair quite a while to get Paul back up the staircase, and with each step he took, he was sure he was going to either throw up or pass out. They finally made it to the compartment where they were to be quartered, and both eased him onto a bunk on one side of the room.

At first Paul was certain he would die. He felt so miserable. As his feeling of sickness got even worse, he was afraid he would not die.

Hack said, "We have to get back to work, so you just stay put."

Paul had trouble even speaking and barely eked out the words "Don't worry. I'm not even going to move while I feel like this."

Tony and Hack disappeared, and Paul closed his eyes, trying to cope with his miserable feeling. He thought to himself, *This is so stupid! Here I was in the North Atlantic on the* Queen Elizabeth, *traveling fast and zigzagging in thirty- to forty-foot waves, and that didn't faze me. Crossing the Irish Channel in mountainous seas, both going to Northern Ireland and coming back, was no problem. Making it across the very choppy English Channel in a landing ship and then into a landing craft that was bouncing around wildly on the high waves still didn't bother me in the least. Here I am on a ship tied up at a dock, just becoming as sick as a dog. I must be going crazy!*

It seemed he had been lying there for hours when Hack returned with Captain Sheridan, who took one look at him and muttered, "You are in bad shape, and I feel sorry that the pharmacy on board doesn't have anything I can give you to help. Your buddy was sent to me to get a replacement for you, and so Evans is down in the hold, working away with Tony. I think the best thing for you is to get out on deck and get some fresh air. Next we have to try to get something down your stomach."

"Captain, sir, I'm afraid that I'll pass out if I even try to lift my head."

Hack said, "There is an old navy remedy." He turned to Captain Sheridan. "If you don't mind, sir, I have a stash of heavy German beer. This is on the q.t. I could get court-martialed for having this, you know. If we get him out on deck and can get some of that beer down his gullet, that should settle his stomach."

Sheridan replied, "Sailor, I promise your secret is as good as gold. I think you have a good solution for this problem. Back home, in the medical literature, we have found that Coca-Cola syrup is a good remedy for nausea, but we are not back home, and we don't have any Coke syrup handy. Let's haul him out of the sack."

The two of them moved Paul out of his bunk and toward the doorway, with him weakly protesting all the way. As soon as they got him out on deck, the fresh sea air caught his nostrils, and almost immediately, he felt better. Harcourt and Sheridan gently moved him onto a raised hatch cover and instructed Paul to sit up straight. Harcourt disappeared for a few minutes and then returned with a large mug of a foamy, dark yellow-brown liquid. He held it up to Paul's lips and ordered, "Guzzle it down, sad sack."

Paul was too weak to protest and started to swallow the beer in little sips and then, as he felt still better, in bigger gulps.

"Kramer, get it down," ordered Captain Sheridan.

"Yes, sir. Thank you, sir. Thank you, Hack," he replied.

He already felt well enough to look around and noticed that the ship was moving and the shore had become a thin, small line in the distance. The sky that had previously been overcast had now changed to being partly cloudy, and the color of the choppy Mediterranean Sea had changed from gray to dark blue. The water was just as rough as it had been in the North Atlantic, but now that the beer had settled his stomach, Paul was nearly ready to eat some food.

Almost as if reading his thoughts, Captain Sheridan turned to Hack and said, "I would really appreciate it if you could get him down to the enlisted men's mess when it is chow time."

Hack gave the captain a sort of sloppy salute and said, "Aye aye, sir. Consider it done."

The captain turned away, and Paul called out to him, "Thanks for your help, sir." Then he turned to Hack. "Hack, you saved my life."

"You can get off your butt tomorrow and get back down to help your buddies in the hold" was Hack's gruff answer, but he was obviously pleased that his patient was recovering. He added, "You know that Admiral Horatio Nelson also suffered from what we call mal de mer. So you are in very good company."

"Right now I feel just about ready to get back to work." Paul ventured.

"Give it the rest of this day to get your sea legs back." was Hack's reply.

When chow time came along, Paul joined other GIs in a line for the mess room he was assigned to. The mess area was immaculately clean, to the point where it seemed to be spotless. The dishes and eating utensils had apparently been scrubbed until they were sparkling. An island in the middle of the room was staffed by a team of cooks and mess personnel who were doling out generous quantities of appetizing food.

When the line reached the island, it split into two, with the food being distributed on both sides. Roast stuffed chicken was served with mouthwatering au gratin potatoes. Bread that tasted like cake and butter was available in plentiful quantities. A very nice salad topped off the meal, while a dessert of genuine vanilla ice cream and fresh apple pie completed the fantastic spread. The US Navy once again lived up to its reputation of being an outstanding outfit, and the food it served, whenever possible, was of the very highest quality.

Paul was really feeling normal now, and all thoughts of his earlier misery were gone from his mind. The following morning, he eagerly reported for breakfast, and once again there was real milk on the tables, as well as butter and sugar. The men and women were served coffee that tasted great along with a dish of bacon and eggs that made all of the GIs blink in surprise. These were real eggs—not the watery powdered kind they had been used to for so long. Home fries cooked with onions was another genuine plus, along with bacon and ham.

As soon as he was finished, he flew down the many flights of stairs to the hold, where he found Tony and Red already at work. It was fairly easy to locate and check off items that were familiar to him. Penicillin was something new that he had not seen available to their outfit in combat, but there it was, now that the war was over, being shipped back to the States. In other areas of the hold, winter clothing and insulated combat boots—something the men in his outfit had desperately needed, especially at the time of the Battle of the Bulge, but had never gotten—were sitting on shelves in plentiful quantities. Somebody in the Quartermaster Corps had screwed up royally.

When the men had a chance to go out on deck, they noticed what appeared to be thin slivers of land to the north and south of them. Hack joined Paul and Tony at the rail at the ship's stern as they looked out over what appeared to be an endless Mediterranean. The white froth of the wake churned up by the ship's propellers trailed behind them, moving them ever closer to home.

Hack pointed to their right and said, "That is the coast of Spain, and it comes down to and ends at Gibraltar. On the opposite side, we have the northern edge of the continent of Africa coming up to meet Spain but never quite reaching it. They are separated by what is called the Strait of Gibraltar."

"Who owns Gibraltar?" Tony asked.

"Technically it is a British territory that shares a land border with Spain in the north," Hack answered. "Historically it has been an important base for the British Armed Forces and is the location for an essential British naval base. The territory covers only 2.53 square miles and shares a land border with Spain of about three-quarters of a mile."

"Didn't Spain try to get it back?" Paul asked.

Hack answered, "Gibraltar, also commonly called the Rock, is of great strategic value to the Allies. The word is that Germany planned to capture the Rock, but Spain was unhappy about letting the German Army onto Spanish soil. The planned operation to grab up the Rock was called Operation Felix by the Germans but was scuttled, it is believed, by the head of Abwehr [German intelligence], Admiral Wilhelm Canaris. This guy was one of the people who tried to resist Hitler."

They looked at the big guns of the fortress that commanded the strait.

"It is a great thing that this place is in Allied hands," Paul commented. "Those Germans could have turned the war around if they had taken this piece of real estate."

The good ship *General George Goethals* passed through the strait without incident, and before they knew it, they were out in the Atlantic Ocean. Here the swells were deeper and wider than they had been earlier. Now that Paul's belly was full, he didn't give a second thought to being queasy.

The color of the water was a deep, dark blue, and the height of the waves reminded all on board that they were in the Atlantic Ocean. Some of Paul's days were taken up in continuing to check medical supplies in the hold, and the rest of the time, he was just plain bored.

One day someone shouted, "There she is—the good old US of A!" Although it was midday, the thin, dark thread on the horizon, which was most certainly land, appeared to be possibly a cloud formation. Eager GIs crowded onto the railings on both sides of the vessel as they approached their beautiful country.

A small fleet of smaller ships approached them. As they neared, they started shooting out huge plumes of water. The wording on them indicated that they were New York fireboats. Large signs on both sides of the vessels read "Welcome home, GIs."

The fireboats circled the *Goethals*, and the crewmen on board shouted out greetings to the troops as well. This spectacular welcome was very stirring to all who watched. As the *General Goethals* and the surrounding fireboats approached New York's harbor, the beautiful Statue of Liberty came into view. This was enough to emotionally hit everyone who was watching this incredible sight. There was not a dry eye on the ship.

Paul was standing at the rail alongside Tony and Kurt. He noted, "I was interested in learning about the Statue of Liberty while in grammar school. She welcomes all returning veterans, immigrants, and visitors. Lady Liberty, as she is called, was originally given to the United States by France in 1885 as a gesture of friendship between the two great nations. In 1886 she was dedicated to commemorate the centennial of the United States. The small patch of land that Lady Liberty stands on was selected by William Tecumseh Sherman and is called Liberty Island. It was originally called Bedloe's Island. There was already a star-shaped fortification here when the Statue of Liberty was placed on it."

Tony interjected. "These fantastic New York fireboats greeted the returning veterans of World War I, and now they are doing it again. I always wanted to be a fireboat crewman."

Two tugboats appeared and soon closed in on the *Goethals*. One positioned itself at the front of the ship, and the other at the stern. They started to gently nudge the *Goethals* into a waiting dock. On the dock, a military band was playing some very stirring selections that would have made John Philip Sousa proud. In very little time, the ship was tied up at the dock, and the debarkation process started almost immediately.

Paul and the people he worked with would be some of the last off the ship, according to the planned schedule. Hurried and frenzied good-byes were said, because all those on

Tug Boat on return trip home.

board knew that once they were on dry land, they would all be scattered to the far winds.

Paul was ordered to report to the separation center at Camp Devens in Massachusetts. He clutched his orders and his travel vouchers in his hand, not even trusting to put them in his pocket. As each GI walked off the ship, he showed his orders to several MPs on either side of the gangplank. One of them looked at the papers and directed Paul to a waiting two-and-a-half-ton truck. A large number seventeen was painted on the side of the canvas. He clambered onto the back, helped up by some already waiting GIs. He scanned the enormous crowd of soldiers, looking for familiar faces, but it was almost impossible to see any of his old buddies. The truck took off with a lurch, and in no time they were driving through downtown Manhattan. What an incredible sight! He had been determined to get down and kiss the ground of the USA as soon as he got off the ship, but in the excitement, he had been distracted. When they arrived at Grand Central Station, they were told by the truck driver to go to track eleven. They tried to run but found it difficult while carrying their bulky barracks bags.

A kindly and helpful conductor waiting at track eleven scanned their papers and bade Paul to board the car he was standing in front of. When Paul got aboard, it was a bit of a shock not to see a single familiar face. The number of civilians on the car was about equal to the number of men and women in uniform. He tried to shove his bulky barracks bag onto the rack above him, but it wouldn't fit. He then eased it into the empty seat next to him and settled down to watch the scenery go by. It was a bit of a pleasant shock to see all sorts of buildings, large and small, completely whole. It seemed as if he were in a very pleasant dream, speeding toward Boston's South Station. In combat, when he had tried to get some needed sleep while cold, hungry, and terrified, he had tried to lull himself into sleeping by fantasizing about what it would be like coming home. What was happening to him now was better than anything he could have imagined. A civilian across the way from him offered him several local newspapers. The only newspaper he had been used to was *Stars and Stripes*. Not only were there very interesting local articles, but all of his favorite comic strips were there, including *The Phantom, Mandrake the Magician, Flash Gordon, Dick Tracy, Blondie, Buck Rogers in the 25ᵗʰ Century A.D.*, and *The Katzenjammer Kids*. He had some serious catching up to do.

Before he knew it, he was on another train heading for Camp Devens. This time the passengers were all dressed in khaki.

Again, try as he might, he could not find a single familiar face. The few last remaining men of his outfit had been scattered at the New York docks. When the train finally stopped, Paul and the rest of the men were assembled into designated units and assigned to various barracks. After a great meal at the mess hall, Paul got back to his barracks and almost fell asleep just sitting on his cot. He slept like a child and woke up the next morning feeling hungry once again. The mess hall turned out a breakfast worthy of praise, and all of the men present practically inhaled the food. Later, they were assembled in front of the barracks, and a captain greeted them.

"Welcome to Camp Devens. I am Captain McIntyre, and I am in charge of this company. Our job is to process the work of your becoming a civilian in the most expeditious way. There is a lot of necessary paperwork involved, and so it may take a little time, we estimate between one to two weeks, or maybe less. First and most important, we have to prepare an Honorable Discharge for you and all the paper work that goes with it. It may not seem important to you now, but later on in civilian life an Honorable discharge may be very significant to your getting a job or a higher education. The Federal Government has set up a program called the "G.I. Bill", which can benefit you in many ways such as purchasing a home or getting an education in an Institution of Higher Learning. The credentials we are preparing for you will be of the utmost importance in making you eligible for these and other benefits you may be entitled to as a Veteran. We also have to process any possibility of your having a disability claim with the Veterans Administration. You will be meeting with trained counselors to help you prepare for what your next steps in civilian life will be. We ask you for your patience and understand you want to contact your loved ones. In your free time, you will be allowed to use one of a battery of telephones that have been set up for this purpose in the Post Exchange. Since we are in what one might call "East Overshoe," all of your calls will be long distance."

"At no charge to you, simply dial "O" for operator' and give this person the telephone number you want to get and say you are calling collect. You can invite your immediate family to visit you on Saturday or Sunday. You will have to tell them that there is no determining the exact day or time that you will be sent home. We will do that just as fast as we can; but, they will just have to be patient a little while longer. It is in your best interest that the critical paperwork we will be preparing be as accurate as possible. Just as soon as this is done, you will be sent home. Good luck, men."

He turned to a first sergeant and said, "Carry on, Sergeant O'Connell."

Sergeant O'Connell faced the group and said, "You now have the rest of the day off so you can get your gear in order, make your phone calls, or get yourself oriented about this camp. Now fall out."

Paul found his way to the post exchange, and upon entering a large reception room, he noticed that one entire wall was lined with telephone booths. There was a line of GIs—men and women—at each booth. He was anxious to call Mom, Dad, and Jerry. It would be great to hear their voices, and maybe they could even come out to the camp and see him.

Might as well do this now. Those lines are not going to get any shorter.

He chose the shortest line, and thankfully it moved along at a reasonable pace until it came to the man in front of him. Apparently he was talking to his girlfriend, and she obviously did not believe in brief conversations. He looked exasperatedly up in the air, figuring, *Leave it to me to find somebody holding up the line.*

At long last, the man left the booth, and Paul settled himself contentedly onto the seat. Excitedly, he dialed *"O"*, and a female voice came on the line,

"Operator. What number do you wish to call?"

"This is Paul Kramer, and I would like to make a collect call to Geneva 1895, please, ma'am."

"One moment please," she replied, and he heard the phone ringing.

Mom picked it up on the first ring, inquiring, "Hello, who is it?"

"This is the Long distance Operator at Camp Devens. Will you accept a collect call from Paul Kramer?"

"Oh yes, yes, yes! Charlie! It's Paul. He's back!"

"One moment, and I will connect you," the operator said. After a moment, the operator announced, "You may begin your conversation now."

"Hello, Ma, it's me, Paul." he replied emotionally.

"Oh, thank God you are home safe! Wait a minute; here's Dad."

His father picked up the phone, and Paul could tell from his voice and Mom's that they were both crying from joy.

"Where are you, my son?" Dad asked.

"I am out at Camp Devens, which is a demobilization center."

"We know," Mom answered. Apparently they were handing the phone back and forth to each other. "Cousin Andrew just returned home. He was out there and told us it was most likely that you would be processed through the same location."

A strange voice came on the phone, asking, "Can you get off the phone, please? I need to make a call."

Mom replied, "We are talking to our son who just got home from overseas."

The other party answered, "Then go right ahead; you are entitled."

Mom got back on the line, saying, "We're sorry about that, Paul. We have a party line, and we are always getting into each other's way when we want to make a call. More important, are we allowed to come out and see you?"

"Absolutely," Paul replied. "The camp is open to visitors on

Saturdays and Sundays. I know Dad works all day on Saturday, so could you come out here this coming Sunday?"

"My darling son, we will be there first thing Sunday morning," Mom answered. "How are you? Are you all right?"

"I'm just fine, Mom. You come to the front gate and ask for Company C, Third Battalion, and go to the post exchange. I will be waiting for you there."

"We will be there, my precious Paul," she answered.

Paul saw the line of waiting men growing at the door of his phone booth.

"I have to get off the phone now. I can't wait until I see you on Sunday. Love you."

"We love you, dear Paul. We will count the minutes until we see you this weekend." Mom replied.

He hung up and wordlessly turned the receiver over to the next waiting soldier.

For the rest of the day, he walked aimlessly around the camp, even going as far as the front gate. *This is where Mom, Dad, and Jerry will come in*, he thought. *Should I surprise them and wait here? There are a few more days to think on that.* He looked down at his uniform. It looked grungy. So what? They wouldn't care about how he looked. *The heck with it.*

He returned to the recreation hall adjacent to the PX. A few games of Ping-Pong showed how rusty he had gotten. Then he meandered over to a baby grand piano sitting in one corner and tried a few tunes. After a short time, men and women gathered around the piano, requesting their favorites.

Before he knew it, it was time for chow. Later, in his bunk, he found falling asleep difficult, what with the excitement of his loved ones coming soon.

Early the next morning, right after chow, he and his entire barracks group reported to a large Nissen hut marked "Processing."

As they entered, each was handed a small card with a number on it. Paul's number was fourteen. Folding chairs lined three sides of the massive room, and there were about six desks in the middle manned by noncoms. The remaining wall was lined with filing cabinets. The men were instructed to be seated until their numbers were called.

It didn't take long for Paul's turn, and he was directed to a desk that was free. A buck sergeant introduced himself as Fred Perez. He got Paul's name and serial number and went to the filing cabinet behind him.

He returned a short time later with a thick folder—apparently Paul's service record. He went through many details of Paul's service, including the time he was in combat, and made many notes. Sergeant Perez stated, "We are going to bring your record up to date, and then we can process your honorable discharge and papers that go with that. In the meantime, we are going to get you a new set of uniforms. One is a dress OD shirt, pants, and a new Eisenhower-style jacket. That is the blouse that is cut off at the waist. The other is a tan outfit with shirt, pants, and field jacket. You'll also get two new hats, several pairs of socks, and a pair of shoes. When you pick up your new uniforms, you'll notice that our emblem for honorably discharged veterans has been sewn on your Eisenhower jacket. This is a Golden Eagle, which most of the men jokingly refer to as a "Ruptured Duck"."

"Following that, with all of your papers processed, you will be given your honorable discharge and all of the important documents associated with it. You will be given two full-size copies—one in white and one in black. You also will be given two wallet-sized copies as well. As soon as you get settled at home, put the original set of honorable discharge papers in a bank vault for safe keeping. You may want to go to a photography store and have them make up some extra copies. You'll need them if you want to take advantage of the GI Education Bill, as well as the GI Home

Bill. Following that, I see that you are entitled to be given the Combat Medic Badge as well as whatever ribbons are designated for you. Any questions?"

Paul was overwhelmed with how great the army was treating him.

Maybe I should sign up for another hitch? he thought. But then he caught himself. "I could never do that to Mom, Dad, and Jerry. They have obviously sweated me out enough."

With most of his paperwork still being processed, and wearing his brand-new uniform, he made his way to the front gate bright and early Sunday morning.

"I guess I'm just compulsive," he thought.

As he approached the guard shack, one of the MPs came out and asked, "Waiting for your family?"

"You've got it," he replied excitedly.

The guard waved him to a place beside the guard shack, and he settled in to wait patiently. Knowing Mom and Dad, he would not have to wait long. Sure enough, in just a few minutes, the familiar royal blue Plymouth rolled up to the camp entrance with Dad at the wheel. He stopped the car to greet the MP, and Paul darted over to greet his loved ones. All four doors flew open, and Mom, Dad, and Jerry jumped out along with an absolutely gorgeous girl. It was his cousin Charnette, who had insisted on accompanying them to the camp. She provoked some appreciative stares and whistles from other GIs in the vicinity. Mom, Dad, Jerry, and Charnette all grabbed Paul hard and squeezed him.

Mom kept saying, "Thank you, dear God, for bringing our precious Paul home to us safely. Thank you for answering our prayers."

Her words broke into sobs of thanks while they all just stood there holding each other and weeping from pure joy.

The MP waited patiently and then finally said, "Soldier, we

would appreciate your moving that vehicle along. You have others backed up here."

Sure enough, there were several cars, all waiting patiently, viewing the emotional scene of reunion.

"Oh sure there," Paul answered, and he jumped into the backseat of the car. He was in such a state of euphoria that no amount of thinking or imagining could have prepared him for this.

Dad, holding the car keys in his hand, turned around to Paul and asked, "Would you like to drive?"

"No thanks, Dad," Paul answered, ensconcing himself back down in the luxurious backseat alongside Charnette.

He directed Dad on how to proceed back to his company location, pointing out his barracks along the way, and then on to the recreation hall. There was a substantial parking lot right next to it, and Dad pulled the car in expertly and parked it between two white lines.

They all went into the recreation hall, sat down at a table, and started to catch up on what had happened since Paul had gone overseas. A small but adequate lunch counter was positioned in a corner of the large room. Paul offered to get a snack for everyone. Dad had a cup of coffee, Mom had tea, and Paul, Charnette, and Jerry drank Cokes. They sat there for hours, catching up on what he had missed at home. He really didn't feel like going into details about the war. How could they understand? He finally found out what had happened to his beloved Zadie, who had passed away the previous February.

No one noticed how much time had transpired until a sergeant major opened the front door partially and called out, "Visitors are getting ready to leave now."

"When can you come home?" Mom asked.

"They are processing my paperwork, and just as soon as they are finished, I can leave."

"Call me when you are ready to leave, please," she urged.

"Absolutely," Paul replied.

Dad ventured, "I could come and get you."

"Thanks, Dad, but this will be a last-minute thing, and I want to leave as soon as I get the green light."

"I respect that," Dad answered.

They noticed that other civilian visitors were starting to get up and head for the door. Wordlessly, the foursome followed suit, and Paul walked them out to the car. He gave everyone in turn a huge hug and a kiss, and then he watched the car disappear down the street, heading toward the gate.

First thing the next morning, as directed, Paul reported back to Sergeant Perez. Once again, he waited patiently until his number was called and then sat down at the sergeant's desk.

Perez picked up a file folder and said, "Everything seems to be in order. First a little word about money. You need to be oriented about how everything is jumping up in cost. When you entered the Army in 1943, the cost of a gallon of gasoline was nineteen cents. Now is it up to twenty-one cents. A loaf of bread that used to cost nine cents is now ten cents. The cost of a new car has gone up from eleven hundred dollars to fourteen hundred dollars. A gallon of milk that was sixty-two cents is now seventy cents. The only good news is that the average annual wage has gone from twenty-five hundred dollars to thirty-one fifty, and the minimum wage is now forty cents an hour, while it was thirty cents an hour back in forty-three. The one thing that hasn't changed is the cost of our three-cent postage stamp."

Perez removed a medium-sized manila envelope and pulled out a sheaf of bills and coins.

"This is your separation pay. Sign here to show you received your money. Now take these forms to your local Social Security office. You are no longer considered an employee of the United States Government and are now entitled to collect unemployment compensation for a predetermined number of weeks. You can collect that until you go back to work or return to college."

He opened another large manila envelope and took out several documents, noting, "These are all of your honorable discharge papers, along with some extra copies."

He opened another envelope and took out a number of service ribbons, saying, "We are giving you your Combat Medic Badge and most of the ribbons you are entitled to. Unfortunately we have run out of some. If you like, bring a copy of your discharge papers to any army–navy store, and you can purchase what you are missing. You are entitled, as I said, to purchase a home on the GI Bill. You have to make your own arrangement with a bank of your choice, but the government will guarantee your loan. You will have to give your bank a copy of your honorable discharge papers. We will even arrange for one of our inspectors to check out the house of your choice. If you desire to return to college, the government will pay for your tuition, books, and equipment. You just need to supply the educational institution with a copy of your honorable discharge papers and us with a periodic record of your academic achievement. Now, do you have any questions?"

"You have been very patient and helpful with me, and I can't express my gratitude to you and the army. Thank you, Sergeant. Does this mean I am free to go?"

"Whenever you want," Perez replied, smiling while shaking Paul's hand.

In a whisk, he was back in line at the phone booths, and when he got through, he simply said, "I'm on my way home."

Paul & Charnette after return in front of Paul's home

The author with his family several years after WW2.

Epilogue

Twenty Years Later

P aul's younger son could barely keep up with his father walking briskly down Newbury Street towards the Boston Commons. At the end of Newbury Street, the pair made a sharp right and turned right into an entrance walking downstairs flanked by travel posters of France into a well known French Patisserie. Paul invited his son to pick out a dessert from the glass display case and sternly instructed him to remain at the table and not talk to any strangers. He always picked the cherry tart because it was the only dessert with which he was familiar. Paul entered the kitchen through the swinging doors. This happened quite frequently and from time to time, Paul's son thought it looked like his father was playing soldier with the couple in the kitchen pretending to hold guns. In later years, Paul's son learned that the woman in the kitchen was Pierrette with her American husband. He also overheard that his father was on very good terms with the local French Consulate. I suspect they knew of his wartime exploits. Paul's wife was affectionately given the nickname "Madame Pussycat" by the consulate. Over the years, Paul and Pierrette and her husband drifted apart and some years later, the Patisserie closed.

Paul went on to become an optometrist, as he had decided at an earlier age. He enrolled in The Massachusetts School of Optometry (which later became The New England College of Optometry) in 1942, after graduating from Dorchester High School. His earnings from his previous summer job paid for his first year's tuition. Although granted a deferment from the Army by his student status, Paul waived it after his first year in Optometry School and enlisted in the Army in 1943, shortly after his eighteenth birthday. This chapter in Paul's life is chronicled in the book you have just read. After the war, Paul returned to Optometry School where he graduated and then became an instructor, Assistant Professor and finally Full Professor. He also managed the graduations and served on the Admissions Committee and as Registrar in later years. He distinguished himself as a Professor who was popular with the students and an expert in his field, publishing extensively both in professional journals and textbooks. He ran a successful private practice at home in addition to his academic responsibilities. He was happily married to and extremely devoted to my mother and proud of the achievements of his two sons and extended family. He was fond of beer and automobiles as long as they were American, hot dogs and baked beans, drive-in movie theaters, hot fudge sundaes, chocolate (still with Hershey Bars kept in a personal stash), rolled beef (which is no longer available), Chinese food (especially Chicago Style Chow Mein), Wild Turkey Manhattans (to which he reverently referred to as "Ho-Ho's"), cowboy stories and movies, Science fiction such as "Mystery Science Theater", Gouda or Muenster cheese (which he affectionately referred to as "Rat Cheese") and smoked salmon. He collected anthologies of Charles Addams' drawings. I remember his nickname for the family automobile, a 1962 Rambler, was "Buddy." He also gave back to the community by volunteering to deliver hot food to recipients of "Meals on Wheels." He was president of his synagogue and later served in his local Jewish War Veteran Post.

My parents were voracious readers completing a book or two per week.

As his friends will remember, it was in Frank's vocabulary to refer to his handwriting as barbaric, developments as revolting and he frequently referred to himself as an ugly old man (with a smile on his face). Growing up as a child, I remember hearing the phrases "immediately if not sooner" and "bail out" never thinking they were common phrases during the War.

He liked to fly the flag as weather permitted. He always removed his hat and held his hand over his heart when the flag passed him during parades. Upon my brother and I asking him what he did during WW-II, his stock answer was, "You're too young..."

He grew up admiring movie stars like Errol Flynn and John Wayne and characters such as Flash Gordon and Buck Rogers. During the war, he became a hero much like them.

Because war is hell, veterans are frequently reluctant to share their experiences. Every veteran has a story which frequently goes untold because they do not want to remember the horrors of War. We are fortunate that Frank committed his memories of his WW-2 adventures to become this book.

Neil Kozol
Sharon, Mass

Photo with second son, Neil circa 1958.

Author working as instructor circa 1960.

Author with a student at The New England College of Optometry 1979

Author supervising The New England College of Optometry graduation.

Author with his wife in later years.

Author's first son, Mark, with author's portrait when unveiled at The New England College of Optometry

Photo taken approximately 15 to 20 years after WW-2

Cap proudly worn by the author 60 years after WW2